DENOTIFIED TRIBES: DIMENSIONS OF CHANGE

DENOTIFIED TRIBES: DIMENSIONS OF CHANGE

Dr. Malli Gandhi

KANISHKA PUBLISHERS, DISTRIBUTORS
NEW DELHI-110 002

KANISHKA PUBLISHERS, DISTRIBUTORS
4697/5-21 A, Ansari Road, Daryaganj
New Delhi-110 002
Phones : 2327 0497, 2328 8285
Fax : 011-2328 8285
E-mail: kanishka_publishing@yahoo.co.in

First Published 2008

ISBN 978-81-8457-065-6

PRINTED IN INDIA

Published by Madan Sachdeva for Kanishka Publishers, Distributors, 4697/5-21A, Ansari Road, Daryaganj, New Delhi-110 002, Typeset by Sunshine Graphics, Delhi, and Printed at Nice Printing Press, Delhi.

To
Mahasweta Devi

Preface

With the establishment of Colonial Rule in India and consequent introduction of machine made goods, the Austro-Asiatic groups were deprived of patronage for their handicrafts and hand made goods. With the loss of patronage for their goods, these Artisan groups lost their livelihood. Many of them were forced to take to crime for earning their livelihood. By the early 19th century, the 'Criminal' activities of the groups became such a serious law and order problem that the Government enacted 'Criminal Tribes Act' to control the 'Criminal' activities of certain communities. Under the said Act, community members of which were generally found to be engaged in 'Criminal' activities viz., house breaking, dacoity, cattle lifting, jewellery snatching etc., were notified as 'Criminal Tribes' in each district on the recommendations of the Superintendent of police of the District concerned. The movements and activities of the 'Criminal Tribes' used to be under surveillance of the Station House Officer (SHO) of the Police Station in which the 'Criminal Tribe' concerned used to live. As a result of the restrictions on the movements of the entire community notified as 'Criminal Tribe' the members of that community became backward economically and educationally. The entire community suffered social stigma of being labeled as 'Criminal Tribe'.

After the advent of independence, the Government of India appointed the Criminal Tribes Enquiry Committee under the Chairmanship of M. Anantha Sayanam Ayyangar. The committee after studying the conditions of the 'Criminal Tribes' in the entire country recommended for the repeal of the Criminal Tribes Act. The Government of India accordingly repealed the Criminal Tribes Act and replaced it with Habitual Offenders Act 1952. The Habitual Offenders Act is a State Government legislation. With the repeal of Criminal Tribes Act, the communities notified under the said Act as 'Criminal Tribes' were denotified with a view to undertake ameliorative measures for the ex-Criminal Tribes. A list of the tribes which were denotified with the repeal of the Criminal Tribes Act was issued by the respective State Governments as the list of Denotified Tribes or Vimuktha Jathis. Thus the list of Denotified Tribes came into existence for each state. The list of Denotified Tribes of the erstwhile Madras State was issued in 1952. There are 66 entries. These entries relate to the Andhra region of the state. Many of these entries do not indicate any community. For example: Gang of Assassins; Sl. No. 20 (Jatur Mixed Gang) Sl. No. 60 (Tankela Ramanas) etc. Most of these entries are repetitions of the same community. Again, Yerukulas find place at Sl. No. 32 (Yerukulas) Sl. No. 33 (Eerukulas) Sl. No. 29 (Urkorchas) Sl. No. 39 (Koravas) Sl. No. 42. (Korachas). Korachas known as Dabbala Yerukas 48: Mondi Korava 52; 63 Nawabpet Korchas; Veyalpad Korachas 65 ; Eerikkalas and Korachas 66. Korava, Koracha and Kaikadi are synonyms for Yerukulas and therefore, all the above entries refers to one community i.e., Yerukula. The sixty six entries in the Denotified tribes list of Andhra region can be identified as the following communities:

1. Malas (Sl. No. 2, 3, 45, 36)
2. Madigas (Sl. No. 16)
3. Harijans (Sl. No. 15)
4. Dombs (Sl. No. 9, 22)
5. Rellis (Sl. No. 29)
6. Vaddar (Sl. No. 14, 26, 31, 34, 53, 55)
7. Paidu (Sl. No. 56)
8. Reddika (Sl. No. 58)
9. Urali Goandars (Sl. No. 62)
10. Mutharacha (Sl. No. 43 & 50)
11. Kepmaris (Sl. No. 37)
12. Mondivagula (Sl. No. 45)
13. Paraliya (Sl. No. 30)
14. Poligar (Sl. No. 1 & 28)
15. Tandari Mandalam
16. Kintali Kalinga
17. Boyas (Sl. No. 4, 12, 25, 35)
18. Chakala (Sl. No. 5)
19. Dommara (Sl. No. 10)
20. Dasara (Sl. No. 6, 7, 13)
21. Jambuvandai (Sl. No. 17)
22. Jogi (Sl. No. 18 & 19)

23. Nokkar (Sl. No. 21)
24. Telaga Pamulas (Sl. No. 27)
25. Konda Dora (Sl. No. 38)
26. Mondi Vagula (Sl. No. 46)
27. Monda Pottas (Sl. No. 49)
28. Mutha Racha (Sl. No. 43 & 50)
29. Nakkala (Sl. No. 51)
30. Pitchikaguntala (Sl. No. 57)
31. Nirshikari (Sl. No. 54)
32. Lambadi (Sl. No. 44, 59)
33. Yerukula (Sl. No. 23, 32, 33, 37, 40, 42, 48, 65, 66, 63, 52)
34. Yanadi (Sl. No. 64)

In respect of Telangana region the following three communities are Denotified.

1. Waddara
2. Dommara
3. Kaikadi (Yerukula)

After the repeal of the Criminal Tribes Act and consequent definition of erstwhile 'Criminal Tribes', the restrictions on the movements of the ex-criminal tribes have been removed and some of these communities managed to get them listed as Scheduled Tribes. For example, Yerukula, Lambadi and Yanadi and several communities have listed as socially and educationally backward classes. The remaining groups were listed as Denotified Tribes which also received attention of the Government for their rehabilitation. The list of nomadic and ex-criminal tribe/groups were popularly known as list of Nomadic Tribes and Denotified Tribes. There are several non-tribal groups in both the lists. The communities listed in the list of Nomadic and Denotified Tribes refer to tribes with the denotification of the erstwhile 'Criminal Tribes' and removal of restriction on their movements. With the launch of various measures for their rehabilitation by the Government and NGOs like the Salvation Army, Bharatiya Adimajati Sevak Sangh etc., the erstwhile criminal tribes and nomadic groups came into contact with the rest of society. Since 1952 these cultural contacts paved the way for adoption of certain traits of backward Telugu castes in rural areas in symbiosis with whom erstwhile criminal and nomadic groups have been living in the rural areas. With the constant interaction for the past 50 years between the erstwhile criminal and nomadic tribes and the rural caste groups has led to assimilation of many of erstwhile criminal and nomadic tribes into the caste system in the rural areas. As a result of this process of acculturisation of several erstwhile 'criminal' and nomadic tribes and by virtue of their residence in rural areas after their rehabilitation and settlement these groups got themselves absorbed into Indian caste system. However, this change from tribe to caste did not take place overnight. This took place over a period of more than four decades.

The study of 'CTs' has not generally been a favourite subject among the academic circles. The present study is an investigative research into the origin and development of these tribes. The 19th Century colonial policies destroyed the age old occupation of a number of communities and as a result they lost livelihood. This has gone into the making of 'CTs'. No government or administration worth its name can remain idle for long towards the plight of these people. The government has to either directly settle and provide employment opportunities to these people or better still encourage private agencies in this direction.

The colonial government sought to improve the lot of these 'CTs' through private agencies such as the Salvation Army, the London Mission, the American Baptist Mission, the Canadaian Mission, Chief Khalsa Diwan, Deo Samaj, Anjuman Islamia, Ahamdia Society, Sanatana Dharma Sabha, Arya Samaj and the Punjab Hindu Sabha in Andhra Pradesh. These tribals were for the most part settled in Stuartpuram (Guntur district), Siddhapuram (Kurnool district) Sitanagaram (Guntur district), Kapparalla Tippa (Bitragunta) Kavali (Nellore district) and Lingala (Mahaboob Nagar district) settlements. The government provided them vacant land so that they will engage and enable themselves in agricultural pursuits. Educational opportunities were also made available for the children of these communities. The Government also granted financial assistance to the Missionary managements for the upkeep of these settlements. The various agencies sought tocater to the educational, health and employment opportunities of the tribes. The present volume consisting of articles on various facets of the 'Criminal Tribes' from the inception till date is based on through research including extensive field work.

Acknowledgements

I am deeply indebted to many people during the course of the present work. Foremost among them are Prof. V. Ramakrishna and Dr. V. Lalitha for their enlightened guidance and sympathetic help throughout my research work. I am very much grateful to Sri Lavanam and Mrs. Hemalatha Lavanam, Samskar, Varni, Andhra Pradesh for their constant support.

I record my deepest sense of gratitude to Prof. Krishna Kumar, Director, NCERT, Prof. G. Ravindra, Joint Director, NCERT and Prof. G.T. Bhandage, Principal, Regional Institute of Education, Mysore for their encouragement and administrative support.

I wish to thank the authorities and staff of Andhra Pradesh State Archives, Hyderabad. Tamil Nadu State Archives, Egmore, Chennai. National Archives, Nehru Memorial Museum and Library, New Delhi and Anthropological Survey of India, Mysore for providing me with necessary documents, records and books.

I am thankful to Sri K. Ganapathi Bhat who took the pain to edit the manuscript and making valuable suggestions. I am also thankful to Prof. B. Krishna Reddy, Head, Department of Folklore and Tribal Studies, Kuppam University, Prof. K.M. Maitry, Department of Tribal Studies, Hampi University, Prof. P. Venkata Rao, Head, Department of Anthropology, University of Hyderabad, Prof. M.L.K. Murthy, Retired Professor, Department of Folklore, University of Hyderabad and Dr. K. Sasidhar Rao, Retired Principal, IASE, Hyderabad and Prasnna for their academic help.

During my field work, a number of people extended their help. I thank all the village elders of the DNT colonies in Andhra Pradesh, Parents and Head Teachers of the DNT schools and the Salvation Army authorities without whose help this work might not have been completed. It is unbecoming on my part if I fail to acknowledge the patient help of Smt. S. Imavathi, RIE, Mysore, Smt. K. Mamata and Smt. K. Surekha for typing the manuscript of the present work.

AUTHOR

Contents

List of Abbreviations

ABM	American Baptist (Telugu) Mission
BASS	Bharatiya Adim Jati Sevak Sangh
CID	Criminal Investigation Department
CTA	Criminal Tribes Act
CTs	Criminal Tribe
DNT	Denotified Tribe
GO	Government Order
IGP	Inspector General of Police
ILTD	Indian Leaf Tobacco Development Company
IPC	Indian Penal Code
NCERT	National Council of Educational Research and Training
NGO	Non Government Organization
NTs	Nomadic Tribes
NWFP	North-West Frontier Province
PWLD	Public Wroks Labour Department
RIE	Regional Institute of Education
SA	Salvation Army
SHO	Station House Officer

Glossary

Agraharam	:	village granted to caste people by government for charity either rent free or at favourable assessment
Alagiri	:	appellation given to Katheras as a class of professional thieves (Pickpockets)
Bidaris	:	carriers
Farm Bailiff	:	village officer
Ganga Raju	:	village head
Gotras	:	clan
Karnam	:	village accountant
Kathiravandlu	:	thieves, pickpockets
Kolukarudu	:	minister
Kuladharma	:	caste duty
Kulapanchayat	:	council of village elders
Mamullu	:	bribe
Moodevi	:	goddess of sleep
Nattu	:	bent grass
Navvy	:	unskilled work
Okkakubettedi	:	betrothal ceremony
Parkuchi	:	a stick with long iron ferrule (dagger)
Patta Land	:	a grant or lease specifying the land given to a cultivator and assessment due on it
Pendli	:	marriage
Pittalavandlu	:	bird trappers
Rangam & Melam	:	the institutions of Yanadi tribe
Ryot	:	peasant
Toddy	:	country liquor
Tolabottu	:	mangalasutra
Veedus	:	religious endowments given to the local temples
Voli	:	bride price
Waddars	:	earth workers

1

Colonial Rule and Criminal Tribes Acts

I

Introduction

Nomadic tribes lived first in forest areas and then shifted to plains. Yerukula, Yanadi, Lambadi (Sugali) Boya, Woddera, Dasari, Koracha, Pamula, Nakkala, Jogi, Konda Dora, Kalla, Relli and Dommaras are considered as nomadic tribes in Andhra Pradesh. These nomadic tribes had to migrate from place to place, from state to state in order to eke out their livelihood. They acquired expertise in handicrafts and petty business. They found it easier and so enjoyed their life. Their lifestyle today is totally transformed. They came to cultivate land and settled gradually in some place which is a hallmark of change among them. However, we can still see the traces of nomadism among them.[1]

The present chapter makes an attempt to study the need for regulation and control of these nomadic, semi-nomadic and 'criminal tribes' (CTs) and passing of certain regulatory acts called as Criminal Tribes Acts (CTA) from 1871 to 1965. The chapter aims at the scrutiny and analysis of various CT Acts. An attempt is made to study how various provisions under the CT Acts affected the 'criminal tribes'. Their life pattern under the CT Acts is also discussed. The chapter closely looks into the major changes or the deviation that took place under the CT Acts and what exactly motivated the British to pass the CT Acts. The main intention of the chapter is to trace the historical background of the CTs which started from nomadism and transformed them to the present state through an evolutionary process.

II

Colonial Rule and Notification of Tribes

The 19th century colonial economic policies destroyed the age old occupations of a number of communities. Specific policies of the administration severely affected communities which were involved in trading. The Salt Policy of the Government destroyed the trade of Koravas, Yerukulas, Brinjaries and Lambadies in Andhra Pradesh.

The Government forest policy (the forest laws of the 1880s) prevented free gazing of the cattle owned by these groups and prevented them from collecting forest produce.[2] The Chenchus of Hyderabad were very much affected by the forest laws.[3] In desperation they turned into bandits.[4] Like Chenchus, many other groups were also badly affected by the colonial forest policies.[5] Lieutenant Balmer in his letter to the Collector dated 22nd May 1865, No. 317, wrote the following about the Yerukulas: "The crimes they are addicted to are dacoity, highway robbery and robbery. They are the most troublesome of our wanderers."[6]

There were widespread and severe famines in 1866, 1876-78 and 1898.[7] It witnessed unprecedented outbreak of dacoity, food riots and looting of markets, house-breakings, cattle-stealing, etc. The Inspector General of Police (IGP) observed in 1877 that "Dacoity as the 'special famine crime' was committed by hungry people, not ordinary criminals."[8]

In 1824, Sir Thomas Munro, the Governor of Madras, observed that there were several thousand men scattered over in our country, whose business from their earliest days has been robbery.[9] The development of roads and railways further destroyed their business activity and in turn they lost their traditional means of livelihood.[10] Mackenzie, in his book, *Mud Bank* writes: "The Yerukulas were originally merchants. Their fore-fathers carried salt, grain and other commodities inland, on the backs of the pack animals, but in the march of progress, rail, and roads came and transportation was taken out of their lands. Their living was gone, they knew no trade and they resorted to crime."[11]

These tribes led a vagrant life in jungles, hills and deserts with no fixed abodes. They wandered about with their bag and baggage and pitched their tents on the out-skirts of a village or a city or in some secluded place.[12] In the absence of any substantial means of living, these people depended on begging, cattle lifting and crop stealing.[13] In earlier times, they felt that their life was much easier. But gradually with the advance of 'civilisation' they realised the real situation and faced hardship in the day today 'criminal' life.[14]

III

Criminal Tribes Acts in Andhra Pradesh

To put down crime, the British Government took stern steps to arrest and punish these people. They could not forget their bad experiences with thugs and pindharis.[15] The British, high caste Hindus and police officers were unable to comprehend or sympathise with the lifestyle of the nomads. Their peculiar social practices, their consumption of alcohol and inferior types of food, their so called laziness and unwillingness to work were the criteria in branding them so. References were made to the immoral women of these communities who would be as a matter of course described as rogues.[16] A gypsy way of life, necessitated by earlier trading activities came to be described as Vagrancy or a lust for wandering. There was a view amongst the British that the 'criminal' tribes looked different from ordinary human beings in their physical appearance.[17] Around the last part of the 19th century, on the basis of increased rate of crime, the administration viewed about the concept of the hereditary principle among the criminals. Instead of as wandering tribes they were classified as CTs. Their number since then increased.[18]

Several theories have been advanced regarding the origin of these CTs. According to one view, they have descended from the gypsies. It was held by some that the CTs owe their origin to the aborigines, who had been displaced from time to time by the incursions of the inhabitants of Central Asia.[19] The Government used to deal with the individuals caught in criminal activities individually or collectively, first under the regulation XXVI of 1793, then under the Act of XXX of 1836 and later, under the Indian Penal Code (IPC) of 1860. Thus, legally until the year 1871, no tribe as a whole was dubbed as CT.[20] When the control of the traditional criminal behaviour on the part of certain tribes became a problem for the British Government, they felt it necessary for preventive and deterrent purposes to treat the entire tribal group legally as a CT. In this way all the members could be kept under continuous watch and vigilance.

The gangs of thugs used to travel by roads in the disguise of merchants and ordinary travellers and used to strangle, plunder and kill innocent travellers on finding opportunities to commit these nefarious acts.[21] Sleeman writes: "Large gangs from Hindustan and the Deccan used to rendezvous in these groves, remain in them for many days together every year and carry their dreadful trade."[22] The operations went on upto 1853 till the thuggery was created.[23] By 1860, the suppression of these pirates was completed. After complete suppression of the thugs and pindharis, the English paid their attention to the nomadic and Gypsy tribes roaming in India.[24]

It is difficult to enumerate all the tribes declared as criminals. The report of the All India CT Inquiry Committee enumerated 136 of them besides the various mixed groups declared as such.[25] A report prepared by the Tribal Cultural Research and Training Institute, (TCR & TI) Tribal Welfare Department, Hyderabad, Andhra Pradesh cited 59 sects of denotified tribes of Andhra Pradesh.[26]

The first criminal tribes Act was passed in 1871 by the Governor General of India in Council. The CT Act was amended in the year 1897. The CT Act II amended received the assent of the Government on 28th January 1897. Another Act of CT came into existence in the year 1911. This Act was repealed in 1923. A new Act was passed in the year 1924. The CT Act of 1924 was again repealed and the Madras Restriction of Habitual Offenders Act was passed in the year 1948. The Criminal Tribes Laws Repeal Act was passed in 1952. The Andhra Pradesh habitual offenders Act was passed in 1962. This Act was abolished in 1965. With the abolition of this Act a number of tribes dubbed as criminal were set free. However, the stigma of 'once a criminal is always a criminal' is still attached to them.

A. *The Criminal Tribes Act of 1871*

Origin of the Criminal Tribes Act 1871

Prior to the enactment of the Act XXVII of 1871, there was no special legislation to deal with the 'criminal' tribes. They were governed by the ordinary law of the land as everybody else was governed. It was reported that the magisterial and police authorities had found it impossible to deal with criminal bands in India. Therefore, the Government of India decided to enact a special legislation and the Act XXVII of 1871 was passed. The Act received the assent of the Governor General of India on 12th October 1871. It is an act for the registration of CTs and Eunuchs.

Main Provisions of the Act

According to Sections 2, 3, 4, 5, 17 and 19 of the 1871 Act, the local Governments were required to report to the Governor General of India the tribes they wished to declare as criminals, reasons for declaration, their fixed places of residence and the areas intended to be restricted under the Act together with a note regarding the arrangements for their means of livelihood. If the Government of India was satisfied, the tribe could be declared criminal under Section 5 of the Act. The District Magistrate had the authority to order the CT members to appear for registration and restriction. The authority was also vested in the local Government to transfer the tribe from one place to another place under certain conditions or place them in reformatory settlements. Village headmen and watchmen had the duty imposed on them to watch the movements of the members of 'criminal' tribes and also to report the offences committed by them. The local police were given authority to inspect their residence and villages. The Act, in brief provided for registration, restriction, control and surveillance of the CTs. The Act was restricted in its application except Section 1 and 20. These sections applied to the whole of British India, the rest of this Act extended to the terrotories and provinces of Bengal, the North West Frontier Province, (NWFP) the Punjab and Avadh.[27] In 1876 by Amending the Act of 1871 it was extended to Lower Bengal as well. As a result of the experience gained by the British Government, the 1871 Act was amended in 1897 (Act II of 1897). The power was delegated to the provincial Governments of notifying tribes. Any action could be taken against a part of the class, gang or tribe also. Under Section 17 (A) of the Act, the local Government was vested with the authority to establish and maintain reformatory settlements and to separate, remove children from their parents. The Government established reformatories and institutions for the CTs. The children of the CTs under the age of 18 and above the age of 4 years were kept in such reformatories. Superintendents were appointed to guard the children. Penalties were enhanced for the repetition of offences as well as breach of rules.[28]

The main aim of the 1871 Act was to keep an eye on the activities of the CTs. The Act also aimed to control the crime and help the members of CTs to reform and rehabilitate themselves. The provincial governments were authorised to declare any group of people whom they suspect as 'incorrigibles' as CTs.[29] In this Act the phrase CT was first coined. The system of registration had begun. This Act provided for the maintenance of a register in which the names and other particulars of the tribe were written. Some of them were required to report at regular intervals to the police station.

It was discovered that the families of these men were usually involved in petty criminal activities. If the men were thrown into prison, the families either had to continue their depredations or suffer great financial and emotional stress. The authorities found that criminals who were released from prison were worse than before. As a result of the experience gained, the Act was amended in 1897.

B. *The Criminal Tribes Act of 1897*

In 1897, the colonial government passed another CT Act. It permitted the local governments of India to establish and maintain settlements for children of CTs. In these settlements they were taught to work. Instructions were given to lead an honest life. Their children were sent to schools. It was hoped that such steps would bring about a complete reformation. If any family failed to furnish the required information they were liable to punishment. They were forced to remain in the settlement until the authorities were fairly certain that they could be trusted to remain honest and law-abiding citizens. Enhanced penalties for repetition of offences and breach of rules were provided.[30]

The CTA II of 1897 was found deficient in many particulars. It got adverse criticism from the Police Commission of 1902-03. Eventually in 1911 a fresh Act (Act III of 1911) was passed. Some new provisions were brought into this Act. The Act made it obligatory on the members of the CTs to register themselves, to allow fingerprints to be taken, to report their action and change of residence. The Government was further vested with the power to restrict the movement of a tribe to any particular area or place of residence; and the power relating to reformatories were further elaborated. As against these stringent provisions, two liberal modifications were made authorising the District Magistrates to grant exemption to reformed members and raising the age limit of children of separation from their parents from four to six years. It was stated that : "Evidently, the activities of the CTs at the time must have been considerably anti-social to secure the consent to the Act of such a liberal statesman and patriot as the late Shri Gopal Krishna Gokhale."[31]

C. *The Criminal Tribes Act of 1911*

Origin of Criminal Tribes Act, 1911

The Criminal Tribes Act, 1911 had its origin in the report of the Indian Police Commission, 1902-03. The Police Commission laid down the principle that it should be the aim of every police system to obtain knowledge of CTs and secure overall supervision on certain gangs addicted to crime. Starting from this principle, the Police Commission declared that the police should have more powers of control on the criminal tribes. Keeping this specific object, the Police Commission recommended certain amendments to the CTA of 1897. The Government of India, in due course of time found many defects in the CT Act of 1897 and repealed the Act. In the place of 1897 Act the CT Act of 1911 was substituted. The CT Act 1911 was more comprehensive than the 1897 Act.

Main Features of the 1911 Act

The main features of the Act were: 1. Notification, 2. Registration 3. Restriction of movements, 4. Settlements, schools, and penalties.[32] If the local governments had reason to believe that any tribe, gang or class of persons or a part of a tribe, gang or class is addicted to the systematic Commission of non-bailable offences, it may, by notification in the local official gazette, declare that such persons or group was a CT (section 3). There are two methods of dealing with these people - registration and settlements. Registration attempted to keep track of them under police surveillance in the communities where they live. Settlement means locating in a special place so that they can be more clearly controlled than by registration. Certain passes were issued to the criminal tribes to leave the place in which they are settled.[33] Schedules were prepared. Personal identification marks, thumb and palm impressions of the tribe were taken into consideration.

Under Section 22 of the Act if any member in a family of the CTs violates the rules they were punished and imprisoned in the jails. On the first conviction one year jail, on the second conviction two years jail sentence and any subsequent conviction to three years rigorous jail imprisonment were made.

Difference between the CT Act of 1871 and 1911

The Criminal Tribes Act of 1871 was only applied to certain provinces in Northern India, namely, Benal, United Provinces, North

West Frontier Province (NWFP) and Punjab. It was not extended to Madras. However, the Criminal Tribes Act 1911 applied throughout British India. The application of CT Act 1871 in certain provinces was not possible to the British Government due to some practical difficulties. The Criminal Tribes Act 1911 was designed to apply the provisions of the criminal Tribes Act in all provinces. One of the specific objectives of the 1911 CT Act was to enlarge the power of control by enabling the Local governments to proclaim CTs on their own authority and provide for the registration of the members without reference to the questions of settlement or the provision of the means of livelihood.[34]

Provisions of the 1911 Act

The CT Act 1911 enabled the Local Government: (1) to declare any tribe, gang or class to be a criminal tribe, if it is satisfied that tribe, gang or class is addicted to the systematic commission of non-bailable offences, (2) to order the registration of the members of any criminal tribe and the taking of their finger impressions and (3) to direct that, every registered member shall report himself at fixed intervals or notify his place of residence and changes thereof. The Local Government can also declare, with the sanction of the Government of India, that a CT shall be restricted in its movements to any specified area or shall be settled in any specified place of residence (Section 12). But before such action was taken, the Government of India must be satisfied that it is expedient to restrict the movements of such tribe or settle them in a place of residence and that the means by which it is proposed that such tribes shall earn their living were adequate. Another important feature of the Act was that the Local Government is authorised to establish industrial, agricultural or reformatory schools and to separate the children from their parents (Section 17). This provision was the most important and useful portion of the Act. It enabled the Local Governments to secure all the children, to educate them and to bring them up in a more wholesome atmosphere than that in which they would have been left if the tribe had not been settled. The government hoped by these means the children would grow up as honest citizens. Under Section 20 of the Act, the Local Government may make rules to carry out the purposes and objects of the Act. Strict penalties and procedures were laid on the members of a CT such as issuing notices, obtaining unnecessary information from the families and taking fingerprints etc.[35]

D. *The Criminal Tribes Act of 1923*

The question of CTs came into review during the year 1919. The CT settelements were the main terms of reference included in the All India Jails Committee. The All Indian Jails Committee was appointed during the year 1919. The Jails Committee emphasised that the settlements were not to be merely another kind of a jail. The CT settlements were such places where there is a provision for economic development. Without enthusiasm, devotion and religious teachings, the economic progress could not be achieved. The committee emphasised that the aim of the settlement should be positive one of the reclamation of the settlers. The CT settlements were not merely the negative one of the protection of the society from their degradation. The committee deprecated segregation and separation of children from their parents only in certain cases. The committee recommended that the most successful settlements would be placed in the industrial places. The settlers were employed as labourers in the industries. Due to the non-availability of land and lack of experience in agricultural methods, the committee did not recommend the opening of agriculture among the CT settlements.[36] The Committee also did not recommend for the industrial settlements because the CTs were not provided work sufficiently, paid less remuneration and were barred from socially useful work. However, for the first time, the Government considered the problem of CTs with greater emphasis. The government laid emphasis on economic development. It paid lesser attention on the penal side.[37]

E. *Criminal Tribes Act of 1924*

On the recommendations of the Indian Jail Enquiry Committee, the CT Act was again amended in 1923. It was applied to the whole of British India in 1924. In many aspects, the 1911 Act was found defective and contained many loop-holes. Basically, in aim and intent, it was preventive and not corrective. There were virtually no attempts in it to reform and rehabilitate the criminals. There was provision for separating children from the parents and giving them proper education. But there were practical difficulties too. Intermixing the parents and children will add new problems. The culture of crime will be continued. Some of the main features of the Act are: 1. Notification, 2. Registration, 3. Restriction of movements, 4. Settlements and Schools of Criminal tribes and 5. Unjust punishments and sentences.[38]

Provisions of the 1924 Act

1. *Registration:* Every member of the designated tribe was categorised as a "Criminal" or as a "potential criminal." The tribes were instructed to register themselves either with the police department or the village administration, the purpose being to locate and keep vigil on them. Every new born child was thus forced to be registered to update records. Failure to register was a punishable offence.
2. *Reporting* : A surveillance system was built up by making every registered person belonging to a "Criminal tribe" report to the police or to the village administration. The movements of each such person were recorded and each one had to get written permission from the authorities to go out of the colony and when returning to it had to furnish information about the purpose and destination (name and address) or the movement. Regardless of whether any crime was indulged in, merely belonging to the "Criminal Tribe" Provided sufficient legal grounds for total vigilance.
3. *Segregation:* Those individuals and families which were really involved in criminal operations never bothered to register themselves or report to the authorities. To exercise effective control and watch over them, active criminals and families were rounded up and sent to special settlements. The management of these settlement was given over to Christian missionaries, who were given magisterial and police powers. Some arable land was made available and the settlers were expected to cultivate it and live on its produce. Reporting to the management thrice a day was a routine instruction; night checks and controls were conducted; some settlements were fenced with barbed wire. In Andhra Pradesh there were five such settlement, established between 1906 and 1917; Sitanagaram and Stuartpuram in Guntur District, Kapparalatippa near Bitragunta in Nellore District, Siddhapuram in Kurnool District and Lingala in Mahaboob Nagar District. The Culture of crime was perpetuated by isolating the members of the tribe and keeping vigilance on them, because the children born in these settlements were socialised only in their values and culture, old people take pride in narrating their brave deeds.

Section 3 of the Act empowered the local government to declare any tribe or class of persons or a part there of, as a criminal tribe, if it has some reason to believe that they are addicted to the commission of non-bailable offences. Sections 4 and 5, empowered the district magistrate to make a regular register of the members of the criminal tribes living within his jurisdiction. The district magistrate called every member of the tribe concerned and asked each one to furnish the information required by him. Section 16 of the Act provided for the establishment of industrial, agricultural, reformatory settlements and schools for criminals. It empowered the local government to place any tribe in any type of settlement. Section 23 of the CT Act declared that any person belonging to this category convicted once for any offence under the IPC, specified in the schedule first, if convicted to the same offence for the second time, he will be punished with imprisonment for ten or not less than seven years and on a third or any subsequent conviction with transportation for life. The instance of getting a pass and reporting oneself to the police and village headman to take forced and free labour from the poor. This gave birth to bribery at the local level.[39]

Though the Act remained in force for about 80 years, it failed in its purpose. The leaders and social reformers realised that the dubbing of a people as CT was a blot on the Indian Society. Nehru stated in 1936: "I am aware of this monstrous provision of criminal tribes Act which constitutes a negation of civil liberty. Wide publicity should be given to its working and an attempt made to have the Act removed from the statute book."[40] B. Pattabhi Seetaramayya, angrily pointed out that: Cattle that are sold and brought in the market, wild animals that are hunted out of villages, worms that are trodden under the feet are not worse treated than criminal tribes.[41] Criticising the CT Act Vennelacunty Raghavaiah stated "the CT Act destroyed domestic peace, embittered human life and led to the false theory i.e., once a criminal is always a criminal."[42] Thakkar Bapa remarked that, "the Criminal Tribes Act is disgracing our statute book."[43]

F. *Madras Restriction of Habitual Offenders Act, 1948*

During the year 1947, under the CT Act 1 of 1947 (Section 23 of CTA) laid down the minimum punishment of 7 years for the second offence and transportation for life for the third and subsequent offences was modified to the maximum of 7 years. The court can award any punishment it considered appropriate for the CTs. It came into force from 29th April 1948. It aims at the control of the criminals who take to crime as a profession. It was taken up after the rules under the Act were published in the Fort St. George Gazette dt. 22nd November 1949. The then Deputy Inspector General of Police Railways and Central Intelligence Department Madras noted: "The application of the Act is very limited. The Act has application only to such criminals—convicted of serious offences and criminal minded persons interned in the settlement. The Government of India published an All India Habitual offender's bill which is an effective-instrument to exercise better control over the criminals."[44]

N.G. Ranga strongly fought for the repellation or abolition of the CT Act in Madras Presidency. He said the CT Act was used to 'suppress political workers' in those days.[45] Two bills were passed in the Central Legislative Assembly. The first bill was sponsored by Venkatsubba Reddiyar who was an MLA to repeal the CT Act. The second bill was sponsored by N.G. Ranga. He proposed to repeal sections 10, 11, 12, 13, 17, 18, 19 and 20 of the Act.[46]

G. *Criminal Tribes Laws (Repeal) Act, 1952 (No. XXIV of 1952)*

This act is called the criminal tribes laws (repeal) Act 1952. The Act extended to the whole of India except the state of Jammu and Kashmir. The CT Act and any other law corresponding to that was repealed on the 31st day of August 1952. However, the central government by its notification in the official Gazettee declared that the said Act or law shall stand repealed in all the States.[47] Though the Act was abolished in India by 1955 in some of the states, the provisions of the Act continued till 1965. The Andhra Pradesh Habitual Offenders Act was passed during the year 1962.

H. *Andhra Pradesh Habitual Offenders Act 1962*

With this Act the Government of Andhra Pradesh formulated some rules.[48] They are:

1. The Superintendent of Police shall from time to time, examine the cases of individuals residing in the area within his jurisdiction.
2. A register is maintained in the settlements. The register shall be placed in the custody of the Superintendent of Police.
3. Every registered offender is supplied with a certificate of identity.
4. Every registered offender shall give his certificate of identity

for examination or inspection when required by any police officer.

5. Every registered offender shall report at the nearest police station.
6. The District Collector or any officer, authorised by him on his behalf may at any time order the finger and palm impressions, footprints and photographs of any registered offender to be taken.
7. With this Act, if any habitual offender is found outside the area, to which his movements have been restricted, he may be arrested without warrant by a police officer.
8. If a registered offender is arrested or convicted, the certificate of identity shall be treated as his personal property and dealt with accordingly.
9. When a village headman receives information that a registered offender of another village has spent a night or part of a night in his village, without a certificate, he shall promptly inform the station house officer. Any registered offender who intends to leave the house in which he is residing, during night between 10.00 p.m. and 5.00 a.m. before his departure, he/she has to inform to the village headman, the date and time at which he intends to leave the house and return and the place to which he/she is going.

IV

Conclusion

For the first time, penal provisions were imposed on CTs in 1871. They were gradually stiffened till 1911. From 1919 onwards there was a tendency to make modifications in favour of CTs. The Act of 1924 was amended by the Act 1 of 1947 in the Indian existing law in relation to the CTs. The government felt that it was the time to repeal the evidently stringent laws without endangering the security of the peaceful citizens and without weakening government authority in the matter of reclamation and reformation of the CTs.

Many of the District Magistrates and Superintendents of Police in Madras presidency did not favour the repellation of the CT Act. But some sympathetic District Magistrates and Superintendents of Police forced the abolition of the CT Act. Social organisations, workers and associations, of the CTs (Bharatiya Adimjati Sevak Sangh, Andhra Rastra Adimjati Sevak Sangh under the leadeship of Takkar

Bapa and Yerukala, Yanadi, Sugali Associations under the leadersship of V. Raghavaiah and other community members) from all the settlements requested the government for the total repel of the CT Act. The District Magistrates and SPs who were against the repeal of the CTA however favoured the notification of CT individuals. They defined terms 'Tribe', Gang', Class' and people addicted to the systematic commission of non-bailable offences.

The first CTA was passed 135 years ago in 1871. It had located, identified and restricted the law abiding citizens in India. The Acts severely penalised and stigmatised honest people in the society. It created an impetus among the tribes. It made the communities to disassociate among themselves. The Act divided the communities into 'criminal' and non-criminal groups without having any social and marital relations. There was a clear separation among the tribal groups. Many individuals and families keenly felt the stigma. There was almost a universal request from the members of the tribes, freedom fighters and social workers for the total removal and abolition of CT Act. There was no single advantage of the CT Act in Madras Presidency. The CT Act created the psychological effect with a stigma of 'criminal' as millions of people particularly their younger generations among the communities were severely affected. They in turn developed anti-social feelings, resentment towards the society for condemning and branding them as 'criminals'. The youngsters with undeserved shame and inferiority complex among their classmates of other castes suffered seriously. On the other hand, the adults in the employment spheres suffered as their employers shied off on getting to know that their employee was a member of the CT.

Various states in India took steps to repeal the Criminal Tribes Act. The Madras Government was the first to take steps to repeal the Act in 1949. The Indian Government appointed a committee in 1949 to study the usefulness of the law. It expressed the view that the Act was against the spirit of the Constitution. The public also moved and as a result the CT Act was repealed in 1965. With the repeal of the Act, about 2,268, 348 persons in the country were legally set free.

After Independence, the Government of free India abolished the Criminal Tribes Act and tried to free the criminal tribes from being "Born criminals". Also asserted that crime can be no profession. In spite of the change in the legal situation, the position of the CTs in the settlements continued and they did not get a chance to change themselves for the better. It is still unfortunate to call the whole tribe or a clan or family criminals. There is no country in the world to our knowledge, whose people practice crime as their occupation. To our surprise, even blind persons are also registered. To reform the CTs, it is necessary to impart them some professional skills of earning a livelihood, for it is hopeless to expect them to be honest without proper food and shelter.

Now the status of the criminal tribes in law is the same as other fellow Indians. Various committees also recommended that suitable steps should be taken for the amelioration of the problem of CTs after the repeal of the Act. The government is now involved in initiating necessary steps to ameliorate the hardships of these groups of people. In spite of all the facilities provided by the Government of India and the states, the social position of the criminal tribes remains the same as before. The stigma still haunts them. These people are unable to free themselves from social bondage.

NOTES

1. See, Chirravuri Nagabushanacharyulu, *Adimavasulu*, (Telugu) Tenali, 1949, p. 60. Also see, *Judicial Department, G.O. No. 917 dated 10th May 1913*, p. 1.
2. See, *Government of Madras, Administrative Report of the Forest Department, Madras Presidency for 1889-90*, Madras, p.27, TNA. Also See, Radhakrishna, Meena, *Dishonoured by History, Criminal Tribes and British Colonial Policy*, Orient Longman, Hyderabad 2001. p.8. Also see, *Judicial Department, G.O.No. 918, dated 10th May 1913*, p. 3.
3. See, Government of Madras, *Development Department, G.O. No. 1634*, dated 6th December, 1922 p.1 TNA. Also see, Government of Madras, *Report on Scheduled Tribes, Welfare of Chenchus – Kurnool district, Material condition, progress for 1959-60*, Kurnool, 1961, pp. 1-5. Also see, *Judicial Department, G.O. No. 924, dated 10th May 1913*, p. 2.
4. In the history of Deccan, while prince Mohammad Masum, son of Aurangazeb, was passing through Kurnool, the Prince gave the Chenchus gold and silver, but they were unconcerned at receiving them. Firishtha, the Mughal chronicler, wrote, the Chenchus were "a wild mountainous people who dressed themselves and lived on honey, roots and flesh of wild animals and had a language not in the least understood by the plain folk". See, *Tour in Hyderabad*, Pamphlet No. 11, by the Secretaries of *Bharatiya Admjati Sevak Sangh*, New Delhi, 1950, p. 3. Also see, *Judicial Department, G.O. No. 918, dated 10th May 1913*, p. 3.

5. See, Government of Madras, *Proceedings of the Chief Conservator of Forests, Proceedings No. 321,* (Press), *dated 15th July 1932,* p. 4. Also see, *Judicial Department, G.O. No. 1161, dated 12th June 1913,* p. 1.
6. Government of Madras, *Hukumnamas and Papers relating to Sriharikota Yanadis, Vol.1, A selection of papers from the old records of the Nellore District,* Nellore, 1915. Also see, *Judicial Department, G.O. No. 1161, dated 12th June 1913.*
7. See, Jagannath Pathy, 'Social Basis of Banditry and the Criminal Tribes Act', *Social Science Probings, Vol. 1, No. 4, December 1984,* p. 497. Also see, *Judicial Department, G.O. No. 1193, dated 18th May 1913,* p. 3.
8. See, Radhakrishna, Meena, "From Tribal Community to Working Class Consciousness : Case of Yerukula Women" Review of Women's Studies, *Economic and Political Weekly, Vol. XXIV, No. 17, April 29, 1989,* pp. 2-3. Also see, *Judicial Department, G.O. No. 1298, dated 30th June 1913,* p. 2.
9. See, Jagannath Pathy, *Op. Cit.* p. 494. Also see, *Judicial Department, G.O. No. 1369, dated 5th July 1913.*
10. See, Government of Madras, *Note Showing the Progress made in the Settlement of Criminal Tribes in the Madras Presidency upto September, 1916,* Madras, 1917. p. 19, TNA. Also see, *Judicial Department, G.O. No. 1379, dated 8th May 1913.*
11. Mildred, E., Mackenzie, *The Mud Bank,* Pensilvania, 1894, p. 60.
12. They felt that if they committed any offence and went to far away places, apprehending them would be very difficult, especially as in those days means of communication were not sufficiently developed. The agencies for detecting crime were not properly organised. Even if they returned to the same place after a few years, it would be difficult to recognise the culprits and establish their guilt. Thus, they were secure and as circumstances were favourable, they developed their technique of committing crimes. See, Vernier Elwin, *The Aboriginals in Oxford Pamphlets on India Affairs, No. 14, Oxford* University Press, Humphrey Milford, 1943, p. 1. Also see, *Judicial Department, G.O. No. 1638, dated 13th August 1913.*
13. Waskom Pickett, J., *Christian Mass Movements in India,* Chicago, 1933, p. 297. Also see, *Judicial Department, G.O. No. 1639, dated 13th August 1913.*
14. *Ibid.,* p. 298. Also see, *Judicial Department, G.O. No. 1645, dated 14th August 1913.*
15. They gathered in gangs to roam across the subcontinent for three or four months of every year. They spend the balance of the year in their home villages appearing as ordinary peasants. Sleeman wrote, "while I was in the civil charge of the district of Narsingpore no robbery or theft could be committed without my becoming acquainted with it ; nor was there a robber or a thief of the ordinary kind in the district, with whose character I had not become acquainted in the discharge of my duty as magistrate." Quoted, in Freetag, Sandra B, 'Crime in the

Social Order of Colonial North India', *Modern Asian Studies, Vol. 25, 2, 1991*, pp. 234-36. Sleeman grouped them mainly in five categories as follows: 1. Fighting men and soldiers lost their jobs and turned into criminals, 2. Communities who were doing the work as village watchman and who took to criminal life, 3. Wild tribes in distress who took to criminal life, 4. Beggars turned to criminals and 5. Some selected castes and tribes who were very poor and considered low in the society took to crime. For other details see Shah P.G., *Vimukta Jatis, Denotified Communities in Western India*, Bombay, 1967, p. 23. Also see, *Judicial Department, G.O. No. 1796, dated 5th September 1913*, p. 2.

16. A. Balmer, the then Superintendent of Police, Nellore stated that the Yerukulas are constantly moving in Nellore district. The Yerukulas migrated to Nellore from Cuddapah and Kurnool Districts. They spread all over the country. A close watch cannot be kept on their encampments. Some live here and others make a visit now and then. These people unite with the occupations of salt and grain carriers with robbery and have friends and agents in every part of the country. Three-fourths of the dacoity and robbery in this district is caused by Yerukulas. In consequence of their roaming habits, the speed with which they travel, the friends they have in all districts, their connection with different gangs, it would be difficult to watch and observe these people. See, *Appendix to the Government Police Report, 1863*, Government of Madras, 1896, pp. 24-25, TNA.
17. See, Ghani, Mohammad Abdul, *Notes on the Criminal Tribes of the Madras Presidency*, Provincial police Training School, Vellore, Madras, 1915, p. 246. Also see, *Judicial Department, G.O. No. 2005, dated 3rd October* 1913.
18. See, Government of Madras, *Home Department, G.O. No. 1675*, dt. 2nd December, 1919, p. 2. Also see, *Judicial Department, G.O. No. 2066, dated 13th October 1913.*
19. David, Macritchie, *Account of the Gypsies of India*, New Delhi, 1962, p. 62. Also see, *Judicial Department, G.O. No. 2120, dated 21st October 1913.*
20. See, Lalitha, V., *The Making of Criminal Tribes patterns and transition*, Madras, 1995, p. 12.
21. See, Taylor, Meadows, *The Confessions of a Thug*, New Delhi, 1988, p. 70. Also see Sleeman, W., *Rambles and recollections of an Indian official*, Delhi, 1915, p. 651 (First published in 1844). Also see, *Judicial Department, G.O. No. 9th December 1913.*
22. See, Sleeman, William, *Ramaseena and a vocabulary of the peculiar language used by Thugs*, Calcutta, 1836, pp. 32-33. Also see, *Judicial Department, G.O. No. 2573, dated 11th December 1913.*
23. See, Sleeman, William, *Op. Cit.*, p. 650. Also see, *Judicial Department, G.O. No. 2573, dated 11th December 1914*, p. 1.
24. Sleeman, William, the hero of the Thugee Department wrote: The system is destroyed, the profession is ruined, the guild is scattered

never again to be associated into a great corporate body. The craft and mystery of the thuggee will no longer be handled down from father to son. See, *Judicial Department, G.O. No. 113, dated 17th January 1914.*

25. Some of the criminal tribes in Bombay Presidency were Berad, Bhamptus, Bauriah, Bhars, Pasis, Bhils, Chapparbands, Dharalas, Kaikadis, Kolis, Lamanis, Mang Garudis, Minas, Sansia, Waddars. Bhamptus travel all over India and commit thefts in crowds. Bauriahs are expert burglars. Bhars and Pasis commit murders. Chapparbands were wanderers. They took to coining. Kaikadis are house-breakers. Kammis are local thieves. Katkaris are crop stealers. Mangs are experts in passing off brass ornaments for gold. Mang Garudis are beggars. Marwar Baoris disguise in Sadhus. Minas are burglars. Pardhis are noted for hunting and poaching. Waghris were addicted to theft and cheating. 47 tribes are notified under the CTA in United Provinces namely the Parsis, Doms, Banjaras, Haburas, Chambars, Nats, Aherias, Bantu, Borya, Sansias, Karwals, Hindu Gosains, Lodhas. Few tribes are, Muslims. Majority members of CTs are Hindus. Gujars, Bhars, Kewats belong to scheduled castes. See, Government of Bombay, *Report of the Criminal Tribes Act Enquiry Committee*, Government Central Press, Bombay, 1239. pp. 12-25. Also See, Government of India, *Report of the Criminal Tribes Enquiry Committee,* United Provinces of India, Allahabad, 1948, pp. 2-4. Also see, *Judicial Department, G.O. No. 381, dated 14th February 1914,* p. 3.

26. These tribes are as follows: Telaga Pamulas, Konda Doras, Boyas, Yanadis, Dommaras, yerukulas, Budabukkalas, Lambadis, Waddars, Donga Dasaries, Pedda Boyas, Nirshikaris, Donga-Ur-Korchas, Kanjarbhatt, etc. Cited from the *files, Superintendent of Police, Crime Branch, Hyderabad, No. 1185/CIB/58 dated 27.2.1958,* APSA.

27. See, *Judicial Department, G.O. No. 1316, dated 4th July 1891,* p. 4. Also See, Government of British India, *Criminal Tribes Act Enquiry Committee Report,* 1871, Delhi, 1872, p. 1.

28. See Raghavaiah, V., The *Problems of Criminal Tribes,* Akhil Bharatiya Adim Jati Seval Sangh (BASS), Delhi, 1943. Also see, *Judicial Department, G.O. No. 461, dated 21st February 1914.*

29. The term 'children' includes all persons under the age of 18 and above the age of four years. See, *Act. No.11 of 1897* passed by the Governor General of India in Council, Madras, 1898, p. 1. TNA. Also See, Semhadri, Y.C., *Denotified Tribes (A Sociological Analysis),* classical publishing company, New Delhi, 1991.

30. On a first conviction to one year, on a second conviction to two years and on any subsequent conviction to three years and any further conviction be liable to whipping. See, Government of India, *Report of the Criminal Tribes Enquiry Committee,* United Provinces of India, 1947, Allahabad, 1948, p. 5. Also see, *Judicial Department, G.O. No. 657, dated 16th March 1914,* p. 3.

31. See, Government of Madras, *Criminal Tribes Act Enquiry Committee*

Report of 1911, Madras 1912, pp. 1-2, TNA. Also see, *Judicial Department, G.O. No. 700, dated 21st March 1914.*

32. See, *Judicial Department, G.O. No.1023, dated 4th May 1914*, p. 3.
33. The earliest criminal tribes settlement in Andhra Pradesh was established by the American Baptist Telugu mission at Kavali in the year 1912. Before that, there was a settlement at Kalichedu in Nellore district for Dommaras and Katheras in the year 1911. Sitanagaram Settlement was established by the Salvation Army in the year 1913. Siddhapuram Settlement was a voluntary settlement established in the year 1914. Stuartpuram settlement was established in the year 1914 by the Salvation Army. Bhummannagadda settlement was an agricultural settlement intended for the Nawabpeta Korchas. Reformatory Settlement in Guntur was established by the Salvation Army. Chintala Devi settlement in Nellore district was established in 1914. The Nizam government opened a settlement for the Donga Waddars, Yerukulas and Chenchus at Lingala in Mahaboobnagar district in 1917. See, *Home Judicial Department, G.O. No. 101, dated 15th January 1917.*
34. See Government of Madras, *A Collection of the Acts of the Indian Legislature and the Governor General for the year 1924 (Act VI of 1924)*, Delhi, 1925. Semhadri, Y.C., *The Ex-Criminal Tribes of India*, National Publishing House, New Delhi, 1979.
35. See, Government of Madras, *Note showing the progress made in the settlement of Criminal Tribes in the Madras Presidency upto September, 1916*, Madras, 1917, p. 1. Also see, *Home Judicial Department, G.O.No. 160, dated 23rd September 1917.*
36. See, *Government of Madras, Madras Criminal Tribes Manual, Criminal Tribes Act VI of 1924 brought upto 31st March 1927, Madras, 1927, p. 1. Also see, Government of Madras, Note Showing the Progress made in the Settlement of Criminal Tribes in the Madras Presidency upto January 1925,* Madras, 1927. p. 3.
37. Government of Madras, *Madras Criminal Tribes Manual, The Criminal Tribes Act, 1924 (VI of 1924) As Amended by the Criminal Tribes (Amendment) Act, 1925 (XXXIII of 1925)*, Supernintendent, Govt. Press, Madras, 1927, p. 1.
38. *Ibid.*
39. *Ibid.*
40. Quoted in Raghavaiah V., *Problems of Criminal Tribes, Op. Cit.*, p. 11.
41. *Government of Madras, Note showing the progress made in the settlement of Criminal Tribes in the Madras Presidency upto September, 1916, Madras, 1917,* p. 3.
42. *Ibid.*
43. *Ibid.*

44. See, Government of Madras, *Administration Report on Habitual Offenders Settlement for the first half year 1953-54*, Madras, 1955, p. 6.

45. The registration of persons under the Madras Restriction of Habitual offenders Act, 1948 was taken up after the rules under the act was published in the Fort St. George Gazettee. 5268 persons were registered under the Act out of which 4,097 were the Ex-Notified Tribes. The Ex-Notified Tribe members belong to the wandering gangs. During the year 1951 a total number of 770 persons were brought under the provisions of the Act. The Act had showed very little effect in controlling crime and criminals. Only some active criminals were kept under strict control by the provisions of the Act. The proposals were submitted to the government. The report of the findings of the CTA Enquiry Committee recommended for the amendment of the Act. The Bombay Habitual offenders Restriction Act, 1947 was more rigorous and comprehensive than the Madras Habitual offenders Act. The amendments were submitted to the government on 1st may 1952 to make the act more useful in its function. The amendment of the act aimed at controlling the crime and criminals in Madras province. See, Government of Madras, *Administration Report on Habitual offenders Settlements for the year 1951-52*. Government Press, Madras, 1953, Also See, *Government of Madras, Home Department, G.O. No. 2900, dt. 8.8.1952.*

46. It was stated in the *Report of the Criminal Tribes Enquiry Committee, United Provinces*, 1947, that "Prof. N.G. Ranga's proposal amounts to willing to wound but afraid to strike, it seeks to retain the best of the CTA and remove its Kernal. In a special penal legislation such as the CTA, the only Justification can be the absolute necessity of provision of coercive and restrictive measures for the protection of society and if these are to be 'deleted or diluted' as Rangas' bill proposes, the raison d'etre of the Act disappears." For details see, Government of India, *Report of the Criminal Tribes Enquiry Committee, United Provinces of India, 1947*, Government Central Press, Allahabad, 1949, pp. 11-12. Also See, Government of India, Home Department *File No. 24/21 1943 Police branch 1943*, p. 1. Also See, Government of India, Police Branch, *The Criminal Tribes Amendment Bill by Prof. N.G. Ranga, File No. 32/3/45*, Delhi, 1945, p. 1. NAI.

47. See, Simhadri, Y.C., *Denotified Tribes, A Sociological Analysis*, Classical Publishing Company New Delhi, 1991, p. 171.

48. *Ibid.*, p. 187.

2

Tribes in Transition: A Study of Denotified Tribes

Introduction

There are some groups of people in India whose 'criminal' propensities are well known and hence are dubbed as 'criminal' tribes. These tribes are kept under a vigilant watch both by the people and the government. The study of these people concerns us rather significantly because they constitute very much a part of the society. They are extremely poor, devoid of formal education and oppressed by fears which arise out of lack of modern knowledge in the society. The present chapter attempts to highlight the conditions of the Dasaries, Dommaras, Nakkalas, Waddars, Sugalis (Lambadis), Yanadis, and Yerukalas and the various aspects of their life. They are called as nomadic semi-nomadic, ex-criminal tribes and denotified communities. They live in "Tandas" (colonies/villages) throughout the State.[1] They are leading a life of misery and suffering. From the stage of nomadism and unsettled life, they should be brought into the main stream of society by providing them regular aid, proper means of livelihood and employment opportunities.[2]

I

Denotified, Nomadic and Semi-nomadic Tribes Dasaries (Katheras)

Dasaries are one of the Denotified communities in Andhra Pradesh. They predominantly inhabited in Bellary district. They are called Aligaries or Capemaries.[3] The appellation 'Alagiri' was given to them as a class of professional thieves (pickpockets). This was applied by the police to the persons suspected by them, whose castes are not known and who give a vacillating account of themselves and who had no place in the census reports. Dasaries were also known as Katheras' an endogamous sect of the Devangas and a subdivision of Gadabas.[4] 'Kathera' is a Telugu word meaning scissors. They were known as 'Katheravandlu'. The appellation seems to have been given to them from the fact that they frequently go to fairs and festivals and busy railway platforms selling knives and scissors.

There are four divisions among them. They are: *(1) Cape Mari Alagiri, (2) Donga Dasari Alagiri, (3) Gudu Dasari Alagiri and (4) Padayachi Alagiri.*[5] The Headquarters of *Cape Mari Alagiri* was located at Tirevellore, Chingleput districts in Tamilnadu. They were also found in Bangalore, Cuddapah, and South Arcot districts.[6] The head of the Cape Maris lived in Tiruvellore. He was attached to *Abbilam Mutt* as paid servant. Their men and women are fair and good-looking. Their language is Telugu. They also speak Tamil and Canaries. *Donga Dasaries or Gudu Dasaries* are called *Mucherikalas.*[7] They are drawn from the Boya, Golla, Waddera and Salia Castes. In Nellore district they are known as ***Kathiravandlu*** (thieves). Their Headman is styled as Gudu.[8] He was responsible for predatory excursions. The headquarters of these people are Cuddapah, Bellary, Kurnool, and Nellore districts. They are found in small numbers throughout Andhra Pradesh. They visit temples in the guise of Byragies (Wandering Sadhus/Sanyasins), with religious symbols. They command respect from the villagers. They are experts in the art of reciting the Vedas. *Padayachi Aligiris or Thogamalai Koravas* are skillful counterfeiters and dexterous in passing coins.[9]

Dasaries are petty thieves and pickpockets in olden days. Hindus of all classes and some Muslims are the members of their fraternity. They are described as a part of the great Satani caste disciples of Chaitanya, a native of Bengal, who introduced the worship of Lord Krishna in south India and died in 1527. Dasaries or Aligiris resemble the Sonariahs and Bhamptas of Bundlekund and Poona.[10] Both men and women are clever.

They are trained in the art of picking pockets and snatching jewels from travellers. Men adopt the disguise of respectable traders. They were well dressed, wearing caste marks and other outward signs of respectability. They gain admission to temples.[11] They acquaint themselves with the names of persons of good social standing and ascertain facts connected with their private life. They take the advantage of these acquaintances and cheat the persons occasionally. Women and children usually dress well, sometimes like Brahmins and sometimes as fashionable well to do family members.[12] They attract the men-folk and deceive them at the end. Starting in a gang of 4 or 5, the men were accompanied by their women and children. They occupy seats in railway compartments. Some of them disguise as traders and others as wandering minstrels. They wait for the opportunity to steal jewels, valuables and leave the train at the next station. The members in the gang unite at a place previously agreed upon.[13]

Though their language is Telugu, they are well acquainted with Hindustani. They take the role of traders in cattle and visit cattle markets. During 'pongal' festival the 'religious Dasari' is frequently seen with his sacred bull asking alms.[14] Before proceeding on a predatory excursion, offerings of sheep and fowls are made to their Goddess 'Gangamma'. They carefully observe omens. Women of all classes with the excepton of 'Malas' and 'Madigas', are admitted to their community. The marriage ceremony is performed by a purohit from the 'Satani' creed.[15] Marriage laws are easily relaxed and polygamy is allowed. Widow marriage is also allowed. Infant marriages are very rare. Dasaries are loyal to one another. Thota, Mekala, Kunchala are some of the well known family names of these people.[16] Dasaries lift children in order to strengthen their community numerically. The children are brought up in an atmosphere where crime is the only source of livelihood. The deplorable economic conditions, prevailing during the 19th century, in the whole of Madras presidency were responsible for the grave crime, committed by Dasaries.[17] It was stated that the Dasaries were dangerous than the Yerukulas. Bawden said: "I should say the Dasaries of Kalichedu were of a more dangerous character of criminals. Most of the absconders and those in jail are from the Dasaries. They need the penal settlement because they do not believe that we are trying to help them."[18]

The socio-economic factors responsible for declaring them as criminal tribe are: (1) Conditions of insecurity prevailing in Madras Presidency. (2) Administrative mismanagement in areas of limitless revenue extortions which resulted in the pauperisation of the country sides and consequent misery of the people. (3) The havoc created by the Rajas and Zamindars. (4) The failure of monsoons, recurring famines and drought situations. (5) The disorder, law and order situation in the state, etc.[19] All the above factors were responsible for the criminal depredations. As Sarada Raju said: "Harassed by rival armies, extortionate renters, Zamindars' and despoiled by gangs of robbers, the condition of the country was indeed deplorable."[20] Under these circumstances mica mines attracted the attention of the government authorities to settle the Dasaries in Nellore District. Kalichedu may aptly be described as the centre of mica mines in Nellore district.[21] This was under the supervision of Mr. Ludwig, local agent of Kalichedu Mica Mines. The settlement was established in 1911 with a total strength of 391 members and later on due to the outbreak of the great war in 1914 led to the closing of the mica mines, hence Kalichedu settlement.[22]

Kalichedu settlement was the first settlement established in Andhra Pradesh in the year 1912. This settlement was meant for Dommaras and Dasaries. A large Kathera gang was raided by the police in the territories of Nizam.[23] They were brought to the Kalichedu settlement. However, as suitable employment could not be provided to them, they began to live on charity. Later on they were shifted to Mypad where they were tried in agricultural occupations.[24]

Some Yerukalas and Dasaries were interned in Kapparalla Tippa and Sitanagaram Settlements. The nature of interaction with other group's of people at Kapparallatippa are different from that of Sitanagaram settlement. People living in these areas are generally responsible for the cultural impact on these people.[25] Distance makes all the difference. Culturally and socially, these people are isolated and segregated from other people.[26] The most formidable task one faces in bringing up these people close to the contemporary world is in setting an ideal tone for ensuring better societal relations between individuals.[27]

Dasaries are not related to the Yerukalas by marriage or by descent. They are declared as a 'criminal' tribe by the then British government and settled them in KapparallaTippa and other settlements.[28] Both the communities are living together in the settlement for a long time. There are cultural contacts between them from the beginning.[29] However the Dasaries are listed under Backward class community. They are economically very poor and deserves to be included in the category of Scheduled Tribes. The social experience of the ex-criminals still adds to their lurking fears of being dominated by the more vociferous strata of the society.[30]

Unless the society provides equal opportunities, normal and equal treatment with others in every sphere of life, the ex-criminals may not come out of their shell. Dominant sections of society should not oppress them. As long as the 'stigma' remains, they cannot become real partners in enjoying their due share of national prosperity.[31]

The psychological barrier that prevents the ex-criminals from identifying themselves with other sections of the society arises out of their 'inferiority complex'. As long as other sections of the society look at them with suspicion, no better atmosphere could prevail. These people cannot have emotional affinity with others as long as they do not acquire sound economic base. A radical change is essential in the very socio-economic fabric of society. Reformatory steps will have to be carried on forever. Change is a continuous process and it has to be pursued with all dedication, zeal and energy.

II

Dommaras Reasons for Declaring Dommaras as a Criminal Tribe

Dommaras are a tribe of tumblers, athletes and mountebanks. Some of them wander about the country, while others have settled down as agricultural labourers. They are experts in making mats, combs and cosmetic articles. They sell their articles to the wholesale merchants. These are a semi-nomadic class of acrobats. They rear pigs. They are the itinerant trading community. They migrate from place to place to show their circus and dance performances. The British Government declared the Dommaras as professional burglars. They used to camp near the villages and towns. They steal pigs, kill them and distribute pork among them. They maintain close contacts with the villagers. In all respects, they resemble the Gypsies in their style of living and that they may also possibly be connected with the Doms of northern India. They are skillful jugglers and snake charmers. Both men and women are clever tumblers, rope and pole dancers. They display their physical feats as they travel about the country. As a tribe they are tall and well built. They are dark in complexion. Shortt said that "the predominant type of countenance which they exhibit is Mongollan. They have some what pointed chin and absence of whiskers, large eyes and prominent cheek bones."[32] The titles used by the headman of the caste are Reddy, Nayudu and Naik. Their suffixes like Raju, Raya, Nayudu and Reddy, etc. mentioned in the epigraphs indicate the process of sanzkritization among the Dommaras.

Dommaras are found predominantly in Northern Circars and Hyderabad. Dommaras are mainly found in Gurazala, Rentachintala, Miriala Guda, Karampudi areas in Guntur district. They were also found in East and West Godavari, Krishna, Nellore, Anantapur and Chittoor districts. Dommaras were convicted by the Colonial Administrators for the petty criminal offences against the stolen property and other sections of Criminal Procedure Code. It was stated that: "The Dommaras are addicted to the systematic commission of cognisible and non-bailable offences. Therefore they are fit persons to be recognised under the Criminal Tribes Act."[33]

The Dommaras adopted acrobatism as their main occupation. They used to exhibit various gymnastic feats, athletic exercises, rope dancing, tumbling and conjuring tricks. By means of these performances they sustained their livelihood. They have no interest in agriculture. Their traditional profession is acrobatism. However, this is not patronised either by the present government or by the people. The Medieval Telugu literature and epigraphs contain interesting information about the various aspects of their life. They throw considerable light on the means of livelihood, their living conditions, caste organisation and various aspects of their life. They are declared as CTs based on the lines of the Maravars of Tinnevelly and Adi-Dravidians in North Arcot district. Abeyance system was introduced to control them.[34]

The original place of Dommaras was Maddalapuram in Cudapah district during Vijayanagar empire.[35] A number of sub-castes existed among the Dommaras. The epigraphical evidence indicate that the Dommaras made endowments to the Temples in the Telugu country.[36] The inscription in Cuddapah mentions that the endowments were made for the religious merit of all members of the 24 kulas among Dommaras.[37] An inscription from Pushpagiri in 1577 A.D. from Cuddapah district refers to the "Veedus" of Dommaras which have religious endowments to the local temples. Dommaras hold Inams in the Telugu country especially in Jammalamadugu, Tadipatri, Proddutur and Macherla areas. They were spread into the Mysore territories also. They are said to have travelled to more than 50 countries as trading clans.[38]

There are two mythological stories about the origin of Dommaras. According to the first mythological story a child who was handed over to the wandering beggar thinking that he will bring ill luck to the family. The beggar consigned the child to a ruined well. The cries of the child attracted the attention of the Gods Parvati and Parameswar. They bestowed on him the right to obtain an earthen drum from a potter's house and rice from each house as alms. The boy who got the blessings of the Divine, was also rejoined to add the profession of acrobatic performer to that of itinerant beggar. It was a popular belief that the Dommaras were the descendants by a concubine. According to another mythological story it was stated that a Reddy's wife delivered a daughter. A hut was improvised and the sister in law of the Reddy contrived that the mother and child should be regarded as out-castes. The father gave all his land and property to the progeny of the other wife and left to these a drum, a pole and a rope. The daughter learnt acrobatic feats and later she became a prostitute and thus earned her livelihood. This is said to account for the practice, of prostitution which is prevalent in Dommara caste.[39] However these mythological stories are not correct, they indicate the process of sanskritisation among them. The Dommara caste appears to be an offshoot of the Doms of Bengal, Bihar and the North Western provinces. In the 1871 census report, it was noted that in many villages, the Doms carried the occupation of weaving. In Jaipur they are employed as horsekeepers, scavengers, and in other works.[40] Fawcett wrote that "these people are an outcaste jungle people, who inhabit the forests on the high lands, fifty to eighty or a hundred miles from the east coast, about Vizagapatnam."[41]

The Dommaras are divided into two groups, viz., Reddy Dommaras and Array Dommaras. The Array Dommaras are also known as the Mahrata Dommaras from the fact of their language being a form of Marathi. They chiefly confined themselves to wandering in the Ceded Districts, the Nizam's Dominions and Mysore province. There is however little distinction between the two classes, and their caste customs appear identical. They are said to be allied to the Lamadies, a statement which perhaps is supported by the legend which tells of 'Mola', the ancestor of the Lambadies, as exhibiting his gymnastic feats before the king. The view is further corroborated by the fact that Lambadies and Dommaras mix freely with each other. The head of the tribe is called the 'multiguru'. He is their high priest and thus exercises supreme jurisdiction over them both in spiritual and temporal matters. His head quarters was located at Chitvel, Pullampet-Taluka of the Cuddapah district in Andhra Pradesh. The position is hereditary and highly respectable.[42]

The language of the Reddy Dommaras is Telugu. The Array Domamras speak Marathi. They have a slang of their own. Their dwellings are some what similar to those of the Koravars and Joggies of Tamil Nadu. Their houses are made of palmyra leaves. Their huts are located on the outskirts of the village. They carry their huts on the backs of donkeys when they migrate from one place to the other.[43]

The men among the Dommaras usually wear trousers made of a coarse white cloth. They also use gaudy shawls, Jackets and Lace turbans. After acrobatic performances, they get presents from the people. The women in the past are generally considered to be the concubines of the poligars. The women of the tribe, are good looking. They are easily identified by their dress and ornaments. The gay clothes, profusion of brass bangles, necklets of cowries make a distinction in the personality of the women. The treatment of Dommara women is very peculiar. From early infancy, they are trained in the mysteries of rope dancing and tumbling. Those who prove themselves adepts are reserved for prostitution and the rest are allowed for marriage. Marriage takes place after puberty. Adultery by women is condoned. If a married women elopes with a man of another caste, fine will be levied, equal to that of the marriage expenses. If she comes back, she is given 'thirtha' (divine water) which makes her as 'Kulambidda' that is, an approval or a license to live in the caste. If an unmarried girl becomes pregnant through a person of the same group, their marriage will be performed. If he refuses for marriage he is declared as an outcaste. Then the women concerned may be married to any person, cutting a few locks of her hair, slightly burning the tip of her tongue with the bit of gold and swallowing 'vibhuti' (sacred ashes). In the social scale they are considered to be the low caste people ranking next to the Malas and Madigas (Harijans).

The Dommaras are notorious for dedicating their girls to become 'Basavis'. The dedication ceremony takes place when the girl attains the age, between 15 and 16 years. The girl is bathed and dressed in new clothes. The girl bows to the elders and receives the blessings from the caste elders. She will be taken to the 'Yellamma' or 'Hanuman' temple beating the drums and singing songs. The 'Yajaman' (Head of the Caste) grants her sanction to lead a life of prostitution. She is declared as harlot and receives from her first lover new clothes, four rupees, a new dwelling (hut) and a cot to sleep. Sometimes the 'Basavis' get themselves tattooed with

Vaishnava symbols of 'sankha' and 'chakra' and after death, their dead bodies would be carried and buried by Dasaries. The children of the 'Basavi', born before marriage are left with her father. The Basavis daughter gets a share in her grand fathers property. Even after death, her children are entitled to her share of property. 'Pattapurani' is the house name of one of the Dommara endogamous sects. A Basavi, who wishes to give up her life of prostitution, may be married in the kudike form. However, she will not be allowed to perform acrobatic feat in public. Her children born before the marriage are left with her father.[44]

Women play a very active role in household and other kinds of work. Men either marry them or keep them as concubines. Polyandry is unknown. The Bride price is 52 rupees. Still it is prevalent among the Dommaras. The marriage ceremonies are most primitive. The bridegroom, along with his trusted friends, goes to the bride's place and make the proposal. The bride and bridegroom should belong to two endogamous groups. The exchange of betel between the two parties is considered as the ratification of the contract. 'Tola Bottu' (mangala sutra) and five toe rings are used for the marriage. The bride groom proceeds to tie the tali; the bride puts one of the five rings on her husband's second toe on the right foot and the Basavi or a married women of the tribe puts the remaining four rings on the brides four other toes. The marriage ceremonies, which are numerous, usually take five days to complete. Child marriages are not performed. Widow remarriage is prevalent. polygamy is common. The relations between the sexes are very lax.[45]

The Dommaras wander about the country and still they are in a semi nomadic stage. Their economic backwardness did not hamper them in the way of making donations to the temples of various deities. The religious endowments instituted by the members of the community, mentioned in the epigraphs were in favour of the Vaishnavite temples like those of Chennakesava and Tiruvengalanatha and Ganapati. They also worship female deities like Yekilidevi, Yellamma, Sunkalamma and Poleramma. Poleramma is their Kuladevata (Mother Goddess). She is invoked and her blessings are solicited on the eve of their activities. The cultural life of Dommaras was very rich. Some of the Dommara women were well versed in varieties of music and dance. They are proficient in musical instruments like the Venna, Dolu and Mridangam.

The interesting feature of Dommaras is that they have relations with the Doms of northern India. The Dommaras are designated as 'Dombari' and 'Domber', which are the derivations from 'Dom', the term by which the very numerous outcastes of northern India are known. They were allied to the Kolties and the Bereahs of Central India and the Dommaras of Bengal. Crooke finds the origin of the Doms in the Dravidian menial castes who were the aborigines of India. In the past they were forced to live on the outskirts of a town, eat spoiled food, wear the clothes of the dead and were excluded from all social intercourses. Some authorities are of the opinion that the existence of such towns as Dompur, Domali, Domigarh, etc. show that there was a Dom kingdom at one time. What ever their origin, they are nomadic people throughout India.[46]

Dommaras who lived in Nellore and Guntur Districts were considered to be the most dangerous criminals in the Madras Presidency. At Kalichedu (mica mines) in Rapur Taluq of Nellore District a criminal tribes' settlement was established for them.[47] The experiment of kalichedu settlement had passed through three stages: (1) Settlement on the mica mines and training in Industrial skills, (2) Leasing out lands and imparting training in methods of agriculture and (3) Settling them as peaceable ryots elsewhere only those who have passed through the above stage.[48]

Kalichedu settlement was closed down in the year 1917, due to the pressures of the 1st World War. They were rehabilitated in different parts of Nellore District by Late Vennela Kunti Raghavaih, well known social worker, and freedom fighter of Nellore district. The nomadic character of Dommaras, the meager means of their livelihood and the prevalence of Basavi system make their life miserable. They earn meager income by selling mats, combs, baskets and whigs. They are very poor and economically backward.[49]

In conclusion, we would like to highlight a very important aspect relating to the Dommaras. Today they are included in the category of Backward Communities List (OBC Category) in Andhra Pradesh. They are no longer considered as a schedule tribe. There is every proof to say that they are a nomadic tribe for all practical purposes. However, it is unfortunate that they are included in the list of backward communities, which deprives them of the benefits of positive discrimination.[50]

III

Nakkalas

Nomadism is as old as mankind. There is historical evidences for the existence of nomadic groups throughout the world. *The Criminal Tribes Act Enquiry Committee Report* stated, "there are certain wandering tribes found in the Madras, Bombay, and in the Hyderabad. They live by hunting, begging, collecting and selling forest produce. They are experts in snaring birds."[51] The World Health Organisation (1964) emphasised the urgent need to study primitive and small populations around the world. There are a good number of nomadic groups like hunters, trappers, artisans, entertainers such as acrobats, magicians, puppeteers, snake charmers, monkey displayers, singers, dancers, fortune tellers, palmists, deity displayers and others.[52] L.H. Morgan points, "It is probable that the great epochs of human progress have been identified more or less directly, with the enlargement of the sources of subsistence."[53] Nomadism cannot be described as a character of individuals. It is a cultural trait which results from want of ambition, or aspiration either total or partial. Nomads constitute a significant part of more than 60 crores population in India.[54] Many of the nomadic, tribal groups are slowly getting extinct. There is an urgent need for demographic and ethnographic investigations. Studies on such populations provide ample opportunities to assess significant changes in human societies. An attempt is made here to study another particular nomadic tribe of Andhra Pradesh, viz. Nakkalas. The literature dealing with them is scarce and very little is known about them. Not much information is provided in the District Gazetteers also. The information regarding Nakkalas is totally based on field survey that has been conducted in Andhra Pradesh. The present information has been gathered from Venkaiah, the President of the Nakkala Welfare Society in Chemudigunta in Venkatachalam Mandalam in Nellore District of Andhra Pradesh. Without his help, it would have been difficult to approach them or to have access to the required information.

There are different appellations in different languages about the Nakkalas. 'Narikorava' or Nakkala is one among the habitual non-pastoral nomadic tribes of South Eastern India. They were mostly found in the towns, cities, and in the villages of Tamil Nadu. In Andhra Pradesh they are called Nakkalas. They hunt jackals.

They are also called as Pusalavandlu (makers of bead necklaces), Pittalavandlu or Guvvalavandlu (bird catchers). They are called Shikaris in Karnataka and Malawalas (necklace sellers) in Hindi speaking areas.[54] Their dialect is closer to that of Marathi and Gujarathi. The Nakkalas are mentioned as a 'criminal' tribe in the *Criminal Tribes Enquiry Committee Report. (1949-50).*[55] Enthoven reported the Vaghris (Narikorava) as one among the endogamous groups of pardhis, who belong to the great predatory Bawari Tribe of Gujarat. They were scattered under different appellations all over India. They claim their origin to the descendants of a Kshatriya family. Their ancestor, a Kshatriya man, married seven wives and they (Narkoravas) are the children of the fourth wife. The children of the first wife are Marwadis and the children of the second wife are Sugalis; the children of the third wife are Marathas, the children of the fourth wife are Narikoravas; the children of the fifth wife are Banjaris; and the children of the sixth wife are Meenas. The children of the seventh wife is not clearly mentioned in the puranas.[56] Some others say, that they are the children of Kaalairaja, king of a Kshatriya family. They are the descendants of Guru Dheenavat. Narikorava is a tribe of Gujarat and people of Mewar. Long ago, these people migrated to the south for livelihood. The geographical connections, linguistic affiliations, dress patterns also give sufficient evidence of their migration. During the year 1922, Nirshikaris of Kurnool, Bellary districts and the Nakkalas were brought under Sections 3 and 10 of the Criminal Tribes Act. They are found in Godavari, Vizagapatnam districts and in the South of the Ganjam district. The headquarters of these people is the Palkonda taluk of the Vizagapatnam district.

Nakkalas are divided into several lineages like linbo, dambo, pawar, pillio, thobanio, darkio, nilaji, lalji, bokku, naval, makiram, govinda, nakkala, datto, damo, jambula, kheto, namo, nanching, calching, sinodi, salio, palhal, manizo, makro, nande, ganibalu, jagat, blutto, khubo and villyo, etc.[57] C.P. Ramaswami Iyer said, "they live by basket-making dealing in horses and ponies, cattle-breeding, fortune telling and various forms of magic."[58]

The family system of Nakkalas is patrilineal. However the women occupies an important place. They lead a life separated from all others. They are rigid and tenacious in following their customs and rules governing their clan. They are very particular about the reputation of their women. They consider it a serious matter if a woman returns home after dusk without an escort. Among them, joint family system is an unusual feature. Presently, nuclear family system has come into existence. Nakkalas have their own type of tribal marriage. Nakkalas prefer consanguineous marriage of both cross-cousin types and rarely uncle niece type. In addition to that the brother-in-law can marry his wife's elder sister. Sometimes father and son can marry brother in Law's sisters and call them accordingly to their relations. Bride price, originally was twelve rupees, now it is increased upto 2000 rupees. Still, it is continued and dowry system has crept into their marriage system. Generally the marriage of a girl takes place before puberty. Child marriages are still prevalent among them. Monogamy is observed in most of the families. But in some cases polygamy is followed. Polyandry is never found in their society. All the wives, irrespective of the number and their children live together. The marriages are performed generally for three days. On the first day they prepare rice pongal and the second day, they eat meat and on the third day the bridegroom will go to the bride's place. Hunting and drinking are common in all the auspicious occasions. Betelnut, rice, vegetables, green gram, onions, garlic will be distributed to all the families in the tribe. In the marriage 'thali' made out of the black beads is tied round the neck of the bride.[59]

The bride and bridegroom take pongal in their hands and keep it under the chin of each other. Another notable custom that prevails among them is that the bridegroom and bride's mother should collide their heads forcefully, so that a sound is heard. Then only the bride's mother accepts the bridegroom as her son-in-law. Those who attend the marriage cry loudly when the 'thali' is tied round the neck of the bride.

Remarriage of widows is permitted among them. Adultery and other contraventions are adjudicated by the panchayat (Council of Headmen). They settle disputes and decide on the amount of fine or punishment to be inflicted on the guilty. If the charge of adultery is established the woman in question will have to take her bath and she is asked to pray to goddess Kanaka Durga. They keep the betel leaves in her hand, tied with a thread. The burning hot iron rod will be placed in her hands. She has to carry a rod and throw it on a heap of hay. If her hands are not hurt she is considered as chaste and vice-versa. If any women has illicit relations with a man of other tribe, she will not be retained in her community.

Birth ceremonies of children are not celebrated. One of the old women of the tribe serves as midwife, and receives a small present in return for her services. Naming of the child depends upon the place where the woman delivers a child. The dead are buried and nothing will be kept along with the dead body. On the eleventh day, after death, they perform the obsequies to which all their kith and kin are invited. If it is a woman, the ceremony is observed on the 12th day as it is supposed that female child takes more to be born than a male child. The ceremony is called 'Dokkukulu Dokkulu'. Nakkalas are short-statured, and have narrow shoulders, narrow chest and long arms. They possess weak bodies. They live under the shade of trees and on pavements close to busy places like markets, bus-stops, railway stations and temples. They live on petty trade of selling needles, small mirrors, kum kum (bindi pointers) combs, etc. Their men wear a loin cloth and rarely a turban whereas a woman wears a low skurt and blouse. Both men and women wear colourful bead necklaces. Tattooing is done on different parts of their bodies.

The 'Nakkalas' are Hindus by religion. Nakkalas are associated with their Goddess like Jagaur, Viraghan, Villaivelo, Nowkhad Devi, Selmahammari, Vaghai Devi. Figures of Goddesses are kept in a bundle of blood soaked clothes as 'Samisatru' or 'Samimoota'.[60] They also worship 'Parvathiswari', Goddess of Hills. D.D. Kosambi stated: "Nearest to Poona city is the Parvati temple, now dedicated to fashionable Brahmin Gods; but many others are known which retain more primitive deities slightly brahmanised, to whom an animal blood sacrifices will be made."[61] Elmore stated that these Gods and Goddesses are almost propitiated with blood or animal sacrifices.[62]

The Nakkalas are still leading a life of nomadism. Piggery, cattle rearing, domestication of birds, selling waste papers and begging, are their occupations. They love hunting. Most of their names are not figured in the voters list today. They are still in the food gathering stage. Nakkalas wherever they are they should be provided with the status of scheduled Tribes and the right to vote because most of them are in the nomadic stage. Political consciousness is not found among them. There is no one educated or politically conscious, in their community, who can represent their case. Another significant factor is that these people are requesting for land to cultivate and earn subsistance. They should be provided with land to cultivate and earn their subsistence. This changing occupational trend towards agriculture is part of their desire to settle down in a permanent habitat.

There is an emerging social consciousness among them to get rid off their nomadic habits by taking to agriculture. The government of Andhra Pradesh recently included them in the list of scheduled tribes category.

IV

Waddars

Ethnic Background

Waddars were known as Katheras or Dasaris. They were also known as Gudu Dasaris or Mucherikalas settled in all districts of Andhra Pradesh. They were drawn from the Boya, Golla, Daddur and saliakas.[62] In Siddhapuram the term "Donga Waddera" is used for these people. The term *'Waddera'* is a corrupt form of the Sanskrit word *'Odhra'*, the name of the country now known as Orissa from where these people are supposed to have migrated.[63] The members of the Woddars were nomadic but majority of them have settled in different parts of the country, especially in Kurnool, Guntur, Krishna, Banaganpally, Chittoor, Cuddapah and Nellore districts of Andhra Pradesh.[64] In Gribble's Cuddapah district manual, this tribe is classified as house-breakers, cut-purses (pick-pockets) and cattle lifters. Gribble, as early as 1875, remarked that these Waddars were the most hardened class of criminals.[65]

These Waddars live in detached settlements, conical huts similar to those of the Dommaras with a low entrance.[66] The huts were far away from any village and most probably they live in selected jungles.[67] They used to wear a waist cloth and an upper cloth and put on *'namam'* and a *'bottu'*.[68] In the name of Kal-Waddars or Matti Waddars, they watch the topography of each house in that village, pitch upon such houses and commit house-breakings. They were skillful to break open any stone or mud wall without much difficulty. They go out in batches to villages for work and commit crimes.[69]

Previously, they lived in Bodducherla, Markapur taluk, Kurnool district and later, in 1890, they came to Kothalur in Vinukonda taluk of Guntur district.[70] This formed as the head quarters of the gang. This can be well cited that Machi Reddy a Kapu criminal (of Cumbum taluk of the then Kurnool district) organised a gang of Woddars. Another criminal by name Vemulanagadu was the head of the other gang. These two parts of the gang were formerly registered as gang no. 83 and 84 of the Criminal Investigation Department (CID).[71] After the death of Vemulanagadu, Machi Reddy became the head of the gang. Their total number was 33. These leaders became old and infirm, lived together for certain time but later split up into small parties headed by their own nominal heads. They occasionally united at marriage celebrations and other occasions. They took to a wandering life committing crimes throughout the ceded districts. Thus a notorious gang settled at Siddhapuram in Kurnool district.

F.S. Mullaly, in his Notes on Criminal Classes of the Madras Presidency, wrote, "in ceded districts some of the Woddars were known as Donga Waddars or 'thieving Waddars' from the fact of their having taken to crime as a profession."[73] These were desperate, and at times very cruel. When any opposition comes across they were ready to inflict severe personal injuries on their victims. Paupa Rao Naidu mentioned about the 14 different divisions of Woddars located in different places. They had their own peculiarities.[74]

In the manual of North Arcot district these Waddars were summed up as natives of the country, quarrying stone, sinking wells, constructing tank bunds and executing other kinds of earth work more rapidly than any other classes.[75] Thurston in his Castes and Tribes of Southern India writes that these people have two sub-divisions according to their occupations. 1. The *Kallu* or *Rathi* Wadars (stone workers) and 2. The *Mannu* Waddars (earth workers).[76] M. Kennedy further subdivides these people as *Bhandi* Waddars (cart men), *Pathrat, Janti* or *Dagdi* Waddars (stone dressers). *Ghatti* Waddars also known as *Donga* (thief) or Takku (cheat) Waddars. *Takku Waddars* (Donga Waddars) were inveterate house breakers and burglars.[77]

All Waddars are not criminals. The 'Donga Waddars' of the ceded districts form a separate section living by means of criminal propencities. The ordinary waddars wander about the country living temporarily where they get work. In Banaganpalli state they were called as *Takku Waddars.* In Chengalpat district they were called as *Kallu Waddars* and in Gudiatham town of North Arcot district they were *Mannu Waddars.* In Kurnool, Bellary, Cuddapah, Chittoor, Anantapur, Nellore and Guntur districts of Andhra Pradesh they were called as *Donga Waddars. Takku Waddars* (Donga Waddars) were inveterate house breakers and burglars.[78] Besides building walls, they were skillful stone-cutters. Under the disguise of mending grind-stones, they used to obtain useful information about the houses to be looked or parties of travellers to be attacked.[79] In committing a highway robbery or dacoity, they were always armed with huge sticks and sometimes use violence in case of defence. Their depredations were usually confined to a radius of 20 miles (32 kms) from their encampment. They seldom set out in large bands for the purpose of committing crimes.[80]

The Waddars are a fine looking people. They are dark in complexion and capable of much endurance and generally hard working. The males are well-built, and wear Vaishnavite trident marks on their foreheads, arms and breasts.[81] As a class they are dirty, thriftless and hard drinkers. They wear scanty clothing. The male's dress consists of *Dhotar* (loin-cloth) or *Cholna* (short-drawers) *Angi* or *Pairan* (shirt) a *Rumal* or a piece of cloth for the head, a *Hachda* (coarse sheet) and *Kambal* (blanket) or shoulder-cloth worn over the shoulders.[82] Women's dress is a sari with the upper end passed over the head and across the bosom. Men do not wear shoes and women do not wear the bodice nor glass bangles on the right hand.[83] They wear brass or kasa bracelets. The looks of the younger women would compare favourably with women of the better class.

The Waddars of Siddhapuram were originally from different parts of Andhra Pradesh. Some of them were related to each other. Kinship plays a very important role in the life of the 'Waddars' of Siddhapuram. They like to live close to their relatives. They also prefer to establish marriage ties within their community itself. They maintain their social ties with their kith and kin in different parts of Andhra Pradesh.

Being exclusively a Telugu sect, their language is a corrupt form of Telugu, but those settled in the Southern districts are conversant with Tamil. They also speak Marathi or Canarese according to the district they live in.[84]

The Woddars hold that they had a number of sub-castes of which eleven are known today. They are as follows: 1. Mannu Waddars-*Earth workers* 2. Kallu Waddars-*Stone workers.* 3. Uppu Waddars-*Salt traders* 4. Bandi Waddars-*Cart users (Gadi Waddars)* 5. Girini Waddars-*Grind Stone workers* 6. Raja Waddars-*Lac-Sellers* 7. Aragu Waddars-*Lac-Sellers* 8. Tudugu Waddars-*Thieves* 9. Uru Waddars-*Town dwellers* 10. Takku Waddars-*Robbers and House breakers* and 11. Ghatti Waddars-*live in forests.*[85]

Mannu Waddars are largely found in the districts of Gulbarga, Mandya and Mysore. They are employed in earth work such as well sinking, construction of railway tracks, irrigation canals, tanks, dams, bridges and its repairs.[86] According to a note, compiled by a sub-inspector of police by name, Rashid-Ulla Khan, from Yeotmal district, they always travel in disguises, so that the distinguishing characteristics were not easily observable.[87] The *Kallu Waddars* are employed in stone Quarries, building constructions, road-metaling and cutting or grind stones.They were more in the districts of Bangalore, Bellary, Chitradurga and Kolar. *Uppu Woddars* trade in salt and tamarind. They are found in Bangalore, Kolar and Chitradurga districts. In Andhra Pradesh, they are found in Chandragiri Mandal of Chittoor district. *Bandi Waddars* are stone workers. They live in huts made of mats, grass, etc. They are accompanied by their families, and pack donkeys. *Girini Waddars* derived their name from their profession of cutting grind stones. *Raja Waddars* are employed in public construction works. *Aragu Waddars* collect and sell forest products like gum and wax. *Tudugu Waddars* are highway robbers. This group of Woddars were referred by Edgar Thurston and Abdul Ghani. *Uru Waddars* weave ropes. *Ghatti Waddars* encamp in the forest or on waste lands. They were also accompanied by their families, pack asses, goats, etc. The Waddars believe that they originally formed a single endogamous group but in due course they were split into a number of smaller endogamous groups. Each sub-caste is named and the name indicates the occupation.[88]

They eat all types of animal food such as rats, fish, pigs, black faced monkeys, Jackals, antelope, fowls, cats, deer, goats and all sorts of birds, crows, sparrows, and squirrels. They eschew beef.[89] They are generally non-vegetarians. They go for begging and hunting. They smoke ganja and tobacco. They are addicted to drinking.[90] They do not hesitate to mix up with Dommaras, Madigas and Malas.[91] Mannu, Kallu and Bandi Waddars interdine with each other.[92]

Social Life

Woddars consists of two types of families, namely, nuclear and extended families. There may be one or two single membered families also. In course of time, they get the nuclear status. There are 300 families of waddars living in Siddhapuram settlement. We have Interviewed the inmates of each and every hut and gathered the information about the present state of affairs. The 300 families comprise of 3000 people. On an average, each family has 1 to 2 acres of land. Some families have more and some have not even one acre of land. Some Waddars do not have permanent huts. Their average monthly income on all sources may be between Rs. 1000-1500.[93]

While doing the construction work, they came in close contact with ordinary Waddars and hence the possibility of inter-marriages between them. The general marriage ceremony among the Waddars is performed in two stages. 1. *Okkakubettedi* (tambulam bettedi) i.e., betrothal and *Pendli* (marriage). This takes place in the presence of elders. Gangaraju (the village head) plays an important role in conducting marriage ceremonies.[94]

When the parents of the boy or a girl find a suitable match for their son or daughter, they exchange betel leaves, betelnuts, turmeric and fruits to the girl's house accompanied by Gangaraju and a few elder members.[92] The relatives of the boy and girl sit in two separate rows facing each other and bargain their demands. After receiving the betelnuts in the presence of village headman, the brahmin fixes the auspicious day for marriage. F.S. Mullaly writes, brahmins exercise spiritual jurisdiction over these people and are consulted in matters connected with marriage and other ceremonies. The marriage ceremony is not a tedious one. It consists of the bride and bridegroom walking three times round a stake placed for the purpose in the ground.[95]

The marriage involves a number of rituals and social ceremonies spread over a period of two days. The important rituals in a marriage are, the *Nalugu, Gangapuja, Dare, Tali, Oli,* and *Muyee*. The *Nalugu* ceremony is performed by five or seven elderly women of their community. The maternal uncle presents new clothes to the bride and the bridegroom. The bridegroom receives two white dhotis and a shawl and the bride a white saree and a blouse.[96]

This crermony is followed by a procession to the village temple where the bridegroom performs puja. After the visit to the temple, food is served at the bridegroom's house. The tali tying is performed accordingly as it is arranged earlier. The ritual is performed by the bride's father who takes rice in both hands and drops it over the head of the bridegroom and the bride. This is followed by tying the tali or mangal sutra. The maternal uncle of the bride plays a dominant role in this function. He presents mettelu a pair of copper or silver toe-rings. The *oli* (bride-price) and *muyee* (gift-giving) ceremonies are generally performed after the feast. Gangaraju begins the oli ceremony. Its cost is Rs. 8. The bridegroom gives Rs. 20 to Gangaraju as a payment to the community God.[97]

It was observed that these Woddars are slowly bringing changes in the institution of marriage. This is due to the Sanskritisation process. The impact of higher castes is felt on these people. On one hand oli system is continued, on the other, the educated Waddar bridegrooms are demanding dowry.[98] Some marriages are taking place in the churches due to the influence of Christianity. Pastor performs the ceremony.

Widow remarriage exists by mutual agreement between the two spouses to live as husband and wife with the approval of the *Kula Panchayat*. No ritual significance is attached to such a marriage. The bridegroom and his party visit the bride's house with saree, ornaments and flowers.[99] The headman performs the ritual. When these Waddars were first settled in Siddhapuram, they had no marriage ceremony. The practice of the tribe was that those members who happened to be out of jail should assort themselves as man and woman locked up in intimate relationship with each other. As some come out of jail and others went in, new alliances were contracted. There was no such thing as stable marriage relationship. This was changed largely through the influence of the Settlement Managers. The marriage ceremony and regular relationship are the order of the day with the Siddhapuram settlers.[100]

Thurston reports polygamy and divorce are freely allowed to men. Divorce is possible at any time but Rs.16 has to be paid to the bride's parents. The Children by the marriage are divided between father and mother as decided by the Kulapanchayat. Divorces are very infrequent occurrences. Infant marriages are allowed but seldom practiced.[101]

Festivals, Ceremonies and Superstitions

Birth ceremony is another happy occasion among the Donga Waddars. Though it is observed among all the castes, the practice varies from caste to caste. It is customary for a Waddar woman to give birth to her first and second child at her natal home under the care of her mother. She is sent to her natal home during the fifth or seventh month of her pregnancy. The Waddars believe that the mother-daughter relationship is the most tender and affectionate one and a pregnant daughter always looks forward to her mother's care during the last stages of her pregnancy like other caste women. The relationship of a daughter-in-law to her mother-in-law is one of great respect. The Waddars feel that a daughter is unwelcome to the family. They pray for son, who perpetuates the family prestige. He toils hard and protect the family from economic difficulties. A girl after marriage becomes the member of other family that is the reason why she is considered to be a loss to the family.

The birth of a child causes pollution to the mother, child and all the other members of her conjugal household. The mother and the child are given a bath on the third, fifth and seventh days. On the 9th day, turmeric paste is applied on the mother before she is given a bath to remove her impurity. No sacred offerings are made. On the 9th day the house is cleaned and purified by sprinkling water mixed with cow dung.[102] The members of the family light a wall-lamp to worship the household deities. They prepare sweet pongal and offer coconut to the household deities. Among Mannu Waddars, the naming of the child is performed on the 11th day.[103] The presentation of hair to the deity is another important ceremony found among them. The temples that the Waddars generally visit are Venkateswara of Tirupati, Penchala Narasimha Swami temple of Penchalakona, Malakonda Swami temple of Pamuru, Veera Brahma Matham of Cuddapth, Mallamkonda Swami temple, Peddamma temple of Nellore, etc.[104]

When the death occurs, they keep the body with its head resting towards south.[105] Valuables are removed from the dead person. The eldest son of the father or the youngest one of the dead burns incense at the feet of the corpse. Rich people erect grave stones and monuments and the others put stones on the grave. The Waddars believe that the spirit of the dead visits the grave on the third day. The food is kept on a leaf and the people move to a distance so that a crow can come and touch it. The Waddars observe ritual pollution caused by death for ten days and participate in the purificatory rituals on the eleventh day. If a death occurs on a Tuesday or Friday, they believe that the spirit of the dead normally remains malevolent for at least three months.

The Waddars are more superstitious and put great faith in omens. Some of their bad omens are: 1. any member sneezing when they are about to start, 2. the meeting of two sudras on their way,

3. a cat crossing their path and 4. the whining of a dog. If any of the above happens, they will put off their expedition. Some of their good omens are: 1. the meeting of one sudra, 2. the neighing of a horse, 3. the braying of an ass and 4. the fight of a swallow across their path.[106]

The Waddars of Siddhapuram perform their religious functions just like the Waddars of Anantapur and Cuddapath districts. But they were not in any way related to either of them by blood relationship.[107] The settlers were accustomed to celebrate Hindu festivals and attend the temple in the settlement for worship and prayers. General meetings were held now and then and moral instructions were given to the settlers by the Managers and police officers. Banjaras who lived there used to enjoy the evenings by singing and dancing. Apart from Waddars, other caste people living in the settlement were 'Donga Dasaris', Dalits, Muslims, Kapus, Chenchus, Reddis, Yerukulas, Sugalis and converted Christians. The Christians who were converted, originally belonged to the backward communities. The converted Christians among the Waddars attended the churches and celebrate Christmas and new year like other Christians.[108]

Criminality -Modus Operandi

The Waddars have never settled and have always been nomads. The women are as criminal as men. They are clever at poultry and other petty thefts. They are very daring. They are adepts in the art of spying and of concealing and disposing of stolen property and also in collecting information useful to their men in the commission of crime. Women are most troublesome and they rescue the males from lawful custody. The children are equally clever at petty thefts.[109]

In committing a highway dacoity, they are always armed with stout sticks and use great violence in times of need. For breach of walls, the implement ordinarily used is the crowbar. It was used by them in their profession as stone-workers. Another implement used by them is called the *parkuchi*, a stick with a long iron ferrule. This is an ineffectual weapon and more oridinarily kept as a means of defence. While committing depredations, they are armed with daggers and battle axes. Some of them will carry baskets to contain the stolen property and others carry pieces of meat to be thrown to any troublesome dog.[110]

The Waddars get information of wealthy persons of a village by making friendship with the low caste people such as Malas, Madigas and Boyas. After acquiring sufficient information they move to a distant place for operation. Gangs are formed from six to seven members or sometimes more. These seven people discuss the plan of action. Some of them guard the lanes, while the more experienced and courageous under Gangaraju rush to the house and sack it. Signals are exchanged by whistles and gestures.[111]

They make holes near bolts to open the doors. They also do the same in the walls big enough to allow a person to pass through. The breach is made at the back or side of the house near the foundations. One peculiarity of these breaches is that their edges are neat and straight as made by them. Where there has been one successful case, there are invariably several signs of unsuccessful attempts in the neighbourhood.[112]

The Waddars mutilate the person by cutting the nose, ear, etc. of owners of property who gave chase to arrest them. In some cases they assaulted the police officers, carried off their carbines and ammunition and even killed them. Escapes from police lock-ups are very frequent. In order to escape from the custody they jump from the running trains. Various articles belonging to higher castes are thrown at or near the scene of the crime to mislead the police.[113]

After commission of crime they carry the property to the out skirts of the village. The cash is always retained and grain is handed over to the toddy shop-keeper for safe custody.[114] Jewels are disposed off to the receivers such as Komatis, Kapus, Gollas, Kammas and Ediga Balijas and Reddis of the place. Some village magistrates and village Taliairies have also acted as receivers. In some cases the property will be buried near the place where the gang is halting. It is not unearthed and taken away with the gang when it moves off, but some days afterwards two or more of the females will return secretly and hide it in some more distant places. As regards the division of stolen property, it is invariably shared equally amongst all except Gangaraju. Males, females and children receive an equal share. Gangaraju receives two shares because he leads the gang.[115]

The Waddars had no fixed place of residence. They frequently escape from surveillance and commit crime. It is felt that a criminal who has no settled abode and whose movements are unknown is more dangerous than a known criminal with a fixed residence. These Waddars live in a hilly and sparsely populated area covered with scrub jungle. To take any action against them in such a locality is out of question.[116] Hence all the members of Waddars were kept at Siddhapuram tank project.[117] The then executive engineer, Kurnool, provided them with work and quarters. Some Donga Waddars settled at Siddhapuram voluntarily, and others were brought from different places as mentioned earlier.[118]

Some of the Waddars lived in Selampad of Guntur Taluk, a distance of 24 km from Guntur. Toddy obtainable in abundance is a special attraction for the criminals of various tribes. It affords opportunities for exchange of criminal intelligence, formation of organisations and disposal of stolen properties. The villagers or higher castes readily receive the stolen properties. It is very difficult for an investigating officer to get clues in any case. Most of the villagers are in hand and glove with them. The rest are terribly afraid of these upper classes because they are upto anything. The villagers stood as sureties for these hardened criminals not minding the forfeiture of bonds in some instances. Under these circumstances, they stepped into Siddhapuram settlement.[119] When the settlers were in need of money, their numerous patrons and receivers of stolen property freely lent them money unhesitatingly. Then they abscond and commit crimes and bring the booty. They are violent criminals. They are a menace to the peaceful public.[120]

Woddars Today

To know their present conditions of the Woddars interviews were conducted. Some of them shared with us their present problems. The Secretary of Ex-Criminal Welfare Association (in Siddhapuram) K.R. Somanna, demanded that the government should include all the ex-criminals in the list of Scheduled Tribes.[121] The Madras Police Department of the colonial era prepared a report on their lifestyle. According to the report, Waddera, Korava, Kathera and Korcha tribes have been wandering tribes, getting involved in 'criminal' offences. They married women from other tribes like Yanadi, Sugali, Chenchu, Yerukula, etc. Waddars claimed that they are the descendants of the foregoing tribes and demanded that they should be included in Scheduled Tribes. Siddhapuram was officially recognised by the government as an ex-CT settlement. Members of other settlements like Bitragunta and Golla Kuppam went to the court to get the status of Scheduled Tribes but still that is not sanctioned.

Government officials are unable to see the strength of this truth. In fact, these settlers have lost confidence in the government officials because their hopes and aspirations are never understood by them. Somanna said, "Old people are not getting pensions, physically handicapped members are not receiving the benefits; the children are neglected."[122] Somanna further said, "We are harassed by the police and forest officers. Still we are suffering with stigma as criminals. Nobody passes in our life without suffering. Everybody is afraid of us but nobody comes to our rescue. What a pathetic and deplorable life we are leading. We are not getting the loans. When we approach revenue officials, we only get empty promises of house loans and other loans. Our country is not a poor country but the corrupt officials are neglecting us. If that is the situation poor will become poorer and the rich will become richer day by day."[123] The settlers questioned about the social justice and its negligence in this land of cultural heritage. Even for bribing these officials again they have to commit theft. The ex-settlers are in the vicious circle of corrupt officers, greedy lawyers and unsympathetic public. They say that their life is always on the verge of danger.

Whenever the police suspect a person he will immediately arrest the person and apply third degree methods. To avoid physical torture and mental harassment the person generally gives the names of other settlers. Taking this as excuse, the police conduct raids on the houses of settlers and loot the same, molest their womenfolk and register false cases against them.[124] Lakshmayya another member in the Woddars community said: "Every night the police are gathering information about our ex-settlement. Recently one of our youngsters was shot dead by police when he was returning from a pilgrimage to Srisailam hill. Whenever and wherever there is a crime, settlers of Siddhapuram will be under severe stress. Police officials always find an easy prey in the settlement whenever they are in need of more cases. Many of our members are still undergoing trials in various courts and are thrown behind bars for no fault of theirs. Who will look after us? Earlier, the police people themselves used to motivate us for committing thefts and burglaries. We were forced to give false witness in various cases. In fact, we are made criminals by the police."[125] Somanna said, "We are really happy that Mr. Bhaskar Rao, the Police Sub-inspector, has been very helpful and the entire settlement heaved a sigh of relief under his benevolent administration. In 1994, the Superintendent of police used to supervise Siddhapuram settlement. When approached, the Superintendent of Police asked us to abstain from criminal activities and such an act alone would fetch us the government's help. We did accordingly and in course of time we got lands and loans."[126]

The state government had taken various measures for their welfare such as: 1. Provision of suitable land for cultivation, 2. Setting up primary school for education, 3. Starting handloom weaving centers as cottage industries, 4. Setting up co-operative societies for supplying credit and other necessities of life, 5. Opening of dispensaries in the area, 6. Construction of pucca houses for habitation, 7. Imparting training for the inmates of industrial and agricultural settlements, etc. Apart from the government, social workers also helped the settlers to engage themselves in gainful occupations and thus lead a life of normal citizens. However, these welfare schemes are not available for them today. They pleaded for the government's help.

The settlement was situated in a forest area at the foot of the Nallamalai hills, and hence snakes and cheetas abound the area. The inhabitants found unsafe to move about after sunset. It is therefore proposed to provide lights in the settlement. The government sanctioned money Rs. 900 during the year 1951-52 for the provision of street lights. The settlement was electrified during the year 1952. The lights were installed on 17-3-1952 in the place of kerosene oil lights in Siddhapuram settlement.[127]

Some time ago, the forest ranger of Bairluti asked them to come and help them in the forest region. Accordingly, many of them from the settlement worked there. They are always ready to involve themselves in any employment. "We only feel that we should be paid according to the rates prevailing. Sometimes this is not so. For example the forest ranger of Byrluti informed us that whatever amount the government earmarks for works of present nature the same amount will be distributed in the settlement. However, the sanction of the government is always lower compared to the existing wage rates."[128]

K.R. Somanna stated that they require congenial atmosphere to strive hard and develop the colony and he was very much satisfied with the present district forest officer and his staff. There is no response from the district collector in any matter and all their attempts to convince him failed. It is their plight. Neither officials nor the politicians are taking interest in their village. K.R. Somanna further explained elaborately the agony faced by the villagers. Even the

Venkatapuram Panchayat in which their village is located is neglecting them. In spite of the drought conditions, to their misfortune Siddhapuram was not considered famine stricken area.

At present the entire three villages are plagued by the evil of illicit liquor.[129] The local liquor barons encourage the settlers in this direction. Whenever the excise people unearth these activities, they are always at the receiving end and the real culprits escape punishment. They amass huge wealth. While they are rolling in luxuries, the settlers are reeling in poverty. Lack of proper employment makes them lay their hand in it. Due to prohibition they stopped manufacturing liquor. "We have almost abandoned the criminal activities and learning how to live by our sweat. Let the government take stringer measures to curb the liquor addicts."[130] Avocations like mat-making and carpet making cannot sustain our families. If industries are established, thereby providing us some gainful employment, we are confident that we can lead a trouble-free life. In recent past the government initiated sericulture programme and we are associated with it. It is regretted that the programme did not succeed. Even to equip ourselves with ration cards. Unless Civil supply officials are bribed we do not get our ration cards. We are in a dilemma as we cannot resume our criminal activities or to get ourselves away from the present scenario.[131]

V

Lambadis (Sugalis)

The Sugalis are not the autochthones of south India. Their original home is believed to be Marwar in Rajasthan. In the 18th century, they had also taken up services under the Maratha rulers of Satara, the Peshwas of Poona, the Nizam of Hyderabad, and the British in their Mysore and Maratha wars. With the advent of the British rule, the Sugalis gave up much of their traditional occupation of transporting goods due to introduction of mechanised transport, laying of roads and rail lines by the then government.[132] Being poor, illiterate and lacking technological skills, they took to crimes like robbery, dacoity, cattle-lifting until the middle of the last century. Therefore, in order to control their criminal activities, they were brought under the perview of the XXVII of 1871 Criminal Tribes Act.[133]

During the year 1912, the then District Magistrate of West Godavari district opined that some provisions of the CT Act (sections

3 and 10) should be made applicable on certain members of the nomadic tribal groups with wandering tendencies.[134] His main intention was to secure the object of implementing the CT Act effectively on the sedentary communities. Some families of Sugalis used to live in Guntur, Krishna, East and West Godavari districts in Andhra Pradesh.[135]

The ostensible means of livelihood of the Sugalis were rearing and trading the cattle. They used to carry the forest produce from the delta lands to the uphill lands. Cultivation was their main occupation along with trading activities. They lived in the uplands for some time in a year and moved down to the delta area during summer season. They used to move along with their flocks doing trading activities. With the commencement of rains, they actively engaged in argicultural activities. They were also involved in manual labour. It was during their migration into the delta land they used to commit a few petty offences such as cattle lifting, crop stealing, etc. in order to eke out their livelihood. Under these circumstances the Sugalis were declared as a CT under Section 10 of the CT Act 1911. The following were the reasons showed by the colonial administrators for declaring/notifying the Sugalis as one of the members of the CTs.[136]

1. Sugalis were addicted to systematic commission of non-bailable offences.
2. Some of the members of the Sugalis were already declared as a 'Criminal Tribe' in the adjacent districts.
3. There were many convictions on their adult males.
4. The Sugalis were suspected of non-bailable offences in property crimes and
5. They were having more convictions and extended convictions.[137]

These accusations of the colonial administration not only ruined the trading skills of the Sugalis but also stigmatised them as a CT until the repellation of the CT Act in 1952. During the year 1953 the Sugalis were denotified.[138] Till 1977, they were treated as a nomadic tribe in all parts of Andhra Pradesh except in Telangana region. However, the list of Scheduled Tribes has been revised by the Scheduled Castes and Scheduled Tribes Commissioner's Orders (Amendment Act) in 1976 in order to remove the areas of restriction in respect of the Sugalis.[139]

VI

Yanadis

Ethnic Background

The Yanadi are one of the major scheduled tribes of Andhra Pradesh. It is presumed that they are the earliest races of Indian peninsula.[140] Thurston suggested that they derived their name from the Sanskrit word Anadi denoting those whose origin is unknown and noted that they were the natives of Sriharikota Island.[141] Now they are predominantly spread over the districts of Nellore, Chittoor and Prakasam. The Yanadi live in symbiosis with non-tribals.[142] Their population, according to 1991 census reports, is 3, 95, 739 in Andhra Pradesh. The total literacy rate among them is 14.78 per cent.[143] The mothertongue of the Yanadis is Telugu. Their culture originated, developed and even today largely flourishes in the lap of nature. But with the passage of time, several negative interaction forces, especially deforestation destroyed their environment which ultimately resulted in shattering the Yanadi life, particularly their economy. However, without suffering any social disorganisation, the Yanadi have successfully adapted themselves the changing environment.[144]

Name of the Tribe and Brief History

The Yanadis are also called as 'Yanadi' or Yenadi. Thurston opined that the Yanadis are a distinct tribe.[145] They had the similar customs that of the Nakkalas of Palakonda taluk in Vishakhapatnam district.[146] The Yanadis are essentially a jungle tribe. They call themselves as 'Yanadi Doras'.[147] They are distinctly homogeneous. The Yanadis were divided into three main groups, viz. 1. Dammala Yanadis (worshippers), 2. Kapu Yanadis (cultivators) and 3. Donga Yanadas (Thieves). Dammala and Kapu yanadis are very honest. They will not mix and dine with the Donga Yanadis. It was the Donga Yanadis who were registered as a 'Criminal Tribe' under Section 16 of the CT Act 1911.[148]

Description of the Tribe

The Yanadi settlements are mostly found on the fringes of forest. Ethnically they are characterised by dark skin, curly to wavy hair, medium statures, long head, broad facial with a short chin, messorrhine and depressed nasal feature, less prominent cheek bones, poor straggling beard over the fore part of their chins and their muscles are soft and flabby. Their dress pattern does not differ from that of neighbouring caste communities. The non-colonialised yanadi live in low, conical and circular huts rudely built with bamboo and palmeara leaves, grass or millet stock, thatched roofs consisting of a single room with a small entrance. Ventilation is very poor in their houses because of small windows. The house can accommodate only a few members. Cooking is usually done outside the hut during the rainy season.[149]

Whether Nomadic or Settled

The Yanadis originally lived in the North-eastern corner of Sriharikota, in Nellore district of Andhra Pradesh. But some scholars believe that the Yanadis are originally from the Chenchu tribe of Nallamala hills and when they left the hills and came down to plains became Yanadis. They lived in 18 villages in Sriharikota. Catching fish and rat in the small rivers, ponds was the ostensible means of livelihood.[150]

The Manner in Which the Yanadi Earn their Livelihood

The Yanadis are very local in their habits. Women and children accompany the males for earning their livelihood.[151] The Yanadis attend the marriage functions regularly and collect the food from the left out plates and leaves. They help the people in domestic and labour work. The Yanadis do the allotted work sincerely. The Yanadis earn their livelihood by committing petty offences and house breaking, etc.[152] It was stated that "although they were permanently settled in villages, they were already a semi-jungle tribe. Whenever the police tried to arrest them, they absconded into the hills, where it was almost impossible to arrest them. They bury their property in the jungles. Raid after raid had been made on the villages but in every case without success."[153] They also earn their livelihood by doing cultivation, cooli work, grazing cattle, village watching and domestic work and by stealing the cattle. They lead their life in abject poverty. They support the large families and under these circumstances they were notified as a CT in Madras Presidency.[154]

Food Habits

They eat all kinds of vegetables that are available in their surroundings as also in the markets. They are non-vegetarians. They catch jackals and eat rabbit, rat, squirrel, fowl, goat, sheep, wild pig, fish and other small animals. They abstain from eating beef. Alcoholic consumption is a common feature among males and among the females during the festivals and at the time of celebrating rites of passage.[155]

Marriage System

The Yanadi consider marriage as a necessary biological and social institution. They have their own rules and regulations which govern the choice of mates. These rules also suggest not only the person whom one may or may not marry but also the person whom one ought to marry. They are : tribal endogamy, sub-tribe endogamy, surname exogamy incest taboos, and preferential marriages. The rules of endogamy compel the Yanadi to select a spouse within the tribe and within the sub-tribe but the rules of exogamy prescribe that an individual must find a spouse outside the surname group. There is also the custom of treating members of the surname groups as siblings, besides the custom of treating some groups as siblings of one another.[156]

The rules, besides providing guidance as to where from a spouse should be obtained, the Yanadi encourage preferences for certain categories of relatives. With regard to such relatives, symmetrical cross-cousin marriages are favoured, because the marriageable persons know each other and because of this, a better understanding is supposed to develop among them later when they marry. However, a person is free to marry either a patrilateral (father's sister's daughter) or a matrilateral (mother's brother's daughter) cross-cousin. If both the cousins are available for marriage, generally it is left to the discretion of the boy so that he can choose any one of them. In practice, matrilateral cross-cousin marriages occur in lower proportion than patrilateral cross-cousin marriages. Further, it can be observed that of all the preferences for certain categories of relatives, unrelated people are mostly preferred. Further, no child marriage has been noted among the Yanadi. Girls are eligible for marriage only after they attain menarche and boys are usually married after the age of 20 years. The payment of bride-price to the bride's parents is inevitable among the Yanadis. Marriage by negotiations, mutual love and elopement are usual modes of acquiring mates. The re-marriage of divorcees, widows and widowers is permitted. The nuclear type of family is more predominant.[157]

Occupations

The Yanadi depend on a seven-fold subsistence pattern of economy such as: 1. gathering, 2. hunting, 3. fishing, 4. fowling, 5. farming, 6. casual or agricultural and cooli labour and 7. firewood-selling.[158] To earn their livelihood, today very few Yanadi families depend upon government service. The Yanadis pursue two or three occupations as primary and secondary ones. They gather fruits, roots, tubers, leaves, honey, firewood and other forest produce. They usually sell the forest produce in the neighbouring villages or towns. Honey collection is one of the important economic pursuits of the Yanadi during the months of March and April. Much of the honey is sold locally after storing the required quantity for their consumption. With regard to hunting, they usually hunt cats, wild doves, mangoose, etc. Big game, however, is absent in the foot-hill zones on the one hand and on the other hand, forest laws forbid hunting in the reserved forest. However, they are traditionally proved to have hunted wild animals like Kaniti (cerves unicolour), Adavi Pandi (susserota cristatus), Kondagorre (Muntiacus Muntjak), Jinka (Axis Axis), and Kondamuchohu (presbytis Entellus). Fishing activities are undertaken in seasonal as well as perennial aquatic zones by adopting different fishing methods. Similarly, for catching patridges and wild doves both traditional and modern methods of fowling are adopted. Farming in small extents is the latest economic activity taken up by the Yanadis. They also work as farm labourers for the neighbouring peasants.[159]

Social Life : Religion

Since the Yanadi have been living in close contact with the Hindu neighbours, they are subjected to Hindu influence through different sources such as affinity with: 1. Hindu Mythology, 2. Hindu Shrines belonging to Saiva and Vaishnava cults.[160] These sources of influence are working simultaneously and they usually combine together to bring about the change of life and culture among the Yanadi. The latter have borrowed several little traditional deities of the neighbouring agricultural castes such as Gurrappa, Muniswami, Patemma, etc. At different festivals they utter the names of Venkateswara, Rama, Krishna, Siva, Anjaneya, Saraswati, Lakshmi, Subramanya, Valliyamma and other deities of Hindu pantheon, especially those of agricultural castes. The impact of Hindu deities and the epics can be seen in the naming pattern of children who are named after Lord Venkateswara, Lord Subramanya, Lord Nataraj, Lord Ganesh and Lakshmi, Parvathi, Sreevalli, Bharathi and epic characters like Krishna, Dharmaraja, Bheema, Arjuna, Sahadeva, Dhananjaya, Yasoda, Sasirekha, etc.[161] Nowadays there is a growing tendency to name their children with modern names among the Yanadi.

The Yanadis go on pilgrimage to the important pilgrimage centres such as Tirupati, Tiruttani, Palani, Melmaruvattur, Sabarimala, etc. Offerings of money are made to the deities such as Lord Venkateswara, Subramanya whose temples are located at Tirupati and Tiruttani respectively for the bestowal of children, redressal of their day-to-day grievances, relief or cure from physical and mental ailments, etc.[162] When their prayers are answered they visit the said temples for offering worship. In case any child is born to them, it is christened after the deity in whose name the oath is taken. Thus, the numerous gods and goddesses that the Yanadis worship are conceptualised in different ways.[163]

Rites and Rituals

Like all other Hindu castes, the Yanadis observe the rites and observances concerning the major crises of life with a view to leading the appropriate way of life so that they can enjoy prosperity and well being of the family and have a desirable future for individual after death. With the exception of life cycle ceremonies and festivals, according to the calendar there is very little spiritual activity in the Yanadi community. The Yanadis celebrate festivals such as Sankranthi, Sivarathri, Ugadi, Sriramanavami, Vanatamama Panduga, Adikrittika, Vinayaka Chavethi, Deevali, Om Sakthimala and Ayyappamala which reflect the Hindu impact in ample measure.[164]

The Yanadi institution is consisting of "Rangam" and the entertainment form of "Melam." This goes into the world view and structural linkages of their society. The Yanadi divide the world into visible and invisible worlds in which living human beings, gods, devils, plants and animals are both benign and malign to them. They simultaneously live in these distinct worlds. There is no end for life, because even after death in visible world, they do live in invisible world and interact with their kinsmen of the visible world. Life is not even cyclic but is considered to terms of extension from visible world to invisible world. In the visible world, the human beings are broadly classified as non-Yanadi (Samsarulu) and Yanadi. The non-Yanadi are again divided into benign and malign. In the invisible world, all things are considered powerful but are divided into gods and devils. This suggests a dichotomous nature of perception of the universe by the Yanadi. "Rangam" is a very recurrent activity in the life of the Yanadi. This was made by them to understand the characteristic behaviour of the Yanadi. The views of the Yanadi on the world is very complex.[165]

Political Organisation: Kulapanchayat

Regarding the system of customary governance in the Yanadi society, the political organisation of the Yanadis falls under 'State less' system as it was no formal government embracing the entire society, the political functions being performed by the settlements and there being no person or group with centralised authority applicable to the tribe as a whole.

The Principle of organisation in the Yanadi society is based on any genealogical associations or units. There is no headman for every clan. All classes is enjoy equal status. In addition, there are no special associations such as military organisation, religious organisation, etc. Hence it is appropriate to place the organisation of the Yanadi settlement under the principle of territory as the main organisation criterion. Thus, the territory unit is the settlement, the smallest unit of organisation represented by family. The Yanadi inhabiting a number of settlements constitute the tribe.[166]

The system of governance resembles that of political system with a hereditary/non-hereditary chief assisted by a body of hierarchically placed officials. It, however, differs from feudalism to democracy in its functioning. The officials have no absolute power to enforce their decision without consulting the elders of the settlement. Further, in the Yanadi settlements, there exists no military organisation which is an indispensable characteristic of any government. Hence, the system is comparable to the caste panchayat (Council). The Panchayat is consisting of a head with a body of elders. The Yanadi interpret their settlement officials in terms of officials of royal kingdom, viz. Raju (King) and Mantri (Minister).[167]

The settlement has a permanent hereditary/non-hereditary headman called Yanadi Pedda (Raju) who presides over the traditional Panchayat (Council). The chief hails from a particular clan which is not the same in all settlements. In general, succession to the office of the Yanadi Pedda is hereditary. Upon his death, the eldest son succeeds him if he is intelligent, is known for his understanding and capability of managing the affairs of the settlement. Otherwise the settlement people select one of the sons of the Yanadi Pedda. The succession to the office of Yanadi Pedda is not characterised by a special ceremony. He is not entitled to any type of regular or voluntary gifts either in kind or cash and compulsory dues such as tribute or tax. But there is a traditional obligation that when liquor is served at the time of dispute in the settlement the Yanadi Pedda is treated first.[168]

In the traditional political structure of Yanadis the Yanadi Pedda is assisted in discharging his duties by Kolukarudu (Minister) and a few elderly persons. The latter express their opinions on the merits of the case and assist the Yanadi Pedda in arriving at a decision. Ordinary disputes are settled by the Panchayat itself, whereas serious offences and complicated disputes are often settled by caste leaders at the village level by the police personnel. The disputes are usually related to adultery, elopement, theft, divorce, abusing, etc. Of late, the culprits are punished as per severity of the crime. There are various rates of fine within the range of maximum and minimum. The fines are imposed in order to compensate the loss and the punishments include apology and ex-communication.[169]

Criminality : Modus Operandi

Women and children accompany the males for committing crime. It was stated that the Yanadis were very local in their habits. All the crimes committed by them were within a day's march from their homes. They confine their operations to the neighbouring places in which they lived.[170] The crimes committed by them were under the security sections of the IPC. House breakings, robbery ánd cattle theft were the crimes frequently committed by them. Although they were permanently settled in villages, they were by nature a semi-jungle tribe. Whenever, the police tried to arrest them, they used to abscond into the villages and hills. It was almost impossible to the police to catch them under such circumstances. It was stated that "Raid after raid has been made on the villages but in every case without any success. They were familiar with every path of the village to the hills where they easily evade the arrest."[171] The Yanadis used to earn their livelihood by the extortion of mauls from their owner's cattle. The owners used to pay to the local Yanadis a few rupees in order to not to steal the cattle. If the owners refused to pay the money then the Yanadis used to steal the cattle one by one. The women and children used to act as spies and informants for the men. The Yanadis never reveal their movements. Under these circumstances A.M.A.G. Galletti, the then District Magistrate notified the Yanadis a criminal tribe under Section 10 (a) of the CT Act,[172] A draft notification was also issued by the then British Government declaring them as a CT in Madras. According to the draft notification it was stated that: "Whereas there is every reason to believe that the tribe of Yanadi known as Donga Yanadis are addicted to the systematic commission of non-bailable offences. The Government in Council in exercise of the powers conferred on him by Section 3 of the CT Act VI of 1924 hereby declares that the Donga Yanadis is a criminal tribe for the purpose of the said Act. Further, under Section 10 of the said Act, the Governor in Council directs that every registered member of the said criminal tribe, report himself at fixed intervals and shall also notify his place of residence and any change or intended change of residence and any absence or intentional absence from his residence."[173]

Yanadis Today

With a view to solve the poverty stricken conditions among the Yanadi community land colonisation schemes were started during the colonial period. The same has been continued even in the post independence period for reformation, reclamation and rehabilitation of the Yanadis. The Government of Andhra Pradesh has also introduced land assignment schemes to provide land for cultivation to the landless Yanadi community members. The District Administration has taken up two colonisation schemes one in Karvetinagar Mandal and the other at Kuppam Mandal. In Karvetinagar Mandal land to the extent of one or two acres was allotted to a few Yanadi families.[174] Loans to the extent of an amount of Rs. 4,000 were sanctioned under DWACRA. The Yanadis in Kuppam Mandal have been cultivated unassigned lands in the forest area.

In addition to this, some of the Yanadi families were given sheep and buffaloes which were disposed off in course of time to meet their financial exigencies. Besides, the developmental schemes under the sectors like education, housing, woman and child development, health and nutrition, roads, electricity, sanitation, etc. are also under implementation level for the benefit of the Yanadis.[175] The expected results of progress and development of the Yanadi families in Andhra Pradesh could not be achieved despite of the efforts of the State and Central Government programmes. Therefore, a decision has been taken by the Government of Andhra Pradesh on 9.9.1997 to establish a separate Integrated Tribal Development Agency for the Yanadi inhabiting districts such as Nellore, Chittoor and Prakasam districts. A Yanadi development plan has been prepared for the improvement and development of Yanadis who were inhabiting in 166 Mandals in Nellore, Chittoor and Prakasam districts.[176] The Government of Andhra Pradesh issued orders (vide G.O. Ms. No. 136 Social Welfare and Tribal Welfare Department dated 19.12.2001) for establishing the ITDA for the Yanadis. The Project is headed by a Project Officer (IAS rank) assisted by Development Officer and other supporting staff to implement various developmental programmes. It is needless to state that the ITDA should take the responsibility of the development of the Yanadis who are still in primitive stage.[177]

VII

Yerukulas

Ethnic Background

In south India, among the various tribes, Yerukulas occupy an important position. According to the 1981 census report the Yerukulas occupy the fourth place out of 33 groups of tribes, and their number was 3,00557. These Yerukulas were found in almost all districts in Andhra Pradesh. However, their number is higher in Rayalaseema and coastal Andhra districts.

The Yerukulas spread all over India with different languages and dialects. They are known by different names in different localities. [178] From the extreme South to the North Arcot district in Madras Presidency, they were called Korvas. From North Arcot district they are called Korchas or Korcha upto the ceded districts. From ceded districts they are called Yerukula. Thurston found, in Calcutta, that these were practicing quack doctors. Writing about Yerukulas, Paupa Rao Naidu observes that "as railways spread all over the country they readily adapted themselves to travelling by them and the opportunities afforded for going quickly far from the scene of a recently committed crime or for stealing from sleeping passengers, were soon availed of."[179] H.A. Stuart stated that he found Yerukulas, a vagrant tribe, in Madras Presidency as well as in many other parts of India.[180] The Yerukulas, Koravas and Korchas were in fact branches of the large Korava community operating in different regions of Madras Preidency. Yerukulas lived and traded in Telugu districts, Koravas in Tamil districts and Korama and Korchas in Karnataka districts.[181] In the Andhra region, these people were called 'Yerukulavandlu' or 'Korachavandlu' but they always speak of themselves as 'Kurru'. In Nellore they speak of one another as Kurru and Kula.[182] It has been suggested that Yeru is connected with 'Erra' meaning red.

In Telugu, Yerukulavandlu means fortunetellers and Oppert suggests that this is the origin of the name Yerukula. He says, "it is highly probable that the name and occupation of the fortune-telling Kurruvandlu or Kulavandlu indicated the Telugu people to call these people 'Yerukulavandlu'.[183] He further connects the word kurru with the root ku a mountain, and Thurston informs that in a Tamil work of the 9th century (Tirumurukairuppadi) Kurru or Kuru is given as the name of a hill tribe.[184] Brown and Wilson in their glossaries, used the word, Erukalvandlu or Erukulawaru, a plural in Telugu for Erukavadu.[185] The Yerukulas are black in complexion. They are muscular and hardy. Both men and women have tattoo marks on their heads and forearms.[186]

Each caste has its own sub-castes and its own caste rules. Social customs, religious beliefs, omens, ordeals and standards of morality vary from tribe to tribe and from one social group to another. Their social customs and religious beliefs are perfectly in tune with their criminal career. From times immemorial, the members of the CTs have been following Hinduism in its crude from. Similarly, Yerukulas also have their own way of living, customs, traditions, superstitions, rituals and ceremonies. These traditions separate them from other population.

Easily identified, traditionally, the Yerukula men dressed in a Gochi, or piece of cloth around the loins and possessed a bag called Vadi Sanchi (made of striped cloth). The Yerukula women wore a black cloth, necklaces and beads made of variegated colours, were common to both men and women.[187] Silver, glass or brass bangles adorned them from the wrist to the elbow. Silver rings on their fingers were also common. The new generation has gradually moved away from these traditional modes of dress and they are increasingly copying the Hindu women. Here we find the Sanskritisation process which M.N. Srinivas talked about. The Yerukulas split up into infinite divisions, some criminal and some non-criminal. They wander over the districts of Nellore, Kurnool, Guntur, Krishna, Godavari and Hyderabad. They are divided into seven main divisions known as Criminal Investigation Department (CID) Gang Nos. IV, V, VI, VIII, IX, X and XIII.[188] To check their criminal tendencies, the Madras colonial government established several CT settlements in various parts of Andhra. Primary education is being imparted to children in these settlements. There are graduates and postgraduates among them.[189]

Originally the Yerukulas were innocent temple servants. Subsequently they took to petty trading and selling of agricultural products in several places. With the development of communications, the Yerukulas discontinued their trade. This disorganisation in their social and economic life made them become petty criminals to make their both ends meet. Generally the Yerukulas feel that it was an absurd thing to work a whole day for six annas. By courage and goodluck one night adventure may bring in thousands of rupees.

Social Life : Family

The Society of the Yerukulas was based on the patriarchal system. Women occupied a relatively important position. Women are treated well in general. Both the joint and the nuclear family system evolved. The decision-making power rested with man. The relationship between married children and the parents is good. Freedom was given to the married members of the family. Even now there are some traces of joint family system among them.

The society of Yerukulas consists of three types of families: nuclear, joint and single membered families. However, the number of nuclear families are more. The population is divided into four age-groups, i.e. 1 to 13, 14 to 21, 21 to 59 and 60 above. The age group of 21-59 represents the highest number of people.[190] Basically the houses are: (1) tataku-itukillu (thatched-brick houses) and (2) penk-utillu (brick houses). The thatched houses are large in number because of the poverty-stricken conditions of the Yerukulas. In all the settlements, the Yerukulas, both men and women are hard working. Both are busy with their work. Generally men go for works like agricultural operations, rickshaw-pulling and work in the industrial establishments (ILTD), etc. Women, when not employed, stay at home and look after household work.

Position of Women and Children

Traditionally, women were greatly oppressed and this has changed a little and for the better. They are expected to show respect to the male members of the family. In general, the brother-in-law or other children accept women as part of their family. They cannot call their husband by name. Yerukulas are particular about the reputation of their womanhood and consider it a serious matter, if any of them return home without an escort after sunset. Debauchery is considered to be the most sinful act and is severely condemned. The fortune - telling women carry a basket, winnow, stick and wicker tray in which coury shells are embeded in a mixture of cow dung and turmeric. The basket presents Kolapuriamma. The women go about the streets calling out 'Yeruko Amma Yeruka' which means 'prophecy, mother, prophecy'.[191] With the coming of the missionaries into the lives of the Yerukulas emphasis was made for their cleanliness to convert the entire family into Christian fold of life. It was observed that: "There were a myriad number of ways in which true women were fashioned out of what the SA (Salvation Army) called 'thievish raw material'. For instance, they were taught to pay attention to their appearances. The SA even helped periodic parades of the 'most neatly dressed woman' (and gave the winners a prize of one rupee each). The women were also not allowed to go outside the settlement camp on a pass if they looked like 'vagrants'. The 'before' and 'after' photographs of women in the missionary (SA) records shows the 'after' version with a completely changed Hinduised appearance, with neatly tied saries, oiled hair with flowers and vermillion marks on their foreheads. Their appearance in the settlement colonies were in fact modified according to the opinions of those of the outside people."[192]

Gotrams or Clans

They have their own 'Gotras' or clans. They are Sathupati, Kavadi, Manepati, Mandragutti.[192] These are all corrupted Tamil words. Sathupati is a corruption of Sattupati which means adorning a Hindu deity with flowers, jewels and vestments. Kavadi means a pole carried on the shoulders with two baskets, pendants hanging from both ends. Manepati is corruption of manpadi which means stitching a pair of shoes and presenting them to the temple.[193] In earlier days, these people were very particular about their gotrams. Of these four major divisions, Sathupati and Kavati gotrams are considered superior. A kavati man (styled as Pothuvadu in Telugu), according to the tradition, can marry into a Sathuputi family as they are endogamous. However, the reverse is not generally acceptable, though there are very few exceptions.

These tribes are said to have many sub-divisions but these refer chiefly to the various occupations they follow. Some of them are, Kavati Yerukulas, Uppu Yerukulas, Dabba Yerukulas, Karrepaku Yerukulas, Parigimugga Yerukulas, Koot Yerukulas, Kotulas, Bhazantri Yerukulas, Ram Yerukulas, Nagi Yerukulas, Suvva Yerukulas, Kunchapuri Yerukulas, Sathupati Yerukulas, Kuddikatti Yerukulas, etc.[194] Some men who were appointed as watch men were called kavali Yerukulas. Some men who maintained their livelihood by taking the business of salt were called Uppu Yerukulas. Dabba Yerukulas prepare bamboo baskets. Pamulas catch snakes and exhibit them in the villages to earn a living. Parigamuggalas' profession is tattooing. Kotulas trap monkeys and perform. They are excellent hunters. Satupati Yerukulas main source of livelihood is preparing baskets. Etapulla Yerukulas main occupation is net weaving. Suvva Yerukulas main occupation is the basket making with iron rods.

In all the settlements among the Yerukulas, there are basically two religious groups, viz., Hindus and Christians. The number of Hindus and converted Christians are large in number.[195] The Hindus worship Venkateswara, Lakshmi, Siva and other gods of Hindu pantheon. The Christians attended the church service. But due to the influence of the SA, ABM American Baptist Telugu Mission and CM (Canadian Mission), there are a good number of people who go to the church though they are traditionally Hindus. Both Hindus and Christians used to celebrate their festivals like Dasera, Deepavali, Pongal, Christmas and the New Year Day. Some of the people who engage in 'criminal' activities are animists. They believe in natural forces and worship all kinds of idols, animals, birds and supernatural forces.

The Kula Dharma (caste duty) of Yerukulas was 'dongatanamu' (thieving). Before going out on a house breaking excursion or a raid on a peaceful village they used to pray to the Modevi (goddess of sleep). The contents of the prayers being that they themselves might be kept alert that a heavy sleep might fall on their victims and that the police would not interrupt their operations. When the Yerukulas first came to settlements it was not easy to get them attempt to ordinary honest work.[196]

Language

These tribes have their own language but no script. The words of Yerukulas and Korvas appear to be taken mainly from other south Indian languages such as Tamil, Telugu and Canarese. The wandering tribes speak more than one language to make friendship with others. But the settled people speak the language of the locality.[197] Those Yerukulas who were spread all over the Andhra region speak only Telugu language. They use slang expressions which are unintelligible to the outsiders.

The Yerukulas in the settlements have their own language. Parents generally talk in Yerukula language. Some of the children learn this from their parents. Language is the factor which contributes to their unity and they recognise very easily the non-Yerukulas. In the settlements the people observe their gotrams or kinship relations very strictly while performing marriages. They identify a certain person by his house name. Thus they follow endogamous rules. Today, inter-caste marriage are also taking place among the Yerukulas.

Food

Goats, sheep, antelope and all sorts of birds, crows, sparrows, squirrels, parrots, etc., serve as articles of food for these people.[198] They are totally nonvegetarians and love hunting. But due to their economic scarcity they are turning into vegetarians. They drink toddy heavily. They eat all varieties of vegetables. They are restricted to eat with other communities like pariahs and muslims.

Marriage System

The type of marriage that prevails among Yerukulas is polygamy. But it is weakening now. They are favouring monogamy. Elders arrange their marriages. They freely admit other caste women into theirs, except those of the lowest order, such as Malas, Madigas and the like. At present, they are admitting these men and women also into their fold. A marriage is generally negotiated between the parents of the bridegroom and the bride and the former promises to pay a voli or bride price of Rs. 3.50 for the first marriage and seven rupees for the remarriage of a man or woman.[199] Child marriages are not allowed. Dr. Shortt stated that "A custom prevails in the tribe whereby the maternal uncle may claim the first two daughters of family as wives for his sons."[200] Generally, the selection of a match was followed in the following manner. First, they, select a suitable bride and the parents of bridegroom visit the bride's house with all elderly persons. The village head was the mediator between the two parties. If they find that the girl is suitable to their bridegroom, they give their acceptance. Instead of brideprice, the dowry system slowly stepped into their life due to the Sanskritisation process. People take dowry according to their social status. It is taken in terms of fields, cash, gold, vehicles and other luxurious goods.

Soon after the selection, they celebrate the occasion with the drinking of toddy in the presence of the village head. Parents of both the parties exchange toddy and also supply one vessel to the head of the kulapanchayat. Feast will follow after drinking. After the betrothal ceremony is over, the parents of both the parties are bound by the contract. Otherwise a meeting is called for and explanation is given accordingly for the breach of the contract. The kulapanchayat gives its judgment and it will be followed strictly.

Generally, for those that follow Hindu customs, a Brahmin priest fixes the marriage muhurtam (auspicious time) and perfoms it. A pastor performs the marriage for converted Christians. The Tali consists of black beads and Talambralu (rice grains spilled over the heads of bride and groom) will follow.[201] Widows are not allowed to participate in the function. Another custom that exists in their family is to make contract between two individuals before the birth of their children. They say to one another: "If your wife should have a girl and mine a boy or vice versa they must marry."[202] But if a Brahmin objects, then there is a scope for its breach.

Puberty

Puberty is a happy occasion to the tribals. If the girl attains puberty, the news is sent to her maternal uncle. The girl 'sits' for five days and observes pollution. Her uncle gives her new clothes, comb, mirror, flowers, kumkum (coloured powder), nuts, bangles, etc., and also arranges for a feast to her. Sweets are distributed to celebrate the occasion.

Divorce

Divorce is rare and, if it takes place, the divorced parties may rake up their differences and become enemies. In the case of elopement, the father of a boy or girl summons a meeting at which the accused is penalised. The man who elopes with the girl is forced to marry her. If a married person elopes with another girl, both woman and man are strictly punished by the village elders in the kulapanchayat. Certain amount of penalty is also fixed on the accused. This system is also implemented on those who have illegal contacts. If a man, already having a wife, does not have children, then he is eligible to take a second wife. He is obliged to pay for the maintenance of the first wife.

Widow Marriage

Widow marriages are quite common in this community. A person who wishes to marry a widow will buy a new saree and accepts her as wife in the presence of others. This is what is called cheerakattukovadamu (wearing the saree).[203] The head of the village acts as a mediator. They celebrate it with drinking toddy.

Birth Ceremonies

In earlier days, immediately after the birth of the child, they burn incense in front of the hut. They purify the hut with cow dung. After this purification, everybody is allowed to see the new-born baby.[204] They also follow certain practices for the safety of the child in order to escape from a supernatural force. They bestow attention on mother and child. They take bath on the nineth day.[205] Toddy and dinner are served. Naming the child will take place after a few months. These names are most probably selected from their ancestors, sometimes their heroes or from their gods and goddesses. Generally, the names are Venkatigadu, Gangadu, Nagi, Ankali, etc. (The slang words in the name was given by the Britishers) After a name is given, a black string is tied to the wrist of the infant. The maternal uncle takes interest in the new-born child. They consider it a good omen if the child is born on the new moon night.[206] If the child is born with an umbilical chord twisted round his neck, they take it as a bad omen and expect death of father or the maternal uncle. They would like to overcome this by killing a fowl and wearing its inner parts round the neck and afterwards burning them along with the umbilical chord.[207]

Disposal of the Dead

If a wandering Yerukula dies, he is buried as quickly as possible, by keeping the head to the North and feet to the South. They cover the corps with new clothes and he is given bath and a coin is placed in one corner. They invite crows thinking that the spirit of the dead is moving around. Exactly after one year, they perform a function and that completes the major death ceremonies. More or less the procedure is followed by converted Christians with minor changes. Some Yerukulas used to plant a Tulasi plant at the place where the body is burried.

Superstitions

Falling of a lizard in front of them is considered badluck and if it chirps on other sides, it is taken as a sign of goodluck. While starting, if any members of his family sneezes once, it is considered to be bad-luck but if it is done repeatedly, it is considered to be good. It is inauspicious to them to see an oil man, a barber, a police constable and a cock-eyed man while they are going. A crow flying towards the right hand side is considered a good omen, but if it flies over the head of the person, it is considered a bad omen. If the crow cries, it is supposed that somebody is coming to their home for a visit. It is unfortunate, when starting on a journey, to see widows, pots of milk, dogs barking and a man leading a bull. Number three is considered ominous and an expedition never consists of three. Sundays are auspicious for weddings while they are inauspicious for crime. Mondays, Wednesdays and Saturdays are unlucky.[208] It is a bad omen to meet with a bundle of wood or cow dung cakes. If they meet a well-dressed widow or a cat it is considered as serious and bad omen.

Weapons

Some Yerukulas possess knives and a kind of 'billhook', called Kodavali, which is a sort of compromise between a sword and sickle. The back of the blade is heavy and renders it capable of dealing a severe blow. With this implement, animals are slaughtered, murders committed and bamboos split. For the purpose of committing burglaries they used an iron instrument called gadikolu or sillukolu.[209]

Kulapanchayat

In the past, the village head played a very important role in tribal communities. He was the person concerned with register for the births and deaths and the new arrivals into the settlements. All the Yerukulas were controlled by him. He was elected on the basis of his popularity, age and the ability to deal with the cases of various types. The Panchayat comprises of five persons. These fives elders of the tribe are called Berumanusom, big people or elders from the council. All the individuals respects their unwritten law and obey the will of Kulapanchayat. Any violation of these conventions is seriously dealt with.

The meetings of the panchayat are held at a common meeting place. The alleged culprit and his people usually sit at the left side and the aggrieved party on the right side or vice versa while the elders sit in between the two parties. The elders secretly decide the type of ordeal to test the guilt of the culprit. It is customary that the accused should dip his fingers into the boiling oil and it is an indication to prove his innocence or guilt. Still there are some traces of this custom. The other system of this sort is lifting a red-hot crow bar from fire and carrying a pot filled with water to its brim without slipping a drop.

The tribal panchayat usually deals with: (1) cases of immorality within the members of the tribe. If any woman is caught red-handed when she is involved in adultery, the husband brings the case to the members of the Kulapanchayat. On an enquiry, the Kulapanchayat decides the punishment. The culprit is expected to bear the cost of it. (2) persons who violate the social custom (3) property disputes (4) marriage disputes (5) disputes pertaining to the division of the parental property (6) to admit new persons and (7) disputes of stolen property, etc.[210]

Criminality-Modus Operandi

We get a fair account of their crimes and causes through the interviews conducted in the settlements. The types of crime they generally commit are: 1. Pickpocketing, 2. Dacoity, 3. House breaking, 4. Animal theft, 5. Railway robbery, 6. Bank looting, 7. Shop snatching, 8. Chain snatching and 9. Rafu (Placing artificial gold instead of real gold and pass it to the customer in the process of bargaining), etc.[211]

The following five factors prompt the people in the settlements to commit crimes. They are: 1. Lack of alternative avenues of livelihood 2. Lack of proper up-bringing of children 3. Their poor economic conditions. 4. Laziness in work and 5. The harassment by the police department even after giving up criminal activities.[212]

When interviewed, one criminal said, "My parents from the beginning belong to Sturtpuram settlement. My father used to commit petty thefts since my childhood and was a drunkard. He died of tuberculosis. My mother died after that. After the death of my parents, I faced acute financial troubles.Then started my criminal life and, in course of time, I grew into a notorious criminal.[213] Another settler revealed that, the police would arrest even the children of the ex-criminals. The police harassment on the children and on the parents will leave strong impact on the tender minds and it would sometimes forcibly make them take to crime.[214]

In the interviews, the 'criminals' narrated several ways of committing crimes. To start with, they choose the place of their operation and gather information through the local people about the potential rich homes. Generally, they go in batches to commit theft. They steal money, gold, silver and other costly goods. Sometimes they act like rich people and go in hired cars to commit robberies. Sometimes they return to their homes without stealing. They have their own code language when they are doing the crime. Some of the words they use are listed below.[215]

Table-1
Code Language Used by the Yerukulas

Sl. No.	*Word*	*Meaning*
1.	*Oluku*	Torchlight
2.	*Sonapam*	Gold
3.	*Kanchakam*	Money
4.	*Bokollu*	police
5.	*Berikeda*	Sub-inspector
6.	*Pullakollu*	Leader of the gang
7.	*Ellavi*	Assistant leader
8.	*Nemati*	Man
9.	*Tella Belupu*	Silver
10.	*Ulli Mukka*	Knife or screw driver

The nature of the 'criminals' in all the settlements is that they never reveal the secrets of their gangs. Whenever they feel the threat to their lives they even sacrifice their life in order to escape from the danger. The fact is that there are nearly 20 batches in all the settlements and each batch is consisting of four to five members. People in one batch should not join another batch until their operation is over. Each batch has its own leader and an assistant. No batch reveals the secrets of the other batches. They commit crimes only in the late nights between 12 O'clock in the midnight of 3 O'clock in the morning. They enter into the houses by making big holes in the walls, breaking locks and windows. They cleverly escape when they find any problem in committing thefts. They call this type of crime as *Chori.* They call it dacoity when they rob the house in front of people in the house by threatening them.

The number of women criminals in these settlements are also large in number. There are only 20 families in which women go for thieving. The crimes they indulge in are pocket picking, suitcase lifting, snatching both from the railway passengers and busy shopping centers. The main reasons for these women to commit crime are, more or less, the same as that of their menfolk. However, in some cases, these women, divorced and widowed, both categories going without subsistence, along with other women who are undergoing imprisonment, take to these criminal activities.

The criminals in all the five settlements have links with some of the other notorious criminals in the state and sometimes even outside. One criminal has narrated how they robbed a rich temple in Simhachalam in Visakhapatnam District of Andhra Pradesh. They went in a gang consisting of twelve members and planned to steal precious jewels and ornaments from the temple. They went to Viskhapatnam and gathered information about the temple. After a week, they went to that place with all kinds of weapons. First, they entered to visit the temple for Darshan and returned. The next day they went the temple and threatened the priest and looted money and Jewellery. Soon after finishing the temple robbery, the priest was killed in the operation but the police got information about them and all of them were nabbed in the settlement and were kept behind bars.[216]

It was reported that the police were responsible in perpetuating crime in the settlements. The police encourage crimes and they claim a lion's share in the looted property. In return, they rescue them in times of need. It is a matter of routine that the police demand money from them. Unable to bear the police harassment, the criminals give false names. When interviewed, a woman criminal stated that police never allow them to stop thieving. They want their *mamullu* (bribe). In order to escape the harassment of the police some criminals are forced to dispose off their property and other belongings such as grain and vessels to bribe the police. In this context, a criminal stated, there were no minimum facilities in the jail. Moreover, the police used to ill-treat his relatives and sometimes committed rapes on their women. In prison he was beaten severely with lathis three times a day. [217]

The mention of a dacoity anywhere in the state makes the police to involve the DNT people even if they are not concerned with it. Radio, TV or the newspaper also emphasise the same. It is a pity, however, that real culprits are never punished. An ex-criminal in an interview gave a graphic account of this. "In *Eenadu* (Telugu daily) there was a statement twenty days back that a theft took place at Mangalagiri (Guntur District), and in that crime it was reported that two young persons by name Golla Sreenu and Venkaiah are involved. It is also reported that both of them belong to Sitanagarm and Stuartpuram settlements."[218] But these two people do not belong to the same place. Unfortunately, the very mention of the place settlement, is associated with criminal activity and this shows the notoriety it assumed over time. An ex-criminal explained that, in Tirupati, a police officer reported to the newspapers that a dacoity and murder was committed by the Stuartpuram settlement people. Consequently they were arrested. But what actually happened was quite contrary to the police officer's public pronouncement. In the CBI enquiry it was later revealed that the criminals of other states were involved in the crime. He further elaborated on how the police used them as pawns in their game.[219]

It is true that the settlements of the DNTs produced a good number of criminals. Among them a notorious criminal who was their hero gained popularity in the one of the settlements. He was the loacal Robinhood and spent a major portion of the stolen wealth on his fellow men, i.e. the poor people. Being an orphan himself, he gave shelter to orphans. This 'hero' was Tiger Nageswara Rao. He becomes so legendary in his own lifetime that songs were composed extolling his philanthropy, kindness, etc. In one of the songs, the atrocities committed on him by the police, who killed him later, were also vividly mentioned.

VIII

Conclusion

The DNT tribes today consists of both 'criminal' and non-criminal families. The Section of non-criminal families are employed in government jobs, industrial establishments, agricultural operations and petty trade. Among the 'criminal' families only a few section of the people only are committing petty offences and tricks of the trade. Also those people who have the criminal background, they are averse to committing crime. The reasons obviously are: 1. Some of their kinsmen are killed by the police. 2. They are unable to bear the ill treatment and harassment either by the Police or from the public. 3. Education has enabled them to realise their folly. 4. They are interested in the future of their children and 5. They want to lead a respectable life by joining the mainstream of life. Gradually they are taking to small jobs and business and changing their lifestyles. But there are not many opportunities either in the private or public sector to provide them with some meaningful occupations, even though the government is providing some succor in the shape of small loans, cattle, rickshaws, etc. It is needless to state that such measures are in adequate.

NOTES

1. Lalitha, V., *Socio-Economic and Administrative Aspects of an Ex-Criminal Tribe,* unpublished M. Phil. thesis, S.V. University, Thirupati, 1982, p. 42.
2. Lavanam and Hemalatha Lavanam, *Notes and Reflections on Our Work in the Rehabilitation of Ex-Criminal Tribes people in settlements* — A paper circulated by Gandhi peace foundation, Vijayawada, 1976, p. 4.
3. Naidu, M., and Paupa Rao, *The Criminal Tribes of India, No. II, A History of Korawas, Erukulas or Kaikadies,* Madras, 1905, p. 80.
4. Naidu, M., and Paupa Rao, 1904 : 81.
5. Kapadia, K.M., 'The Criminal Tribes of India', *Sociological Bulletin I & II (March,1952),* pp. 14-15.
6. Majumdar, D. N., *Races and Cultures of India,* The Universal Publishers Ltd., Lucknow, 1961, p. 384.
7. Bharal, G.P., 'Denotified Communities and Their Problems of Rehabilitation' *The Journal of Social Work, Vol. XXVII, No. 4, January, 1968,* p. 5.
8. Bhargava, B. S., *The Criminal Tribes: A Social and Economic Study of the Principal Criminal Tribes and Castes in North India,* Ethnographic and Folk Culture Society, Lucknow 1949, p. 17.
9. Raghaviah, V., *The problem of Criminal Tribes,* Akhil Bhartiya Adim Jati Sevak Sangh (BASS), Delhi, 1943.
10. Apte J.S., 'Talwada Ashram School, An Experiment in Tribal Education', *Vanyajati, Vol. No. 2, April, 1960.*
11. Biswas, P.C., *The Ex-Criminal Tribes of Delhi State,* Unpublished Ph.D. thesis, University of Delhi, I960.

12. Edwards, S. M., *Crime in India,* London, 1924, OUP, p. 106. Also See, Bawden, *Written Statement, on the working condition of CT Settlements in Madras presidency,* Madras, 1918.
13. Darrow, Clarence, *Crime: Its causes and Treatment,* London, 1934. p. 34
14. Chang, Dac. H., *Criminology – A Cross Cultural Perspective, Vols.1 & 2,* New Delhi, 1976. p. 27.
15. Singh Jaspal, *Reformation of Ex-Criminal Tribes,* paper presented to the Police Academy Hyderabad, 1978.
16. Hatch, W.J., *The Land Pirates of India,* Seeley Service and Company, London,1928, p. 263.
17. Haikerwal, Bijoy Sankar, *Economic and Social Aspects of Crime in India,* George Allen and Unwin Ltd., London: 1934.
18. See, Gillin, John Lewis, *Criminology and Penology,* The Mcmillan Company, New York, 1945, p. 20.
19. See Government of Madras, *Administration Reports of the Inspector General of Police from 1904-1920, Madras,* Collected from Tamil Nadu Archives TNA.
20. Sarada Raju, A., *Economic Conditions of Madras presidency 1800-1850,* Madras, 1941, p. 13.
21. Lalitha 1982:19.
22. See Government of Madras, *Madras State Administration Reports During the Years 1912 to 1920, Madras, TNA.*
23. See Government of India, *The Report of the Criminal Tribes Act Enquiry Committee, 1949-50,* Government Central Press, Delhi, 1951.
24. See Government of Madras, *Report of the Indian Jails Committee, 1918-20,* Government Press, Simla.
25. See Govrnment of Madras, *Home Department, G.O. No. 1161, dt. 12th June, 1913.*
26. See Government of Madras, *Home Department, G.O. No. 1638, dt. 13th August 1912.*
27. See Government of Madras, *Judicial Department, G.O.No. 2000 dt 3.2.1912,* TNA, Madras.
28. For details see *The Hindu,* dt. July 3rd, 1913.
29. For details see *Indian Patriot,* dt. 20th March, 1913.
30. Venugopalarao, S., *Crime, Society and Police,* Indian Express, dt. 9-6-77.
31. Simhadri, Y.C., *The Ex-Criminal Tribes of India,* National Publishing House, New Delhi, 1979, p. 7. Also see Simhadri, Y.C., Scheduled Castes and Denotified Tribes, *The Journal of Social work, Vol. XXX VII No. 4, January, 1977.*
32. See, *Public Works Labour Department, G. O. No. 779 (L) dt. 26th March 1936.*
33. Mullaly, F.S., *Notes on Criminal Classes of the Madras Presidency,* Madras 1912, p. 72.
34. *Ibid.,* 73.

35. *Papa Kavi, Chenna Basava Puranam,* pp. 90-91. Also see, Soma Reddy, "The Life of Dommaras as Reflected in the Literature and Epigraphs of Medieval Telugu Country", *Proceedings of AP History Congress.*
36. *Ibid.,* p. 30.
37. Mullalay, F.S., *Notes on Criminal Classes of The Madras Presidency,* Madras, 1912, p. 71.
38. 'Veedus' are the troupes which the Dommaras organised into divisions. The heads of these 'Veedus' made endowments in that capacity on behalf of the respective 'Veedus'.
39. Nanjundaiah, H., and Rao Bahadur L.K., Anantha Krishna Iyer, *The Mysore Tribes and Castes Vol. II,* Mysore, 1928, p. 142.
40. Nanjundaiah, H., and Rao Bahadur L.K., Anantha Krishna Iyer, *The Mysore Tribes and Castes Vol. III, Mysore,* 1928, p. 142.
41. *Ibid.,* p. 140.
42. Thurston, Edgar, *Castes and Tribes of Southern India,* Madras,1909, reprinted Cosmo Publications, Delhi, 1975.
43. Government of Madras, *Madras Manual,* Vol. I, 1901.
44. Information in this regard is mainly collected through the oral testimony conducted during the field study in Nellore District.
45. Bhargava, B.S., *The Criminal Tribes: A Social and Economic Study of the Principal Criminal Tribes and Castes in North India,* Ethnographic and Folk Culture Society, Lucknow, 1949.
46. *Ibid.,* p. 8.
47. Government of Madras, *Administration Report of the Inspector General of Police, Madras 1912,* Government Superintendent press, Madras, 1913.
48. See Government of Madras, *Public Works (Labour) Department, G.O. No. 7065-A/29-1, dt. 29.4.1929, Also see,* Government of Madras, *Home Department, G.O. No. 373, dt. 28.1.1937.*
49. Government of Madras, *Home Department, G.O. No. 2217, dt. 21.4.1939, Also see* Government of Madras, *Home Department, G.O. No. 3092, dt. 5.6.1939. Also see Government of Madras, Home Department, G.O. No. 868L, dt. 15.3.1930. Also see Home Department, G.O. No. 1862 L, dt. 28.8.1933. Public Works (Labour) Department, G.O. No. 7065, dt. 29.4.1924.*
50. *Home Department, G.O. No.1162, dt.11.5.1936 and Public Works (Labour) Department, G.O. No. 7065A, 29th April 1929, Also see Public Works (Labour) Department, G.O. No. 779(L) dt. 26.3.1936. Public Works (Labour) Department, G.O. No. Ms. 779 L., dated 26th March 1936, and Fort St. George Gazette, Notification No. 71, dt. 19th January 1937, Part. I,* p. 118.
51. Government of Madras, *Administration Report of the Inspector General of Police,* 1922, Government Central Press, Madras 1923. Also see, the Criminal Tribes Act Enquiry Committee Report, 1949-50, Madras, 1951.
52. See Chirravuri Nagabhushanacharyulu, "Nomadism in Andhra Pradesh", *The Andhra Pradesh Nomadic Tribes Welfare Conference, Guntur, 1967.*
53. See Morgan, L.H., *Ancient Society,* New York, 1877.

54. See Chirravuri Nagabhushanacharyulu, *1967* : p. 98. See Deep Kumar, V.S., *"Nakkalas"* unpublished Doctoral thesis, Sri Venkateswara University, Tirupati, 1985.
55. See Ayyangar, *Criminal Tribes Enquiry Committee Report,* 1949-50 Government Press, New Delhi, 1951.
56. *Ibid.*
57. All these are house names of the Nakkalas. Information is collected from the 20 families of Nakkalas in Nellore District.
58. See C.P. Ramaswami Ayyar, Foreword in the *"Gypsies"* by Chamanlal, New Delhi, 1962.
59. See Frederick, Mullaly S., *"Criminal Classes of Madras Presidency", Madras,* 1892, p. 23.
60. *Samisatru' or 'Samimoota'* is a sacred bundle which will be preserved for generations together. It is very essential for the performance of marriages. The eldest son inherits this sacred treasure. Others cannot touch it. Otherwise purification ceremony has to be performed as a penance.
61. See Kosambi, D.D., *An Introduction to the Study of the Indian History,* Bombay, 1975, p. 40. Also see Elmore, W.T., *Dravidian Gods in Modern Hinduism,* New Delhi, 1984, p. 10.
62. All these are the different connotations of the nomadic tribal population in Andhra Pradesh. These are not actually Yerukulas. They left Yerukulas and kidnapped and abducted the children of other castes and expanded their families. Presently, the government has included them in the BC—A cetegory/Group. Still their habits, traditions, customs are all equal to that of the nomadic tribal population. The Waddars have interdining and marital relations with other nomadic tribal population in AP also. Somanna's plea to the government is to include them in the list of scheduled tribes. Interview with K.R. Somanna, Siddhapuram, dated 24.11.2006.

    See Lalitha, V., *The Making of Criminal Tribes : Patterns and Transition,* New Era Publications, Madras, 1995, p. 74.

    The Waddars are not a part and parcel of Yerukulas. However, the Waddars or Dasaries living in Kapparalla Tippa Village in Nellore District claim that they are the descendents of the Yerukulas due to some inter-caste marriages. A lot of research has to be conducted to prove sociologically and anthropologically that Waddars are the offshoots of Yerukalas in Andhra Pradesh. Due to their poor economic conditions and other qualities of the other tribal groups, the government should notify them as one of the Scheduled Tribe Groups in A.P.
63. See Government of Madras, *Home Judicial Department, G.O. No. 1279, 10th June 1915,* p. 1, TNA.

    See Government of Madras, *Home Judicial Department, G.O. No. 1140 dated 20.5.1920, p.1, TNA.* Also see Government of Madras, *Home Judicial Department, G.O. No. 1279, 10th June 1915,* p. 1, TNA.

64. Ramachandra Sastri, E., *History of The Criminal Thieves in Madras Presidency,* Madras, 1929, pp. 17-18.
65. See Government of Madras, *Public Works (Labour) Department* (hereafter PWLD) G.O. No. 2146, dt. 28th August 1928, p. 2, APSA.
66. Houses were constructed to the Waddars within an enclosure of 540 feet by 340 feet fenced with split bamboo to a height of 10 feet. The huts were constructed in six blocks. Each hut measured 12 feet by 10 feet. It was thatched with grass. An open space of 60 feet left between the huts on all sides. These houses were very poor. They were made of tatee and mud walls with thatched roofs. When the Waddars were in better circumstances they would be made to repair their own places and kept them clean of jungle growth. See Government of Madras, *Home (Judicial) Department, G.O. No. 1860 dated 5th September 1917,* p. 1. Also See Government of Madras, *Home Department, G.O. No. 2661 dated 25.10.1920,* p. 3, NAI.
67. Mullaly, F.S., *Notes on Criminal Classes of the Madras Presidency,* Madras, 1912, p. 28.
68. See Government of Madras, *PWLD, G.O. No. 2146, 28th August 1928,* p. 2, APSA.
69. See Government of Madras, *PWLD, G.O. No. 2146, 28th August 1928,* p. 1, APSA.
70. See Government of Madras, *Home Judicial Department, G.O. No. 1279, 10th June 1915,* p.1, TNA. Also see Government of Madras, *Home Department, G.O. No. 3570, dated 27.1.1951,* pp. 3-5, NAI.
71. Withinshaw, L., Memorandum on Donga Waddars in *Note Showing the Progress Made in the Settlement of Criminal Tribes in the Madras Presidency upto January 1926,* Government Press, Madras, 1927, p. 36.
    See. Public Works Department, G.O. No. 1977 L., dated 10-7-1929, Memorandum on Donga Waddars Prepared by L.Withinslaw, the then district Superintendent of Police Madras, Madras, 1918.
72. Gayer, G.W., *Lecturers on Some Criminal Tribes of India and Religious Mendicants,* (2nd edition), Principal Police Training School, Central Provinces, 1910, p. 46. Also see Abdul Ghani Mohammed, *Notes on the Criminal Tribes of the Madras Presidency,* Vellore, 1915, p. 124.
    GOM. Law (General) Department, G.O. No. 69, Dated 5.1.1929 and GOM. Law (General) Department G.O. No. 2973, Dated 31.7.1929.
73. Mullaly, F.S., *Op. Cit.,* p. 80.
74. Naidu, M. and Paupa Rao, *The Criminal Tribes of India, No. II, A History of Korawars,* Erukulas or Kaikarees, Madras, 1905.
75. See *Note Showing the Progress Made in the Settlement of Criminal Tribes in the Madras Presidency upto September 1916,* Madras 1917, p. 36. Also See V. Lalitha, *Op. Cit.,* p. 49.
76. Thurston, Edgar, *Castes and Tribes of Southern India,* Cosmo Publications, New Delhi, 1909, Vol. V, p. 422.

77. Kennedy, M., *The Criminal Classes in India,* New Delhi, 1985, p. 165.
78. Takku Waddars were experts in stone cutting. During the year 1945, R. Dorai Swami Ayyar sanctioned advances to start the industry. They were permitted to cartage stones from Nallamalai hills to the colony and from there to Atmakur and neighbouring villages for sale. See Government of Madras, *Home Department, G.O. No. 504, dt. 15.2.1945,* pp. 1-2, NAI.
79. See Government of Madras, *PWLD, G.O. No. 2146 28th August 1928,* p. 2, *APSA.*
80. Gayer, G.W., *Police Lectures on Some Criminal Tribes of India and Religious Mendicants, (2nd edition),* Principal Police Training School, Central Provinces, 1910, p. 35. Also See F.S. Mullaly, *Op. Cit.,* p. 22.
81. Ghani, Muhammad Abdul, *Notes on the Criminal Tribes of Madras Presidency,* Vellore, 1915, pp. 124-25.
82. Kennedy, M., *Op. Cit,* p. 167.
83. The Waddars never wear shoes of any kind on their feet, though sandals may be worn nor do their women wear cholis or jackets. Their legend is that ages past rats stole all their shoes and cholis and as their forefathers were deprived of them, they may not use them and that is why they are inveterate enemies of the rats and dig them up and eat them whenever they can. See Gayer, G.W., *Op. Cit.,* p. 36. P.B. Thomas, the then Deputy Commissioner of Police, writes in 1899 that : "I am not aware of these people using any peculiar shoes. They use slippers (sandals) worn by riots and the lower classes. These they get by stealing". See Kamala Manohar Rao, *Op. Cit.,* pp. 121-22.
84. Mullaly, F.S., *Op. Cit.,* p. 79.
85. Kennedy, M., *Op. Cit.,* p. 11.
86. See *Hukumnamas and Papers relating to Sriharikota Yanadis, Vol.1, Selection of Papers from the Old Records of the Nellore District,* Nellore, 1915, p. 44, A.P. Gazetteers Office, Hyderabad.
87. Gayer, G.W., *Op. Cit.,* p. 47.
88. During the early part of the 20th century their trade suffered due to frequent droughts in the area of their operation. The land which a few of them possessed hardly gave enough for their sustenance. Under these conditions, they migrated to Venkatagiri, Puttur, Nellore and Cuddapah.
89. Ramachandra Sastri, E., *History of the Criminal Tribes in Madras Presidency,* Madras, 1929, p. 19.
90. Shashi, P.S., Varma, P.S. *Op. Cit.,* p. 87.
91. Ramachandra Sastri, E., *A Socio-History of ex-Criminal Communities, OBCs,* New Delhi, 1991, p. 21.
92. Government of India, *Gazetteers of Bombay State,* Dharwar District, Vol. XXI, 1884, Bombay, p. 64.

93. Interview with K.R. Somanna, Siddhapuram Settlement, 24, 11, 2006.
94. Chandrasekhar Bhat, *Ethnicity and Mobility,* New Delhi, 1984, p. 103.
95. See Syed Siraj Ul Hassan, *Castes and the Tribes of H.E.H., the Nizam Dominions,* Delhi, 1909, p. 649.
96. Mullaly, F.S., *Op. Cit.,* p. 81.
97. Gayer, W.G. *Op. Cit.,* p. 48.
98. See Lalitha, V., *Op. Cit,* p. 59.
99. Their marriages are arranged by the Kulapanchayat. Though they are particular in observing their Gotrams in their marriages, slowly the intercaste marriages are taking place nowadays.
100. Lalitha, V., *Op. Cit.,* p. 59.
101. Thurston 1909: 424 Also See Government of Madras, *PWLD, G.O. No. 137dated 19.1.1927,* p. 6, APSA. Also see Government of Madras, *Home Department, G.O. No. 6170, dated 22.12.1938,* p. 3, NAI.
102. See Ghani, Mohammed Abdul, *Op. Cit.,* p. 126.
103. See Lalitha, V., The Making of Criminal Tribes, *Op.Cit.,* p. 60.
104. Bhat, Chandrasekhar, *Ethnicity and Mobility,* New Delhi, 1984, p. 100.
105. Syed Siraj-ul Hassan, *Op. Cit.,* p. 193.
106. See Mohammad Abdul Ghani, *Op. Cit.,* p. 126.
107. See Government of Madras, *Home Judicial Department, G.O. No. 1279, dt. 10th June 1915,* p. 4, TNA.
108. Some of the converted Christians among the Waddar families came from Kapparallatippa settlement. The population of Hindus are more in number. 200 families of Hindus are converted to Christianity. This is because they are transferred from other settlements, managed by Christian missionaries. They are always at cross with the Muslims who are still treating these Waddars as 'criminals'. See Government of Madras, *PWLD, G.O. No. 2671 dated 6.12.1934,* p. 6, APSA.
109. Government of Madras, *Home Judicial Department, G.O. No. 1279, 10th June 1915,* p. 1, TNA.
110. See Kennedy, M., *Op. Cit.,* p. 172.
111. The modus operandi of these Waddars is that they go to the busy shops on the pretext of purchasing provisions. They engage the shop-keeper in bargaining to divert his attention. They steal goods or money when opportunity comes. If the shopkeeper finds the loss and chase them, they conveniently thrust the box in the bags of others, whom they have already arranged and concealed themselves in order to throw the blame on others. The offences they generally commit are road thefts, highway dacoities, house-breakings, bank robberies, forest thefts, animal thefts and pickpocketing, etc.
112. See Mullaly, F.S., *Op. Cit.,* p. 80.
113. Women are not, as a rule, ill-treated and the mangal-sutra, the Hindu married woman's insignia and toe rings are never touched. Kennedy, M., *Op. Cit.,* p. 170.

114. Mullaly, F.S., *Op. Cit.*, p. 81.
115. Gayer, G.W., *Op. Cit.*, p. 47.
116. Withinshaw, L. Memorandum on Donga Waddars in *Note Showing the progress made in the Settlement of the Criminal Tribes in the Madras Presidency, upto September 1916,* Government Press, Madras, 1917, pp. 36-37.
117. See Aiyappan, A., *Report on the Socio-Economic Conditions of the Aboriginal Tribes of the Province of Madras,* Madras, 1948, p. 38.
118. As the work provided by the Public Works Department completed by 1918, the Government allotted a block of forest land measuring 650 acres in 1917. On 1st April 1919, 65 males, 65 females and 74 children were on the rolls of the settlement. See *Note Showing the progress made in the Settlement of Criminal Tribes in the Madras Presidency upto January 1926, Government Press, Madras, 1926,* p. 29, TNA.
119. See Government of Madras, *PWLD, G.O. No. 1201, dated 22.5.1935,* p. 5, APSA.
120. All possible efforts to control their activities under Criminal Tribes Act were not successful. Ordinary prosecutions under Criminal Tribes Act was not effective. Hence their movements were restricted to Siddhapuram. They were made to work regularly under the supervision of the Manager. The habit of heavy drinking was systematically controlled. See Government of Madras, *Home Department, G.O. No. 2500, dated 16.5.1938,* pp. 1-5, NAI.
121. Interview with K.R. Somanna, *Ibid.*
122. For example, a police officer lost his revolver and arrested the son-in-law of Somanna, for the same. The Officer demanded a bribe of Rs.10,000 to release him. Since he could not pay the bribe, his son-in-law was sentenced to seven years imprisonment.
123. Interview with E. Lakshmayya, Siddhapuram, dated 24.11.2006.
124. Mr. Bhaskar Rao initiated many steps for our welfare. He transformed the entire atmosphere in the colony. He was instrumental in looking after prohibition and advised us to keep ourselves away from politicians. He instructed us to freely cast our votes – Interview with K.R. Somanna, *Op. Cit.*
125. Interview with Wodde Lakshmanna, Siddhapuram, dated 22.11.2006. The Forest Manager assured the ex-criminals that he would provide work for them in all the schemes designed by the Local Mandal Revenue Officer, Block Development Officer and Integrated Tribal Development Agency. He said, "We should strive hard to earn money in a legitimate way." He said that the schemes were framed and financed by the Government and asked them not to play truants to work.
126. "Political parties of all shades approach us very often and ask us to associate with them and lure us into their trap by promising us jobs and bright future." Interview with K.R. Somanna, *Op. Cit.* In the Waddar

community of Siddhapuram, three sects of people are living. They are 1. Gadidala, 2. Santhamuchu, 3. Donga Waddar. Siddhapuram has been divided into three blocks. 1. Jandrapeta, 2. Gummadipeta, 3. Santhamuchupeta.

127. Somanna continued to say that poverty was the main cause for the Waddars to commit crime. In his opinion, District Forest Officer's and police officers are responsible for the continuation of crime. If they are helpful like the present District Forest Officer, their problems will be solved. Otherwise lion's share in their booty will go to them. "In fact our miseries and suffering are the real base for the luxuries of these notorious officials."
128. Interview with Erragadindla Ramdas, Siddhapuram Settlement, dated 24.11.2006.
129. Interview with K.R. Somanna, an ex-criminal settler, Siddhapuram, Atmakur Mandal, Kurnool District, dated 24th November 2006.
130. Interview with wodde Lakshmanna, an ex-criminal settler, Siddhapuram, Atmakur Mandal, Kurnool District, dated 24th November, 2006.
131. Interview with Erragadindla Ramdas, an ex-criminal settler, Siddhapuram, Atmakur Mandal Kurnool District, dated 24th November, 2006.
132. The Sugalis are not the autochthones of south India. Their original home is believed to be Marwar in Rajasthan. In the 18th century, they had also taken up service under the Maratha rulers of Satara, the Peshwas of Poona, the Nizam of Hyderabad, and the British in their Mysore and Maratha wars. With the advent of the British rule, the Sugalis gave up much of their traditional occupation of transporting goods due to introduction of mechanised transport, laying of roads and rail lines by the then government. Being poor, illiterate and lacking technological skills, they took to crimes like robbery, dacoity, cattle-lifting until the middle of the last century. Therefore, in order to control their criminal activities, they were brought under the preview of the XXVII of 1871 Criminal Tribes Act. See Krishna Reddy B., A Tribe in Transition: *The Sugalis of Rayalaseema region in Andhra Pradesh,* Unpublished Ph. D. Thesis, S.V. University, Tirupati, 1984, p. 8. Also see, Krishna Reddy, B., "Forests and Sugalis in Andhra Pradesh, Historical and Anthropological Perspectives," *Man in India,* 71:4, pp. 611 to 621.
133. See Krishna Reddy, B., "A Note on the Worship of Hindu Deities of Banjaras", *Man and Life, Vol. 18, Nos. 1 and 2,* pp. 45-53. Also See, Krishna Reddy, B. and Ramachandra Reddy M. An Ethnographic Account of the Banjaras, *Vanyajati Vol. XXV, No. 2,* pp. 19-23.
134. See *Public Works and Labour Department, G.O. No. 1425 L.,* dated 4.7.1932.

135. See *Public Works and Labour Department G.O. No. 1426 L., dt 4th July 1932.* Application of Sections 3 and 10 of the Criminal Tribes Act on Donga Lambadis was laid by M.E.R., Wood, Esq., I.C.S., the then Collector of Krishna district, and the Secretary to Government.
136. See Public Works and Labour Department, G.O. No. R.O.C. – CI.516/ A -32 dated 12th March 1932.
137. See, C.B. Cunningham, Esq, C.S.I., Inspector-General of Police to the Secretary to Government of Madras, dated 1st June 1932, RC No. 267-2/state/32.
138. They had been notified as a Criminal Tribe in *G.O. No. 648, Judicial, dated 16th November 1925.* See Kurup, A.M. and B.K. Roy Burman, Lambada: A Scheduled Tribe of Andhra Pradesh, *Census of India Monograph, 1961.*
139. Venkatesh, K., Sivaram, P., Bhaskar, D.S., "Socio-Economic Conditions of Sugalis in an Andhra Tanda", *Vanyajati, Vol. XXXVIII, No. 4,* pp. 6-16.
140. For details see B. Krishna Reddy, 'Change and Continuity in Denotified Tribal Community: The case of Yanadi in Andhra Pradesh', paper presented in the National Seminar on Denotified – Nomadic Tribes in India: Issues and Perspectives held at Department of Sociology, University of Pune, 5th and 6th January 2007, p. 1.
141. Thurston, Edgar, *Castes and Tribes of Southern India, Vol. 3,* Madras, 1909, p. 301.
142. Reddy, P.C., *The Yanadis of Madras Presidency,* Unpublished Ph.D. thesis, Lucknow University, p. 7.
143. Government of India, *Census Report, Special Tables for Scheduled Castes and Scheduled Tribes,* 1991, Government Press, New Delhi, p. 22.
144. For details see, B. Krishna Reddy, 'National Seminar on Denotified Tribes in Andhra Pradesh' held at Kuppam University, Department of Folklore Studies, Dravidian University, Kuppam 2006 (sponsored by NT-DNT Commission, New Delhi).
145. See Thurston, Edgar, *Castes and Tribes of Southern India, Vol. 3,* Madras, 1909, p. 302.
146. See *Judicial Department, G.O. No. 28, dt.15th January 1926.*
147. See *Judicial department, G.O. No. 1080, dt. 25.9.1922.*
148. It was clearly stated in the *Government Order No. 28, Judicial Department, dt.15. 1. 1926* that "the Yanadis in general are a jungle tribe. It is not advisable to bring them under the criminal Tribes Act."
149. See Gousia Begam, S., The Yanadis : *A Study in marriage, family and Inter-community linkages,* Unpublished dissertation, submitted to S.V. University, Tirupati, 1986.
150. See *Judicial Department, G.O. No. 28, dt.15.1.1926,* p. 6.
151. See *Public Works Labour Department, G.O. No.1962, L., dt.16th September 1932,* p. 4.
152. The notification had been published in the *Fort St. George Gazette dt.*

30th August 1932, Notification No. 306, dt. 30th August 1932, p. 1435, Part-I.

153. *Home Department, G.O. No. 4140 C/36-3, dated 2.7.1937, p. 4.*
154. See *Public Works and Labour Department, G.O. No.1764 L, dated 19th August 1932,* p. 1.
155. Pulla Reddy, A., 'Ethnographic note on the Yanadi tribe of Andhra Pradesh', *Vanyajathi, Vol. No. XXXII,* Bharatiya Adimajati Sevak Sangh, New Delhi.
156. Pratap, D.R., *"Andhra Pradesh Adimajatulu"* (in Telugu), Director, TCR & TI, Hyderabad.
157. See, B. Krishna Reddy, Change and Continuity in Denotified Tribal Community: The Case of Yanadi in Andhra Pradesh, paper presented in the National Seminar on Denotified – Nomadic Tribes in India: Issues and Perspectives held at the Department of Sociology, University of Pune, Pune on 5th and 6th January 2007, pp. 3-4.
158. *Ibid,* p. 5.
159. *Ibid,* p. 6.
160. Raghavaiah, V., *The Yanadi,* Akhil Bhartiya Adim Jati Sevak Sangh, New Delhi, 1962, p. 19.
161. Vasulu, T.S., *Demographic study of a genetic Isolate, Genetic implications of Demography of Yanadis,* Unpublished monograph, Anthropological Survey of India, Mysore,1980.
162. Saheb, S.A.A., Yanadies: Ethnographic profile of the tribes (ed) K.S. Singh, *People of India, Vol.* 2, Tamil Nadu, Anthropological Survey of India, Kolkata, 2004.
163. Saheb S.A.A., *Shamanism mother Goddess cult among the Irulas of Tamil Nadu,* Anthropological Survey of India, Mysore, 1993.
164. Ramesham, *Andhra Pradesh District Gazatteers, Chittoor,* The Director, Government Press, Andhra Pradesh, Hyderabad, 1979.
165. See Sudhakar Rao, N., "A Structural Perspective of Yanadis Two forms of Entertainment: Melam and Keelugurralu"; *The Eastern Anthropologist, Vol. 50, No. 1, 1997,* pp. 27-46. Also see, Sudhakara Rao, N. 'Rangam of Yanadi of Sriharikota', *The Eastern Anthropologist, 36, 3, 1983,* pp. 223-26.
166. Sudhakar Reddy, B.V., *Tradition and Transition : A Study of Socio-cultural change among the Yanadis of Andhra Pradesh,* Unpublished Ph.D. thesis, S.V. University, Tirupati.
167. See Krishna Reddy, B. 'Change and Continuity in Denotified Tribal Community : The case of Yanadi in Andhra Pradesh', paper presented in the National Seminar on Denotified – Nomadic Tribes in India: Issues and Perspectives held at Department of Sociology, University of Pune, 5-6 January 2007, p. 6.
168. *Ibid.*
169. See Krishna Reddy, B., National Seminar on Denotified Tribes in Andhra

Pradesh held at Department of Folklore Studies, Dravidian University Kuppam, 2006 (sponsored by NT-DNT Commission, New Delhi).

170. See *Public Works and Labour Department, G.O. No. 1962 L. dated 6th September 1932*, p. 1.

171. See Government of Madras, *Fort St. George Gazettee dated 30th August 1932 Notification No. 306, Part I*, p. 1435.

172. See *Judicial Department, G.O. No. 28 dated 15th January 1926*, p. 1. In this connection, the attention was invited to PWLD G.O. No. 2738 L., dated 13.12.1934 wherein Rule 12 of the CTA was amended so as to provide for the absence of CT members from their residence.

173. See Government of Madras, *Fort St. George Gazettee dated 15th December 1925, Notification No. 214, Judicial, dated 9th December 1925, Part I*, p. 2358.

174. See, Sudhakara Reddy, P., *The Displaced Yanadis of Sriharikota Island: A Study in Socio-cultural Continuity and Change*, Unpublished Ph.D. thesis, S.V.University, Tirupati, 1981.

175. Agarwal, Binod, Sudhakar Rao C.N., and Gurivi Reddy P.C. , *Yanadi Response to Change: An Attempt to action Anthropology*, Concept Publishers, New Delhi, 1985.

176. Krishna Reddy, B., Change and continuity in Denotified Tribal Community: The case of Yanadi in Andhra Pradesh, paper presented in the *National Seminar on Denotified and Nomadic Tribes in India; Issues and Perspectives* held at Department of Sociology, University of Pune, 5-6 January 2007.

177. *Ibid*, p. 7.

178. These people are called 'Yerukulas' in Telugu, 'Kaikadi' in Marathi, 'Korava' in Tamil and 'Korama', 'Koracha' and 'Kurwi' in Carnatic districts. The Yerukulas are the Telugu division of the great South Indian Tribe 'Koravas'. Paupa Rao Nayudu's *"History of the Koravas"* and Edgar Thurston's *"Castes and Tribes of Southern India, Vol. III"*, gives some details about this tribe. The Yerukulas were split up into infinite divisions-some 'criminal' and some non-'criminal' speaking different languages and having different customs. The Yerukulas were recognised as a separate tribe or gang in South India. Its members were known in the Telugu districts of Andhra Pradesh as 'Donga Yerukulas (Thieving Yerukulas). For details see, Naidu, M., and Paupa Rao, The Criminal Tribes of India, No. II, *A History of Korawars, Erukulas or Kaikaries*, Madras, 1905, p. 18. Also see Thurston, Edgar, *Castes and Tribes of Southern India, Vol. III*, Madras, 1909, Cosmo Publications, Delhi, 1975, p. 39.

179. The different divisions of the Koravar tribe was grown more and more distinct as time went on. Many divisions among the Koravas contained permanent settlements and villages. Some Koravars used to carry grain and salt to the neighbouring districts in Tamil Nadu. They were always nomadic in their habits. They were originally grain carriers.

They used to travel with their pack bullocks. Some of them even do it now. The spread of railways, the increase in population and other causes took away the means of livelihood of these people and similar other gypsy tribes in the Telugu districts of Andhra Pradesh. It became difficult for the gypsies to make an honest living in a nomadic state in India as it became very difficult in Europe. In due course of time, the nomads in India were compelled to disappear from the places where they were existing. It was stated that "all the wandering tribes in Madras Presidency are criminal, because they could not make a honest living. See *Home (Judicial) Department, G.O. No. 2294, dated 7th October 1919,* p. 1. However, the British Government declared the Yerukalas as a 'Criminal' tribe. The government applied on them the Provisions of section 10(b) of the Criminal Tribes Act of 1911. Instructions were issued to the local police for the Preparation of registers of the members of the tribes in the districts in which they were found. Thus during the year 1913, in Guntur and Nellore districts of Andhra Pradesh alone six gangs of Yerukulas were notified. The Government immediately restricted their movements to certain specified areas of Andhra Pradesh. P.B.Thomas, the then Deputy Inspector-General of Police in charge of the Criminal Investigation Department, gave an account of their 'Wandering' habits and the nature of the offences to which they were addicted. His report showed that they did not have any legitimate means of livelihood.

180. The Yerukulas were settled in different parts in Andhra Pradesh. All the settled Yerukulas were not necessarily 'criminals' by profession. But all the Yerukulas were included in the list of Criminal Tribes Act of 1911. They were settled mainly in the districts of Nellore, Guntur, Kurnool, Krishna, Godavari, Vizagapatnam and Nizam dominions in Andhra Pradesh. They formed into a distinct division from the South Indian Korava tribe. It was reported that: "If there was any objection to their being known as a distinct 'tribe' they may be described as a distinct 'gang'; See *Judicial Department, G.O. No. 1062 dated 8th May 1914,* p. 4. It is important to note that the members of the tribe lead a nomadic life, begging and stealing. They ostensibly followed the occupations of basket making, carrying salt and grain and selling edible leaves, etc. They possessed a small area of land, which was insufficient to provide a livelihood for them. P.B.Thomas wrote that: "Owing to alternative circumstances they have gradually deprived of their occupation as carriers of grain and other merchandise, and been driven to dishonest practices. For this reason the Governor in council has strong hopes that, given the means of making a living, they will in a short span of time abandon their predatory habits."

181. The Madras police used to identify the Yerukulas as convicts. The police knew some of the adult males among the Yerukulas. Their names were

recorded in the police stations as suspected criminals. The full details and fingerprints of all the identified males of the Yerukulas were taken and kept in by the Police Department. The Yerukulas were also divided into certain gangs. The total number of males among the Yerukulas in the beginning districts were was 1000. They were addicted to 'criminal' habits. They did not have sufficient means of livelihood. They were registered under non-bailable offences. They did not have a nominal or actual place of residence. Many of them were out of view. Most of them were arrested and sent to jail. The yerukulas used to wander in small groups preparing mats, baskets, selling kariapauk leaves (collected in the jungles) carrying salt, grain and begging, etc. The Government of India had established by the Salvation Army in 1912 an Industrial settlement for the Yerukula tribe at Sitanagaram in Guntur district of Andhra Pradesh for their reception and maintenance. The American Baptist Mission at Kavali in Nellore district also established a settlement with of the support Government. In these two settlements the Yerukulas in the beginning were accommodated and provided with some agricultural work.

182. Thurston, Edgar, *Castes and Tribes of Southern India, Vol. III,* Cosmo Publications, Madras, 1909, p. 146.

183. Gustav, Oppert, The Original Inhabitants of Bharatavarsha or India, New York, 1978, p. 8. The colonial government declared Yerukulas as a criminal tribe during the year 1910. The Government applied on them the provisions of section 10(b) of the CT Act of 1911. Instructions were given by the District Magistrates to register the members of the yerukulas in the districts where .hey were found. During the year 1913 in Guntur and Nellore districts, six gangs of Yerukulas were notified under the Criminal Tribes Act of 1911. The Government immediately restricted their movements to the specified areas. See, Judicial Department, *G.O. No. 917 dated 10th May 1913 and Judicial Department, G.O. No. 1714, dated 4th July 1916.*

184. Thurston 1909: 275.

185. This is mentioned in *Hukumnamas and papers relating to Sriharikota Yanadis, Vol.1, A Selection of Papers from the old records of the Nellore District,* Nellore, 1915, p. 42.

186. Generally women and children are very active. They used to wander with a few cattle and portable huts. They used to accompany their males for work. The life of the Yerukula women were better than the women from Kepmaris, Nakkalas, Yanadis, Dommaras and Dasaris. During the year 1910, the women and children were also brought under security sections of 401 and 402 and some efforts were started to reclaim the women and children of Yerukulas. See *Judicial Department, G.O. No. 1635, dated 15th July 1913.*

187. Partha Sarthy, Jakka, *The Yerukula: An Ethnographic Study*, Anthropological Survey of India, Calcutta, 1988, p. 65.

188. There was no question about the homogeneity of the Yerukulas. All the Yerukulas belong to the four classes or gotras among them. They are known as *Satupati, Menapati, Kaveti and Mendragutte.* The Yerukulas are a homogeneous tribe. They maintain their blood relationships wherever they live. It was stated that "there was blood and marriage relationship between the members of the gangs Nos. IV, VI, VIII and IX. The members of Gangs Nos. V, X and XIII were also known to be related to each other. The members of each of these two main groups had been proved by convictions. They have been jointly associated in crime. They were in all probability connected by blood or marriage. The different divisions of the Yerukula Tribe (The CID Gang Nos. IV, V, VI, VIII, IX, X and XIII) used to wander in the following districts. Gang Nos. V and X used to wander in the districts of Nellore and Bellary. Gang No. IV in Godavari District. Gang No. VI, VIII and IX were found in Guntur district and Gang No. XIII used to live in Kurnool district.

189. A brief description of the Yerukulas and their gangs was given by A.G. Cardew the then Acting Secretary to the Government of Madras in his official communication to the Secretary to the Government of India, Home Department, No. 1299, dated 30th June 1913. According to this note it was stated that:

    1. *Criminal Investigation Department Gang No. IV:* The Yerukulas in this gang was consisting of 51 donkeys and 6 monkeys. The donkeys and monkeys were used for the purpose of carrying portable huts of the Yerukulas. The monkeys were used as performing animals to assist in begging. The Yerukulas in this gang were described themselves as " Bidari" Yerukulas or "Carriers". They Possessed pack bullocks. The gang was numbered by the then CID department as Gang No. 53.
    2. *Criminal Investigation Department Gang No. V:* TheYerukulas in the gang owned 8½ acres of wet land in KOVVUR taluk in Nellore District. (about 20 miles from Vemulapad.) They had 4 cows, 116 goats and 84 donkeys. There were 48 males out of which, 19 members were convicted of dacoity, robbery, housebreaking and theft. 14 males were arrested under the security sections. They were having only one temporary hut on the land. The whole of the land and cattle are owned by seven persons. These 7 members were the leaders of the gang. They were nomadic and do not have any means of subsistence. The Yerukulas in this gang were is related to criminal Investigation Department gangs No. X and XIII.
    3. *Criminal Investigation Department Gang No. VI:* The Yerukulas in

this gang had 17 donkeys. They were "Bidari" Yerukulas related to Criminal Investigation Department Gang No. IV . The total number of males is this gang was 48.

4. *Criminal Investigation Department Gang No. VIII:* The Yerukulas in this gang possessed 633 cattle and 192 donkeys. They were "Bidari" Yerukulas related to gang Nos. IV and VI. Yerukulas in this gang were arrested under the Security sections. They were sent to jail. The cattle owned by them were not sufficient for their support. The Yerukulas in the gang were experts in – cattle lifting.
5. *Criminal Investigation Department Gang No. IX:* The Yerukulas in this gang possessed 4 donkeys and 10 pigs. They were "Bidari" Yerukulas related to Gangs Nos. IV, VI, and VIII. The total number of males in this gang was 68.
6. *Criminal Investigation Department Gang No. X:* The Yerukulas in this gang owned 14 acres of weland in Vemulapad in Nellore district. They also possessed 6 acres of dry land. They owned 64 cattle, 160 goats, 12 buffaloes, 2 pigs and 77 donkeys. They were "Bidari" Yerukulas but do not do any "Bidari" work. There were 61 males in the gang. They were having only two temporary huts. The gang lead a nomadic life like the rest of the tribe.
7. *Criminal Investigation Department Gang No. XIII:* They owned 47 cattle, 68 goats and 6 acres of dry land in Kurnool District. There were 47 males in the gang. The gang is entirely nomadic. They were related to Gangs Nos. V and X. The Criminal Investigation Department Gang No. IV had never had any nominal home. It wandered through Godavari, Krishna and Ganjam districts. The Criminal Investigation Department Gang No. VI lived in Guntur district (Ongole), but did not possessed any land. The Criminal Investigation Department Gang No. VIII lived in Guntur District (Bapatla), They did not possess any land.The Criminal Investigation Department Gang No. IX lived in Guntur District (Vinukonda), but did not possess any land. The Criminal Investigation Department Gang No. X had a nominal home with a little land in Nellore (Vemulapad) District. The Criminal Investigation Department Gang No. XIII usually lived in Kurnool but they did not possess any land. The Salvation Army established a settlement at Sitanagaram near Bezawada. The settlement was an agriculture settlement. It was a suitable place to settle the Gangs Nos. IV, VI, VIII and IX. They all used to move in their neighbourhood. The Yerukulas developed bad criminal habits very slowly. Gangs Nos. V and X own land near Kavali in Nellore where the American Baptist (Telugu) Mission settled some of theYerukulas. Gang No.V was provided work at Mica Mines at Kalichedu where Donga Dasaris already started their work on

the Mica Mines owned by a German firm. The manager took strong personal interest in their reclamation. The Salvation Army settlements at Sitanagaram and Kavali was consisted of 864 members in the beginning. The criminal investigation Department Gang No. XIII had a small branch of the tribe in Bellary where the Government established a settlement for Yerukulas at Rudrapad. It was proposed to hand over the settlement to the Salvation Army.

The Government had considered financial aid to the settlement established by the American Baptist Mission at Kavali for the reclamation of Donga Yerukulas. The settlement at Kavali was opened in October 1912. It consisted 55 families (nearly 200 persons). A number of 20 families of the same tribe were sent to the settlement. The American Baptist Mission made arrangements to provide the settlers with the means of livelihood by providing *(a)* weaving *(b)* Fiber-Cleaning and bundling *(c)* Market Gardening. The collector had assigned to the Baptist Mission about 100 acres of dry land on the understanding that it will be irrigated with deep well water. Land was allotted to such Yerukulas whose character was found good. To place the settlement on a satisfactory footing, the Baptist Mission incurred an amount of rupees 5000 on buildings, water supply, and to maintain the settlers, development of the settlement, etc. The government sanctioned the money subjected to the proviso that no person should be converted to adopt Christianity as a condition of admission to the settlement. The District Magistrate reported every year through the Inspector General of Police on the progress of the settlement under provision of section 12 of the criminal tribes Act 1911. The Yerukulas were restricted their movements to the areas Comprised within the industrial settlement established by the Salvation Army at Sitanagaram in Guntur District, and the area comprised within the settlement established by the American Baptist Mission at Kavali in Nellore District.

190. See Simhadri Y.C., *'The Ex-Criminal Tribes of India'*, National Publishing House, New Delhi, 1979, p. 64.
191. See Hatch, W.J., *The Land Pirates of India*, Seeley Service and Co., London, 1928.
192. See Memorandum on Donga Yerukulas prepared by Mr. P.B. Thomas, Deputy Inspector-General of Police, Railways and Criminal Investigation Department, in *Judicial Department, G.O. No. 1299 dated 30th June 1913*, p. 1.
193. Thurston 1909 : 451 and Paupa Rao and Naidu 1905 : 2.
194. *See Judicial Department, G.O. No.784, dated 25th April 1913, Annexure III*, p. 10.

195. See Joseph, A., 'Yerukula Traditional Justice', *Tribal, Vol. 4, No. 1,* p.11.
196. The Government of India in its notification declared the Yerukulas as criminal tribes. It was stated that : "Whereas there is reason to belive that the gangs of Yerukulas described below are addicted to the systematic Commission of non-bailable offences. The Governor in Council, in exercise of the Powers conferred on him by section 3 of the Criminal Tribes Act, 1911 (III of 1911), hereby declares that each of the said gangs is a criminal tribe for the purpose of the said Act." The following table shows the restriction of the movements of the yerukulas under their Local leaders.

Table-2

Restriction of the Movements of 'Donga' Yerukulas in AP

Gang No.	*Name of the Leaders Local Leader (s)*	*Restrictions of Movements of the gangs to specific areas/Localities*
I	Manupati Pichigadu and Manupati Kasigadu	Movements confined to Godavari District.
II	Batchu Guravadu	Movements restricted to Nellore District. The head quarters of the Gang was located in Kovur Taluk, Nellore district.
III	Kavati Kotadu	Guntur District.
IV	Karredula Narasigadu	Guntur District.
V	Bande Guravadu	Guntur District.
VI	Avula Pedda Subbadu	Headquarters of the gang was located in Nellore District, Vemulapadu Village, Kanigiri district.
VII	Avula Subbadu	Headquarters of the gang was located in Kurnool Dist.

Further it was notified that under section 10(b) of the said Act, the Governor in Council directed that every registered member of each of the said criminal tribes shall in the prescribed manner notify his place of residence and any change or intended change of residence and any absence or intended absence from his residence."

197. Note 1916: 36. Also see, Government of Madras, *Hukumnamas and papers relating to Sriharikota Yanadis, Vol.1, A selection of Papers from the old records of the Nellore District,* Nellore 1915, Appendix 1-3.
198. Lalitha, 1995: 72.
199. Sherring, M.A., *The Tribes and Castes of Madras Presidency,* New Delhi, 1975, p. 18.
200. See, Government of Madras, *Bulletin, Vol. V, No.1, Anthropology, Vision of the Uralis and Sholagas; More Marriage Customs in Southern India, Hook-Swinging, Paliyans,* The Superintendent Government Press, Madras,

1903, pp. 23-24. The value of a wife is fixed at 20 pagodas. The maternal uncle's right to the first two daughters are valued at 8 out of 20 pagodas.

201. See Government of Madras, *Madras Government Museum Bulletin, Vol. IV, No. 3, Anthropology,* Madras, 1903, p. 165.
202. Thurston 1909: 456 and Paupa Rao and Naidu 1905: 6.
203. Syed Siraj-ul-Hassan writes, "The ritual is vogue. Widow marriage is simple and consists in dressing the widow in new clothes, putting bangles on her arms and taking her home etc": See Syed Siral-ul-Hassan *'Castes and the Tribes of H.E.H. the Nizam Dominions,* Delhi, 1909, p. 18.
204. Writing about Yerukulas, T.Cain informs us that immediately the woman feels the birth-pains, she informs her husband, who takes some of her clothes, puts them on and places the same on his head. She retires into a dark room where there is only very dim light and lies down on the bed, covering herself up with a long cloth. When the child is born, it is washed and placed on the cot besides the father. Asafoetida, Jaggery (molasses) and other articles are given not to the mother but to the father. See Kamala Manohar Rao, *'Bulletin of Tribal Cultural Research and Training Institute'*, Madras, 1901, pp. 114-15.
205. Gustav Oppert 1978, p. 14.
206. It is considered that children born in such auspicious circumstances will become expert thieves. Thurston, 1909: 492.
207. Paupa Rao and Naidu 1905: 17.
208. See Abdul Gafoor syed Khaja, *Tribes and Tribal Welfare in Hyderabad,* Government Press, Madras, 1915, p. 49.
209. Each family had its snares for edible birds and nets for game, such as hares, etc. and they use them to catch the birds and other pet animals. The men go out for hunting with these and bring back live birds and small animals which they kill and eat or sell for grain or money. This is a means of livelihood and source of income in addition to basket and mat making. Kamala Manohar Rao, 1901: 118.
210. Lalitha 1995: 168. Also see, *Home Department, G.O. No. 3467, dated 30.12.1943. Home Department, G.O. No. 1837, dated 13.6.1944 and Home Department G.O. No. 2214 dated 26.7.1946.* They wander over the districts of Nellore, Kurnool, Guntur, Krishna, Godavari and Hyderabad. They were divided into seven main divisions knows as Criminal investigation department gangs Nos. IV, V, VI, VIII, IX, X and XIII. These members have been conceited of non-bailable offences. None of them have nominal or actual place of residence. Many of them were constantly hiding. Some were out of view and others went to jails. The gangs wander about in small parties professing to live by basket making, selling "Kariapauk" leaves (collected in the jungles and used in cooking), begging and carrying salt and grain.

211. Since 1897 the yerukulas were registered in serious offences. It was stated that they were always committing pickpockets. They frequently visit the fairs and festivals, towns and railway stations like most of the regular criminal gangs. They were addicted to crimes accompanied by violence such as dacoity, highway robbery and burglaries. For details see, *Home (Judicial) Department, G.O. No. 757, dated 4th April 1917. Also see, Home Judicial Department G.O. No. 920 dated 2nd May 1917.*
212. See *Home (Judicial) Department, G.O. No. 1006, dated 14th May 1917 and Home (Judicial) Department, G.O. No. 1485, dated 19th July 1917. Also See Home (Judicial) Department, G.O. No. 1516, dated 24th July 1917 and Home (judicial) Department, G.O. No. 1850, dated 4th September 1917.* The yerukulas got the bad reputation for the highway robberies and dacoities they used to commit in the vicinities of their encampments. It was reported that: "In Nellore, the highway roads were so unsafe in those days wherein some parts of the districts, the Magistrates issued special licenses of arms and weapons to travellers for their protection. The crimes committed by them was usually accompanied by the show or violence." Therefore, repressive measures were taken by the government by using sections 400 and 402 to restrict their movements in the presidency.
213. Interview with an ex-'criminal' Stuartpuram (Betapudi) Settlement dated 6.2.2007.
214. Interview with an ex-'criminal' in Kapparalla Tippa (Bitragunta) Settlement dated 4.2.2007.
215. Interview with an ex-'criminal' in the Sitanagaram Settlement (Tadepalli) dated 8.2.2007.
216. Interview with an ex-'criminal' in Stuartpuram Settlement, dated 6.2.2007.
217. Interview with an ex-'criminal' in Sitanagaram settlement, dated 8.2.2007.
218. Interview with an ex-'criminal' in Stuartpuram settlement, dated 6.2.2007.
219. *Ibid.*

3

Establishment of Criminal Tribes Settlements in Andhra: A Historical Survey

Introduction

The aims and objectives of the Chapter is to present: 1. a brief historical background and concept of CT settlements, 2. the role of the Christian Missionaries, 3. official policy, 4. settlement patterns and 5. the progress made in the settlements in Andhra Pradesh over a period of time. Source materials for this are Government records collected from the State Archives Andhra Pradesh (Hyderabad), Tamil Nadu (Chennai) and National Archives (New Delhi). The archival sources like Law (General) Department, Home Department, Revenue Department, Public Works (Labour) Department, Judicial Department, Development Department, Forest Department, Missionary sources, published books and government reports constitute the major source for the present chapter.

I

Historical Background and Concept of CT Settlements

India is the only country in the world where the British Government in 19th century branded certain tribes as 'criminal' tribes, inferring that they were criminals by birth and crime was their profession. 1. To contain them, one of the programmes implemented by the then Government was to gather active criminals belonging to those tribes at one place, like an open air jail, but along with their families. Often, Christian Missionaries were given the management of these 'criminal' settlements with magisterial powers. In such a situation, a culture of crime developed. As crime is anti-social, there has been always a clash with the rest of the society. According to

Hindu Varna system, when crime is attributed as a profession of a particular group of people that becomes a part of design by the divine. It becomes very difficult to make them understand reason and change. Some of the people belonging to other social categories involved in crime do not have the stigma of criminality unlike the Denotified Communities/Tribes in India. When the British Government branded certain castes, communities and tribes as criminals it meant that those thus branded would become so considered by birth and profession. Perhaps, the CTA had an implicit assertion that a woman from criminal family would necessarily conceive a criminal embryo. The Denotified Tribes (DNTs) have been included in this category whereas other criminals escaped the branding.

The problem of crime is a major issue faced by mankind, though it varies its form from place to place and period to period, according to the value system of people. Crime on the streets, in towns, banks or on trains have become a common topic for discussion in every part of the country. It is as old as human-failing as the birth of mankind itself. In India or elsewhere in the world, the mass media are filled daily with lurid descriptions of genocide, sensational robberies, gangsterism, police politician collusion in matters associated with corruption, unthinkable embezzlements of public funds by respected financial officers, etc. Y. C. Simhardri stated : "In any society, the social structure is usually responsible for the confronting and non-confronting behaviour of people."[2] Clarence Darrow points that, "Crime is an act forbidden by law of the land, and one which is considered sufficiently serious to warrant providing penalties for its commission."[3]

It is unfortunate to call the whole tribe or a clan or family as criminals. There is no country in the world, to our knowledge, whose people practice crime as their occupation. Biswas stated : "It is very likely that the present ex-criminal tribes of India are the off-shoots of Thugs, and that after the creation of Thagi department by the then government of India, the migratory habits of these people were stopped and many of them consequently settled in different provinces of India."[4]

The idea of CT settlements was first started in 1868. The CT settlements were coincided on the same lines as those attempted by the Thuggee and Dacoity Department in 1931 in north India. J.V.

Stephens the member of the viceroy's council, in charge of law and order stated: "The special feature of India is the caste system. A family of carpenters will be carpenters, a century or five centuries, hence, if they last so long. When a man tells you that he is an offender against the law, he has been so from the beginning and will be so to the end. Reform is impossible, for it is his trade, his caste almost I may say his religion to commit crime."[5]

This was the background for the establishment of criminal tribes' settlements in India. The government started this work on two assumptions. First, all persons born in a particular group or caste are criminal by birth and secondly once a criminal one is always a criminal. These two assumptions led to the idea that the so-called CTs were dangerous elements in the society, should be protected from them.[6] The criminal Tribes village writes Booth Tucker, "is like a rabbit warren. When the ferret appears at one end, they escaped at the other. They will sleep in the open air, in places from which they can observe all comers. They will scatter themselves over a wide area amongst out of the way of villages, where police supervision is impossible."[7]

The CT Act was the handiwork of the British Colonialism by classifying certain social groups as CTs, the British had sought to gain control over them in order to deploy them for vigilance over other groups that were rebelling or conspiring against foreign domination. The Criminal Tribes Acts developed the culture of settlements. The CT Acts are the root cause of the emergence of the CT Settlements. The CT Act and Settlements ruined the culture of civility and sociability. The settlements were islands of slavery in the midst of Independent India. The abolition of the CTA and Settlements is the contribution of the freedom struggle. The freedom struggle was thrust forward to shed the residual chains of the CTA and the abolition of the structures of the settlements.

II

Role of the Christian Missionaries

Criminal tribes' settlements were established in such districts where grave crime was prevalent. In order to provide a settled life government opened settlements. The Salvation Army, London Mission, Canadian Mission and the American Baptist (Telugu) Mission were entrusted with the management of the Criminal

Settlements.[8] These missions had three main objectives: 1. to implement the CT Act effectively and control the inmates of the settlements within the framework of the CT Act, which reduced the inmates virtually to slaves of the management; 2. to convert the inmates to christianity and 3. to provide some opportunities of employment to the adults and education to their children.

The government found the successful work done by the Missionaries such as the Salvation Army (SA). The SA was the first organisation that stepped into the activities among the CTs. They started their work with the Doms rehabilitation in Uttar Pradesh.[9] The Madras government invited the SA to take charge of the CTs and homes. Dadabhai Naoroji said: "The Salvation Army's help has been requisitioned from time to time. Whether it is SA or whether it is any other reforming body, the religious zeal is very often a necessary element in pursuing difficult task of people of this kind and winning them from evil ways."[10] William Booth Tucker, the SA Officer in Andhra managed successfully two settlements in Guṇtur District, one at Sitanagaram (1913) and the other at Stuartpuram (1914). The Lieutenant Governor of United Provinces, John Hewett, said; "The most gratifying feature of the history of criminal tribes has been the success of the Salvation Army settlements. Booth Tucker and other self-sacrificing members of the organisation were on the way to turn the criminals from hopeless enemies of mankind into useful citizens."[11]

Conversion to Christianity as a means of controlling crime is doubtless overrated by both missionaries and public officials and underrated by many police officers. Crime among the under privileged is not so much a problem of a specific group as a disease of the social organism.[12] It was stated that: "All are convinced that Christianity is true and offers the only salvation to Yerukulas, Waddars, Yanadis and Gollas. Some have worshipped their idols so long it will require a few years to banish them from their minds. Some enjoy their sins too much to give them up all at once. But all will be Christians in five years or ten."[13] There were four main reasons for the conversion of Yerukulas and Waddars into christianity. They were: 1. The changed lives of out caste converts, 2. The loss of faith in Hinduism 3. The influence of the schools and churches and 4. to liberate themselves from the criminal laws.

III

Official Policy

About the management of the CT settlements there was a debate in Madras Legislative Assembly as to why should Christian Missionaries alone should be given the management work of the CTs. Because of the dedication and zeal of the Christian Missionaries, their interest in the reformation, rehabilitation of the depressed classes and, in addition to that, their interest in evangelisation were responsible for handing over the CTS to these people.[14]

The different laws on the so-called CTs have been influenced by the colonial considerations of political mechanism and economic needs. The colonial administrators believed that maintenance of law and order would be a mere exercise in vacuum unless a better control could be achieved over the indigenous population. It was then imperative that a stray and shifting population could not be conductive to the so-called 'good' government and the colonial notion of 'pax Britannica'. In order to achieve this, unlike in the west where legislation regulated incidences of crime, in India, interception of crime was attempted. The colonial government here tried to confine would-be-male factors to settlements.[15] Some wandering tribes without any fixed habitat became dubbed as 'criminal' and were set up in settlements. It was stated that : "If the local government has reason to believe that any tribe, gang or class of persons or any part of a tribe gang or class is addicted to the systematic commission of offences it may declare that such tribe, gang or class or part of the tribe, gang or class as a criminal tribe."[16] A broader economic structure had grown up around the life of the settlements. Stolen-proterty dealers, corrupt officials, investors in crime and greedy lawyers all exploited the situation. These tribes are found in almost all parts of India. The total population of these tribes in India was estimated in different states totaling approximately more than eight million population.

The primary object of a 'Criminal settlement' is reformation but not segregation or confinement. Its management has fallen into the hands of the police. The police and the government officers had no training for the reclamation of criminals. Their duty is to inspire trust in the criminal classes. In the non governmental agencies the government will get the help of self-sacrificing men. They are prepared to devote their lives to the reformatory work. The government officers who are keenly interested in the reclamation service are transferred sometimes when suitable substitutes may not be found to carry on the work. It is noticed that the work of the non governmental agency for management has been successful. The consideration is its economy. The government cannot get skilled service for the remuneration actually it pays to the non-official agencies. The manager of a settlement has full freedom to undertake the responsibility of the CTs in the settlements. But the non-official manager enjoys independence and prestige. He refuses to inform unimportant matters to higher authorities for decision. To maintain peace and order, the government officials will take the help of the police. The work of reclamation is more likely to be done effectively by men who make it their main object in life than by public servants. The public servants may not show the necessary interest on the reclamation work.[17] The Government opined that : "The experiences gained in other provinces indicate that organizations like Salvation Army carried out the reclamation work with less money and got good results."[18]

Registration was made to every member of the designated tribe was categorised as a "Criminal" or as a "Potential Criminal". The Criminal Tribes were instructed to register themselves either with the police department or the village administration, the purpose being to locate and keep vigil on them. Every new born child was thus forced to be registered to update records. Failure to register was a punishable offence. The CTs were asked to report themselves at the nearest police station at fixed intervals. A surveillance system was built up by making every registered person belonging to a CT or settlement report to the police or to the village administration. The movements of each settler were recorded and each one had to get written permission (Passes) from the authorities to go out of the settlement and when returning to the settlement had to furnish information about the purpose and destination or the movement. Regardless of whether any crime was indulged in, merely belonging to the 'Criminal tribe or settlement' provided sufficient legal grounds for total vigilance. Of course those individuals and families which were really involved in criminal operations never bothered to register themselves or report to the authorities. To exercise effective control and watch over them, active criminals and families were rounded up and sent to special settlements. The management of these settlements was given over to Christian missionaries, who were given police powers. Some arable land was made available and the settlers were expected to cultivate it and live on its produce. Reporting to the management thrice a day was a routine instruction, night checks and controls were conducted. Some settlements were fenced with barbed wires.[19] In Andhra Pradesh there were five such settlements established between 1908 and 1917. The culture of crime was perpetuated by isolating the members of the settlements who enjoyed independence and prestige.[19]

IV

Settlement Patterns

The Colonial Government felt that penal, agricultural, industrial and reformatory settlements were the best sources for the reformation work on these criminal classes.[20] The Madras Government felt that agricultural and industrial settlements are the best sources for reclamation work because in the cooli work, the labourers do little work. If a man is given a small plot of land he goes to the land early in the morning and works till late. Even if he has other works to perform, he will spare some time to work in his plot. Hence the government made it compulsory in all settlements that agriculture should be the main industry. Each family was distributed a block of dry land and a piece of wet land to maintain themselves. If any one is found to neglect his land he was given punishment with harsh work such as breaking stones, digging earth, etc. and the land was taken away from him and given to another. The Government considered that, in course of time, a patta for his land may be given to the settler.[21]

In industrial settlements, the following piece work was given: 1. Silk worm rearing 2. Silk reeling, spinning and weaving 3. Wool spinning or weaving 4. Carpet making 5. Cotton weaving and warping 6. Carpentry and Blacksmithy 7. Shoe making 8. Tailoring 9. Mat and basket making 10. Coir picking 11. Pottery 12. Fitting and metal work 13. Stone breaking, dressing, quarrying or mining 14. Gardening 15. Building and repairing buildings 16. Making of bags and boxes 17. Poultry farming and sheep farming and 18. Scavenging, etc.[22]

The Government decided to establish the settlements during the year 1910. A total number of 25 tribes living in twenty districts were declared by the Government as criminal tribes. Seven CT settlements were established under the Act upto the end of the year 1915. Five settlements were managed by the SA, one by the ABM at Kavali and the others were under the official management.[23] The following classes of settlements and institutions have been established by the SA: 1. Agricultural settlements, 2. Mixed Agro-industrial settlements, 3. Industrial settlements, 4. Homes for released prisoners, 5. Homes for Juvenile Adult Released prisoners and 6. Homes for children, etc.

The settlements were equipped with all infrastructural facilities for the administrative staff. The settlements were directly administered by the government. All the infrastructure was kept under its control. The missionary management were asked to pay a nominal rent to the government for using the infrastructure and the buildings.[24] The Manager was the sole incharge of the settlement where he was appointed. Clerks had to assist the manager for the administrative correspondence and other work. Peons looked after the administrative works. The midwife used to assist the doctor and looked after the delivery cases. The compounder used to supply the required medicines who attended the hospital. The agricultural maistries helped the settlers in instructing the unskilled labourers in doing agricultural work. The ward boy assisted the doctors and attended the hospital work regularly. The teachers has to run the school and watchers used to look into the whereabouts of the settlers. The scavengers had to sweep the managers' bungalow, offices, schools, hospital, etc.

V

Progress Made in the Settlements

CT settlements in Andhra Pradesh were well known. The earliest settlement was Kalichedu settlement established for Dasaries, Dommaras and Yerukulas. This was an *industrial settlement.* Kavali settlement was an *agricultural settlement* established by the ABM. Sitanagaram settlement was an *industrial settlement* established by SA in 1913. Siddhapuram settlement was a *voluntary settlement* established in 1913. Bethapudi settlement, known as Stuartpuram, was established in 1914 by SA. Bhumannagadda settlement was an *agricultural settlement* intended for the Nowabpeta Korachas by the SA in the same year. A *reformatory settlement* in Guntur was established by SA, intended to be a home for the prisoners undergoing imprisonment in Madras Presidency. Chintal Devi settlement was established by the Government for the settlement of Kanjar Bhats who belonged to Bombay presidency.[25]

A. *Kalichedu Settlement : Origin*

Kalichedu settlement was started during the year 1911 in Nellore district. Mr. Ludwig who was the then local manager of M/s H. Brandt Mica Mines Company opened the 'settlement'. Kalichedu settlement was opened with 200 people belonging to Katheras or Dasaris.[26] They had faced a number of difficulties in the beginning. The government provided a police constable, hospital and school during the year 1915. Mr. Ludwig strove hard for the progress of the settlement.[27]

Notification of Katheras and Dasaris

Katheras were not accustomed to hard work in the beginning. They were notified as a 'criminal tribe' along with the other people (Dasaris) living in Kurnool, Guntur, Godavari and Krishna districts. Their movements were restricted to Kalichedu settlement. They were identified as CTs with the Dommaras of Nellore district.[28]

Satisfactory Condition of the Colony Until the Outbreak of the War

The settlement worked very well until the outbreak of the European War in 1914. The Company's work on the mines was closed due to the outbreak of the European War. The settlers were thrown out of work. Some of the Dasaris were transferred to Kavali settlement in order to provide them suitable employment during the year 1916. They were provided with unskilled labour. They were given repair works for the Govt. buildings, road construction work and other contract works provided by the Public Works Department.[29] The settlers acquired great skill in mica mines work and there was a great demand for them in the neighbouring villages. Agriculture, mat-making were some of the other industries provided to them.[30]

Employment in Tea Gardens

Some families of Dasaris immigrated to Assam for the sake of employment in the tea gardens. The United Planters' Association of south India recruited some of the Dasaris in their estates on voluntary basis.[31] Coffee-picking, weeding, road-work, etc. were given to them. The turnout of these people was very satisfactory. The Dasaries who were working in the estates complained of ill-treatment by the managers. They escaped from the estates and returned back to Kalichedu.[32]

Agriculture at Kalichedu

The managers often complained about the difficulty of providing employment to Dasaries. They were not self-supporting. During the year 1920 agriculture was taken up by them.[33] 40 acres of dry land was brought under cultivation during the year 1921. Some of them did not know how to cultivate their lands. They were engaged in the works provided by District Boards, Public Works Department, etc. A textile industry was opened in Kalichedu during the year 1921. The Dasaries prepared excellent date mats and were sold in the market.[34]

Kalichedu School

A school was opened in Kalichedu during the year 1917. Competent teachers were employed in the school. During the year 1920, there were 400 children studying in the school. 39 bright children were transferred to SA School at Nellore during the year 1921 from the settlement school. The government paid a grant of Rs. 3 per each child who were kept under the care of the SA.[35]

The settlement management authorities could not provide sufficient work for the Dasaries for a number of years. There was an increase in the number of absconders from Kalichedu during the year 1930. The inefficient police encouraged the Dasaries to commit crime. Therefore, the government decided to close down the Kalichedu settlement and transfered them to Stuartpuram settlement. The settlement failed due to non-availability of employment for the tribes, weak administration, corrupt police, etc.[36]

B. *Bhumannagadda Settlement (Chittoor District) : Origin*

The settlement was opened for the Nawabpeta Korachas during the year 1913. The SA took the management of the settlement during the year 1915. The government handed over 855 acres of land to settle the Nawabpeta Korachas. Adjutant Allan the SA Manager took the responsibility of the 550 members of the Korachas. The SA took the control of the settlement from the Police Department during the year 1916. Booth Tucker said: "The police were interfering in the management of the settlement even after it had been handed over to the Salvation Army."[37] Adjutant Allan the then manager of the settlement did not understand Telugu. There was a communication gap between the settlers and the manager. The manager was totally ignorant of the nature, manners and customs of the settlers. He did not know how to deal with the settlers. He granted free passes to the settlers. Frequently there were a number of people absconding from the settlement. The SA authorities were not satisfied with his performance.[38] Captain Swami Das was appointed as the manager of the settlement during the year 1920. Subsequently Captain Green and Lieutenant Premanandam became the managers of the Settlement. They gradually improved the conditions of the settlement. Since 1925 the management of the settlement began to run smoothly.[39]

Women at the Settlement

The women in the settlement was very active. They played a very important role in the settlement. They used to sell Karepauk leaves in the neighbouring villages. It was stated that : Women formed an important factor in the settlement. They generally came and went as they liked and acted as spies and informants to their leaders. They used to go out on the pretext of selling Karepauk leaves. But really speaking they frequently go to spy out on the land and to keep themselves in touch with the absconding members. The women have been formally placed in the settlements and many of them have been registered. It was hoped that the industrial training for the tearing women in the settlements will further tends to put down crime."[40]

Employment

Agriculture was the main occupation of the settlers. During the year 1926, the settlers cultivated 700 acres of land. Dams were constructed in the settlement for the agricultural purpose of the settlers. Booth Tucker, the Salvation Army officer further improved their agricultural activities. The settlers were also provided with weaving and silk industries to support their income.[41] The Korachas made ropes, baskets, traded sheep, goats, etc. However, the settlement was not self-supporting. The SA provided a special recurring grant of Rs. 5000 per month for the supervision of the settlement.[42]

School

For the education of the children of the Korachas an elementary school was opened in the settlement. 57 children attended the school regularly. Weaving and sericulture industries were introduced to the school children. The children carried the sericulture work regularly. Sewing, thread drawing and other activities in the sericulture programme were also taught by the teachers.[43]

Success of the Settlement

The overall progress of the settlement was not satisfactory. Under the management of Adjutant Allen the settlement did not progress much. There were fights among the Korachas and the settlement was disturbed due to the outside influence. There were a number of absconders from the settlement. The managers who succeeded Captain Green and Swami Das did not show much interest in the improvement of the settlement. The settlement remained backward in all respects. The strength of the settlement gradually decreased since 1930. During the year 1931 there were 152 females, 135 children and 161 males in the settlement. Since then the settlement faced a number of obstacles in its progress.[44]

C. *Bitragunta Refomatory Settlement, Kappalla Tippa and Kavali Settlements—Nellore District: Origin*

Kavali settlement was started for the Yerukalas of Nellore district in October, 1912, on voluntary basis with 152 persons. Rev. Bullard of the American Baptist Mission opened the settlement.[45] In 1912, Rev. Bullard, with the permission of the police authorities, took charge of 20 yerukala families and opened the Industrial Yerukala settlement at Kavali. Enroute they changed their mind, and wishing to escape and going to Kalichedu the Yerukalas went to Mr. Bullard and pretended their desire to conversion to Christianity.[46] This was agreed upon by Bullard. The District Magistrate gave his consent to settle the Yerukalas in Kavali. The ABM readily accepted the proposal to provide as far as possible, the necessary conditions for social, industrial, educational and hygienic improvement of the Kavali settlement.[47] Rev. Bullard wanted to keep all of them under his direct supervision so that he could experiment and rehabilitate them until the mission achieved its goal. He provided them with looms, warping macaines and a building to work and store the materials. He also planned to start a silk factory but it did not fructify due to climatic reasons. From the outside, the Kavali settlement had to face enormous problems. None of the Yerukalas were accustomed to any kind of settled labour.[48]

Difficulties in Finding Remunerative and Profitable Work at Kavali

The strength of the settlement increased to 55 families by the end of the year 1913. In January, 1914 the settlement has subsequently notified as one established under section 16 of the CT Act.[49] Minor industries such as weaving, fibre work, gardening, stone quarrying mat and basket making and tile manufacturing were introduced. However, the progress of the 'settlement' was slow. It was difficult to find remunerative and profitable work on account of the nature of the soil and the Yerukalas were found wanting in skilled work. In spite of the best efforts in agriculture, Kavali settlement was unable to develop as a self-supporting unit.

Land for Agriculture

The Yerukalas were provided 950 acres of land for agricultural purpose. The land was located at Kavali and Bitragunta reserve forest. Tools were provided for the Yerukalas to cultivate the land. The efforts made by them was not successful due to the reason that the soil was unfit for cultivation.[50]

Health

The birthrate during the year 1915 was 36 per mille. The settlers complained of the excessive mortality at the settlement. The sub. Assistant surgeon Kavali used to pay periodical visits. The Government paid him an allowance of Rs. 10 per month. The death rate during the year 1915 was 47 per mille. Black scourge (Euly lostomiasis) was very much prevalent among the settlers during the year 1916. No special efforts were taken to eliminate the disease.

Strength

The strength of the settlement at the end of 1915 was 257 men, 244 women and 330 children, a total of 831 persons of whom 743 were present in the settlement. About 200 people were transferred to the Stuartpuram settlement.

Under Taking to Bear the Net Cost of the Settlement

S.D. Bawden succeeded Mr. Bullard. The government was impressed by the efforts made by Bawden. During the year 1915 the Labour Department recruited some of the Yerukalas to work in the estates in the Anamalais. The Yerukalas were also provided work in the United Planters Association Company of south India.[51] A total number of 72 families of the Yerukalas were given employment in the company. The strength of the Yerukalas in Kavali during the year 1915 was 600. Since then the strength of the settlement increased gradually.[52]

Progress After 1916

Bullard was an expert in agriculture. The then District Magistrate granted him 100 acres of waste land for the purpose of opening the settlement. Bullard irrigated the land provided to him with deep well water. The District Magistrate kept 55 families of the Yerukalas under his supervision who were escaped from Kalichedu.[53] The government sanctioned a non-recurring grant of Rs. 5000 for the opening of the settlement. During the year 1914 the settlement was notified as a criminal tribe settlement.[54]

Reformatory Work Among the Children

A school was constructed in Kavali during the year 1914. The attendance of the children was made compulsory for all the children (6 to 12 years) in the Village.[55] A boarding school was also constructed for the benefit of the school going children. Boys and girls were separated from their parents in order to protect the children from the influence of their parents.[56] During the year 1920, there were 90 boys and 70 girls attending the school regularly. A night school was opened in the village for the education of the youth in (children who were above the age of 12 years) the Kavali settlement.[57]

The Yerukalas used to attend the religious services conducted by the American Baptist Church in the settlement. A daily morning prayer and a service on Sundays were organized by the manager.The Yerukalas only attended the church and showed required respect for the Managers. The Yerukalas did not pay attention to the gospels given by the Baptist church fathers. Mr. Bullard used to stress the importance of moral discipline to convert the Yerukalas. The Hindu members of the tribe constructed a temple and appointed a priest to conduct regular bhajans in the settlement.[58]

New Settlements at Allur and Bitragunta

During the year 1916, the entire cost of the maintenance of the Yerukalas was met by the government. The net cost of running of the Kavali settlement was 11,674 Rupees.[59] The District Magistrate, the Inspector General of Police and the Manager felt that there was no further prospects of the settlement. The settlement was not self-supporting. They recommended for shifting over the Kavali settlement to Allur.[60]

In December, 1916, Kavali settlement transferred some of the Yerukalas to Bitragunta where the Bitragunta Reformatory Settlement was already commenced in January, 1917. The Government accepted the proposal of the District Magistrate to transfer 75 families of Yerukalas to the experimental settlement, 50 of whom had to be sent from Kavali and the rest from kalichedu.[61] The agricultural settlement at Bitragunta was declared to be a part of Kavali settlement. This was under the supervision of Bawden who worked hard to make the Yerukalas a self-respecting and self-supporting people. The Government believed that education of settlers' children would be the best possible way to solve the problem of reclaiming the CTs.[62] With regard to incorrigibles, Mr. Bawden wanted a separate settlement subject to certain conditions: (1) Incorrigibles should not be allowed to escape; (2) when a man absconded from Kavali, Bitragunta or Allur settlements for the second or third time, his family should be sent to the penal settlement and (3) no community food was allowed.[63]

In 1919 the settlement had a strength of 1860 members of whom 138 were at Allur, 363 at Bitragunta and 1058 at Kavali. The rest being out of view, in prison or on leave. The process of transferring well behaved Yerukalas from Kavali to the new settlements continued and in 1920 there were 153 settlers at Allur, 443 at Bitragunta and 916 at Kavali.[64] The Yerukalas at Kavali were subjected to a strict discipline and the wages given to them were inadequate. Kavali settlement was disciplinary and probationary and the work that was available there was almost entirely coolie work. Mr. Moir, the then Commissioner of labour investigated the economic conditions at Kavali in 1921 and reported that the unsatisfactory conditions at Kavali were due to two reasons, namely: (1) a far too rapid increase in the strength of the settlement and (2) unjustifiable optimism regarding the agricultural possibilities of the settlement.[65]

According to Moir, reduction in strength is the only solution to the problem. The Government decided to convert the settlement at Kavali into a penal or reformatory settlement. The one at Guntur being discontinued. Only incorrigibles were kept at Kavali and the rest were transferred to Allur swamp area. Rev. Bawden had a serious quarrel with Singapeta people which resulted in a riot, and a serious criminal case was filed against him at the magistrate Court, Kovur.[66]

During the year 1918, the Yerukalas cultivated 85 acres of land. The crops cultivated by them were gram and cholam. The health conditions of the Yerukalas was very poor. The birth rate during 1920 was 36 per *mille*. The Yerukalas complained of the excessive morality in the settlement. The annual death rate was 29 per *mille* during the year 1921. The sub-assistant surgeon Kavali visited the settlement periodically to provide medical assistance for them. The death rate during the year 1925 was 47 per mille. Special measures were taken to eliminate the 'black scourge' ankylostomiasis which was rampant in Bitragunta, Allur and Kavali.[67]

Special constables were appointed from the settlers themselves. The settlers discontinued the practice of escaping from the village. The settlement was not having a fence or a compound wall. The night roll call was completely stopped. The special constables were highly respected by the Yerukalas. The strength of the Yerukalas during the year 1925 was 300 men, 290 women and 380 children with a total of 970 persons.[68]

The government proposed for closing down the settlement at Kavali. The settlers were well disciplined and a lot of progress was made by them. The Government considered only the future of the Yerukalas. Since there was no scope of making the village an agricultural settlement or making the village self-supporting the Government finally decided to close the Kavali settlement.[69]

Why did the Government close the Kavali settlement when it was in the flourishing condition? There were conflicting questions among the Yerukalas, Managers, Baptist Mission authorities, the Inspector General of Police and the District Magistrates. They were not happy in selecting Allur as a suitable place to shift the settlement from Kavali. But the Government appointed a Committee consisting of Inspector General of Police, the District Magistrate and Mr. Bawden. The Committee inspected Allur swamp lands and finally recommended for the shifting of the settlement to the new site. The settlement was shifted to the Eastern part of Bitragunta railway station near the 130th mile stone at the northern road of Madras - Vijayawada highway. The Government started the new settlement as an experimental settlement. The settlement was named as Bitragunta reformatory settlement. The settlement was declared as a part of the Kavali settlement. The government had sanctioned an advance of Rs. 7500 for the purchasing of cattle, seeds, plough, etc. for the settlers.[70] The government also opened a subsidiary settlement at Allur.

The new settlements (one at Allur and the other at Bitragunta) distributed the Yerukalas and Katheras. The cost of expenditure became more on the part of three installments. To reduce the expenditure the Government closed Kalichedu settlement.[71] A large number of Yerukalas were brought to Kavali during the year 1929. There were 1350 people on the rolls. The Government increased the maintenance charges of the Yerukalas. One acre of land was given to each family in these villages.[72]

Some of the Yerukalas who behaved well were transferred to other settlements. The settlers were subjected to strict discipline. The settlers were paid low wages to the actual quantity of work turned out by them. Men used to be paid 7 annas and women were paid 6 annas per day. The managers adopted a policy to pay according to the turnout of the work done by the poor Yerukalas. The managers often complained that it was very difficult for them to provide suitable work for them. A large number of Yerukalas absconded from the three places due to strict discipline, lack of employment and low wages paid to them. It was stated that, "In many of the cases the settlers were suspected merely because they happened to be criminal tribe members."[73]

The villagers started earning their livelihood by their hard work and labour contracts during the year 1928. The juveniles were given training by the managers to earn their living. Boy scouts and girl guides were started in the schools. Night schools were regularly organised in the settlement for men and women who could not attend the school during the day time. There were 3000 Yerukalas in all the three villages during the year 1929. The domestic industries were completely stopped by the villagers (mat making, weaving, basket making, etc.) due to the low money they got from them. Mr. Moir said, "Every escape or conviction represents a total failure in that individual case; every return from jail a beginning anew."[74]

The villagers were paid low wages for the contract works during the year 1930. The workers in each gang were guarded by the maistries and the special constables. The villagers used to camp out for doing the work. Some of the Yerukalas took the opportunity of absconding from the camp. Further, they used to walk a number of miles every day. It caused them physical exertion and low earning due to the wastage of time in walking.[75]

The conditions of the three villages during the year 1931 was very poor. There was no work for them. The lands provided to the villagers were submerged in the water. In order to solve the employment problem of the villagers a large number of the Yerukalas were transferred to other settlements. The panchayats were organised in the three villages to control their behaviour. The members of the Panchayat was taken from the villagers themselves.[76] The total strength of the three villages during the year 1932 was 3500. The death rate was 18 per cent, and the birth rate was 45 per cent. Intra-mural industries were started. A weaving maistry was appointed to instruct them in weaving clothes. Miss. Bullard had done excellent work for the reformatory work among the children in the villages.[77]

A tractor was purchased by the agricultural department for ploughing the swamp lands. Side drains were dug to divert the flood water in order to protect the lands from submersion of water. To protect the crops flood banks were constructed. The superintending engineer visited the lands and installed a pumping plant during the year 1933. In 1934 the management of the settlement was taken over by the Police department and the Inspector of Police became the manager of the settlement since then.[78]

During the year 1939 the then Labour Commissioner Madras transferred some of the Yerukalas from Kavali to Sitanagaram. They were provided work in the Kistna Cement Works at Tadepalli. The Yerukalas were kept at Kaza. They were provided quarrying and stone breaking works, garden cultivation work, etc.[79] During the year 1940, the settlement was managed by one manager, two clerks, one peon, one mid wife, one compounder, two agricultural maistries, one ward boy, five teachers, 10 watchmen, two scavengers and one sweeper.[80] With the repeal of the CTA the inhabitants were left free in September, 1948 and the Settlement Office was abolished and the outpost at Bitragunta was converted into a pucka police station in January, 1949.[81]

D. *Sitanagaram Settlement (Guntur District)*

Origin

The Salvation Army took up the question of the formation of the settlements for the reclamation of CTs during the year 1910. A small settlement was formed at Sitanagaram. In the beginning, some Yerukula women whose husbands and relatives were in jail placed in the settlement. During the year 1912, the then British Government sanctioned an amount of Rs. 5000 as a special non-recurring grant to the SA to start the settlement.[82] An extent of 87 acres of land was also provided to the SA free of cost with occupancy rights. (It was relinquished by the Madras and Southern Mahratta Railway Company).[83] The government had permitted the SA, 1. to adopt persuasive methods to settle the Yerukalas, 2. If the persuasive, methods of the SA failed to apply the provisions of the CT Act to settle down the Yerukalas in Sitanagaram. However, the persuasive methods of the Salvation Army was failed. The Government declared the Yerukalas living in Godavari and Guntur districts as CTs. Their movements were restricted under Section 12 of the CT Act 1911.

The progress of Sitanagaram settlement was very fast. It was necessitated to the then British Government for the formation of another settlement to control the overflow of the settlers in Sitanagaram. Thus the settlement at Bethapudi was opened as an axilary settlement.[84]

Location of Sitanagaram

Sitanagaram settlement is situated in Guntur district. Lying on the South Bank of the Krishna that emerges from a corridor in the Palnad hills and empties into the Bay of Bengal in a broad sweeping curve, this is largely a flat, deltaic plain. It is bounded by Prakasam and Nellore districts in the South and in the West by Prakasam and Krishna districts.[85] Guntur is a rich and surplus district. As Robert Eric Frykenberg said, "Its plain is a luxurious carpet of green all the year round: Sugarcane, rice and other staple crops are interspersed all over the district being fed by irrigation canals. Cash crops like tobacco fetch foreign exchange from Britain, America, Soviet Russia and East European countries. The main line of the railways, joined by subsidiary lines at Vijayawada, connect the district with the leading industrial commercial and other popular centres of India."[86]

The grand trunk road, running from Calcutta to Madras passes through Guntur. Physiographically, Guntur district may be divided into three district regions, viz., the Main Land, the Costal belt and the Delta region. Besides the three principal castes of Brahmins, Kshatriyas and Vaisyas, the Sudras comprise both advanced and backward classes in addition to Scheduled castes and Scheduled tribes. Lambadies, Yerukalas, Yanadis, and Chenchus are wandering tribes, all living in their own settlements in close proximity to forests and speaking their own dialects.

Occupation of the 'Settlers'

The main occupation provided for the Yerukalas in the settlement was quarrying. But the settlers were not accustomed to do hard labour. They did not accept to take up the work. The government considered quarrying as a salutary form of employment. This work was introduced to bring discipline and industrious nature among the settlers.[87] The government sanctioned an amount of Rs.10,000 during the year 1914 for the development of quarrying industry in the settlement. The manager said : "The work could be done only by the able bodied people. There were in the settlement some men and women who were unfit to do quarrying. There was no other work on which they could be usefully employed."[88]

The manager however provided hand-spinning and handloom weaving which were the most suitable occupations for the settlers. Training was given for men and women in hand spinning and handloom weaving. This provided the settlers with sufficient work. Khadi cloth was produced. The Labour Department used to purchase the cloth. The cloth was supplied to the surrounding 'Scheduled Caste' people. The Commissioner of Labour said, "There will be no difficulty in finding a market for the Khadi produced by the settlers as it can be utilised for the supply of clothing to the Scheduled Caste pupils eligible for the ameliorative work of the Labour Department."[89] The government found the market for the Khadi cloth produced by the settlers. The government fixed the selling price of the clothing. The manager said: "It is proposed to introduce spinning and weaving in the settlement for the unregistered settlers. They are at liberty to go anywhere they like in quest of work. Some of them have already left the settlement. "It is not possible to provide work for others in the settlement itself. "[90]

The industries introduced in Sitanagaram settlement were 1. sock-making for the police department, 2. mat making and 3. weaving of Madras handkerchiefs. It was stated : "The settlers need so much to produce an undefined amount of cloth. The cloth will be sold to the department for a certain amount of rupees. The wages are to be paid by the Department for the unstated amount of cloth. There is no indication of estimated out-turn or the requirement of the department. The scheme was a badly cooked dish of figures heavily spiced, with manipulation which the government was not prepared to serve."[91]

Land to the extent of 84-06 acres was given at Sitanagaram to the SA, free of charge, for occupancy rights and free of assessment. The government recommended that persuasive methods should be adopted in respect of the Yerukala settlers and in case those methods failed, they could apply the provisions of the CTA. The persuasive methods having failed completely in their case, the CT settlement was established in the year 1913 with the handful of men who were released from jail. Section 12 of the Act restricted the movements of these people. The Yerukalas of Godavari and Guntur were brought under the provisions of the CTA. Their number became unmanageable and therefore the British government established another settlement at Bethapudi which came to be known as Stuartpuram (Bethapudi) Settlement subsequently.[92]

Division of Sitanagaram into Two Settlements

In October, 1915, the Sitanagaram Settlement was divided into two parts, namely, Sainayapuram and Kondapet Settlement, each under the management of a European SA Officer.[93] This division was made for the effective supervision of the settlement. It was only an internal arrangement. Agriculture was the chief means of livelihood and other main occupations practiced was stone quarrying by the Yerukalas even today. The work was further developed by the SA with the establishment of Train links to the quarries.Weaving, silk spinning, Carpentry, Sewing and other subsidiary industries were provided for the Settlers. They also had shown interest in mat and basket making. In 1914, only 40 acres of land was cultivated due to non-availability of agricultural land. However, during the same year, the government realising the need for more land, handed over a larger tract of fertile land, to SA for the purpose of Parcelling it out to the Settlers for cultivation.[94]

Escapes and Crime

In the initial stages, there were a large number of absconders from among the settlers. The DIG of Police, Railways and CID were entrusted with the general supervision and control of all the settlements in Madras presidency. Mr. Hannygton the DIG, Madras reported that captain Robilliard of the SA at Stuartpuram was a person of a exceptionally high calibre. Since there was demand for more land for the settlers, the government gave more land for agricultural pursuits. Supervision was also strictly enforced. This minimised the number of absconders. The population of the settlement at the end of the year 1915 comprised of 301 men, 271 women, and 337 children with a total of 909 members.[95] Fear of floods and indolent habits kept the settlers away from taking full advantage of the 130 acres of land granted to them for agricultural purposes. The annual report during the year 1916 showed that they were dependent mainly on the quarry work.[96]

School and Education

An elementary school was started by the SA in April, 1913. A night school was also opened. It continued to do commendable work. The weaving section attached to the school possessed five looms.The school provided employment to the pupils who attended the school regularly in the early part of the day. The other cottage industries such as mat making, smithy and carpentry were also instituted in the settlement.[97]

Progress After 1916

The conditions of the settlement, during the year 1917, was very bad. The settlement had to grapple with two successively serious epidemics during the year 1917. As a result of cholera and smallpox the settlers became restless and began to abscond in large numbers.[98] The government, dissatisfied with the working condition of the settlement decided to abolish it during the year 1917. It was decided to slowly deplete the strength of the settlers by periodical transfers of the inmates to other settlements more favourably to the agricultural settlements. A total number of 100 families were transferred to Stuartpuram settlement.[99]

During the year 1919, the Labour Commissioner took charge of all the CT settlements. There was gradual improvement in the general condition of all the settlements.[100] Availability of employment and a fairly good rainfall were responsible for this improvement. This showed a marked decline in the incidence of crime. This established notion that wherever there was economic distress the incidence of petty crimes would increase; otherwise; the phenomenon would be the same.

The year 1921-22 was marked for the special efforts of the government to send the children to attend the school. There were 70 boys and 57 girls of school going age children out of which 48 boys and 57 girls attended the school regularly. A night school was also maintained in the settlement.[101] The general behaviour of the settlers was so satisfactory that fourteen families were released from the settlement as a reward to their good conduct. This was a good augury, and a good system followed by the government. The released persons were asked to go to their native places. Paradoxically some people remained in the settlement even after their release. This showed firstly, that the settlers developed an emotional attachment for the settlements; secondly, when they were interned, the settlers lost their property and were afraid of going back to their native places; and thirdly, the settlement, Manager used to provide them with some kind of employment for keeping their body and soul together. Weaving, carpet making, stone-dressing and other miscellaneous jobs kept them busy throughout the year. The cottage industries were in a flourishing condition and the settlers took real interest in cultivating lands also.[102]

There was an increase in the number of the settlers during the year 1925. The Rudrapad korachas and a few settlers from Bhumannagadda settlement were brought to Sitanagaram settlement. The total number of people during the year 1925 was 1,110 members. All the settlers were provided with work. The total earnings of the settlers was 28,000. Carpet industry was introduced in the settlement by Mr Moir. A maistry was employed in the settlement to assist the settlers in carpet industry.[103]

The strength of the settlement during the year 1927 was 1,092. There were 41 absconders from the settlement. The total earnings of the settlers were Rs.37,000. There were 396 children in the settlement. The average attendance of the school was 120. Cholera was prevalent in the settlement and in the neighbouring villages. The settlement was without a doctor. The sub-assistant surgeon, Mangalagiri used to visit the hospital twice in a week to met the medical needs of the settlers.[104] The behaviour of the settlers was satisfactory. 14 families were released from the settlement as a reward of their good conduct. A stone dressing maistri was appointed to teach masonry work in the settlement. This was to develop skilled labour among the settlers. The total strength of the settlers increased to 1107 during the year 1929-30. 200 acres of land was cultivated by the settlers.[105] The settlers extended their cultivation upto Undavalli Lanka during the year 1932. Weaving, carpet-making, stone-dressing kept the settlers busy throughout the year.[106] Their earnings were fairly good. They were successful in carpet industry.[107] They had earned an amount of Rs. 2,700 by selling the carpets in nearby places.[108] The then Commissioner of Labour Mr. T.G. Rutherford provided work for the settlers in Cement Cos. Ltd., Bombay. They had opened up a limestone deposits in Kaza. The settlers in Sitanagaram and Bitragunta were employed on the quarry work in the limestone deposits. The unfavourable seasonal and economic conditions of the year 1934, contributed to the increased volume of crime.[109]

Hospital : Health Conditions in Sitanagaram Settlement

A dispensary was established during the year 1915. The number of patients attended the settlement dispensary during the year 1933-34 was 990. The average attendance of the patients was 33. The dispensary was very popular and useful for the settlers. But there was no medical officer working in the settlement. The patients were sent to Mangalagiri hospital. The equipment in the hospital was inadequate. A sub-assistant surgeon used to visit the settlement hospital. The settlement was situated at a distance of 8 miles from Mangalagiri and 2 miles from Bezawada. Much difficulty was felt by the Medical Officer for the treatment of urgent cases such as accidents in quarry work, etc. During the year 1933 a sub-assistant surgeon and a compounder were appointed in the settlement.[110]

The economic depression was further aggravated by the failure of crops during the year 1934. The carpet industry was closed in the settlement during the year 1933. No provisions were made by the government to purchase the looms and other articles. The materials of the settlers were sold in public auction.[111] In 1937, there was a little improvement in the economic situation. There was considerable amount of employment in most parts of the presidency. Effective control exercised by the anti-crime measures, the co-operation rendered by the village vigilance committees, the interest showed by the members of the public, the valuable services of the Criminal Intelligence Branch and the concomitant change in the attitude of the CTS and also the effective work by the rank and file of the police, cumulatively contributed to an appreciable decrease in crime. In addition, the movements of the Yerukalas and some of the Kanjar Bhats was restricted to Sitanagaram settlement.[112]

The then Commissioner of Labour Mr. G.W. Priestly transferred some of the settlers of Bitragunta to Sitanagaram. The abolition proposals of the Bitragunta settlement was started in 1937. The government proposed to construct a new settlement called Chintaladevi settlement during the year 1937. The government wanted to close the Bitragunta settlement due to two reasons. 1. The expenditure incurred on the settlement was more. 2. The settlers depended heavily on the maintenance cost of the government without doing any hard work.[113]

The next Labour Commissioner was Mr. Ramakrishna. During his tenure, the settlers were provided employment in Andhra Cotton Mills, Cement Company, Associated Cement Cos. Ltd., etc. on piece work basis.[114] A total number of 100 settlers – (50 men and 50 women) were provided work in the settlement. Men used to be paid 5 annas a day and women were paid 3 annas per day.[115] The settlers were provided railway passes to attend to the work daily in neighbouring places. The Assistant Manager of the Settlement supervised the settlers efficiently during the year 1940. All the settlers were put within the enclosure of the barbed wire fencing. The settlers were made to work on quarrying, stone dressing, etc. Big stones were transported to the settlement from the adjoining hills on tram line.[116]

Carpentry was introduced in the school and regular classes were held in the carpentry work. Tools and materials were purchased and supplied to the school during the year 1939. During the year 1940, the quarry work in the Public Works Department had become very small. They could not provide work for all the settlers. Private contractors was requested to provide work for the settlers. The work in the quarries was stopped due to the expiry of the lease to the Guntur District Board. 50% of the settlers suffered without any work. The settlers were provided work in the Kistna Cement Works at Kaza. The settlers were sent to Kaza on temporary 'O' passes issued for 15 days. The police also arranged bandobust during the nights with the help of the maistries appointed in the settlement. (The quarry work in the settlement was actually provided by the companies in Bombay. The Mining work in the settlements was taken by these companies for lease and got rich profits out of the labour of the settlers). Some other settlers were sent to Piduguralla for work.[117]

During the year 1941-42, The drainage system in the settlement was improved. The level of the roads were raised to prevent water stagnation. The conditions of the houses were improved. The settlers constructed their houses with stone and mud. The settlers developed in all aspects.[118] The settlers were self-supporting. Due to unsatisfactory monsoons the agricultural operations made by the settlers was not successful. The settlers cultivated only 83 acres of land.

The managers faced many difficulties to get the work from the settlers in the beginning. Only a small portion of the land was cultivated by the settlers. A cattle pound was constructed in the settlement during the same year. Pumpsets were also provided to keep the wells in the settlement.

During the year 1942, the then Labour Commissioner provided employment to some more settlers in the cement company at Vijayawada. The settlers were transferred to Sitanagaram from Bitragunta settlement. The settlers were provided railway passes to attend the work in the limestone quarries. The factory was very near to Tadepalli railway station. The Bitragunta settlers were employed on Company's quarries. The managers used to give strict instructions to the settlers before they proceeded to the quarry work. The settlers were paid 8 to 10 annas a day for men and 4 to 5 annas a day for women. A tramline was laid to the settlement. Big lumps of rocks were carried to the settlement. The settlers were asked to break the rocks. The settlers were kept in the barbed wire enclosures. The settlers were also asked to make the transport arrangements in handcarts on the double-shafted carriers managed by two men.[119]

Mr. L., Underwood, the Deputy Inspector General of Police, C.I.D. and Railways, Madras requested the then Secretary of the Madras government to sanction a library for children and supply of other literatures to the settlement school.[120] The school at Sitanagaram was upgraded to an upper primary school in 1946. The D.I.G. of Police also requested for maintenance allowance to the released settlers, which was also conceded by the government during the year 1947.

In 1948, the law and order situation was under control although there was some increase in petty crimes. The abrogation of the CTA in that year in addition to large scale premature release of criminals from prison, deteriorating economic situation, widespread labour and agrarian unrest, better reporting of cases, were considered as the main cause for the slight increase in crime. Dacoity, robbery, house breaking and other petty crimes also slightly increased. This was the sum position in all most all the districts in the province.[121]

Pursuant to the introduction of Prohibition, the moral and material well being of the settlers improved. The health and hygiene of the settlers were considered satisfactory due to the establishment of rural dispensaries. All the internees under the CTA, who did not come under the purview of 'Habitual offenders' as defined in Section 2(4) of the Habitual offender's Act 1948, were released from the settlements. However most of the released settlers continued to stay on in the settlements. Concessions regarding education, free clothing and other facilities were given to all the children of the internees as well as to those of the voluntary settlers as usual.[122]

During the year 1949, there was an increase in the total number of crimes by about 5 per cent in comparison with the figures of 1940. General economic depression, consequent upon the shortage of foodstuffs and their soaring prices, abolition of the CTA, campaigning of a free and proper registration of crimes and the pre-occupation of the police in dealing with the communist upsurge in the country in 1948, again led to the upward swing in the crime rate of Habitual offenders.The Habitual offenders Act came into force on 29th April, 1948 in the presidency.[123]

During the year 1952 Sitanagaram settlement was managed by four managers, viz., Syed Abdul Gaffar, T. Govindarajulu, K. Sreemantham, and K.V.R. Patnaik, acted as the managers of the settlement. There were 246 settlers in the settlement (71 men, 73 women and 102 children). The strength of the internees under Section 2(4) of the Madras Restriction of Habitual Offenders Act, 1948 was 30 members.[124] Many of the settlers were permanently released from the settlement. The settlers cultivated 203 acres of land. 64 families in the settlement were provided land for cultivation. Each family was given 2 ½ acres. Cholam, hemp, red-gram, sajja and turmeric crops were grown by the settlers. The crops yielded good results. Agricultural officers were recruited for the settlement.[125] There was no organised industry in the settlement during the year 1955. The quarry industry in the settlement was abandoned. The workers were employed as bandy drivers, and as manual labourers in quarries. Goat and sheep rearing, petty shopping, rearing buffalos for milk, poultry rearing, shoe making, employment as watchers and employment in the ferry, etc., were other main sources of income for the Yerukalas in Sitanagaram. The health conditions of the settlers during the year 1960 was satisfactory. There were no epidemics in the settlement. An Ayurvedic Rural Dispensary was opened in the settlement. One L.I.M. doctor was appointed in the hospital. He was assisted by a midwife and a ward boy. They worked satisfactorily in the settlement. The school in Sitanagaram worked with six standards during the year 1965. The strength of the school was 78 children. A total number of 8 children studied in the outside schools, 3 were given training in midwifery. 1 boy studied M.B.B.S. in the medical college, Guntur. One person was selected as a sub-inspector of police from the settlement. The Sitanagaram settlement Tenants Co-operative Society worked in the settlement satisfactorily.[126] The settlers were given cows, bulls, buffaloes, goats and sheep by the government. Agricultural advances were also provided to the settlers. The economic conditions of the settlers from 1970 onwards was quite satisfactory. The settlers were engaged in different kinds of employment. They managed to earn their livelihood. The general behaviour of the settlers was very good. Pumpsets were installed on the Krishna river bund, on the main canal bund, on either side to provide wet cultivation in the settlement. The superintending engineer, Vijayawada provided regular water for the settlers' lands. The settlers cultivated their lands located at Tadepalli, Gundimedu Lanka and Undavalli Lanka. The District Collector, Guntur leased out these lands to the settlers. A police station was also established at Tadepalli. The police station was situated 1 km from the settlement. The District Superintendent of Police, Guntur and the Incharge Sub-inspector of Sitanagaram Settlements used to visit the settlement regularly to prevent crime among the settlers. The government did not chalk out any programme as there were no industries in the settlement and the settlement was converted into a free colony.[127] However, the registration of persons in the settlement continued under the Madras Restriction of Habitual Offenders Act, 1948.

The special feature of Sitanagaram settlement was that it was a penal settlement. Mr. Bawden, the Manager of Bitragunta Reformatory settlement, scheduled it as a penal settlement for the incorrigible members of the CTs. When Sir Harold Stuart visited the Sitanagaram settlement, he was asked by the Manager, Mr. Duboulay— "Do you advocate the starting of another settlement where the reformed men will be provided for?" It was a penal settlement, so many settlers were transferred to Stuartpuram from Sitanagaram settlement.[128]

As a Settlement, which was converted into a free colony after the repeal of the CTA, was very near to the city of Vijayawada it was exposed to many employment potentialities for the settlers. The equipment, workshops, and other appliances were simply rusting under a roof for a long time. Thanks to the work of Lavanam and

Hemalatha Lavanam who did lot of work and due to this a significant change could be seen among them to day.

The major problem faced by the settlers and non-settlers was their living in the same settlement, side by side. The settlers were given land for cultivation, whereas the non settlers did not have even a piece of land, though their ancestors lived in the settlement under the management of the SA. It was because of their good conduct they were released and denied any land. In other words, the non settlers were punished for their good conduct. However, they maintain close contact with the settlers. The government, in all fairness, should have taken a sympathetic stand for these helpless non-settlers and provided them with pattas for cultivation and house-building. There are 49 families of the settlers constituting a total population of 1071 people in Sitanagaram Settlement.

Among the 150 families who were interned in Sitanagaram Settlement, the government discharged them from the purview of the CTA and asked them to leave the settlement. Out of a total number of 1205 members- 44 acres of land, was leased out to the settlement management. Further another 66.77 acres of land, was leased out to the settlement management and allotted to Ramakrishna Vidyalaya High School, Maganti Annapurna Devi Primary School, Sri Venkateswara Swami Temple, for formation of the Krishna Bundh and also for an assignment to three political sufferers.[129]

Agriculture is the main occupation of the settlers of the Sitanagaram Settlement even today. The government extended full remission of fees to the children of the notified tribes and sanctioned grant of residential and industrial scholarships. Irrigation facilities were provided by erecting two lift irrigation-pumpsets on the northern side of the Buckingham Canal. Crops, such as paddy, turmeric, chillies and ground nut were raised on the land here. A rural dispensary which was running in the settlement was very useful to the settlers. Small Scale Industries, such as, carpentry, smithy, mat making, basket-making, weaving existed in the settlement previously, but these are now defunct. Even in quarry work, individual exploitation is prevalent. Instead of giving the right of the management of the quarry work to an individual, if it is entrusted to the society, this evil can be eradicated. The tribal welfare Department, Guntur District, conducted a detailed survey of the settlement in the month of June, 1986. The survey covered 45 families.

We are able to collect data for 40 families, as the remaining families have left the settlement. There are no habitual offenders at present in the colony. All the colonists have sprung up with voluntary settlers.[130]

E. *Stuartpuram Settlement (Guntur District)*

Stuartpuram is in between Bapatla (Guntur district) and Chirala (Prakasam District) on the Madras-New Delhi Grand Trunk Rail Road. Stuartpuram settlement was called as a good conduct settlement. It means men who behaved well at Sitanagaram were sent to this place and the misbehaved were taken to Sitanagaram. The strength, in the beginning of the settlement was 691 consisting of 200 males, 196 females and 295 children. It was named after Stuart, the then Home member for the Madras Government.[131]

Origin of Stuartpuram Settlement

The Yerukulas of Guntur district, used to camp near the village of Bethapudi, Bapatla Taluk, Guntur district, from December to August every year. They carried grain for the ryots of Ongole, Bapatla and Tenali Taluks during the months. They grazed their cattle at Vinukonda in Guntur district from August to December. The Yerukulas used to commit petty offences when they had no work. But the police became more active and attentive to the offences which the Yerukulas committed during the year 1913. The Yerukulas took shelter under the SA in order to escape the punishment given by the local police.[132] The government in order to settle the Yerukulas in the beginning gave 1,860 acres of land and money grants to the SA during the year 1915. There was a good amount of unalloted sandy soil in Bapatla. The Government had allotted a portion of land to the Salvation Army in order to settle the Yerukulas. The Salvation Army reclaimed the land and brought it under cultivation. During the year 1915, the number of the Yerukulas increased due to the reason that some of the Yerukulas were brought from Sitanagaram and Kalichedu. But the Yerukulas were suspected without any reason. The neighbouring villagers complained the police repeatedly about their 'criminal' behaviour. The police took the complaints made by the neighbouring riots of Bapatla very seriously and notified the Yerukulas as one of the CTs. Their movements were restricted to the surrounding places of Bapatla.[133] The then Inspector General of Police stated : "the Government had reason to believe that crime had on the whole increased in the vicinity of Bapatla and that some at least of the increase was due to the propensity of the Bethapudi settlement of the Salvation Army and the Bapatla Yanadi settlement, a small concern under the management of the Bapatla Church Panchayat."[134]

Agitation in 1915

Every year the inhabitants of Bapatla and the neighbouring villagers agitated and protested the government to remove the settlements from Betapudi. They often complained against the Yerukulas living silently in the settlement. They were unhappy due to the reason that the land was provided to the settlers. They wanted to grab the land from the government. On careful enquiry the Government was convinced that the Yerukulas were not responsible for any offence in the neighbourhood. The agitation was set up by certain rich landlords due to unworthy and selfish motives. Adequate protection was provided to the settlers by the government.

Notification of Stuartpuram Settlement Under CT Act.

In 1915, the Bethapudi settlement was declared as one of the CT settlements established under the Criminal Tribes Act.[135] In the beginning, the Yerukulas were not under anybody's control. They used to come from different places to the settlement.[136]

Occupation of the Yerukulas

Agriculture was the chief occupation of the Yerukulas in Stuartpuram. A large extent of land was brought under cultivation by them. The Government provided irrigation facilities to improve their cultivation. Coconut and mulberry trees were planted by the SA. The Yerukulas got money from the sale of mats, cooly labour and trading of cattle. The inmates whose conduct was good were appointed as watchmen. They used to give regular information about the Yerukulas to the Managers. The Yerukulas considered the post of watchman very honourable. The watchman maintained good discipline among the settlers.[137]

The Manager

The first Manager of the settlement was captain Robilliard. Robilliard was an intelligent person. He was an expert in agricultural activities. He was an expert in gardening. He had gained lot of experience in rubber plantation work in the East. He developed the settlement on admirable lines. The government congratulated him for the useful work he had done in the settlement.[138]

Strength

The strength of the stuartpuram during the year 1915 was 302 men, 323 women, 243 boys and 238 girls. The total strength of the Yerukulas was 1,106 members. There was plenty of work and space for the other Yerukulas in the settlement. The government in order to maintain discipline among the Yerukulas enforced strict rules. The number of the strength in the settlement did not increase. However, the settlement suffered with bureaucratic measures, application of CT acts, rapid influx of turbulent elements, bad character of the managers, police and the surrounding people. The Government also transferred some of the Yerukula members from Kavali settlement.[139]

Self-Supporting Stage of Stuartpuram

The settlement flourished with agriculture. All the Yerukulas were self-contended. The settlement was self-supporting. The SA received the recurring grant made by the government very late to run the settlement. The SA also suffered severe financial constraints to run the settlements due to lack of proper grants. The settlement was outstanding in its administration in Guntur District. The features of the settlement was remarkable. There were also many defects in the administration of the settlement. There were many defects in the registration of the Yerukulas under the CT Act.[140]

The Yerukulas who were innocent and could not commit even a single crime and who do not have any relation or association with the Yerukulas who were registered were also registered under the CT Act. Except being Yerukulas they were branded as CTs and were placed in the settlements. This lead Stuartpuram settlement very crowded. The settlement was beyond the capacity of the SA to properly administer it. The good conduct Yerukulas were mixed up with other bad characters such as professional robbers and dacoits in the settlement. Though this mistake was found by the Government nothing was done to improve the conditions of the settlement and the entire responsibility was handed over to the SA to set right the conditions of the settlement.

The strength of the Yerukulas gradually increased in the settlement. The strength of the settlement during the year 1925 was 1500. The SA had given land pattas to 140 yerukulas. The Yerukulas got the right to cultivate the allotted portion of the land without anybody's interference. The land was allotted on the condition that the settlers have to behave on the satisfactory lines under the guidance of the SA.

Extension of the Stuartpuram

Paddy cultivation was the main occupation of the settlers. The Yerukulas extended the cultivation on satisfactory lines. During the year 1920, the settlers cultivated 500 acres of land. "Settlement pattas" were provided to them. Water supply was plentiful. The crops were successful. The settlement was filled with coconut, eucalyptus, mulberry, etc. The settlers' achievements were very encouraging. Food crops such as ragi, paddy was cultivated by the Yerukulas. Steady progress was maintained by the Yerukulas every year. During good seasons the Yerukulas cultivated their lands without fail.[141]

Irrigation Difficulties

The Yerukulas had faced many difficulties during the year 1925. Owing to the bad season and lack of timely rains the Yerukulas did not cultivate their lands. The settlement did not have proper irrigation facilities. The water from Krishna canal was not released. The Yerukulas did not irrigate their lands because of lack of water in the Romperu drain. A dam was constructed across the Romperu.[142] The Government Promised the Yerukulas for the continuous supply of water during the cultivation periods. But the settlers experienced the false promises of the government. The Government later constructed the Perali drain. But the Executive engineer did not take proper interest to complete the construction of the dam on time. Thus Yerukulas faced many problems to cultivate their lands.

Plantation Work Industry

The primary objective of the settlement was to make the Yerukulas into self-supporting cultivators. The plantation work was started by the government with the help of the Yerukulas. They had worked hard to develop the plants. It was stated: "The Salvation Army should be directed to the primary objective of the settlement. Instead of developing the land already placed at their disposal, the Salvation Army seems to have fallen a victim to the experimental enterprise of Mr. Robilliard, whose enthusiasm as a planter has outrun the objects of his appointment."[143]

The Government had developed the plantation industry in the settlement in order to boost up the income of the Yerukulas.

The following plantation work was developed in Stuartpurm. 1. Plantation of forest tress, 2. Casuarina plantation, 3. Coconut plantation, 4. Rubber estates, 5. The Mulberries 6. the Eucalyptus plantation, etc.[144] Mr. Davis the then Collector of Guntur inspected the settlement and said : "We would like to open 100 acres of land by the sea for the purpose of planting forest trees."[145] The land was free from any kind of revenue. The Government constructed roads for carting the timber. The trees were cut by the forest department. The Yerukulas were not allowed to take the forest wood and products. The Government auctioned the forest trees to private contractors. The then District Forest Officer said: "The axe men to fell coupes in the reserves often have to be brought from a distance. I see no reason why the Yerukulas should not be trained in this branch of forestry and in any case the plantation work attached to the settlement would afford some means of employment in the case of bad seasons."[146]

A lot of waste land was available in the settlement. The Government planted another 100 acres of land with coconut plants. It was suggested to plant 50 plants per one acre. The plant was grown in an area of 40 × 40m. The coconut palms yielded well. It was reported that : "while travelling from Madras to Bapatla if any one notices outside the view near Stuartpuram the coconut palms used to attract the viewers." Mr. Gordon Brown the then expert in coconut industry and Inspector of Federated Malay stated: "Having a large space I suggest casuarinas planting as a cash crop between the coconuts. We can plant the same number and at the end of three years we could clear a space around each tree."[147]

R.W. Davis, the then collector of Guntur handed over the Vedullapalli forest reserve to the SA for the casuarina plantation work. Money was also sanctioned to the SA to develop the plantation work in the settlement. The Government asked the SA not to collect any money from the Yerukulas. But the SA regarded the forest reserve and the casuarina plants as its property. The SA contracted the lands and casuarina plants to the private land holders to bring the plants to maturity. The forest department leased out some portion of the land to the private owners. The forest department favoured eucalyptus and coconut plantation in Stuartpuram. The government understood that the SA and the forest department leased out the lands to private contractors. The produce of the land was taken away by the SA. The casuarina plantation work was a commercial enterprise for the Yerukulas in Stuartpuram.[148]

Extension of Dry Cultivation

Mr. Moir another Labour Commissioner suggested for the dry cultivation in Stuartpuram. Advances were given to the Yerukulas for the purchase of cattle for the purpose of manure. The coconut plants brought the profit of Rs. 1 per each tree every day. It has given a profit of Rs. 5000 per year from the 100 acres. There was considerable amount of land for the plantation work in Stuartpuram. The plantation work was undertaken serioursly by the Yerukulas.[149]

The government also planted a portion of land with casuarina plants, coconut plants, rubber plants and eucalyptus plants in Stuartpuram. The casuarina plants were planted three years ahead of the coconut plants. The government realised the successfulness of the plantations. The casuarina plants work was made in Stuartpuram as a cash crop.[150] The casuarina plants were used as wind breakers on the rubber estate. The rubber plantations did very well. The mulberries were intermixed with the casuarina plants. Brunter the then Officer from the Federated Malay said : "The whole settlement was fermented with rubber, coconut, mulberry and casuarina plants."[151] The salvation army planted eucalyptus plants in the settlement. Booth Tucker the then Commissioner of the Salvation Army said: " I advise you to go for eucalyptus and mulberries as these are trees with a great future and they have as you know a great advantage of croping so that you can cut them at intervals of ten to fifteen years and they spring up from the same roots without the necessity of replanting".[152] Eucalyptus plants do not require so much watering. The cost of growing eucalyptus was met by the government. The government got profits from the plantation work in the settlement. During the year 1916, the Government undertook the work of planting the cash crops and plantation work in the settlement.[153]

The fertile land was not inexhaustible in the settlement. The bad seasons had a disastrous effect on the economic conditions of the Yerukulas. There was a lot of demand for fuel in the North-East states. The settlers supplied the required fuel. The plantation work was taken up by the Yerukulas on large scale in the sandy area around Bapatla. The Yerukulas accustomed to the plantation work, watering and filling. The Yerukulas were provided with sufficient work as a means of employment during the bad seasons. The burden of supporting the settlement during the bad seasons was wholly on the SA. One way plantation work provided regular employment. Only new settlers got benefited out of the work. However, the plantation industry was taken up by the SA and the Government as a temporary measure only.[154]

A block of 360 acres of dry land and 1500 acres in the Romperu Swamp were placed at the disposal of the SA in 1914. The SA employed agricultural maistries from old settlers. They used to instruct the new settlers on the techniques of cultivation. The settlers cultivated paddy, ragi, and groundnut. They got money from mats, ropes, baskets, curry leaf, tomato and green gram cultivation. They were also given road work, stone quarrying, drain digging and other works from Public Works Department. Their income during the year 1915 was Rs. 19,520.08. The manager leased out lands to the settlers. Harold Stuart noted : "The case of Stuartpuram settlement is unfairly. This settlement was most successful having the best land. Its progress appeared fast." Bazlulla, the agricultural officer, set up a scheme for casuarinas and for tomato canning. Robilliard favoured planting coconut and eucalyptus. In order to ensure a better supply of water, a dam across the river Romperu was built in 1919. There was an increase of the settlers income from Rs. 84,189,05 to Rs. 1,03,109.08 (sic) during the year 1923-24.

Progress of the Settlement Since 1925

George Paddison proposed to build a bund in order to protect the fields from submersion of water from the swamp. The cyclone in November 1927 ruined the whole crop of paddy. Robilliard, in his record showed that some of the settlers resorted to begging. A number of settlers had given evidence that they were regularly cultivating the land. The Tahsildar of Bapatla visited the settlement and issued permanent pattas to the settlers' lands who had been regularly cultivating for a period of three years and against whom there was no complaint of crime.[155]

A Karnam (Village Officer) was appointed on full time basis to look after the land records, measurements, allotments and supervision of the cattle. The government gave up land cess over the settlers lands to encourage cultivation. When they asked to go to work they refused. Then an order was given that no kind of passes were given to the settlers, not even for purchasing rice. Thus they were made to go to work. The cases of escapes and of overstays of leave were more in number in the settlement. Marjori Banks, suggested the construction of a lock up at the settlement during the year 1916. Absconders were rigorously prosecuted. The practice of issuing passes made some of the settlers to abscond from the settlement.[156]

A store was opened in the settlement during the year 1919. There were many ways to cheat the settlers in all ways. In the store, two kinds of rice were available. One broken rice (Nukalu) and whole rice. The Yerukalas were cheated many times by giving poor quality rice with dust and stones in the store rice. The SA was also responsible for the opening of a railway station in 1921. The opening of the railway station extended their income by introducing the cultivation of tomato growing.[157]

In addition to agricultural activity and labour work, the Yerukalas were also provided work in an industry by name Indian Leaf Tobacco Department (ILTD), opened at nearby village Ramanagar (Epurupalem) in 1915.[158] Men used to be paid wages at the rate of 8 annas per day (48 annas per weak, i.e. Rs. 3. (16 Annas made a rupee in those days) and women used to be paid 7 annas per day (42 per week, Rs. 2.62).[159] The Yerukalas were employed in pounding paddy belonging to the Komatis at Chirala, Perala, Epurupalem, Bapatla and in carting stones from Karamchedu during the year 1920. Some settlers worked in settlement gardens. The manager engaged them in filling up of pits. Every year the tobacco cultivation expanded on the sandy area.

A co-operative society was organised with 290 share holders before 1927. The main purpose for which co-operative societies were organised were 1. acquisition of house sites on the easy payment system, 2. loans for agricultural purposes, 3. cultivation and reclamation of land etc.[160] During the year 1930, the settlers were sent on 'O' passes to the Kodanda Rama Mica Mines in the Rapur taluk of Nellore district for employment.[161]

A beat post was opened prior to 1956 to check the physical presence of the criminals in the settlement. C.B. Cunningham, the then Inspector General of Police, Madras, wrote: "Many habitual criminals have been reformed and are being reformed here. The police should come to the manager with their problems and difficulties as a fellow worker and colleague."[162]

New forms were introduced in the settlement to facilitate the identification of unregistered persons. There were lapses and fighting amongst the settlers. This was largely due to the sale of toddy in neighbouring villages. Old men and women received subsistence allowance under two categories. 1. Widows with children and 2. women whose husbands absconded or in jail.[163] The Administration Report for the year 1933-34 stated : "the cash given at present may be misused. The certainty of getting food would be appreciated by those in real need."[164] During the year 1936, nearly 168 families were released on 'O' passes and permitted to live in a newly formed colony near Chirala adjoining to the premises of the ILTD company.[165]

The Salvation Army thought that education was essential for the Yerukalas of this settlement and therefore, started an elementary school in 1916. Out of 481 children in the settlement, 250 children were school going during the year 1916. Class books, maps, slates and slated pencils, pictures of animals and plants, a globe, Ananda primer and Ananda readers for standards I, II and III and garden implements were purchased by the manager. A boarding school was established for the sake of 1. orphan children, 2. children whose parents were in jail and 3. children of parents just returned from jails. The SA dissuaded the parents from meeting their children.

The SA established peons for the reformation of the children of ex-settlers. The Headmaster was with a certificate of higher grade training. Mackenzie, the Salvation Army official, wanted to change the structure of the building to create a new atmosphere in the settlement. The closing down of the Stuartpuram Boarding School (1926) was a severe blow on the settlers children. The Salvation Army constructed a church in the year 1915. Dowson, the then Deputy Inspector General of Police, Madras said: "The Kiddies looked fat and happy. The settlement is in a most flourishing condition."[166]

The SA opened a new girls' school for women's education during the year 1921. During the year 1926, few girls were transferred to Nellore Industrial school. The settlers had a brigade of scouts since 1923. A small bugle band had been formed and equipment supplied. A post office was opened in the settlement during the year 1934. The supply of mid day meals was started from December 1947. Separate hostels are also being maintained by the SA for these children. There are nearly 155 students in these hostels today. In the hostels there are 101 boys and 54 girls studying in class I to the SSC (10th class). In the year 1958, the Salvation Army combined with the Inspector General of Police, opened a new high school for the children of the settlers. The strength of the high school as per the annual record of the year 2005 is 277.

Death rate was high during the year 1915 due to influenza. A new hospital was built by the government. Cooked food was distributed to the settlers upto September 30th 1919. During the year 1920 there was a great effect of Malaria in Stuartpuram. The sub-assistant surgeon was called bi-weekly from Bapatla and medicines were supplied for diseases like dysentery, cholera, malaria, fever, smallpox, beriberi, boils, heart diseases, stomach ache, etc.[167] The National Health Week was celebrated for the first time during the year 1927. V. Sitarama Ayyar took a keen interest in the well-being of the settlers. G.R. Premayya, a non-official visitor made the following remarks : "It is a great blessing to the settlers to have an experienced compounder and a midwife living in the settlement."[168]

Records were maintained for the births and deaths in the settlement. There was a serious attack of smallpox in the settlement during the year 1950. In the beginning, the police used to consult the SA for the whereabouts of the settlers.[169] The police could not enter the settlement without the permission of the manager of the SA. In spite of the manager and local police, there used to be constant fights between the settlers. Maintenance of peace and order was a very big problem. Those settlers who found themselves criminally active and uncontrollable, were brought under restrictions and Penalties of Section 10 of the Madras Habitual Offenders Act 1948.[170] The then Commissioner of Labour stated: "The settlers were not incorrigibles and they were not confined behind barbed wires. No special police staff was employed to watch the settlers."[171]

After Independence, Indian government removed all the powers of the SA. The authority of the management was shifted to the Tribal Welfare Department. There has been an overall change in the settlement at present. More than 200 members received even university education. This is obviously due to the awareness among the youth. In addition to the SA, other social workers namely Gora, Lavanam, Hemalatha Lavanam and M.V.Thomas endeavoured hard to reform these people.[172] During the years 1983-85, the Andhra

Pradesh government implemented a scheme to improve these settlers economically. It is noteworthy that there were freedom fighters in the settlement. Mention may be made of Madigani Dattu, Devara Konda Hanumantha Rao who inspired the settlers with the spirit of nationalism and introduced Gandhian ideology to them. In the modern period during the freedom struggle the British government tried to humiliate the educated upper middle class congress leaders by placing them in the prison cells along with the criminals of Denotified tribes. This had an indirect message to the freedom fighters that their act too was an act of crime and that they did not get any better treatment in Jails. Deverakonda Raju was identified as the most notorious criminal in the eyes of the colonial government. He was famously called Sardar as he was believed to have perfected the art of crime and the art of stealing. When in jail he could meet and interact with the leaders of freedom struggle when the latter were placed in his cell. Some of the leaders took advantage, interacted with the habitual criminals and promised them that they would help in the repealing of the CT Act after independence. Devarakonda Raju was one of those many who attracted towards freedom struggle and freedom fighters like Gandhiji. Raju soon developed a different attitude and he was the first person in Stuartpuram who shaped himself as a nationalist while in jail. After his release from the jail he changed his dress into Khadi and wore a Gandhi cap. He started enlightening the Stuartpuram inhabitants on the nature of freedom struggle and leaders like Gandhiji. He even unsuccessfully tried to organise a meeting of leaders of freedom struggle in Stuartpuram. This kind of exposure to the freedom struggle for some of the inmates of DNT settlements generated a new ethos among them. But the managers of the settlement nipped it in the bud. Under the influence of freedom struggle Devarakonda Raju took a pledge that he would not commit crime again. Also he took a resolve to educate his children. His son Devarakonda Hanumantha Rao later became a convenor of ST Cell in the provincial Congress Committee.

Political consciousness in the settlement has increased over the years and a number of them are active political workers today. In the year 1975, the panchayat system was introduced in Stuartpuram. This was under Murukonda Padu Panchayat. From the year 1981-82 it is under Betapudi Panchayat. There are nearly 10,000 voters. The Stuartpuram ex-settlers are trying to have a separate constituency but this is yet to come into existence. The youth who are working in various private and public employment are very keen on the development of Stuartpuram. They organised "Yerukula Ekalavya Samithi" an organisation which is the centre for many activities.[173]

F. *Siddapuram Settlement (Kurnool District): Origin and Progress upto 1927*

Siddhapuram Settlement is in between Atmakur and Srisailam road. The settlement is situated in the midst of Nallamalai forest of Andhra Pradesh. Siddhapuram was a voluntary settlement. The site of the settlement was shifted to the interior village in the forest area about 13 km east of Venkatapuram village (which is on Atmakur - Srisailam road). It is in Atmakur police station limits and about 12 kms east of Atmakur town. The change of the settlement to the new site contributed to the health and comfort of the Waddars. In January 1927 the site of the settlement was shifted to the present place.[174] The strength of Siddapuram in the beginning was 112 (30 men, 40 women and 42 children).[175]

Occupations

Before coming to Siddhapuram, the Waddars had a meager income. They led a hand-to-mouth existence in the surrounding areas. Their earnings from agricultural operations were insufficient to maintain their families. The British government constructed a huge water reservoir to cultivate the lands attached to the settlement. Every year the crop yield has been dismally low. The manual work is not fetching more than Rs. 15 per day. The primary occupations of the Waddars of Siddapuram were: 1. agriculture, 2. manual work, 3. cutting wood and processing it, 4. daily labour work, 5. basket and mat making, 6. petty business and 7. quarrying.[176] The settlement was kept under the charge of a sub-inspector of police assisted by a constable. The sub-inspector was a key person to manage the settlement. The items of work suitable for employment of Waddars in Siddhapuram were: 1. earth work in connection with the clearance. 2. earth work for excavating distributary channels.[177]

Apart from the subsidiary industries, the main source of livelihood for the Waddars was agriculture. Thousand and sixty six acres of land were distributed to the settlers in the beginning.[178] In addition to these settlers, some other Waddars belonging to Guntur, Hyderabad, Krishna, East and West Godavari districts, Lingala, Chittoor, Nellore, Hubli and Betamcharla was transferred to this settlement. They were also provided more than 175 acres of land and labour works.[179] They were provided with bullocks. Horse gram and cholum were cultivated among other crops and some vegetables like brinjals, green chillies, etc. were grown by the Woddars. The tamarind crop gave them encouragement to get more money.[180] Implements were provided for repairs. They were given seeds for their crops. Fodder was supplied to the cattle. Maistries were appointed to instruct them about the value of land and the knowledge of the production of various crops.[181] Agricultural loans were granted to the Waddars by the then labour Commissioner Mr. Moir.[182] The loans were used for purchase of cattle and carts. A survey was conducted by the Revenue department. According to it, temporary pattas were sanctioned for a period of five years to the settlers.[183] Later on permanent pattas were provided. The government supplied Ongole breeding bulls in 1932 to the Waddars to improve the live stock. Cows were given as gifts to the Waddars who showed interest in agriculture.[184] As the bulk of the Waddars were highly ignorant of farm practices, two farm servants were appointed to help them in addition to the agricultural maistries.

Till January 1942, Waddars maintained themselves by doing cooli work such as road repairs, improvements to schools and managers' quarters, tank revetment, and repairs to the police lines. The average earning of a male was annas 3 per day (18 paise) and a female annas 2 ½ per day (15 paise).[185] They had sufficient scope to earn a living by doing; 1. cooli work; 2. cultivation of their own lands and also of the ryots, 3. ploughing and weeding operations, 4. re-ploughing of land after harvest, clearing of lands overgrown with grass. 5. cutting fuel and selling it in head loads. 6. cutting grass and selling it as fodder, 7. cutting 'tangedu' wood and removing its bark and 8. repairs of roads, etc.[186.]

In addition to this, they were given daily labour such as breaking clods, spreading earth, supply of water to the machinery, pushing empties and loaded wagons at the site of the *Navy*, etc.[187] The settlers earned money from various heads of the public works department such as: 1. construction work, 2 forest contract work, 3. cultivation , 4. spining, 5. weaving, 6. clearance of jungle, 7. sale of cattle, etc.[188]

During the year 1954, about 1,300 Waddars were employed during the tobacco season. The Siddhapuram tank is one of the biggest tanks in Kurnool district with a tank bed of 504.06 acres with abundant facilities for fishing.[189] Mr. Turner of the Krishna cement works, Mangalagiri, had kindly consented to provide work for some Waddars in the limestone quarries at Kaza in Krishna district. Thus some families of Waddars were sent to Kaza.[190]

Cottage Industries

During the year 1920, the Siddhapuram colony's advisory committee resolved to provide a match factory on cottage industries scale in the colony to provide subsidiary occupation to the Waddars. The settlers had a large airy wool shed with 12 looms and prepared cumblies. The looms were all locally made. During the year 1920 the Waddars made 182 cumblies.[191]

Progress of the Wool Industry

The weaving industry was vital to the success of the settlement which supplied guaze cloth for hospitals. There was no demand for the cumblies produced here.[192] Due to the following reasons weaving industry was closed.[193] 1. Because of unfavourable fluctuation in the yarn market. 2. The cloth of finer counts was available in market at cheaper rate. There was difficulty in finding a market for the coarse cloth manufactured in the settlement. 3. There was no scope for unlimited expenditure. 4. The settlers were not evincing much interest in the industry because of low wages.[194]

Sericulture programme was developed but failed. The men at Siddhapuram draw a hill allowance at the rate of 3/10ths of their pay. During the year 1925 a co-operative society was also formed in the settlement.[195] It can be observed that every year a few member of the settlers used to abondon the settlement. The causes of such an action was the periodic outbreak of famines in neighbouring regions accentuated by the consequent steep rise in prices and lack of work during this period which forced some of them to leave the settlement. Added to this, lack of irrigation facilities resulted in the failure of crops. It had become a recurring feature and hence they quit the area in quest of some work outside their place of residence. Above all some of them willfully left the settlement since they found themselves unfit for any manual work which was nothing but drudgery to them. They had been inclined towards the practice of crime which almost became their second nature by the time they were brought to Siddhapuram settlement. Though such a tendency was not rampant among settlers, we cannot totally, rule out the existence of this tendency in any one of the criminal tribes settlement.

For the education of the Waddar children a school was constructed during the year 1915. Education was imparted in the three R's and no attempt had been made to give them industrial training. The attendance was fairly regular. Taylor, the then labour commissioner, said: "The children look well-cared-for and show satisfactory knowledge of their subjects."[196]

The educated Waddars were sent to teachers' training institute in Kurnool and were appointed as teachers in the school. The girls were taught sewing. They had the proficiency in making their own jackets. During the year 1938, the school was developed into a first grade elementary school.[197] The government sanctioned to open the sixth standard in the settlement school at Siddhapuram during 1947-48 and to convert one higher elementary grade teacher's post into a secondary grade post.[198] The strength of the high school as per the annual record of the year 2007 was 158. At present, the location and condition of the school at Siddhapuram is deplorable. There are only two graduates in the Settlement who are still unemployed.

A medical officer was appointed on Siddhapuram tank project and all the sick Waddars were treated by him. Malaria was a common disease in forest areas and hence also in Siddhapuram. The sub-assistant surgeon of Atmakur used to visit the settlement four times in a month. A dispensary with a compundery was opened in April 1929. The common diseases treated in the settlement were bronchitis, fever, pneumonia, dyspepsia, smallpox, common cold, digestive disorders, throat complaints, ulcers and skin diseases, etc.[199] Here, we want to cite one interesting factor. In those days 'health week' was celebrated every year and the manager awarded prizes for the cleanest house Rs. 6 as 1st prize and for the healthiest baby Rs. 2 as 1st prize.[200] The prizes were an incentive to the settlers to keep their huts and surroundings clean and to devote attention to the health of their babies. The condition of the village at present is really pathetic. The only hospital established in 1929 became dysfunctional and women die at the time of delivery. For medical help at present they have to rush to Atmakur. They pleaded for a hospital.

It is an interesting factor that the manager of Siddhapuram settlement was instructed to keep a record of all the settlers living in the settlement with a brief note of their history, associations, avocations, movements, conduct and behaviour with a view to help the police to have a proper control and watch over them. Police go round in the nights regularly and check the settlers to find out whether they go out in the nights for committing crimes.[201] The managers of the settlement reposed confidence in the settlers and made them understand that they were ryots and not criminals. The then labour commissioner Mr. Moir said: "The success of this settlement was due to the efficient and tactful management of K. Subramana Ayyar the then Inspector General of Police".[202]

Until March 1937, it was a voluntary settlement. In 1937, the government declared the settlement as a regular CT Settlement. Upto 1941 the administration of the settlement was under the control of the Commissioner of Labour. From 1943 onwards the administration was taken over by the D.I.G. of Police. The administrative control of the settlement was transferred to the Harijan welfare department in June 1954. In 1955, the management was handed over to the social welfare department. In 1965 it was brought under revenue department in the cadre of Deputy Tahsildar. Finally, in 1976, it was declared as a free colony.

In Siddhapuram, there are 300 families. These 300 families comprise 2000 people. On an average, each family has 1 to 2 acres of land. In some cases people do not have even one acre of land. Some Waddars do not have permanent huts. The average monthly income on all sources may be between Rs. 1000 to 2500. Criminal gangs are very active in Siddhapuram in the olden days and these people have relations with other Settlements.[203] The reasons for their criminal propensity among a few Waddar families are: 1. Lack of alternative avenues of livelihood, 2. Lack of proper up-bringing of children, 3. Poor economic conditions, 4. Easy going mentality, 5. Harassment of the police and forest departments even after they have given up their criminal activities.[204]

The police conduct raids on the houses of the settlers and loot the same, molest their womenfolk and register false cases against them. To escape from this torture, the settlers unnecessarily own the responsibility of crime. The secretary of ex-criminals welfare association in Siddhapuram K.R. Somanna explained about the inhuman behaviour and harassment of the police department. Many of the members were undergoing trials in various courts and are imprisoned.[205] In addition to the police harassment, the forest department officials apprehend the settlers whenever they go to the forest which adds to the their misery.[206]

The hospital, school, roads, and the entire surroundings of Siddhapuram is in a deplorable condition. There has been an over all change in the settlement at present. K. R. Somanna said that they are happy and occasionally the individual officials evince interest in them. For example, Mr. Bhaskar Rao, the police sub-inspector, has been very helpful and the entire settlement heaved a sigh of relief under his benevolent administration.[207] However the present condition of the settlement is very pathetic.

G. *Lingala Settlement*

In India many CT settlements were established in the year 1911 by the British government to wean the CTs away from crime. These were agricultural, industrial, reformatory and voluntary settlements. The management was entrusted to voluntary agencies like the Salvation Army, the American Baptist Telugu Mission, London Mission, Chief Khalsa Diwan, Deo Samaj, etc. The government also took the responsibility of some of the settlements. They were known as voluntary settlements. In addition to them, the native states were interested in the reclamation of the CTs and castes. For examples, the industrial settlement in Bijapur under the Bombay Presidency was established for CTs. The paper mill industry in Bijapur absorbed many CTs. As it was remarked by an Indian Civil Servant, O.H.B. Starti, (Officer in-charge of the CTs settlers of Bijapur) that "wonderful results were achieved in controlling and reforming the criminal tribes of Bijapur".

In Andhra Pradesh the only settlement, established in the princely state was Lingala settlement (Nizam's dominions). It is about 104 miles from the capital of the state. It looks like a modern village with permanently built structures including a hospital, police station, jails, schools for boys and girls, work looms, bungalows for the officials and a temple.[208] The Nizam's administration created an opportunity for them to learn spinning and weaving, carpentry, brick making, laundering and other such useful works. Some of them became proficient in starting business enterprises for themselves and were successful in carrying these trades. Some of the families chose to take up animal or cattle farming. They also cultivated agricultural lands. The Nizam's Government supplied them with oxen, implements, seeds and provisions. The settlers felt contented and showed no signs of running away.

Lingala settlement is located in the Nallamalai forest in Mahaboob Nagar district of Andhra Pradesh. The name 'Lingala' connotes a peculiar meaning because nine 'Saiva temples' sourrounded the settlement. (Including Umamaheswaram and Srisailam temples). The main reasons for establishing the CT settlement at Lingala by the then Nizam Er-Us-Man Nawab Khan (1911-40) were firstly the absconders from other settlements used to take shelter in the Nizam's dominions. They were creating problems in the Nizam's dominions. Secondly, the Chencus who lived in Nallamalai forests, depended on the forest produce. The scarcity of food some times made them to way lay passengers and rob them. Thirdly, the Sugails, a nomadic tribe of Hyderabad were creating trouble in the surrounding villages. It was the responsibility of the Nizam to settle all these three tribes in order to maintain peace and tranquility in his dominions. Fourthly, the CT settlements in the Madras Presidency were exemplary because they were maintained by the missionaries. All these factors made the Nizam to bestow his attention to wean the Wandering and nomadic tribes away from the criminal propensity and make them lead a normal life. The Lingala settlement has a hospital, police station, schools for boys and girls, post office and a temple. The children are well clothed, fed and taught at the expense of the state. They are sent to the workshops to learn the work for which they are best fitted. They are experts in weaving, carpentry, tile, brick making and laundering. Many families have farming plots given to them by the Nizam's Government.

A group of Nizam Waddars, originally belonged to Hyderabad state, migrated to Lingala and Nizam Sagar settlements. They distinguish themselves as Nizam Waddars. They lived by daily labour. They were not regular in their work. Some of them were convicted for burglaries and thefts. They were declared as a CT during the years 1913, 1915 and 1921. Several Christian missionaries and philanthropic socieiteis who worked for the moral upliftment of the CTs managed the CT settiements. The following missionaries may be cited: (1) The Canadian mission, (2) Chief Khalsa Diwan, (3) Deo Samaj, (4) Anjuman-Islamia, (5) Ahmedia Society (6) Ahmedia Anjuman Isad-I-Islam, (7) Sanatana Dharma Sabha (8) Arya Samaj (9) The Punjab Hindu Sabha (10) The servants of Indian Society, (11) The Ramakrishna Mission (12) The Salvation Army (13) The American Baptist Telugu Mission, (14) The Brahma Samaj and (15) The Social Service League. The government and non-government bodies dealing with these classes were as follows: (1) The Director of Public Instruction, (2) The Board of Revenue, (3) The Depressed Class Mission Madras and Saidpet, (4) Mr Kesava Pillai, Gooty (5) The Indian Christian Association, Madras (6) The Theosophical Society, Adyar (7) S. D. Bawaden and (8) A. H. Curtis. In addition to these the British Government and the Nizam Government managed CT settlements in Andhra Pradesh.[209]

Lingala Settlement comprised of three tribes, namely, Yerukalas, Chencus and Lambadas. Among the South Indian Tribes, the Yerukalas occupy an important place. They are one of the largest tribes of Andhra Pradesh. These people are found throughout the Madras Presidency.[209] Yerukalas in Lingala originated from Karnataka region. Others came from Lingsoor, Raichur, Adilabad, Nizamabad and Gulbarga. A few of them came from Stuartpuram settlement. The police department guided these settlers initially.[210] The second tribe that settled in Lingala settlement was Chenchus, a non-Aryan tribe dwelling in the hilly tracks.[124] The Chenchus are of semi-nomadic nature and considered as one of the earliest of the South Indian tribes. The Chenchus are divided into five endogamous groups. 1. *Telugu Chenchus*. 2. *Adavi Chenchus*, 3. *Krishna Chenchus*, 4. *Bonta Chenchus* and 5. *Deva Chenchus*. The *Telugu Chenchus* and Krishna Chenchus are beggars. They collect alms by dancing and singing songs in the plains. The *Adavi Chenchus* are to be found in large numbers in the neighbourhood of Srisailam on the banks of river Krishna. *Deva chenchus* and *Bonta Chenchus* worship Lingamma, Peddamma, Balamma, Yellamma, Pochamma and Lord Venkateshwara of Tirupati. They name their children as Yellamma and Pochamma. They are confined to the secluded parts of the forest and earn their livelihood by hunting. These people, to some extent were notorious in way laying passengers.[211] Hence, they were brought to the Lingala settlement by the Nizam's Government.

The Chenchus originated from Komati Kunta, Rayavaram, Chanpet, Peddur and Kotteru of Telangana region. The Nizam's government brought the Yerukalas and Chenchus and provided for each family five acres of land with "*Lavani Patta*" and supplied them with necessary agricultural tools[212] The Banjaras, (Lambadas or Sugalis) are the original inhabitants in Andhra Pradesh.[213] They mostly live in the districts in Telangana, Kurnool, Warangal and Adilabad districts of Andhra Pradesh. The Lambadas are an intelligent, good looking, well built, sturdy people. They have weathered many a storm during their journey from their original home in Rajasthan to several districts of Andhra Pradesh.[214] They speak a peculiar dialect, an admixture of Punjabi and Gujarati. Originally nomads, they are mostly agriculturists. Their songs are closely associated with harvest. During their nomadic life they used to indulge in petty thieving. All these three tribes, viz., Yerukalas, Chenchus and Banjaras are living at present in Lingala settlement. These three tribes are intertwined with each other to the extent that they have marital relations. Some examples of these marriages are cited by them.[215]

Andhra Rashtra Adimajati Sevak Sangh (Under the presidentship of Vennalacunti Raghavaiah and under the vice presidentship of Palapartiveeraiah) stopped malpractices like slave trade and ordeal tests in Lingala settlement. The sale of tribal women to buyers from Punjab (for amounts ranging from two to five thousand rupees) right under the nose of the police department was prevalent. The Sangh took active measures to stop such practices. The Sangh suggested tightening the penal code sections relating to slavery. It was approved by the central law department. It was considered by the Home ministry. With the active support and efforts of the Sangh they became experts in weaving, carpentry, tile and brick-making and laundering. Many families are given farming plots by the Nizam's Government. They also discouraged tribal ordeals like dipping the hand in the boiling oil and lifting the hot iron bars in their hands.[216]

Today, the settlers are engaged either in cultivation, business or manual labour. They have mainly depended on forest produce. Yerukulas bring bamboo from the forest and they are experts in basket making. Chenchus depend primarily for their livelihood upon forest produce and to some extent agricultural work. The Sugalis are engaged in manual labour because they are more hard working. The officers who deal with these people have neither time nor interest to bestow necessary attention on them with the result that they are discontented with their life. Even for those who have taken to cultivation, there are no sufficient irrigational facilities. Borewells are not constructed. Moreover, the land is a dry land. The rainfall is scanty in this region. On the whole they are not much satisfied with the income they get. There is plenty of waste land in the vicinity which can be provided to them along with groundwater facilities as an alternative measure. Another important issue is their main source of income is derived through the preparation and sale of country liquor. Due to the recent ban on liquor by Andhra Pradesh Government, they have lost their main livelihood. They are looking for alternative means like making of gum, match, bamboo work and preparing paper, preparation of match boxes as small scale industries mainly based on the raw materials available in the forest and a small section of them are committing petty crimes (rafu).[217]

With regard to educational facilities in Lingala settlement there is government school and a residential hostel both for boys and girls.[133] Almost all the parents expressed their dissatisfaction with their school. Their economic conditions are not conducive for their proper growth. Some of the parents still feel, that education for their children is a sheer waste of time and energy. They are worried about the employment of their children with 7th or 10th class qualifications. There are very few who have studied up to Engineering, Medicine and other professional courses.

The medical facilities are by and large poor. There is a hospital which was established by the then Nizam Government, which is disfunctional. Generally, the Chenchus are knowledgeable in using herbal medicines. Unfortunately, this practice has been declining in the recent years. They expressed that the Chenchus from Kurnool, Khammam and Dornala have the knowledge of these medicinal plants. They pleaded for a hospital. There is a general awareness among these people about their problems. They want to struggle with the government to get their demands conceded. Although Girijan co-operative society is established to supply the consumer goods, its benefits are cornered to the well to do sections in the village.[218]

The members of the settlement are facing problems from the forest department. The main problem is that rich people from surrounding areas like Achammapeta and other places are given preferences by the forest officers and they are the real beneficiaries of the government schemes. Moreover, the facilities provided by the government are also meagre. What should be done in this context is that the economic rehabilitation should be combined with social education. Inculcating social values should be preceded by necessary economic measures to provide them with basic necessities. To raise them to a higher level of social values, one will have to inspire confidence in them about the right path they should take in their effort. They should be made aware of the vast potentialities that lie dormant in them. In spite of the development activities undertaken by the government, an atmosphere of general discontent prevails in the settlement. They are not fully convinced that the government is showing as much care and attention on them as they should. When compared to other settlements, the settlement in Lingala is lagging behind, the exception being Siddhapuram settlement, in Kurnool district. The social workers are also not evincing proper interest in this settlement.

To sum up, a large share of allotment of these tribals should be spent on their economics rehabilitation. As it was stated by the Planning Commission about the DNTs 2/3rd of the allotment should be spent on welfare schemes such as hawking business, selling gum and other forest products. They should be provided with alternative means of livelihood. It is a stunning paradox that till today no sociologist or anthropologist has done a complete survey of these people. Officials and non-officials who guide and control the destinies of crores of Indians are unable to solve the problems and suggest measures for the cure of their long standing ills. If this is the position, concerted action on all fronts is a pressing need. The feeling of a 'Psychological barrier' will have to be removed among the DNTs. A more responsible and human approach will go a long way in stimulating a change among the DNTs.

VI

Conclusion

The present position seems to be not quite encouraging in the development and the overall conditions of the DNTs their colonies, and the overall socio-economic and cultural conditions of the DNT in their settlements. Still a few families are committing crimes in all the settlements. This can be attributed to the poverty of these people. The government should come forward to provide them with alternative means of livelihood. Though the government is taking some immediate rehabilitation measures such as providing them buffaloes, rickshaws, provision shops, loans, etc. these measures can hardly be a permanent solution. However, the following few observations are made below with a view to improve the rehabilitation development programmes for the welfare of these DNTs of Andhra Pradesh.

1. The DNTs should be provided with enough land and bank loans to make them self-sufficient.

2. Small scale industries such as basket making, weaving, mat making, brick making and the like should be encouraged.
3. Dairy farming, piggery, poultry are useful schemes in their economic development. The government has to provide financial assistance on loan cum subsidy basis.
4. Arrangements should be made with banks to sanction loans to the DNTs who are interested in setting up of small business such as soda shops, tea-stalls, provision stores or fancy stores, etc.
5. They may be given employment such as constables, peons, bus conductors, etc. Such a step if taken, would not only provide them with a respectable livelihood but also take them away from the atmosphere of the settlement.
6. Stolen property dealers, corrupt police officials, investors in crime and greedy advocates should be strictly dealt with.
7. Industries may be established in the DNT settlements on the waste lands so that a large number of people will get employment opportunities.
8. Educational facilities as they exist today are not adequate. A few more schools, (English medium) colleges, Industrial Training Institutes (ITIs) It's and a univerisity may be established and all these schools (upto junior-Degree stages) should be provided with the necessary infrastructural facilities.
9. Regular water supply should be provided for the DNT settlement lands so as to enable them to irrigate their lands. They should not lose interest in cultivation.
10. The state government should provide the DNTs with certain measures for the welfare of the DNTs such as: 1. Provision of suitable land for cultivation, 2. Setting up upper-primary schools for education, 3. Starting handloom, weaving centers as cottage industries, 4. Setting up co-operative societies for supplying credit and other necessaries, of the life, 5. Opening of dispensaries, 6. Construction of pucca houses for habitation, 7. Imparting training for the inmates of industrial agricultural settlements, etc. These facilities were not provided by the government. The government should immediately take up these measures to improve their conditions.
11. Waddars, Dasaries, Dommaras, Nakkalas and others have different connotations in different districts. For example,

the Waddars are called as Gollas, Yera Gollas, Katheras, Dasaries, etc. Unfortunately, these communities are not in the list of Scheduled Tribes. Hence they are losing the opportunities for reservation both in educational institutions and in jobs. Unemployed people are found in all the settlements. So, it is suggested that the government should take measures in giving them the status of Scheduled Tribes. For this purpose, they have gone even to the court. So far no justice has been made to them. The human rights commission, The National Commission for DNT and semi nomadic Tribes, Ministry of Social Justice and Empowerment should help them in getting the required social justice to these communities.

12. The water facilities available in the DNT colonies/ settlements are not adequate. They should be provided with sufficient water facilities to encourage them to grow the cash and commercial crops. For example the water tank in Siddhapuram DNT colony became dysfunctional. If it functions well it is useful for 20 villages of surrounding areas.
13. At present, the entire villages of the DNT Communities plagued by the evil of illicit liquor. Lack of employment makes them take to this practice. Self-employment opportunities should be provided for the women of the DNT communities.
14. The stigma of their being 'criminals' constrained them more glaringly, as people always suspect a person who has spent some time in the DNT settlements colonies. No doubt, this is a serious psychological problem. To get rid of the stigma attached to them will take longer time. The terms such as 'Criminal Tribes', 'Settlements' should be removed.
15. Reformation should not be merely materialistic. They should be instilled with self-confidence and their faith in humanity should not be shaken. Rehabilitation programmes concerning these people should be entrusted to the educational institutions as part of their extension programmes or reputed social service organisations whose approach is always humanitarian. Such people help them in the rehabilitative work. One of the main problems identified by the field experiences is about the social treatment

meted out to the families of the DNT tribes. For generations together, the DNT families and their members have been labbled as criminals and have suffered dishonour and social negligence. The reasons are not far to seek here given the background of the socially despicable avocation as practiced by some of the people belonging to DNT tribes. The children and women, in particular have suffered ignominy from mainstream society. The stigma of criminality is still one of the major impediments in the smooth run of educational progress of children and youth. Children often faced a kind of social alienation in most walks of social life. Social alienation particularly in young age hampers the growth of psycho-social faculties of the children. Social practices of the mainstream society have denied opportunities for the children coming from the so-called DNT families residing in the settlement areas. The approaches of the government often times remain impersonal and lack human element and eye on social cohesiveness in its approach. However, there can be education without even the formal modes and methods of schooling. But mere efforts on mainstream socialisation does not open wide social canvas for the children because there is already a hostile attitude in the outside society. The school or the process of schooling in settlement areas or settlement schools may be used as instruments or tools to impart social culture, feelings of common fraternity, community approach, adjustment mentality, atmosphere of working and learning together and finally moral dynamics of social and cultural behaviour. The schools in the DNT settlement areas are to be treated or perceived from a different angle where they are expected to combine the role of an instructor, change agent, catalyst and humanism.

The main problem in the government schools or those run by private parties is that there is a general schooling atmosphere that best suits the needs of the children from the mainstream society. This kind of atmosphere need not always be congenial to the requirements of social and cultural transformation of the children who are already suffering the social stigma and are alienated. When the government is taking care to mainstream the differently-abled children through advocating their admission into ordinary schools, so that these children too will have the necessary advantage of 'feel good' factor and forget the physical constraints. The same approach may perhaps be extended without any reservations in the case of the children who are socially alienated. However, in the present case, efforts shall be directed towards the direction of mingling ordinary children with the children of these tribes in separate schools with residential facilities. Since the DNTs too are considered under the general item of 'tribes' by the planners and policy makers, the scope for public sanctions for the welfare of these relatively ignored tribes is limited and confined. Among the socially and economically backward classes majority of the families wish to retain some of their children at home without sending to school. They have their own family and economic reasons for not sending their wards to centers of learning. Barring further discussion on this, the point of reference here is that children from the so-called DNT families (whether reformed or not) have a tendency of not going to school or dropping out school if already admitted, for, there is an unwritten feeling among these children that they will receive not only education, but also social humiliation from co-learners as well as teachers (sometimes). Secluded, aloof and separated they feel happier than being insulted in the rest of the society. It is very important that the ice should be broken. So special schools or shaping the existing schools/facilities as special schools for an ideal social integration are necessary. The need is that the children in these settlement areas may be exposed to a kind of development education where aspects of social development, mainstreaming and unhindered socialisation will combine to keep the morale of the learners on a higher pedestal. Along with prescribed and formatted curriculum, realistic or scientific knowledge, social outlook and personality development may be included in the general teaching atmosphere of the schools in settlements. Efforts are to be made to encourage ordinary students from outside the settlement to get admitted into these schools so that the dichotomy between the criminal (reformed or not) and the others may get diluted in the course of time.

Even though the CT Act was repealed in the post independent era (1952,) nobody took a keen interest in the execution of the government decision in making the settlements as free colonies. Thus all the five settlements in Andhra Pradesh (Sitanagaram, Stuartpuram, Kapparallattippa, Siddhapuram and Lingala settlements) remained as ex-criminal settlements. The life conditions in the settlements were not changed. Out of these five colonies

Stuartpuram is under the control of the Salvation Army. The other four settlements were taken over by the government towards the end of colonial rule. They were put under the revenue jurisdiction, and under the social welfare department control. The government is the legal owner of all land and house sites in all the colonies. But in Stuartpuram the Salvation Army is holding the key position even now. After Independence, the Madras government appointed a committee under the chairmanship of Mr. Vepa Ramesam I.C.S. The committee recommended to make all the settlements as free colonies/villages and distributed house sites to the occupants. It also recommended distribution of land to all those bonafied inhabitants who have been living there. The Government notified through a GO in 1976 that all the DNT settlements would be considered as free colonies. Consequently the government took control over all the lands in the DNT colonies and distributed some portion of the land in the name of local inhabitants with ownership rights. Thus they started enjoying self-respect as the rightful owners of property on par with other members of the mainstream society.

Another important aspect concerning the DNTs is that a very small portion of them who were listed under ST category and who joined in the public employment were happy with their families. There was thus more clamor for public placements. The DNT families understood the importance of education, their children would definitely get good jobs. The government is also providing them some facilities including free boarding, lodging, fees, books, etc. These facilities are not being given to all the DNT families because some of them under BCA category. These facilities should be extended to the other DNT communities also. The parents of the children wanted to send their children to English medium schools or convents in the local areas. Some of the programmes that can be implemented by the Government and Non-governmental bodies are: 1. Designing common programmes for the people of the colonies and surrounding villages. 2. Integrated approach where the benefits would be shared by the reformed families and other families 3. Youth exposure programmes 4. Providing work opportunities 5. Common health and education programmes 6. Organisation of women groups 7. Suitable agro-based programmes 8. Establishment of research and reference institutes with emphasis on documentation, preservation and preparation of training modules 9. Conduct of periodic awareness programmes and workshops, meetings on human rights issues and active interaction with the inmates, educated families, public officials, social activists and academicians.

The Denotified tribes still feel the pinch of the harassment for all the trivial and petty quarrels even at the domestic front. Their main contention is the stigma attached to them. They are unhappy with the attitude of the bureaucrats and public. The normal individuals among them assuming their right to question which was hitherto denied to them. They are more vigorous and passionate in the act of questioning every minute aberration in their normal social life. They are vociferously question all the irregularities in the out side society. They have been unconsciously given to a staunch belief that they are morally superior to others. This is no fault of theirs. The public and the government, unnecessarily involves in the routine lifestyles and problems of the DNT families. As long as this continues they cannot enjoy self-respect and human rights. Morality is more individual than social. If personal morality is socialised, we can talk of social and public morality. Without fulfilling this, any talk about the latter becomes an exercise of envoid. Individual can be a moral human being when he or she is certain that their life is safe in the surrounding society and their needs are met through their hard work.

The Denotified tribes are leading a decent and dignified life. They hate their old habits. When they came out of the womb of crime and reformed themselves they had to encounter the out side institutions, social structures and individuals where elements of white collar criminality crept in. When they have tried to distance themselves from criminalisation of individuals, they were simultaneously facing the criminalisation of institutions, social structures and polity outside. While individual crime had an eagle's eye over it, the institutionalised crime had a protective cover in the democratic Indian polity.

NOTES

1. The total population of these tribes in India was estimated in different states totaling approximately more than eight million population.
2. Y. C. Simhadri, 'Changing Criminal behaviour of an ex-criminal tribe in an Indian Village in the *Journal of Criminology, Vol. 4, No. 1, January 1976*, p. 4.
3. Darrow, Clarence, *Crime : its Causes and Treatment*, London, 1934, pp. 7-8.
4. Biswas, P. C., *The Ex-criminal Tribes of Delhi State*, Unpublished Ph.D., thesis, University of Delhi, 1960, p. 188.

5. Government of Bombay, *Report of the Criminal Tribes Act Enquiry Committee,* Government central press, Bombay, 1939, p. 20. Also see, *Report of the Criminal Tribes Enquiry Committee,* United Provinces of India, 1947, Allahabad, 1948, p. 4, TNA.
6. Government of Madras, *Home Department, G.O. No. 1675, dt 2nd December 1919,* p. 9.
7. Booth Tucker, F., *Criminocurology or the Indian Crime and What to do with him – A Report of the work of the Salvation Army among the Criminal Tribes, Habituals and Released Prisoners in India,* London, n.d. p. 14.
8. Government of Madras, *Note Showing the progress Made in the settlement of criminal Tribes in the Madras presidency upto September,* 1916, Madras, 1917, p. 6.
9. Simhadri, Y.C., *The Ex-Criminal Tribes of India* National Publishing House, New Delhi, 1979, p. 35.
10. See Government of Madras, *Home Department, G.O. No. 1675,* dt. 2nd December 1919, p. 14.
11. See Government of Madras, *Home Department, G.O. No. 1675,* dt. 2nd December 1919, p. 6
12. Pickett, Waskom, J., *Christian Mass Movements in India,* Chicago, 1933, p. 297.
13. *Ibid.,* p. 298.
14. Government of Madras, *Note Showing the Progress Made in the settlement of Criminal Tribes in the Madras Presidency upto January 1926,* Madras, 1927, p. 3.
15. Mukhopadhyay, Anandita, 'Criminal Tribes and British Policy, 1871-1928', Un published M. Phil thesis submitted to Jawaharlal Nehru University, New Delhi, 1988, pp. 30-35.
16. Government of Madras, *Madras Criminal Tribes Manual, brought upto 31st March 1927,* Government Superintendent Press, Madras 1927, p. 3.
17. Government of Madras, *Note Showing the Progress Made in the settlement of Criminal Tribes in the Madras presidency upto January 1926,* Madras, 1927, p. 6.
18. Booth Tucker, F., *Criminology or the Indian Crime and what to do with him, A Report on the work of Salvation Army among the Criminal Tribes, Habituals and released prisoners of India,* London, n. p. 18.
19. Lalitha, V., *The Making of Criminal Tribes : Patterns and Transition,* New Era Publications, Madras, 1995, p.·14.
20. Radhakrishana, Meena, Colonialism, Evolutionism and Anthropology-A Critique of the History of Ideas 1850-1930', *Research-in-Progress papers, History and society, NMML.,* New Delhi, June, 1997. Also see Radhakrishna, Meena, Surveillance and Settlements under the Criminal Tribes Act in Madras', *Indian Economic and Social History Review, 29, 2, 1992.* Also see, Radhakrishna, Meena, 'Colonial Construction of a

Criminal Tribe: The Itinerant Trading Communities of Madras presidency' in *Neera Chandhoke (ed). Historical Trajectory: Essays in Honour of Ravinder Kumar, Tulika*, New Delhi, 2000.

21. See Government of Madras, *Public Works (Labour) Department, G.O. No. 1551, dt. 20th July 1927*, pp. 5-6, APSA.
22. Government of Madras, *Madras Criminal Tribes Manual brought upto 31st March 1927*, Government Superintendent Press, Madras, 1927, p. 6.
23. Government of Madras, *Note Showing the progress made in the settlement of Criminal tribes in the Madras Presidency upto September 1916*, Madras, 1917, p. 9. The settlements had a uniform structure with the following facilities and equipments.

Table : 3

The Structure and Staff of DNT Settlements

Quarters		
A and A-1	:	Manager's Quarters
B	:	Office building
C and C-1	:	A Hall for Mid-day Meals and a Kitchen
D.	:	Clerks' quarters
E.	:	Compounder and Midwife's Quarters
F.	:	School Building
G and G-1	:	Roll call shed and settlers' huts
H.	:	Dispensary and Store room
I.	:	Teachers and Maistries' quarters, etc.

The settlements were also equipped with settlers' huts and a lock-up. The following staff members were appointed in the settlements by the government:

Settlement Staff	
(a)	Inspector (Managers)
(b)	Clerks
(c)	Peons
(d)	Compounders
(e)	Teachers
(f)	Watchers
(g)	Scavengers
(h)	Midwife
(i)	Ward boy
(j)	Agricultural Instructors/Maistries
(k)	Sweepers, etc.

24. Booth Tucker, F., *Criminocurology or the Indian crime and what to do with him, A Report on the work of Salvation Army among the criminal Tribes, Habituals and released Prisoners of India*, London, n.d. p. 20.

25. See Government of Madras, *Law (General) Department, G.O. No. 1803, dt. 24th July 1920.*
26. See Government of Madras, *Judicial Department, G.O. No. 924, dt. 10th May 1913.* The members were removed to the kavali settlement, Nellore District. Also see Boswell, *Nellore District Manual,* Madras, 1973.
27. See, Government of Madras, *Home (Judicial) Department,G.O. No. 681, dt. 26th March 1917.* Some of the Dasaries were Transferred to Hubli Settlement.
28. Government of Madras, *Home (Judicial) Department, G.O. No. 681, dt. 26th March 1917. Also see Home (Judicial) Department, G.O. No. 2293, dt. 7.10. 1919.* Lalitha V., *Socio-Economic and Administrative Aspects of an Ex-Criminal Tribe, A case study of Kapparalla Tippa,* Unpublished M. Phil Dissertation Submitted. to Sri Venkateswara University, Tirupati 1975.
29. Government of Madras, *Judicial Department, G.O. No. 616, dated 13th May 1922.*
30. Government of Madras, *Judicial (Police) Department, G.O. No. 658, dated. 15th December 1924.*
31. Government of Madras, *Note Showing the Progress Made in the Settlement of Criminal Tribes in the Madras presidency upto January 1926,* Madras, 1927, p. 10.
32. *Ibid.*
33. See Government of Madras, *Home Department, G.O. No. 2797, dated 2nd July 1940.*
34. See Government of Madras, *Home Department, G.O. No. 5303, dated 2nd July 1940.*
35. See Government of Madras, *Home Department, G.O. No. 4714, dated 22nd November 1940.*
36. See, Government of Madras, *Home Department, G.O. No. 2048, dt. May 4th 1940.*
37. Government of Madras, *Judicial Department, G.O. No. 918, dated 10th May 1913.* Also see, *Judicial Department, G.O. No. 1796, dated 5th September, 1913 and Home (Judicial) Department, G.O. No. 414, dated 20th February 1918 and Judicial Department, G.O. No. 52, dated 31st January 1923.* In October 1915, the then district magistrate reported that two headman of the Koracha tribe by name Puli Bangaru Bojjigadu and Koneti Venkatigadu were the heads of two forts. The entire settlement was split up into two groups. They obstructed the whole development of the settlement. They prevented the people from working on the tank project. The manager removed Bojjigadu to Sitanagaram Settlement in Gaunter District. For other details See Government of Madras, *Judicial Department, G.O. No. 520, dt. 2nd March 1914.* (Report on the settlement of Criminal Gangs in Chittoor district)
38. Government of Madras, *Judicial Department, G.O. No. 381, dated 10th July 1925 and Judicial Department, G.O. No. 592, date 20th October 1925.*

The strength of the settlement at the end of the year 1915 was 161 males, 152 females and 135 children with a total population of 448 people.

39. Government of Madras, *Note showing the progress made in the settlement of Criminal Tribes in the Madras Presidency upto September,* 1916, Madras 1917, p. 12.
40. *Ibid.*
41. Government of Madras, *Judicial Deparment, G.O. No. 1869, dated 30th July 1927.*
42. Government of Madras, *Judicial Department, G.O. No. 562, dated* 23rd October 1929.
43. Government of Madras, *Judicial Department, G.O. No. 506, dt. 22nd October 1934.*
44. Government of Madras, *Judicial Department G.O. No. 643, dt. 28th November 1935.*
45. Government of Madras, *Note showing the progress made in the settlement of Criminal tribes in the Madras Presidency upto January 1925,* Madras 1927, p. 17.
46. *Ibid.*
47. See Government of Madras, *Home (Judicial) Department, G.O. No. 1937, dt. 13th September 1917.*
48. See, Government of Madras, *Home (Judicial) Department, G.O. No. 2874, dated 6th December 1916. Government of Madras, Judicial Department, G.O. No. 784, dated 25th April 1913.*
49. Government of Madras, *Judicial Department, G.O. No. 917, dated 10th May 1913 and Judicial Department, G.O. No. 1714 dated 4th July 1916.*
50. Government of Madras, *Home (Judicial) Deparment, G.O. No. 212, dated 1st February 1917.*
51. See, Government of Madras, *Home (Judicial) Department, G.O. No. 373L., dated 14th February 1934, p. 6. Government of Madras, Home Judicial Department, G.O. No. 24, dt. 5th January 1918,* p. 2.
52. Government of Madras, *Public Works and Labour Department, G.O. No. 1794 L., dated. 15th July 1931,* p. 8.
53. Government of Madras, *Judicial (Police) Department, G.O. No. 377, dated 26th July 1923,* p. 3.
54. See Government of Madras, *Home (Judicial) Department, G.O. No. 1017, dated 30th April 1918,* p. 4. *Also see* Government of Madras, *Home Department, G.O. No. 1004, dt. 27th April 1918,* p. 4.
55. See, Government of Madras, *Home (Judicial) Department, G.O. No. 1004, dt. 27th April 1940,* p. 1. *Also See,* Government of Madras, *Home Department, G.O. No. 242, dated 1st February 1917.*
56. Government of Madras, *Home Department, G.O. No. 1059, dated 15th January 1940,* p. 1.

57. Government of Madras, *Home Department, G.O. No. 1269-G, dt. 15th January 1940* p. 3.
58. Government of Madras, *Home Department, G.O. No. 1004, dt. 13th August 1940,* p. 1.
59. Government of Madras, *Public Works Labour Department, G.O. No. 5248, dt. 5th August 1940.*
60. Government of Madras, *Law (General) Department, G.O. No. 1714, dt. 22nd October 1921,* p. 4. The sub-settlements at Allur and Bitragunta were started in 1917. The services of the manager was given freely by the ABM missionaries. The population of the settlement at the end of the year 1917 was 1,393. The nature of employment of the inmates were contracts, agriculture, carpentry, weaving, limekiln, cooliework, stone quarrying and fire wood cutting. See Government of Madras, *Home (Judicial) Department, G.O. No. 2294, dt. 7th October 1919,* p. 6.
61. Also see, Government of Madras, *Public works and Labour Department, G.O. No. 1551 L. Dated, 20th July 1927,* p. 3.
62. Government of Madras, *Public Works and Labour Department, G.O. No. 1654 L., dt. 6th July 1928,* p. 1.
63. Government of Madras, *Public Works and Labour Department, G.O. No. 2394 L., dated 23rd August 1929,* p. 1.
64. Government of Madras, *Public works and Labour Department, G.O. No. 2338 L., dated 19th August 1930,* p. 1. *Also see, Law (general) department, G.O. No. 666, dt. 26th February 1923,* p. 4.
65. Government of Madras, *Public Works and Labour Department, G.O. No. 1926 L., dated 30th July 1931,* p. 1. *Also see, Law (General) Department, G.O. No. 993, dt. 8th April, 1922.*
66. Government of Madras, *Public Works and Labour Department, G.O. No. 34 10 L., dt. 3. 12.1930, p. 2. Also see, Public works (Labour) department, G.O. No. 296 L., dt. 8th November 1923,* p. 4.
67. Government of Madras, *Public Works and Labour Department, G.O. No. 1426 L., dt. 27th January 1931,* p. 3.
68. Government of Madras, *Public Works and Labour Department, G.O. No. 1350 L., dt. 18th May 1931,* p. 1.
69. Government of Madras, *Public Works and Labour Department, G.O. No. 1364 L., dt. 20th May 1931,* p. 1.
70. Government of Madras, *Public Works and Labour Department, G.O. No. 413 L., dt. 16th February 1931,* p. 1. *Also see Judicial Department, G.O. No. 2874, dt. 6th December 1916, and Judicial department, G.O. No. 212, dt. 1st February 1917.*
71. Government of Madras, *Public Works and Labour Department, G.O. No. 194 L., dt. 24th January 1933,* p. 2.
72. Government of Madras, *Public Works and Labour Department, G.O. No. 427 L., dt. 20th February 1933,* p. 4.

73. Government of Madras, *Public Works and Labour Department, G.O. No. 5554, dt. 17th November 1938,* p. 2.
74. Government of Madras, *Public Works and Labour Department, G.O. No. 5860, dt. 7th December 1938,* p. 1.
75. Government of Madras, *Administration Report of the Labour Department for the year ending 31st March 1933, Madras 1934,* pp. 25-26.
76. Government of Madras, *Public Works and Labour Department, G.O. No. 373 L., 14th February 1934,* p. 4.
77. Lalitha, V., *Making of Criminal Tribes Patterns and Transition,* New Era Publication, Madras, 1995, p. 18.
78. Until 1933 Kavali Reformatory settlement and Bitragunta Settlements were under the management and control of the American Baptist Mission. The total population of the settlement on 31st March 1933 was 1,111 people out of which 378 were men, 287 were women and 446 were children. The Employment for the Yerukulas in Kavali was inadequate and a number of Yerukulas continued to be employed on unremunerative labour. See Government of Madras, *Administration Report of the Labour Department for the year ending 31st March 1933,* Madras, 1934, pp. 24-25, TNA.
79. Government of Madras, *Home Department, G.O. No. 1059, dt. 1st January 1940,* p. 1.
80. *Ibid.*
81. Lalitha V., *Socio-Economic and Administrative Aspects of an ex-criminal Tribe,* Unpublished M.Phil Thesis, Tirupati University, 1977, p. 32.
82. In making the grants the Government recommended first Persuasive methods should be adopted to settle the families of Yerukula tribe. If the persuasion failed, then to apply the Provisions of the CT Act.
83. Sitanagaram settlement was the first of its kind in Madras Presidency. It was actually opened in the month of January 1913 with a few men who were released from the Jail before their arrival to Sitanagaram. The Government adopted some persuasive methods to settle the Yerukulas. Since the persuasive methods adopted by the government failed the Government submitted the proposals to declare the Yerukulas as the CTs under the CTA and restricted their movements under section 12 of the 1911 Act. The recommendation of the Government was carried out immediately. The Yerukulas of Godavari and Guntur districts were restricted in their movements to the areas comprised within the settlement area. See *Government of Madras, Note showing the progress made in the settlement of Criminal Tribes in the Madras presidency upto Septembers 1916,* Madras 1917, p. 5.
84. *Note, 1925* : 1.8
85. V. Lalitha, *The Making of Criminal Tribes Patterns and Transition,* New Era Publications, Madras, 1995, p. 143.
86. Robert Eric Frykenberg, Manual of Guntur District 1960:17.

87. *Home (Judicial), Department G.O. No. 1420, dt. 9th July 1917,* p. 1.
88. *Home (Judicial) Department G.O. No. 1225, dt. 20th May 1918,* p. 1.
89. *Home (Judicial) Department G.O. No. 1234, dt. 22nd May 1918.* p. 1.
90. *Home (Judicial) Department G.O. No. 927, dt. 20th April 1918.* p. 3.
91. *Home (Judicial) Department G.O. No. 2715, dt. 6th December 1918,* p. 1.
92. *Home (Judicial) Department G.O. No. 2615, dt. 13th December 1917,* p. 1.
93. *Judicial Department, G.O. No. 573, dt. 29th February 1916,* p. 1.
94. *Home (Judicial) Department G.O. No. 2373, dt. 4th October 1916,* p. 3.
95. *Home (Judicial) Department G.O. No. 625 dt. 18th March 1918.*
96. The then District magistrate, Guntur, inspected Sitangaram in November 1916, and reported that the place was in a very insanitary condition owing to floods. The government appointed a committee consisting of the Deputy Inspector-General of Police (CID and Railways), the Executive Engineer, the Manager of the settlement and the District Magistate. The Committe recommended: 1. Improvement of Sainyapuram by thinning out the village, 2. Building of new huts at Kondapet, 3. Construction of a road and improvement of drainage, and 4. construction of a well. *Home Judicail department, G.O. No. 22, dt. 5th January 1920,* p. 1.
97. The children attended the school regularly. The strenth of the school at the end of the year 1915 was 92. See, *Home (Judicial), G.O. No. 795, dt. 4th April, 1918,* p. 1.
98. A.G. Cardew the then Govt. Officer on the settlements visited Sitanagaram during the year 1917. There was a through discontentment among the Yerukulas in Sitanagarm. The Government carefully examined the question whether Sitanagaram should be completely closed and to transfer the Yerukulas to Stuartpuram and Guntur. The then SA Manager adopted new ventures to settle the Yerukalas in Sitanagaram. But all his ventures were terminated by the Government and the Yerukalas. In the Month of February 1915 a number of Yerukalas formed into gangs walked out of Sitanagaram defied the management. The then district Magistrate remarked "I regret that I cannot regard the working of the settlement as satisfactory." *See Home (Judicial) Department G.O. No. 946, dt. 27th April 1918,* p. 1.
99. *Home (Judicial) Department, G.O. No. 216 dt. 23rd September, 1918.*
100. The Annual report on CTs during the year 1918-19 showed that the condition of Sitanagaram under the administration of the new management progressed satisfactory. The total Strength of Yerukulas in Sitanagaram on 31st March 1919 was 720 People of whom 122 Yerukulas were absconded. The school contained 94 children due to severe influenza epidemic. *Home (Judicial) Department, G.O. No. 2233 dt. 29th September 1919,* p. 1.
101. Law (General) Department, *G.O. No. 2454, dt. 7th October 1922, p.1.* The future of the Sitanagaram came up for consideration during the

year 1920-21. The new manager enforced better discipline among the Yerukulas. The debts incurred were wiped off gradually. The then Inspector General of Police said: "the settlement should be continued. The early difficulties were mainly due to mismanagement of the missionaries". After careful considerations of all the circumstances, the Government ordered the management authorities to retain Sitanagaram permanently.

102. Employment was freely available for the Yerukulas throughout the year. The wages earned by them amounted to Rs. 22,600. The strength of the Yerukulas during the year 1922 was 728 people out of which 58 people were absconded. There were 70 boys, 57 girls of school-going age children. All of them attended the school regularly. A night school was also maintained at Sitanagaram. A total number of 83 acres were cultivated by the Yerukulas. Agricultural operations were successful. A new masonry drain was built. The level of the road was raised. Housing conditions were improved. The Yerukulas showed improvement in all directions. The government congratulated Adjutant and Mrs. Mabe for their continuous and good hard work for improving the conditions of the Yerukulas. See, *Law (General) Department, G.O. No. 2314, dt. 19th September 1922,* p. 4. *Also See Home Department, G.O. No. 2451, dated 3rd June 1940,* p. 1.
103. *Home Department, G.O. No. 2150 (c), dated 20th August 1936,* p. 1.
104. *Public Works (Labour) Department, G.O. No. 2172 B, dated 25th August 1933.*
105. *Public Works (Labour) Department, G.O. No. 5649, dt. 5th March 1936,* p. 1.
106. *Ibid,* p. 4.
107. *Home Department, G.O. No. 372, date January 28th 1937.*
108. Government of Madras, *Administration Report of the Labour Department for the year ending 31st March 1938.*
109. Government of Madras, *Administration Report on Habitual Offenders Settlements for 1951-52,* Madras 1953, p. 5.
110. *Home Department, G.O. No. 2900, dt. 8th August 1952,* p. 4. The District Medical Board Guntur Contributed an amount of Rs. 25 per month for the maintenance of the hospital. The government have also sanctioned an amount of Rs. 500 to the SA manager for the purchase of equipment for the hospital. See, *Note showing the progress made in the settlement of criminal Tribes in Madras Presidency upto Septembers 1916,* Madras, 1917, p. 6.
111. *Home Department, G.O. No. 2900, dt. 8th August 1952,* p. 4.
112. *Home Department, G.O. No. 1837, dt. 13th June 1944,* p. 1.
113. *Home Department, G.O. No. 2214, dt. 26th July 1946,* p. 3.
114. *Home Department. G.O. No. 3953, dt. 20th July 1939,* p. 1.
115. The Manager of Sitanagaram Settlement during the year 1938 was S.V.V. Gopala Rao Nayudu. The population of the Yerukulas in

Sitanagaram on 31st December 1938 was 298 people (195 men and 103 children). In addition to the above people there were 763 people (110 men, 167 women and 484 children) who were exempted and unregistered. They were freed from the restriction of the CT Act. A total number of 163 acres of land was brought under cultivation by the Yurukalas. The crop raised in Sitanagaram did not thrive well. The Yield was very poor. See Government of Madras, Home Department, *G.O. No. 3953, dt. 20th July* 1939 pp. 31-32 Government of Madras.

116. *Government of Madras, Administration Report on Kallar Reclamation, Korava Reclamation, Yenadi Reclamation (Criminal Tribes) and settlements for 1947-1948,* superintendent Government Press, Madras, 1949, pp. 36-39.
117. *Ibid,* p. 37.
118. *Ibid,* p. 38.
119. *Home Department, G.O. No. 2960, dt. 2nd August 1948,* p. 22.
120. Government of Madras, *Administration Report on Kallar Reclamation, Korava Reclamation, Yanadi Reclamation (Criminal Tribes) and settlements for 1948-49,* Madras, 1950, pp. 14-15.
120. *Home Department, G.O. No. 3587, dt. 16th November 1946.* p. 38.
121. *Ibid,* p. 34.
122. *Ibid,* p. 35.
123. Administration Report on Kallar Reclamation, Korava Reclamation, Yanadi Reclamation and settlements for 1950-51, Govt. Press, Madras, 1952.
124. Government of Madras, *Administration Report on Habitual offenders Settlements for 1951-52,* Madras 1953, p. 1.
125. See *Home Department, G.O. No.* 2900, dt. 8th August 1952. pp. 4-5.
126. V., Lalitha, 'A Profile of Sitanagarams settlement', *proceedings of Andhra Pradesh History Congress, 17th session held at Guntur, 1986,* pp. 171-177.
127. Government of Madras, *Administration Report on Kallar Recelamation, Korava Reclamation, Yanadi Reclamation (Criminal Tribes) and Settlements for 1949-50,* Superintendent Govt. Press, Madras, 1951, pp. 11-12.
128. Lalitha, 1995 : p. 144.
129. Hemalatha Lavanam, *Jeevana Prabhatam (Telugu),* Vijayawada, 1984, p. 3. Also by the same author *Nerastula Samskarana (Reform of the criminals)* (Telugu), Vijayawada, 1985, p. 4 and *Problems of Denotified Tribes – An Experiment on Stuartpuram,* Vijayawada, 1975.
130. Lalitha 1995 : p. 147.
131. See Captain Robilliard of the Salvation Army, Manager of the Stuartpuram Criminal Tribes Settlement, Bapatla, Madras, *Written Statement on the Work of Sturtpuram Settlement,* p. 6 Stuartpuram settlement was opened on the 1st June, 1914. Few families lived at No. 8 division, known then as Ratnapuram in a few dilapidated huts. Since the settlement was opened by Mr. Stuart the then acting chief

secretary to Government of Madras, It was called as Stuartpuram settlement.

132. Government of Madras, *Note showing the progress made in the settlement of Criminal Tribes in the Madras Presidency upto September, 1916,* Madras, 1917, p. 7.
133. See *Home (Judicial) Department, G.O. No. 1093, dt. 16th May 1918,* p. 1.
134. *Note, 1916,* p. 7.
135. See *Home (Judicial) Department, G.O. No. 305, dated 7th February 1918,* p. 1.
136. See *Home (Judicial) Department, G.O. No. 3003, dated 3rd December, 1920,* p. 1.
137. See *Home (Judicial) Department, G.O. No. 1298, dated 6th September 1921,* p. 1.
138. See *Home (Judicial) Department, G.O. No. 357, dated 13th May 1921,* p. 2.
139. See *Home (Judicial) Department, G.O. No. 2233, dated 29th September 1919,* p. 4.
140. See *Home (Judicial) Department, G.O. No. 2150, dated 20th August 1936,* p. 1.
141. See *Home (Judicial) Department, G.O. No. 716, dated 30th March 1917,* p. 1.
142. Note, 1925, p. 8.
143. *Home (Judicial) Department, G.O. No. 212, dt. 1st February 1917,* p. 3. *Also see Home Judicial Department G.O. No. 1579, dt. 1st August 1917,* p. 1.
144. See *Judicial Department, G.O. No. 2491, dated 12th October 1915,* p. 1.
145. *Also see Home (Judicial) Department, G.O. No. 1579, dated 1st August 1917,* p. 1.
146. See *Home (Judicial) Department, G.O. No. 305, dated 7th February 1918,* p. 1.
147. See *Home (Judicial) Department, Memorandum No. 2123/A-4, dt 25th September 1917,* TNA.
148. See *Home (Judicial) Department, G.O. No. 625, dt. 18th March 1918,* p. 1.
149. See *Home (Judicial) Department, G.O. No. 818, dated 5th April 1918,* p. 2.
150. See *Home (Judicial) Department, G.O. No. 1234, dated 22nd March 1918,* p. 3. See *Home (Judicial) Department, G.O. No. 1402, dated 13th June 1918,* p. 1.
151. See *Home (Judicial) Department, G.O. No. 1224, dated 20th May 1918,* p. 3.
152. See *Home (Judicial) Department, G.O. No. 1402, dated 13th June 1918,* p. 4.
153. See *Home (Judicial) Department, G.O. No. 795, dated 4th April 1918,* p. 3.
154. See *Home (Judicial) Department, G.O. No. 2163, dated 23rd September 1918,* p. 1. *Also see Judicial Department, G.O. No. 553, dt. 28th April 1922,* p. 1.
155. See Government of Madras, *Public Works and Labour Department, G.O. No. 1654 L., dt. 6th July 1928,* p. 3. *Also see Home (Judicial) Department, G.O. No. 475, dated 19th February 1920,* p. 2.
156. See *Home (Judicial) Department, G.O. No. 2074, dated 18th August 1916,* p. 1.
157. See *Home (Judicial) Department, G.O. No. 475, dated 19th February 1920.*
158. See, Meena Radha Krishna, 'From Tribal Community to Working class consciousness case of Yerukula women', *Economic and Political Weekly, Vol. XXIV, No. 17, April 29, 1989,* pp. 3-4.

159. See *Law (General) Department, G.O. No. 3187, dated, 14-11-1924,* p. 1, APSA.
160. See *Public Works (Labour) Department, G.O. No. 1551, dated, 20th July 1927,* p. 4.
161. See, *Public Works (Labour) Department, G.O. No. 170, dated 21st January 1931,* p. 3. APSA. *Also see Public Works and Labour Department, G.O. No. 1623 L., dt., 1st August 1932,* p. 1.
162. See *Public works (Labour) Department, G.O. No. 1926, dated 30th July 1931,* p. 3. APSA. *Also see, Public Works and Labour Department, G.O. No. 1662 L., dated 1st August 1932,* p. 1.
163. See *Public Works (Labour) Department, G.O. No. 170, dated 21st January 1931,* p. 4. APSA. *Also see Public works and Labour Department, G.O. No. 1452 L., dated 24th June 1935,* p. 1.
164. See Government of Madras, *Administration Report of the Inspector General of Police, During the Year 1936,* Government Superintendent Press, Madras, 1937, p. 1. Also see, *Home (Judicial) Department, G.O. No. 716, dated 30th March 1917,* p. 2., APSA.
165. See *Public Works (Labour) Department, G.O. No. 2671, dated 6th December 1934,* p. 4. *Also see Public Works and Labour Department, G.O. No. 1551L., dated 20th July 1927,* p. 3.
166. See, *Law (General) Department, G.O. No. 1714, dt. 22nd October 1921,* p. 4. APSA. The Manager of the Settlement during the year 1937-38 was Major H. Stevens.
167. *Home Department (Judicial) G.O. No. 2615, dated 13th December 1917,* p. 1. *Also see Home Department Judicial, G.O. No. 1592, dt. 13th August 1917,* p. 1.
168. See *Public Works (Labour) Department, G.O. No. 973L, dated 3rd April 1928,* p. 1. The Manager of Stuartpuram Settlement during the year 1950-51 was Brigadier F. Ratna Singh.
169. See Government of Madras, *Administration Report on Habitual Offenders Settlements for 1951-52,* Superintendent Government Press, Madras, 1953, p. 1.
170. See Government of Madras, *Administrative Report on Habitual Offenders settlements for the year 1952-53,* Government Superintendent Press, Madras 1954, p. 10.
171. See Government of Madras, *Administration Report on Kallar Reclamation, Korava Reclamation, Yenadi Reclamation (Criminal Tribes) and settlements for 1947-48,* Superintendent Government Press, Madras, 1949, p. 14.
172. See Lavanam and Hemalatha Lavanam, 'The Criminal background of Stuartpurm, Althiest Centre Vijayawada, pp. 10-14. Also see by the same authors, *Mrutyma Amrutargamaya,* Autobiography of Smt. Hemaltha Lavanam, Visalandra Publications, Vijayawada 2004, pp. 1-10 (Telugu).
173. See *Public Works (Labour) Department, G.O. No. 137, dated 19.1. 1927,* p. 1, APSA.

174. Siddhapuram Settlement was started during the year 1913 for the benefit of Waddars. The Waddars were employed by the Public Works Department on the Siddapuram tank Project in Kurnool district. The Government settled the Waddars as agricultural labourers. A block of 650 acres of forest land was allotted for the opening of the settlement by the government in 1918.
175. See *Home (Judicial) Department, G.O. No.1860, dated 25th October 1920,* The Siddhapuram tank project work was completed during the year 1919. The Government did not provide any work for the waddars. The strength of the waddars in Siddhapuram during the year 1920 was 65 males, 65 females and 74 children. 150 acres of forest land was distributed to the Waddars. However, only 15 acres were brought under cultivation by them. Cumbly-weabing was started as a subsidiary industry for the waddars. See *Home Department, G.O. No. 2661, dated 25th October 1920,* p. 1.
176. The wool industry was developed in Siddhapuram during the year 1920. There were 12 looms working during the year 1921. The Waddars manufactured 182 comblies. The cumblies were sold locally. A wool shed was constructed and a total number of 18 males and 15 females were engaged in the wool shed. The males were given 5 annas and the females were paid 3 annas per day. See *Public works (Labour) Department, G.O. No. 137, dated. 19th January 1927,* p. 1.
177. Owing to unfavourable seasons the cultivation activities of the waddars was a great failure. Some waddars were employed in weaving industry. There was no market for the cumblies prepared by the Waddars. The police department refused to purchase the cumblies prepared by the Waddars.
178. See *Public Works (Labour) Department, G.O. No. 1843, dated 25th August 1927,* p. 1. *Also see public Works and Labour Department, G.O. No. 1764, dt 19th August 1932,* p. 3.
179. See *Public Works (Labour) department, G.O. No. 2190, dated 28th July 1930,* p. 7. *Also see, Public Works (Labour) department, G.O. No. 2671, dated 6th December 1934,* p. 4.
180. See *Public Works (Labour) Department, G.O. No. 2671, dated 6th December 1934,* p. 5. *Also see Home Department, G.O. No. 1123, Miscellaneous series, dated 26th June 1936,* p. 1.
181. See *Home Department, G.O. No. 1217, dated 6th March 1939,* p. 4. *Also see, Home Department, G.O. No. 3889, dated 23rd September 1940,* p. 1.
182. See *Home Department G.O. No. 568, dated 23rd February 1944,* p. 1.
183. See *Home Department, G.O. No. 2113, dated 12th May 1927,* p. 1.
184. See *Public Works (Labour) Department, GO No. 2671, dated 6th December 1934,* p. 5. APSA.
185. See *Home Department, G.O. No. 568, dt. 23rd February 1944,* p. 1. TNA.
186. See, *Home Department, G.O. No. 2113, dt. 13th July 1944,* p. 1.

187. See, *Home department, G.O. No. 3889, dated 23rd September* 1940, p. 2.
188. See *Home department, G.O. No. 2482, dated 9th July 1940,* p. 1.
189. The following were the Managers of the settlement during the year 1951-52: N. R. Vasudeva Nayudu was the manager of the settlement during the year 1938. Janab Syed Abdul Gaffar was appointed upto 3rd August 1951, Later, V. Ramanathaiah upto 2nd May 1951. G. Audiseshiah (Accountant in Charge) from 3rd May 1951 to 11th May 1951, T. Gopala Rao from 12th May 1951 to 1st October 1951, G. Sreenivasulu Naidu from 2nd October 1951, T. Govindarajulu from 4th to 18th August 1951, K. Sreemantham (Accountant in charge) from 19th August to 7th November 1951, K.V. R. Patnaik form 8th November to 2nd December 1951 and T. Govinda Rajulu form 3rd December 1951 to 9th March 1952. These managers were constantly absent from many days and the responsibility of the administration of the waddars were given charge to the Accountants in the office. The Inspector of police Atmakur used to supervise the settlement. The total population of waddars on 31st March 1952 in Siddhapuram was 613 people consisting of 172 males, 173 females and 268 Children. See Government of Madras, *Administration Report on Habitual offenders Settlements for 1951-52,* Government Superintendent Press, Madras 1953, p. 4. Also see, Government of Madras, *Report on Habitual offenders settlement for 1953-54,* Government Superintendent Press, Madras, 1955, p. 6.
190. See *Home Department, Memorandum No. 29831-G/47-7 dated 4th December* 1947, p. 1.
191. See *Home Department, Memorandum No. 5539-G/ 48-2,dated 11th February* 1948.
192. See *Home Department, G.O. No. 2960, dated 2nd August 1948,* p. 3.
193. See *Home Department, G.O. No. 2877, dated 10th July 1940,* p. 1.
194. *See Home Department, G.O. No. 2482, dated 1st January 1940,* p. 1.
195. *See Home Department, G.O. No. 2877, dated 10th July 1940,* p. 3.
196. See *Development Department, G.O. No. 238, dated 31st January 1940,* p. 1.
197. See, *Education and Public Health Department, GO No. 204, dated 29th January 1937,* p. 4.
198. Government of Madras, *Administration Report on Habitual Offenders Settlements for 1951-52,* Madras 1953, p. 6.
199. Sew *Law (General) Department, G.O. No. 3187, dated 14.11.1924,* p.1. APSA.
200. See, *Public Works (Labour) Department, G.O. No. 1551, dated 20th July 1927,* p. 4.
201. See *Public Works (Labour) Department, G.O. No. 170, dated 21.1.1931,* p. 3. APSA
202. See, *Public Works (Labour) Department, G.O. No. 1926, dated 30th July 1931,* p. 4. APSA

203. See, *Public Works (Labour) Department, G.O. No. 170, dated 21.1.1931,* p. 4. APSA.
204. See, *Administration Report of the Inspector General of Police, 1936,* Madras, 1937, p. 26.
205. Interview with K.R. Samanna an ex-settler of Siddapuram Settlement dt. 22.11.2006
206. *Ibid.*
207. *Ibid.*
208. Haikerwal, B.S., *"Economic and Social Aspects of Crime in India", Lucknow, 1934,* p. 166. Also see, Government Andhra Pradesh, *Report on the Administration of the District Police of H.E.H. The Nizams Government, 1918*: 27-28.
209. *Home Judicial Department, G.O. No. 1678,* Dated 13th March 1916.
210. The remnants of a Fort, jail, Post Office and temple are still there in Lingala. One bungalow is used as the present post office. It shows how much attention the Nizam's government paid on Lingala settlements. Yerukulas were brought from the surrounding areas and were kept in the jail which was called as *'Juramfis'*. They used to get the written permission of the police officers to leave the settlement for going to some other place. For this, the well known social worker Sangam Laxmi Bayamma pleaded for their freedom. Then the 'Juramfis' was removed.
211. Haikerwal, B.S., *op. cit.,* p. 166.
212. Lalitha, V., *'The Making of Criminal Tribes Patterns and Transition', Madras, 1995,* p. 49. Also see, Govt of Andhra Pradesh, *Report on the Administration of the District Police of H.E.H. The Nizams Government, 1918*: 24.
213. Edgar Thurston, *'Castes and Tribes of Southern India', Vol. 3, Madras, 1909.*
214. Sayyad Siraz-ul Hassan, *"The Castes and Tribes of the H.E.H. The Nizam's Domination"*, New Delhi, 1989.
215. Government of Madras, *The Chenchus and the Madras Police,* Madras, Part I and Part II Madras, 1921.
216. Giridawar, an Officer in-Charge was responsible in supplying them agricultural implements. Interview with Peram Hussain, ex-sarpanch in the settlement, Lingala, 20-10-2006. Palaparti Veeraiah, *"What we did" an article on "* Andhra Rastra Adimjati Sevak Sangh published in the report of the 7th Conference from scheduled tribes and tribal (scheduled) areas Guntur, Andhra Pradesh, 9th and 10th November 1964, New Delhi.
217. Interview with M. David, Lingala settlement, 20.10.2006.
218. Kapila Vatsayan, Traditions of Indian Folk dance, 1976. Samata, R.K. and L. Shayam Sundar, 'The Lambadas their Socio-Psychological and Agro-Economic Characteristics", *Man in India, Vol. 65, No. 3, September 1985.*

4

Criminal Tribes Settlements: The Role of Christian Missionaries

I

Introduction

The British Government framed the CTA of 1871 to prevent crime which was supposed to be committed by some nomodic and wandering tribes in India. Prior to that, the British rulers dealt with the 'criminals' according to the regulation XXVI of 1793 and Act XXX of 1836. Later on the Indian Penal Code came into existence in 1860. It was in 1871 the CTA was passed and later it was amended in the years 1897, 1911, 1924. The Act of 1911, empowered the local governments to declare a tribe to be a CT. During the first half of the 19th century, north India was plagued by thugs and dacoits. The Government of India took special measures to suppress crime and improve the situation. This was entrusted in 1830, to a new Department, popularly known as Thaggi and Dacoity department. There are many criminals and wandering tribes of India who from times immemorial have earned their livelihood by practicing nefarious acts of the same kind, which the gypsies in Europe adopted until the 2nd half of the 19th Century. These tribes are known as CTs, because men and women were born within its fold.[1]

II

Official Policy of the Government

To reform these people it was necessary to teach them some means of earning a livelihood. Unless this objective was achieved, one cannot expect the ex-'criminals' to be free from crime. Therefore, a scheme was worked out to deal with them separately from ordinary criminals. This scheme is called the establishment of CT Settlements' in India. Under Part II of the CT Act the local governments were empowered, with the consent of the government of India, to settle any notified criminal tribe in a definite locality where endeavours were made to convert the settlers into respectable citizens. A supervisory agency was required to enforce discipline and to organise employment. The British government was of the opinion that the management should be placed under the non-official agencies. They were also of the opinion that, as far as possible, some professed religious or philanthropic agency should be attached to each settlement. Secondly, the settlement should be within the linguistic area where the settlers follow their language.[2]

The policy in establishing settlements was to provide the settlers adequate means of earning and honest livelihood. Agriculture being the main occupation of our country, the possession of land was considered a potent agent of self-respect. The government sanctioned land in the name of philanthropic agencies to support the settlers. The government wanted to assign a position of the land to a settler when he proved himself to be an industrious person and a person with good conduct. Intermediate Industries such as silkworm rearing, weaving, mat and rope-making and gardening were also introduced (for the weaker members or for the settlers in their spare time) by the managers of the settlements.[3]

III

The Beginning of the Salvation Army's Work in India

The direct control over settlements had been entrusted to the district Magistrates, the Commissioner and the Deputy Inspector General of Police, but the management was given to the philanthropic agencies like Salvation Army, American Baptist Mission, London Mission, Canadian Mission, etc. The SA was very active in India for organising the work for the poor and depressed classes. William Booth Tucker took the Gospel of Jesus to them. Frederick Booth Tucker listened to the speeches of William Booth Tucker in London and felt that fire in his own heart which was kindled afresh. Then he became the officer of the SA and Telugu country in Madras Presidency. With his influence he became the Officer of the SA and entered into the Telugu land. He wore the prison dress of criminals and declared that his stay in jail was a time of rich spiritual refreshment. An important Government Representative, Mr.Tweedy, (Commissioner of

Rohilkhand), attended the SA meeting at Bareilly in 1908. He spoke to Commissioner Booth Tucker about the possibilities of work among the CTs in India. Booth Tucker visited Gorakhpur where three hundred families of CTs were living under the police care. The SA began its work with the group and succeeded in starting agricultural and industrial settlements for CTs in five provinces of India. It had also opened houses and schools for the children of these tribes. By 1923, the SA had 24 centres for the care of 'Criminal' Tribes consisting of about 7,840 people in total. Booth Tucker strove hard for the upliftment of CTs and to see their children become useful citizens of India. Thus the SA established homes for destitute and innumerable welfare activities such as educational, medical and industrial. He took the care of homeless and unfed the drunkard, the criminal, and the harlot. They believed in conversion to Christianity and persuaded people accordingly. Social service without spiritual impulse was in their view, ' Body without soul."[4]

After coming out of prison-cells the ex-criminals found themselves cursed with the brand of the Jailbird: 'Far from home, character gone, and with no one to fall back upon for counsel, or to give them a helping hand."[5] This contamination of prison life, made the SA to take up the work of criminal rehabilitation. When Mr. Tweedy, then Commissioner of Rohilkhand and member of the government of the United Provinces requested Booth Tucker to take up this work, the latter started an experiment with Doms. At several places, they continued the same kind of work.[6] (Fazalpur, Kanth, Bareily, Sahebzunj, Gorkhpur, Kalyanpur and many other places.) In Punjab, many philanthropic societies worked for the uplift of the CTs placed in the Settlements : (1) Canadian Mission (2) Chief Khalsa Diwan (3) Dosamaj (4) Anjuman Islamia (5) Ahmedia Society (6) Ahmedia Anjuman Ishand-I Islam (7) Sanatana Dharma Sabha (8) Arya Samaj (9) The Punjab Hindu Sabha. Thus, the SA opened Settlements in almost all the states in India and abroad.[7] (Telugu speaking areas in Madras, Uganda, Philadelphia, Nepal, Bombay, Orissa, Travancore, Bengal, Madras,Tiruvanantapuram, etc).

In Madras Presidency, the SA started several settlements and proved to be very successful. Thus, the policy pursued is to take charge of wandering tribes and interning them into the settlements. The inmates were carefully supervised. They were given honest employment. Their children were sent to schools. During nights they should return to their huts and spend their time within the enclosures under a strict guard. The settlements served the CTs more or less like open Jails than reformatories. The government started these settlements on two assumptions. Kapadia said : 'People born in a particular group, irrespective of caste, creed, sex, age were considered to be criminals', secondly the policy of 'once a criminal always a criminal' was followed.[8]

The SA was incharge of Sitanagaram and Stuartpuram settlements in Andhra Pradesh and many other settlements in Madras City.[9] A nucleus was formed at Sitanagaram by keeping some women there belonging to Yerukulas whose male relatives happened to be in prison. In December 1912 the Madras Government sanctioned the grant, both recurring and non-recurring, to the SA to assist the undertaking. Major Mackenizie of the SA took charge of and responsibility of Sitanagaram settlement.[10] Their number became unmanageable. Therefore, the British Government established another settlement at Bethapudi which came to be known as Stuartpuram settlement subsequently. Agriculture was the chief means of livelihood and the other main occupation practiced was stone quarrying at Sitanagaram. Hannyngton, the then Deputy Inspector General of Police Madras presidency, reported that the work done by Bawden of ABM in Kavali settlement and Robilliard of SA at Stuartpuram was of exceptionally high order. As there was demand for more land from the settlers the Government gave more land for agriculture. Supervision was strictly enforced. This minimized the number of absconders. Schools were started in the settlements. The weavers attached to the school containing looms provided employment for pupils who attended the schools. The other small-scale handicraft industries such as mat making, smithy and carpentry were instituted in the settlement.[11]

In the year 1917, the SA decided to close Sitanagaram settlement. The settlement has faced two serious epidemics, cholera and small-pox. The settlers became restless and began absconding in large numbers. Later on, due to the availability of employment, a fairly good rainfall caused for the improvement of the settlement. The settlement manager used to provide them some kind of employment for their maintenance.[12] Weaving, carpet making, stone-dressing and other miscellaneous avenues of employment kept them busy throughout the year. The special feature of Sitanagaram was that it was a penal settlement, scheduled for the incorrigible members of CTs. The conditions were good until the control and supervision was transferred to the government. When the settlers could not find proper employment, the SA and the government initiated steps, in consultation with the managers of the settlement, to send them to Anamallais to work in the plantations.[13]

IV

The Beginning of the American Baptist (Telugu) Missions' Work for Crimanal Tribes

The ABM Union, having carried on missions on the eastern side of the Bay of Bengal from 1814 to 1835, resolved to establish its Mission among the Telugus. Rev. S.S. Day landed at Vizagapatnam in 1836. He went to Madras and from there he established the missionary work at Nellore in February, 1836. Rev. Day returned to America in 1845. He was broken in health due to disease and non-availability of missionary families to keep his family in Nellore, during his absence.[14] Later on, Lynam Jewett offered his services. In 1860, Jewett spent three months in Ongole and baptised many converts from the outcaste weavers belonging to Mala (Harijan) Community. By 1926, the number on the church rolls went upto 1,40,000. Later on they formed new stations in Kurnool, Cumbum, Narasaraopet, Bapatla, Vinukonda, Podili and other places.[15]

The, ABM missionaries tried to seize control of education to mould the minds of men at their most impressionable age. Many of the so-called untouchables fell under the spell of their influence to gain status which they had lost in Hindu Society. Thus Christianity offered educational and material advantages.[16] More significantly, it gave them a feeling of self-respect and equality in an otherwise unequal society based on ritual hierarchy and economic inequality. For instance, Kavali settlement was commenced when the twenty Yerukala families came to Bullerd, asking him to admit them into the Mission and signified their willingness to become Christians. He considered it as his duty to take interest in them. Further more, Mr. Bullard had been planning to establish a settlement for the depressed classes at Kavali. He expressed his desire to the District Magistrate and the Superintendent of Police, Nellore, Diwan Bahadur R. Ramachandra Rao and C.M. Akkinson respectively. Both of them were favourable. He initiated the matter with J. M. Backer of Ongole and J. Heitriches of Ramapatnam. They gave their approval and provided temporary financial assistance to a tune of Rs. 1,200 towards employment of the Yerukala families.[17]

Such a work at Kavali was exceptionally good, the place being a notably healthy one, with abundance of unoccupied wasteland in the surrounding villages, which was cultivable or reclaimable with enough water supply. Furthermore, the ABM Mission also had adequate accommodation for the purposes of supervision, schooling and industrial work, to make a beginning. The ABM readily accepted the proposal to provide as far as possible, the necessary conditions for social, industrial, educational and hygienic improvement of the criminal settlement, if the government is willing to grant an initial sum of Rs. 100, per family and a recurring grant of Rs. 50 per annum per family as well as a permanent grant of 3 to 5 acres of land, unoccupied but tillable or reclaimable per family, anywhere within a workable distance of their settlement. Bullard wanted to keep all the settlers under his direct supervision so that he may initiate his experiments and rehabilitate them until the Mission achieved its goal. The brightest feature of the settlement was the school, ably managed by Miss Bullard, Diwan Bahadur R Ramachandra Rao. The then District Magistrate, Nellore, wrote to the Chief Secretary, Govt. of Madras, that "About 40 children turned out and impressed me favourably. They are bright and clean and are strong in contrast with the other children."[18]

In 1914, Bawden took charge of the settlement and earned the reputation of an efficient manager. In January, 1917, Bitragunta reformatory settlement was established both with the Yerukalas and Dasaries. He kept the members of the settlement busy throughout the year. With regard to their religion and religious beliefs, these settlers were afraid of evil spirits, but generally not god-fearing. Righteousness will only be acquired by means of worshipping God. They believed that the solution lies in the faith of God. Settlers who wished to participate in the daily routine, morning rollcall and morning prayers were arranged together. Sunday used to be a holiday. A minimum of two hours in the morning and one in the afternoon were set apart for preaching. Churches were established and at Bitragunta many members of the settlement became Christians. Evangelists were arranged for each of these settlements. In Kavali and Allur churches there were many Yerukulas and Dasaries members of the settlement became Baptists. Rev. Bewden said that neither compulsion nor pressure was brought upon the settlers to become Christians. When Mr. Mitche Innes questioned Bawden about the religion of the settlement, the latter said that "some of the settlers were Hindus. They were mostly animists."[19]

Surprisingly, in the year 1915, some of the Yerukulas gave a petition to the Chief Secretary, Government of Madras. They stated that they were brought from their native places and made members of Kavali settlement. In addition to the denial of the necessities of life, the ex-'criminals' represented their hardships to the authorities. A petitioner remarked: "If we ask the manager of the settlement why we are so unjustly treated, he beats us. Every morning, men and women were asked to attend the congregations, while children were left alone in the huts, unattended. Thus are we tortured in the settlement by the managers", says the petitioner.[20]

The Petitioners humbly prayed the Governor to protect them from the hands of the settlement managers. Their clan consisted of five gangs. They were not allowed to visit their homeland to pay taxes.[21] This was not the first or the last petition, but they requested the government to allow them to go back to their own native villages.[22] They submitted another petition to the Governor-in-Council, Madras, about coercion in religious matters. Botchu Venkaiah, Guravaiah, Kampa Peda Nagaiah stated in the petition that the settlers were compelled to attend the morning rollcall in the church premises and they are asked to remove their head-wear (turbans) during the prayer hours. If they refuse to do prayers, they were detained for an hour as a punishment.[23] Children also were asked to do prayers at home and in the school. Sunday Prayers were compulsory.[24] Thus, the petitioners humbly begged the authorities to investigate their difficulties and give them freedom of caste and religion.[25] The Bombay Enquiry Committee of 1939 made a systematic study of the working of the criminal settlements under the Christian missionary organizations.[26] The Committee strongly condemned the missionaries on the following grounds: 1. Scriptural instructions were compulsory in the schools. 2. Discrimination was shown by the Mission Societies in favour of the Christian settlers as against non-Christians. 3. The Mission Societies had obviously an interest in propagating their faith and 4. The Settlement accounts were misused by the missionaries.[27] For example, in Sholapur settlement, pamphlets were frequently published at a cost of Rs. 500 and the cost was charged to settlement accounts.[28]

V

Politics of the Salvation Army

General William Booth was the founder of the SA. Commissioner Booth Tucker was the SA Officer to India.[29] The Salvation Army came to India for the first time during the year 1882. The SA worked among 26,000,000 people in several districts of Andhra Pradesh and in India.[30] Brigadier Blowers was the in charge of the Army's work in Madras and the Telugu Country. Later Mildred Mackenzie was appointed as Incharge of SA in the Telugu Country. Brigadier Blowers told Mackenzie, "You have to start a new venture at a place near the town of Bapatla."[31]

The SA managers quickly adopted the Indian way. They learned to love the Telugu people. One SA manager stated: "I loved them as soon as I saw them."[32] They took Telugu names while entering into the Telugu field. They wore Indian garments. European clothes were discarded. The turban, dhoti, coat and shoulder cloth were adopted. Food was taken in Indian style. The SA officers quickly learned the Indian etiquette. The greatest barrier to the missionary was the language. The desire to speak with the people, helped by a natural linguistic ability made this task easier. They gradually picked up the native language (Telugu) and used the language. By repeated usage of the language, they were able to speak, and understand Telugu and made others to understand.

The SA relied on the noisy methods of street demonstration, flags, singing and excitement. Further, the men had to go to work, the women urged to keep themselves clean and tidy. The Salvation Army thought a man, who cannot talk, cannot exhort or convince the people is not suitable for bringing reformation.[33] The SA officers gave training to the cadets in Chinaganjam Training Centre. The training was for nine months. After completion of their training they were sent to the respective villages to teach the Christian way. The Officers kept in touch with the cadets. The visiting officers enquired the problems of young people living in surroundings and provided more comforts.[34] Within a number of 'lower' Sudra castes, typical mass movements had developed. The largest accession is from the Yerukalas. Next came the Waddars and then the Yanadis and Gollas. These castes move more rapidly and on a wider front. Many families of Yerukalas were converted to Christianity. It was stated that: "All are convinced that Christianity is true and offers the only Salvation of Yerukalas. Some have worshipped their idols so long it will require a few years to banish them from their minds. Some enjoy their sins too much to give them up all at once. But all will be Christians in five or ten years."[35] There were three main reasons for the conversions of Yerukulas and Waddars into Christianity. They were: (1) The changed lives of out caste converts, (2) The loss of faith in Hinduism, and (3) The influence of the schools and churches.[36] The SA converted many Hindus in Chellakoor. What would it mean if we accept Christianity? Asked the Hindus. The SA Officer replied: "It means to break with old life, giving up idols, giving up all old practices of witchcraft and superstition, breaking with every harmful practice, abstaining from intoxicating liquor.[37] Chellakoor became the SA village. A hall was built for worship. An officer was sent into preach. This made the Hindu priests angry.[38]

The Tenali division is a caste bound place. Hindu influence was very strong. There is no place for a Christian. In a village called 'Ithanagarapadu' the SA manager converted many Hindus into Christianity. Ithanagarapadu became the centre of Christianity to 'throw away the horror of darkness, idolatory, witchcraft and superstition'. Appicuttla was six miles away from Bapatla. The SA manager said: "It may mean little to the reader but speaks volumes to one who has laboured there."[39] The old life of drinking, revelry, witchcraft and demon worship with all its exciting horrors retained a hold on their minds. It was the most discouraging place of the district. Disheartened about the whole village one SA officer said: "Money and time could be used more profitably elsewhere."[40]

For the Hindus a Brahmin or the Dasary was to perform the marriage ceremony according to Hindu rites. The SA maintained that "It was not lawful for any member of Christian body to marry under Hindu vows. A Christian should marry in Christian way under Christian vows."[41] Notice was served to the disloyal members. It was stated that : "Those, who claim to be Christian and inform to the Hindu priests to perform the marriages, the Hindu priest is acting contrary to the Christian Marriage Act. In doing so the Hindu priest is liable for prosecution."[42]

The Christian Marriage Act of 1872, strengthened and upheld the law of Christian marriage; a severe penalty was given upon one performing unauthorised marriage between persons-one, or both of whom is (or/are) a Christian (or Christians).[43] One SA officer said:

"Christian standards must be held high, there must be no lowering of our principles. . . . Our people generally accepted the rule of no mixed marriages. A Christian Community, thus a new Christian family began."[44]

The Hindus were backed for this. They performed the marriages. Charges were filed before the Magistrate. The Magistrates were thoroughly frightened. Such cases were simply sent to the higher courts for decision.[45] The SA put the young Indian men and women on a period of probation. They were taught the SA doctrine, the ten Commandments, the plan of Salvation, and the sanctity of marriage vows were explained to them.[46] The managers after completing the probation period granted permission for marriage. The SA flag waved over the couple. Many people gather for open marriages. It aroused sensational interest. The surrounding neighbourhood realised that the status of a Christian couldn't be ignored.

The summer season brought an awful situation in the rural parts of India. Cholera, the dreadful disease. It is believed to be a Goddess. The Goddess was referred to as "Ammah"(mother). She was the mother of terror and must be appeased. The priests 'persuaded' their rites to leave her the village. The sickness spread house to house. The dead and the dying lay side by side. The medical authorities went from house to house pouring medicine down the throats of all who had any hope of recovery. The dead were taken for burial. In one grave the SA Officer buried 30 bodies.[47] The SA opened its offices at three centres in the Telugu country namely Nellore, Bapatla and Elore. The SA called it a social movement. The SA worked in Kavali and Bhogulpur in the Godavari Delta. The places were noted for its rowdy elements. Drinking resulted to fighting. The people were husky, hard headed, hardworking and hardliving.[48] They gospelled in the marketplaces. The SA worked for the labouring classes, agriculturists and the depressed classes.

The SA embarked with new ventrues in India in 1910. The Government had approached the Army asking their help with certain social problems. This was considered as the most demanding work from the SA. The Government found the successful work done by the Missionaries such as the SA, the American Baptist Telugu Mission and other Philantrophic agencies in reforming these people. The SA was the first organisation that stepped into the activities of the CTs of the country.[49] They started their work with the 'Doms' rehabilitation in Uttar Pradesh.[50] The successful management by the SA attracted the attention of all the state Governments in India. The Madras Government invited the SA to take charge of some of the managements connected with the CT settlements and homes. As Dadabhoy Naroji said: "The Salvation Army's help has been requisitioned from time to time. Whether it is Salvation Army or whether it is any other reforming body, the religious zeal is very often a necessary element in pursuing difficult task of people of this kind and winning them from evil ways."[51] William Booth Tucker, the founder of Salvation Army in India, was known for his selfless service.[52] Thus the SA in Andhra managed successfully two settlements in Guntur district, one at Seethanagaram (1913) and the other at Stuartpuram (1914).[53]

An important contact made by the Salvation Army in 1910 was with a wandering gang of Yerukula tribe people. They were known to the then Government as hereditary 'criminals'. The police had their record and many heads of the families were lodged in jail. The Superintendents of Police in Krishna, Nellore, Guntur and Chittor districts with the then Home Member of the Madras Government Harold Stuart approached the SA. They asked the SA to take charge of the settlements for these tribes. They understood that SA could deal the problem in settling the wandering people in industrial and agricultural colonies. It was stated that : "The Yerukalas was originally merchants. Their fore-fathers carried salt, grain and other commodities, on the backs of pack animals, but in the march of progress, railroads came and transportation was taken out of their hands. Their living was gone; they knew no trade; they resorted to crime."[54]

The SA Officer Mackenzie was appointed as Superintendent to work on CTs in Telugu country of Madras presidency in 1913. First he started with 5000 men, women and children. The first settlement opened by the SA in Madras presidency was at Seethanagaram. The settlement is near the old railway colony near Bezwada.[55] Mackenzie was given liberty to visit the Jails. He talked with the men in the Jails. He selected the people from the Jails as the first settlers for the colony. The men promised to come to settlement with their wives, children and families under SA authority. Only those people willing to come and live in the settlement were selected.[56] The settlers arrived in chains. They were escorted by the police. The SA removed their chains. Under the loyal authority of the SA they were left free within the limits of the colony. New batches were brought. The tribes protested and said: "They had never done anything wrong. It was the police, who were the real offenders."[57] Large gangs were brought into the settlement with donkeys. These tribes men transported salt from the Government salt pans to the interior places from the sea coast. On their journeys across the country they were associated with an illicit trade. They used to dispose the stolen property of other gangs. Thus they were brought into the settlements.[58]

The SA faced the difficulty of finding employment for these tribes. More than 1000 people needed employment. The public works department, Bezawada entrusted the SA with deepening the irrigation canal work. The settlers were trained in stone quarrying. They climbed the rocks and blast the stones. They brought several tons of stone at once. Others processed the large quantities of broken stones. Others were employed in farm work. Hundreds of acres of farm land were at the disposal of the settlers. They were involved in other occupations like basket making, mat making, rope making, cotton weaving and spinning silk.[59] Good wages were paid.

The early days of the SA were filled with stress, struggle and despair. Discipline for these people was very difficult. Sir Harold Stuart told Macanzie: "I give you 20 years to carry out the reformation of these criminal tribes."[60] Rules were made and enforced. Alcoholic drink was banned. Sometimes drink was smuggled. This resulted to fighting. Games, competitions, entertainments were encouraged. They cannot listen to anything more than a few minutes. Questions were asked and answers were given. The people were indisciplined. They had loud conversation. The manager complained: "...Failure, defeat, gloom, depression of spirit was upon me... to escape from it all I looked up to the hill that rose, several hundred feet, by the side of the colony and decided to climb to the top. I reached the top of the hill: The sky was blue, the air clear, I looked down on my hopeless task, then in my helplessness, looked up into the face of my heavenly father."[61] The managers thought that was 'not the end of their struggle with the powers of evil, but it was the beginning of new strength and confidence' for them. The settlers were allowed to go out on a pass. The pass was issued and signed by the manager. If any Yerukula Tribe was found without a pass, the police used to arrest them. New assistants were entered into the colony. They quarreled with some people in a nearby place - Bezawada. Some people who were saved from jail showed no gratitude. They used to abscond very shortly.

The police caught hold of them and brought back to jail. When asked what was their native village they grimly replied: "Rajamundry Central Jail."[62]

Some showed their loyalty to their manager and his good advices. This influenced them in the difficult situations. The settlers showed their loyalty to the management for their work. As one manager stated: "In all my years in the midst of the settlers I never missed anything of my personal belongings. I never locked the doors while living in the settlement."[63]

It was therefore a shock and grief to the manager when the police complained on them of certain theft cases. Two offsprings were made from the original settlement Seethanagaram. 1. The prisoners home of Guntur–1913–1917; 2. The Stuartpuram Settlement–1914.[64] The prisoners home dealt with security of prisoners who had no means of support. The Government allowed the SA to bring out such men from jail. Their families were allowed to live in the prisoners home Guntur. The home was started in 1913. It worked for three years. During the war period 1914-18 the jails were opened for men who wished to join up in the labour corps. The prisoners home was closed. The people remained in the prisoners home were sent to others settlements.[65] The second settlement for the criminal tribes opened in the Telugu country was Stuartpuram settlement. Stuartpuram is in Bapatna (Guntur district) and Chirala (Prakasam district) on the Madras–New Delhi grand trunk railroad. The strength, in the beginning of the settlement, was 591 consisting of 200 males, 196 females and 295 children.[66] It was named after Stuart, the then Home member for the Madras Government.[67]

The SA introduced agriculture to transform their lifestyle. A block of 360 acres of dry land and 1500 acres in the Romperu Swamp were placed at the disposal of the SA in 1914. The new people who were brought from various places were also provided more than 525 acres of land. The SA employed some agricultural mastries from old settlers.[68] They used to instruct the new settlers on the techniques of cultivation. In order to give a better supply of water to bring greater area under cultivation a dam across the river Romperu was built in June 1919.[69] The next manager of the SA was Pearson. He constructed canals, wells and introduced new implements in agriculture. During the year 1924, the SA handed over some mango, cashewnut, coconut and other plantations to the settlers in order to boost up their incomes.[70] George Paddison proposed to build a bund in order to protect the fields from submersion of water from the swamp. The object of the pumping installation was two fold. 1. To provide water for irrigation at times of scarce supply. 2. To irrigate an additional area of land.[71]

The SA was also responsible for the opening of a railway station in 1921. It was stated that the opening of the railway station extended their income by introducing the cultivation of tomato growing.[72] The crop was excellent for them and they began to supply the corp to distant places.[73] In addition to the agricultural activity and labour work, the settlers were also provided work in an industry by name Indian Leaf Tobacco Department (ILTD), opened at a nearby village Ramanagar (Epurupalem) in 1915, and thereby created employment to these Yerukulas.[74]

The SA Officer gather the children who are not working in the fields, who are watching the village herds. They taught them the elementary rules of learning. Family prayers were conducted by the officers at night. Children read the scriptures. In this way the SA's educational work in Telugu country started. This method was pursued where no schools existed.[75] The bright young boys and girls were taken further in their search for knowledge. The first Boy's Boarding School was opened in Bapatla. Christian teachers were appointed. The headmaster was a Salvationist. The boarding school came with 60 Telugu boys. They were selected from surrounding villages. The manager and his wife became 'Father' and 'Mother' to the children.[76] Vocational training was included in the school curriculum. Weaving was introduced in the school. Weaving masters were employed. The boys produced their cloth for dhotis. Cloth was produced for marketing. It helped the school expenses. Weaving was introduced as a home industry in many villages.[77]

The SA thought that education was compulsory for the Yerukalas in the CT settlements and, therefore, started an elementary schools in 1916. Out of 481 children in Startpuram settlement alone, 250 children were school going during the year 1916.[78] The management of the schools and the employment of the school teachers were left entirely to the discretion of the SA. An interesting feature of that time was that qualified teachers were appointed in the settlement schools from the Yerukulas. Both men and women, were appointed as teachers in the school.[79] In the year 1958, the SA combined with the Inspector General of Police, opened a new high school for the children of the CT settlers. At present, more than 150 members in the settlements even received University education. This is obviously to some extent due to the efforts of the SA.

Death rate was high during the year 1915 due to influenza in CT settlements. New hospitals were built by the SA. Sub-assistant surgeon was called bi-weekly from the nearest towns and medicines were supplied for diseases like dysentery, cholera, malaria, fever, smallpox, beriberi, boils, heart diseases, stomachaches.[80] The SA paid special attention in times of cyclones, drought and other natural calamities. For the maintenance of huts, the Government of Madras used to sanction money from time to time on an average cost of Rs. 16 per hut to each family.[81]

In the beginning, the police used to consult the SA for the whereabouts of the settlers. The police could not enter the settlements without the permission of the manager of the SA.[82] The managers visited the other settlements in the presidency as well as the settlement in Bombay and Nizam dominions. This is for the exchange of ideas, on rehabilitation and reclamation policies of different managements.[83] After Independence, Indian Government removed all the powers of the SA. The authority of the managements of the CT settlements was shifted to the tribal welfare department. But still the SA continues doing its work in stuartpuram settlement. A manager, his wife and some wardens are looking after the medical dispensary, church, schools and hospitals. In the hostel there are 101 boys and 54 girls studying for 1st to S.S.C. It is also collecting land revenue for 600 acres of land which kept under its control. The settlers have a lot of faith in the SA due to its zeal, in its reformative services.[84]

VI

Conclusion

Likewise, throughout the country the Christian missionaries took up the responsibilities of ameliorating the conditions of not only ex-criminals, but also many backward communities. Their motive was proselytisation to the Christian religion. Sher Singh Sher pointed out "the Christian missionaries became unpopular for zeal of religious propagation and for getting profits from the land, labour and capital of the settlements and as a result the situation of settlers became just like that of the Hawaiian who said to a Christian missionary, when the white man came, you had the Bible and we owned the land, now we have the Bible and you have the land." Nevertheless, their services to the cause of the upliftment of CTs were laudable. The Indian Government, in recognition of the value of their work, bestowed upon a number of SA Officers Kaisar-I-Hind medals. Furthermore, some of the ex-criminals still remember the missionaries and their services. The missionaries did not consider their work among these tribes as charity. It was not their business to pay these people wages or maintain them. The Salvation Army, The American Baptist Mission and other agencies were looked upon with suspicion. However, they lived with them, clothed in their attire, and mixed with them closely in performing their duties. Their sincerity, determination of purpose and devotion to the cause made them successful in their efforts. However, their efforts were not intended to solve this thorny problems on a permanent footing. Their efforts should have been followed up by more enduring and serious rehabilitative measures by the Government. Also that the ex-criminals, though benefited by the efforts of the missionaries, their settlement life was an obstacle for them to come into the mainstream society. This was not realised by them nor by the Government. This aspect of the problems still remains unsolved, in all the settlements.

NOTES

1. Bhowmick, P.K, *The Lodhas of West Bengal*, Calcutta, 1963.
2. Booth Tucker, *Frederik, Jean Gold Servant of India*, London, 1964.
3. Edwards, S. M., *Crime in India*, OUP, London, 1924.
4. Booth Tucker 1964 : 24.
5. Sandall Robert 1955 : 17.
6. Fishman, A.T., *For the Purpose*, New York, n.d.
7. M.E., Mackenzie 1959 : 6.
8. Kapadia 1952 : 19.
9. Lalitha, V., *Socio-Economic and Administrative Aspects of An Ex-Criminal Tribe*, Unpublished M.Phil.Thesis, submitted to Srivenkateswara University, Tirupathi, 1977.
10. Government of Madras, *Administration Report of The Inspector General of Police, Madras 1912 to 1914*, Government press, Madrs, 1915. TNA.
11. Bawden, S D., *Yerukala Industrial Settlement – Kavali, Indian Jails Committee Report 1919-20*, Vol. III (Written Statement).
12. Mullay F.S., *The Criminal Classes of Madras Presidency*, Madras 1912.
13. Sandall, Robert., *The History of the Salvation Army*, New York, 1955.
14. Government of Madras, *Madras Administrative Reports of Madras Presidency 1871 to 1914*, Government Press, Madras 1915, TNA.
15. Judicial Department G.O. No. 209, dt. 28-1-1914.

16. *Judicial Department G.O. No. 784, dt. 25.4.1913,*
17. *Judicial Department G.O. No. 1161, dt. 12.6.1913.*
18. *Judicial Department G.O. No. 2000, dt. 3.2.1912,*
19. *Judicial Department G.O. No. 2568, dt. 25.10.1915.*
20. Lalitha 1977 : 15.
21. Bombay Criminal Tribes Enquiry Committee Report 1939 : 21
22. Vanikar, P.G., Missionary approach to Tribal Welfare – *Tribal Souvenir,* n.d.
23. Sher Singh Sher 1965 : 44.
24. Raghaviah V., *The Problem of Criminal Tribes,* Akhil Bhartiya Adim – Jati Sevak Sangh (BASS), Delhi, 1943.
25. Haikerwal, Bejoy Shanker, *Economic and Social Aspects of Crime in India,* George Allen and Unwin Ltd., London, 1934.
26. Majumdar, *D.N., Races and Cultures of India,* Bombay, 1961 (Fourth Revised edition reprinted in 1965).
27. Max Weber, *Religion of India,* 1958.
28. Government of India, *Report of the Criminal Tribes Act Enquiry Committee 1949-50,* Government Press, New Delhi.
29. Frederick Booth Tucker, *Jean Gould, Servant of India,* London, 1964, p. 10.
30. Booth Tucker, Fredrick, *Mukti Fauj or 40 years with the Salvation Army in India and Ceylon,* Marshall Brothers, London, n.d., p. 3.
31. Mackenzie, Mildred, *The Mud Bank,* Pennsylvania, 1959, p. 24.
32. *Ibid.,* p. 24.
33. *Home Judicial Department, GO. No. 1482, dt. 22nd June 1918,* p. 4, TNA.
34. Lessons, lecturers, classes were held out of doors to the cadets. Textbooks were supplied. The Bible, the SA handbook of doctrine, regulations for officers, Early church history, Finney's Revival lecturers and other devotional books were also supplied. They were good for mind and soul. People well versed in English acted as translators. Jean Gould, *Bharata Desa Sainya Sevakudu, (Telugu),* Madras n.d., p. 8.
35. Waskom Pickett, J., *Christian Mass Movements in India,* Chicago, 1933, p. 297.
36. *Ibid.,* p. 298.
37. Mackenzie, Mildred, *The Mud Bank, Op cit.,* p. 39.
38. Ganta Raja Rao, *The History of the Salvation Army in Andhra,* (Telugu) Madras, 1933, p. 19.
39. Mackenzie, Mildred, *Op cit.,* p. 45.
40. *Ibid.*
41. The War Cry, Salvation Army Monthly, August, *1938,* p. 2.
42. *Ibid.*
43. Waskom Pickett, J., *Christian Mass Movements in India, Chicago, 1933,* p. 297.
44. Mackenzie, Mildred, *Op cit.,* p. 47.

45. *Ibid.*, p. 46.
46. Mackenzie, Mildred, *Op cit.*, p. 46.
47. Ganta Raja Rao, *The History of Salvation Army in Andhra, Opcit.*, p. 26.
48. The War Cry, Salvation Army Monthly, August, 1937, p. 6.
49. Government of Madras, *Note Showing the Progress made in the settlement of Criminal Tribes in the Madras Presidency upto January, 1925*, Madras, 1926, pp. 1-2.
50. Dom's are North Indian CTs. The prestige of the SA with the Government was such that William Booth Tucker, the SA influential Officer, was awarded the prestigious title Kaiser-I-Hind by the viceroy in recognition of his services. Under his stewardship, the SA launched many experiments. Based on the past History of the SA, the Government invited them and entrusted them with the reformatory Job. *Home Department, G.O. No. 1675, 2nd December 1919*, p. 10, *NAI.*
51. Home Department, G.O. No. 1675, 2nd December 1919, p.14, APSA.
52. A former Governor of Bengal also remarked that: "The greatest credit is due to the Salvation Army now being achieved". Robert Sandal, *The History of the SA, Vol. 3, On Social Reform and Welfare Work*, New York, 1955, p. 276.
53. The following classes of settlements and institutions have been established by the SA:
    1. Agricultural settlements.
    2. Mixed Agro-Industrial Settlements.
    3. Industrial Settlements.
    4. Homes for released prisoners.
    5. Homes for Children.
    6. Homes for Juvenile Adult Released prisoners.
    7. Schools for training, weaving and silk reeling.
    8. Depots for disposing of goods and obtaining orders.
    9. Plantations of Mulberry and Eucalyptus,
    10. Factory for handlooms, warping, reeling and twisting machines, and 16 Agro-Industrial settlements were under the control of the SA. The main industries on which the CTs concentrated were handloom weaving and silk, Industrial homes, homes for Juvenile adults were opened for adult prisoners. The Madras and United provinces Governments were the only ones which have the Industrial homes for Children of CTs. There were altogether 6 Schools of this Character. See, Booth Tucker, *Criminology or the Indian Crime and what to do with him n.d.*, pp. 50-51.
54. Government of Madras, *Note Showing the Progress made in the Settlement of Criminal Tribes in the Madras Presidency upto September 1916*, Madras 1917, pp. 21-22, TNA. The different divisions wandering in the districts were Nos. V and X in Nellore and Bellary, No. IV in Godavari, No.VI, VIII and IX in Guntur and No. XIII in Kurnool.

55. Lalitha V., *The Making of Criminal Tribes Patterns and Transition,* New Era Publications, Madras, 1995, p. 143.
56. *Ibid.*
57. Captain Robilliard of the Salvation Army, Manager of the Stuartpuram Criminal tribes settlement, Bapatla, Madras. *Written Statement on the Work of Stuartpuram Settlement,* p. 64.
58. Home Judicial Department, G.O. No. 2074, 18th August 1916, p. 1., *TNA.*
59. Lalitha, V., "A profile of Seethanagaram Settlement", *Proceedings of Andhra Pradesh History Congress,* Guntur, 1987, p. 80.
60. The reformatory work was handed over to the missionaries due to the following reasons. 1. Effective control, 2. Individual Knowledge of Each inmate to exercise a personal influence, 3. To take a paternal interest in them and 4. Assign lands for all the members of a small settlement. *Home Judicial Department, G.O. No. 1537, 27th July 1917,* p. 2, *TNA.*
61. Smith, Solveig, *By Love Compelled, The Story of 100 years of the Salvation Army in India and Adjacent counties,* Salvationist Publishing, St. Alboans, Landon, 1981, p. 44.
62. See, Mackenzie, Mildred, *Op.Cit.,* p. 79.
63. *Ibid.*
64. Government of Madras, *Note Showing the Progress made in the Settlement of Criminal Tribes in the Madras Presidency upto January 1925,* Madras, 1927, p. 3.
65. Smith, Solveig, *Op. Cit.,* p. 48.
66. *Law (General) Department, G.O. No. 1714, 22nd October, 1921,* p. 8, APSA.
67. *Law (General) Department, G.O. No. 13187, 14th Nov. 1924,* p. 1, APSA.
68. *Law (General) Department, G.O. No. 1327, February 14th 1925,* p.1, APSA.
69. It was hoped that by the construction of the dam, the settlement lands would be assured of a continuous supply of water during the cultivation season. But there was no justification for such optimism. In addition to this, the manager suggested the construction of a dam across the perali Drain. Government of Madras, *Note Showing the Progress made in the Settlement of Criminal Tribes in the Madras presidency upto 1926,* Madras, 1926, p. 9.
70. The Government, in the year 1917-18, had considered the question of establishing cauarina plantation in an adjacent forest reserve. The government passed a condition that the plantation remained their property. Booth Tucker reported that the condition laid by the Government was not acceptable. He did not undertake the work. However, the district magistrate, Guntur was against the proposal since the proposal was a loss to the Government. Later Mr. Moir, the

next Labour Commissioner, condemned the proposal of establishing Casuarina plantation. Instead of causuarian plantation, he suggested for purchasing of cattle for manure purpose. Then the Government agreed with Mr. Moir. See, Government of Madras, *Note Showing the progress made in the Settlement of Criminal Tribes in the Madras Presidency upto January 1925*, Madras, 1926, p. 9.

71. *Public Works (Labour) Department, GO.No.268, 5th February 1927*, p. 2. APSA. The pumping plant was located at 21/2 of miles distance from the settlement. The manager now and then visited the pumping plant. He could not spare time or physical energy for work. Therefore the Government sanctioned a pony for the use of the manager to supervise the working of the pumping plant. *Public Works (Labour) Department, G.O. No. 2192, 4th September 1928*, p.1, APSA.
72. Mildred Mackenzie, *Op.Cit.*, p. 84.
73. *Law (General) Department, G.O. No. 171114, dt. 22.10.1921*, p. 6, APSA
74. *Home Department, G.O. No. 2074, dt. 18th August, 1916*, p. 1.
75. *The War Cry*, Salvation Army Monthly, May 1937, Madras, p. 1.
76. *Ibid.*, p. 3.
77. *Law (General) Department, G.O. No. 3187, dt. 14th November 1924*, p. 1, *APSA*.
78. *Note showing the progress, Op.cit., p. 7.*
79. Mildred Mackenzie, *Op.Cit., p. 85.*
80. *Law (General) Department, G.O. No. 1714, 22nd October, 1921*, p. 6, APSA. It was recorded that during the year 1925 the number of deaths were innumerable in the settlement. The consequences was that large number of Yerukulas absconded from the settlement.
81. *PWLD, G.O. No. 1996, Dt. 16th January 1933*, pp. 5-6, APSA.
82. See, V. Lalitha, *Op.Cit.*, p. 46. One Head Constable and Ten Constables were appointed in connection with the reclamation of the Criminal classes in Stuartpuram during the year 1926. *PWLD, G.O. No.* 576, p. 1, APSA.
83. *See Public Works Labour Department*, G.O. No. 1926, 30th July, 1931, p. 3, APSA. The manager visited from Bezawada to Lingala settlement, Secunderabad, Hotgi, Sholapur, Bijapur, Bagalkot, Gaddak, Gaddak Falls, Hubli, Tirichunapoly, Madurai, Tinnevelly, Kulasekarapuram, Tanjore, Borstol Institute, Aziznagar, Pallavaram, Kavali,, Bitrangunta and Allur.
84. Interview with P. Jakkaraiah, the Manager of Stuartpuram Settlement, Stuartpuram, dt. 2.2.1991.

5

Denotified Tribes: Problems of Rehabilitation

I

Introduction

Criminality of the CTs was a result of the function of the Indian social structure. They appear to be in a period of transition and are increasingly adopting legitimate means of achieving goals and seeking more identity with the larger society.[1] Crime in a country of India's size and population is a gigantic problem. It is bound to increase quantitatively and qualitatively with the growth of population, economic development and breakdown of traditional institutions and values.[2]

After the enactment of the CTA in 1871, the whole tribe was declared as 'CTs'. The members of such tribes were sent to the settlements established exclusively for them, where they were taught trades and professions. Every effort was made to wean them away from their old ways and habits.[3] There were some philanthropic social organisations that came forward in response to the call of government to undertake the task of rehabilitation of the CTs in India, viz., the Salvation Army, the London Mission, the American Baptist Mission, the Canadian Mission, Chief Khalsa Diwan, Deosamaj, Anjuman Islamia, Ahmedia Society, Sanatana Dharm Sabha, Arya Samaj and the Punjab Hindu Sabha, etc. Some settlements were run by government itself.[4] Among these settlements, there were Agricultural settlements, Industrial settlements, Reformatory settlements, Ordinary settlements and Voluntary settlements. In the Madras Presidency the SA and the ABM took the reformation work to provide a settled life for the various CTs. They are the Kavali settlement, in Nellore District, Bethapudi or Stuartpuram settlement, Sitanagaram settlement in Guntur district, Siddhapuram settlement in Kurnool district, Aziz Nagar settlement in South Arcot district, Kulasekhara patnam settlement in Tinnevelly district, and Kallar settlement in Madurai district in addition to other institutions such as schools and homes for the children of these tribes spread all over the Presidency.[5] In Andhra region the earliest settlements were established at Kalichedu and Kavali which date back to the year 1912. Thus the reformation work started with the missionaries in Andhra Pradesh.

II

Historical Background of the reformation of Denotified Tribes

The reformation work for the Kathera tribe was started by Mr. Ludvig a, local agent of Kalichedu mica mines. It was closed down later due to the bankruptcy of mica mines in a very short span of time. Later, Kavali settlement was established in October 1912 at Kavali in Nellore District.[6] Rev. E. Bullard with the permission of the police authorities took charge of 20 Yerukula families and opened an Industrial Yerukula settlement at Kavali.[7] In the words of K. M. Kapadia, at Kavali on the other hand, where mainly cooly work in mending roads, repairing tank bunds, clearing channels and the like was provided, the sums earned were not sufficient for living, with the result that about 40 per cent of the adult population of the settlement either absconded or were in jail for absconding. The ultimate success of the settlement lay in the weaning away of the children away from the habits of their parents and fixing them up in some occupation.[8] In December 1916, Kavali criminal settlement transferred some of the settlers to Allur and subsequently the Allur settlement was started. In January, 1917, in the same manner Bitragunta reformatory settlement was commenced with some Kathera families from Kalichedu and some Yerukula families from Kavali settlements. This is known as Kapparalla Tippa settlement.[9] Strong barbed wire fencings at a height of 12 feet were constructed around 30 acres of land of the settlements.[10] The inhabitants were provided with agricultural implements and were working as garden coolies. Within the enclosure, vegetables were grown. All these settlements were under the management of, Mr. Bawden. From him the management of the settlement was taken over by the police department and the Inspector of police. After the repeal of the CTA in the year 1952 the CT settlements were abolished. The Social Welfare and Tribal Welfare departments were given charge of these settlements (Colonies).

The reformation of Yerukulas in Guntur District was started with Robilliard of the SA manager. Named after the governor of Madras Presidency, it was Sir Harold Start himself who handed over the first group of the Yerukulas with the words, "take these, Salvation Army—I give you twenty years to do for them what has to be done."[11] Stuartpuram has only one caste of 'criminals', namely Yerukulas, who comprise—5 to 10 gangs. These yerukulas are found all over Andhra Pradesh. After Abolition of the Act, the government extended the full fee concessions to the children of the notified tribes and sanctioned grant of residential and industrial scholarships.[12] Even after the abolition of the Act, the administration was completely in the hands of SA with the full support of the government of Andhra Pradesh. The government and revenue authorities took some lucrative means in this regard. Mr. M.V. Thomas, the then superintendent of police, Sri Lavanam and Hemalatha Lavanam, Andhra Rastra Adim Jati Sevak Sangh, Andhra Rastra Yerukula Samiti and others took keen interest in the rehabilitation programme of these Yerukulas. Thus the behaviour pattern of the Yerukulas changed since the inception of the settlements.

Sitanagaram settlement is in the Guntur district. It is interesting to know that though it is included in Guntur district, it is close to the city of Vijayawada. This is situated in between the river Krishna and Buckingham Canal and on eastern side of Vijayawada-Madras railway line. In October, 1915, Sitanagaram settlement itself was divided into two namely Saineyapuram and Kondapet.[13] This is also an agricultural settlement. But it was considered as a penal settlement, where the incorrigibles were kept. The reformation work was started with Mr. Bawden, the then Manager of Bitragunta reformatory settlement. Now it is a free colony, exposed to many opportunities for employing Yerukulas who are living there. Sri Lavanam and Hemalatha Lavanam are doing immense service to bring about a change among these Yerukulas and a remarkable change is already noticeable.

Siddhapuram settlement was started in the year in 1913 for the benefit of reformation work in Waddars employed by the public works department on the Siddhapuram tank project in the Kurnool district. These Dongawoddars were a criminal tribe, the government applied at them the provisions of section 10(b) of the CT Act. In addition to Woddars, certain number of Chenchus, Sugalis, Boyas were also interned. The reformation work was carried by the government itself as it was a voluntary settlement. In addition to the above, reformation activities were also carried in Chintal Devi settlement in Nellore district for Kanjar Bhats of Bombay presidency and Bommanigada settlement in Chittoor district which also worked for the reformation and rehabilitation of the denotified tribes in the respective areas.

III

Problems of Rehabilitation Among the Denotified Tribes

How far the reformation and rehabilitation programmes started by the Government, non-governmental organisations and the missionaries were successful? There are many illusions about the success of the programmes initiated by the state and central government organisations for the DNTs in India. But all the efforts made so far itself should be considered to be the beginning of success. A philosophical understanding is necessary for the organisations who are involved in the rehabilitation work of the DNTs. This gradually produces the results with their constant and consistent effort. This will also give satisfaction and encouragement. What is required at present is the programmes, projects initiated for the rehabilitation of the DNTs should be carried in consultation with the local people. In some of the colonies, agricultural projects will be a great success (for example, Stuartpuram and Lingala settlements). In some of the colonies (Sitanagaram, Siddhapuram and Bitragunta) training programmes such as tailoring training, beedi making and other small scale industrial programmes will be useful and bring fruitful results. The women and grown up children may be involved in such programmes.

At present, there are a number of educated boys and girls in the DNT colonies. They wish to go for jobs in railway recruitment, bank, police, RTC, home guards, PWD, teaching and other recruitments. They require sufficient training to qualify the recruitment examinations. They feel it very difficult to compete for jobs. Therefore, the government may start at least one coaching centre in all the DNT colonies so as to enable them to attend and take the required competitive skills. This will provide them moral courage to go for various jobs available with the state and public sector enterprises.

All the DNT colonies have a good number of school going children. Children at the primary and secondary education requires sufficient care and educational support. They require more educational support to what they learn at school. Children from the first standard have the enthusiasm to go for English medium education. Looking at their enthusiasm English medium schools, residential schools, may be opened in the colonies.

The women and girl children should be provided with tailoring, weaving, knitting and painting programmes. These programmes are not only advantageous for them but also a large number of women who are very poor and who do not have any employment opportunities will be attracted easily to go for this type of programmes. These programmes will generate a new culture in the community, i.e. 'Yearn for Living'.

The lands distributed to the DNTs by the government are in a bad shape. The colonists have lost their interest in agricultural work due to non-availability of water in the canals/ bunds constructed in their colonies. For many years, due to faulty water supply, the DNTs are not cultivating their lands. As a part of the agricultural programme, the Gram Panchayats, Municipalities and Mandal Panchayats should repair the field channels and water pipes. Regular water supply from the canals should be given to the colonists. The increase in the crop will contribute considerably to the economy of the community.

There are also a good number of aged people in these colonies. Their conditions are pathetic. Many of them cannot support themselves. Their children are unemployed. Old-age pensions should be provided regularly to support themselves. The 'right to life' should be given to the destitute, aged and lonely persons in these colonies.

So far as the progress of the DNT colonies before and after independence is concerned, it was very slow. A few settlement population only succeeded partially in terms of education, employment and other opportunities. However, psychologically and culturally the character of the DNT communities is very much progressive. Today, everybody who were afraid to come to the DNT colonies (as this was considered to be 'won't be good place') from neighbouring villages are also coming and mingling with the DNTs. This is the great social transformation taking place in DNT colonies. The isolation of the DNTs is broken. They started to integrate with the rest of the society. The individual DNT community members want to equip themselves with skills and to improve themselves with the functions of the members of the rest of the communities. Every family member is ready to promise for a bright future. The government under these circumstances should provide opportunities and guidance. There is also an urgent need to integrate the settlements into a big community with the rest of the people. The Panchayats should come out with developmental plans keeping in view of the requirements of the colonies. This is of course a gigantic task. However, keeping in view of the brighter future of the colonists, every possible effort should be made by the local bodies and the State Government. This is also the constitutional obligations and aspirations of many deprived population in the country. Mutual partnership in the development of the country with people will not only provide better results but also rebuild the society. Thus the communities from the weaker sections go stronger, healthier to eradicate poverty and disease. A sea change has to take place in the life of the DNTs today. What they require urgently is freedom from poverty, unemployment, stigma, harassment and culture of 'crime'. It is the human right of these people to educate themselves and to equip themselves to join the mainstream of society and lead a dignified life.

There is a need to understand the theoretical and philosophical problems of the DNT communities. They are not anti-social. They should be treated respectfully on par with the rest of the surrounding society. They were exploited for generations due to their ignorance and indecent ways of life. People belonging to other social categories who are involved in crime do not have the stigma of criminality unlike the DNTs.

The police visit the DNT colonies in order to enquire the whereabouts of the convicts. This has the psychological bearing on the minds of the children, parents and womenfolk of the DNT family members. Sometimes the police also indulge in rough treatment of the parents, children and the womenfolk. In order to escape from the harsh treatment of the police, the convicts escape from the colonies. Thus the offenders leave their family members for a long time. They will be totally cut off from their family life. Their children were left orphans. When the children grow up naturally to support the families, they also follow the same tradition. The simple solution to the entire problem is that the police authorities should be trained in the better ways of investigative methods for the petty crimes committed by a few DNT members. Free and fair exchange of views between community leaders, educated members in the communities and the reputed social workers, panchayat members will not only give fruitful results in the changing behaviour of the colonists and the experiment of reformation will be successful. There is another dimension of the duties of a transferable government officials also. Once the officer gets transferred, there is no guarantee that the succeeding officer would continue the efforts of the predecessor. While treating the DNTs the police authorities should continue with the original zeal and sympathy. They should not degrade their morale and in their methods of investigation.

The public in India should be educated. Public meetings in the DNT colonies to know about the ills of social evils like dacoity, robbery, theft and other illegal activities should be made aware to the public by involving the community, Gram Panchayat, community leaders and educated members. The DNTs also should understand that 'crime is no profession'. Radio, TV and theatre programmes should be encouraged to cover the problems and solutions of the DNTs. This will help to solve their problems to some extent in a proper social context. Gandhian methods of approach to the problems of the DNTs should be taken up by the government. Leaders like Vinoba Bhave in 1960 and Jayaprakash Narayan in 1972 adopted Gandhian techniques to solve the problems of Chambal Valley dacoits.

The educated youth in the DNT colonies has a greater role and responsibility in the reformation process. The schools in the colonies can organise national camp programmes. The youth should work against the famine. Various organisations like Yerukula Ekalavya Samiti, Yanadi Welfare Association, Sugali Welfare Associations, etc. should mobilise and work against the total eradication of poverty among the DNTs. Camps which promote awareness of social responsibiliy and citizenship should be encouraged. The educated youth should bring a vision of change in their colonies. The children of the schools should be mixed with the children of other communities to work freely together in their environments. Attempts of this social mixture of people will bring a proper outlook in their way of life.

Some educated members in Stuartpuram organised regular annual Yerukula conferences in different parts of Andhra Pradesh upto 1980. These Conferences demanded the total repeal of the CT Act, the ban on illicit liquor, the problems of the community members, etc. The organisation published newspapers, weeklies, pamphlets and submitted memoranda to the government to solve their problems. The organisation did a commendable work in the reformation of the DNTs till recently. However, due to the financial problems of the leaders the organisation stopped working effectively.

Still the traces of backwardness can be glaringly seen among the families of DNTs. In order to support the income for the family even children are sold to distant places like Bombay, Punjab and other places. School going children are used in their nefarious activities. Illicit liquor is freely sold in many of the houses. A good rapport with the residents of these DNT colonies will solve many problems of rehabilitation. The government officials working in the reformatory process of DNTs should use the rapport building approach.

Children and family members should come forward with important decisions that would guide them in the reformation work. Public should be encouraged not to accept anything from the families who were involved in crime (as the offering may be a part of the proceedings of the stolen property) and not to talk to any male and female member of the DNT households if they are involved in any offence. This type of an act will definitely have a positive impact in the minds of the people. The woes and agonies and the narrative descriptions of the deeds of their elder members should be projected on the theatre and all the family members should contribute in the development of 'social engineering' in the DNT colonies.

The DNTs have undergone trials for the offences committed by them such as bank robberies, theft cases, dacoities and house breakings. These robberies involved a large amount of money, gold and other valuables. Their crimes were given vide publicity. Majority of the suspects were surrendered along with the booty before the police and ministerial members. However, even after surrender and completing the prescribed years of punishment, the stigma still haunts them. Many of the old offenders have changed their hearts and pleading the government to allow them to lead a respectable and peaceful life.

A gentleman's agreement should be adopted between the police officials and community members with regard to the voluntary surrenders of some of the DNTs in their colonies. The police should clearly mention in the charge sheets about their voluntary surrenders. But for the reasons best known, the police officials violate these agreements and mention that the suspects were arrested by the police at the cine theatres, bus stations and railway stations, etc. A good number of DNTs were converted to Christianity and leading a respectable life by gospelling and by adopting other avenues of life. The goodness of these people have to be encouraged to come out of their past habits. Many a time, the officials do not co-operate in this respect. It becomes a big setback to the reformation process. The police should not go to the colonies to arrest them but just to go to them to inquire about their well being. The DNTs will encourage this attitude of the authorities and a tremendous improvement can be seen in the colonies by such an act of the officials.

Some of the DNT members had also set up defence in the courts. Some of them pleaded guilty and accepted the sentence with a sense of repentance. They have spent their entire life in prisons and were released when they are old. Even on them the police became rapacious and suspect them. Thus they too are becoming hardened. They are also hiring lawyers to argue that they did not commit the offences. The role of the police in the reformation activities was definitely not to condone crime or criminals. They should behave as the custodians of civil society. They should recognise the urge among the DNTs to reform themselves. Reformation of the DNTs demands a highly reasonable civilian attitude from the police in dealing with the DNTs. They should leave the things to the court of law. They also should recognise the willingness and efforts of the DNTs to come out of the cob-web of crime. Reformation is not one sided. It is multisided. When the society is demanding the DNTs to be honest, then all those concerned with them also should be honest.

The government should come up with a rehabilitation package for those living in the DNT colonies who were voluntarily surrendered. Social ignominy forced them to give up the 'criminal' life. In this regard, Hemalatha Lavanam said, "What they now need is a rehabilitation package to lead a normal life." The police officials should not harass the surrendered persons.[14]

The denotified tribes who are the first time offenders should be handed over to the reputed non-governmental organisations instead of sending them to juvenile homes or jails. The Chief Justice of Andhra Pradesh High court B.S.A. Swamy said, "If the first time offenders are sent to juvenile or remand homes, there is every chance that they would become more hardened criminals in the company of others. Counselling centres should be opened to provide counselling to the needy persons in the DNT colonies. Further, the police should adopt a humane approach to their rehabilitation. Also the DNTs should not think that the police were their enemies. No one in the society wanted to lead a criminal life but circumstances forced them to that way of life. Even after the denotification of CTs they were still discriminated in their daily life and treated with suspicion."[15] The government should adopt a humane approach to the problems of the DNTs and help them to eke out their livelihood through agriculture and small scale industrial work. M.V. Thomas, incharge of prisons of Hyderabad Urban Development Authority said that "a rational and humane approach should be adopted in dealing with DNTs."[16] The attempts made by the government and the NGOs has only touched the fringes of the problem leaving a large area of rehabilitation problem unattended. The DNTs and their colonies have been neglected by the Central and State Governments. The rehabilitation of the DNTs—not only economic rehabilitation, but also social and cultural rehabilitation. As far as economic rehabilitation is concerned the DNTs are not poor in the sense that they also can earn money by doing hard work. Avenues can be shown for them to earn through socially and culturally accepted means according to their existing abilities. A distressing factor is that whenever the menfolk are sent to jail for minor or major offences, some womenfolk work as coolies to keep the family going. The DNTs have a different tale to narrate. They say that after taking so much risk in committing an offence, they are left with nothing but police beatings and imprisonment. After getting the booty, a criminal has to share it with the village elder, the police officer and the dealer who buys the booty. Besides he has to pay exhorbitantly to the advocate who defends his case in the court of law. What little is left after these cuts, the offenders spend on drinking and eating. It was reported that, "despite the fact that they have a record which is socially unacceptable, the offenders in these DNT colonies want to live like any other ordinary citizens ably with education to their children."[17] Crime is no monopoly of a particular social group, people or community. Other people drawn from other social categories too commit crime. But the public attitude is that all crimes are committed by the DNT community members. The DNT members still attend the police stations to put their signatures and thumb impressions for their old recorded crime sheets.

Even though the CT Act was repealed in the post independent era (in 1952), nobody took keen interest in the execution of the Government's decision in making DNT settlements as free colonies. Thus all the five settlements in Andhra Pradesh - Stuartpuram, Sitanagaram, Kapparallatippa, Siddhapuram and Lingala remained as ex-criminal settlements. The basic structure of life in all the colonies was not changed.[18] Out of these five colonies Stuartpuram is still under the influence of the SA. The other four colonies were taken over by the government towards the end of the colonial rule. They were put under the police jurisdiction for some time. Later on the colonies were handed over to the revenue department. Presently the colonies were under the direct control of the Social Tribal Welfare Department. The government was the legal owner of all land and house sites in all the colonies. After India became free from colonial yoke, the Madras Government appointed a committee under the chairmanship of Mr.Vepa Ramesam ICS. The Committee recommended to make all DNT colonies as free villages and distribute house sites to the occupants.[19] The committee also recommended distribution of land to all those bona fide inhabitants who have been living there. Since 1976 all the DNT colonies were considered as free village communities. Consequently the government departments took control over all lands in DNT colonies and distributed the same in the name of local inhabitants with ownership rights.

As a people divorced from the set norms of society, these denotified people need adequate measures for their integration with the rest of the society. Their rehabilitation says G.P. Bharal largely depends on how far they are integrated into society. This requires change in the attitude of the society. [20] The main cause of criminality was economic while the social and political aspects contributed their part. In most cases it was found to be a historical accident. The persons left with no other means of livelihood became 'criminals'.[21] Even now there are some people who have the stigma of criminality.[22] After the repeal of the CT Act a good number of people were freed from the stigma of criminality. The Government of India made some suggestions for their ameliorative measures. Now almost all tribes are included in the Scheduled Castes, Tribes and Backward Classes on the basis of their economic backwardness according to their place in the society. They should be resettled and gradually integrated with the rest of the society. Proper education especially for their children should be given for their future employment. Economic rehabilitation should precede the social and cultural rehabilitations.[23]

The ultimate aim is to resocialise the offender, to readjust him to the society and to rehabilitate and change him. The rehabilitative programmes concerning these persons entrusted either to educational institutions or to hand over to reputed social service organisations who can evince real interest in them.[24] The growing apprehension among them of the future for their children should be dispelled and their responsiveness be channeled into purposive activities for their own betterment. The whole issue of rehabilitation hinges totally on the complex process of convincing them of the futility of stealing and thieving as panaccea for their ills and transforming them into people who can eke out their livelihood through the sweat of their brows. Since their problems originate in the social and economic basis, the main thrust of rehabilitation should be socio-economic in nature. Tempered rehabilitation has to be with a human approach to the entire question.

The following suggestions are made with a view to bring about an improvement in the programme for the welfare of denotified tribes of Andhra Pradesh: (1) The government has to conduct sample surveys to know about their present position pertaining to their livelihood, state of literacy, housing and other activities. Guntur district has already done this type of survey and sent an action plan to the government. (2) Large share of expenditure should be spent on their economic development. Some kind of lawful employment should be provided for them as an alternative means of livelihood. (3) 'D' Form pattas, issued to them should be converted into loanable pattas. And also those members of denotified tribes in various ex-settlements who have real interest and aptitude for cultivation should be provided land and other facilities. (4) A number of denotified tribes work as labourers in construction and road works, extracting stones from quarries etc., like in Sitanagaram settlement. Labour contract societies should be organised in consultation with members of these communities, least favourism, nepotism should prevail. (5) Brick-making, mat-weaving, nawara-making, dress-making centers or the cottage industries which require least technical skill and guidance should be encouraged in the DNT colonies. (6) Dairy farming, piggery, poultry are very useful in the economic development. They should be given priority. These are to be organised on the co-operative basis for which the government should provide financial assistance on loan-cum-subsidy basis. (7) As the fellow members in the society the denotified tribes also like jobs which give them immediate remunerations, industrial employment should be provided by absorbing them or created for them in large-scale, this will give them satisfaction. For example in Sitanagaram settlement, many of them are provided with jobs and Crime has reduced to the minimum. They may be recruited into the department of police as constables, water boys, sweepers, etc. Some of them are already employed as watchman with good reputation. (8) Arrangements should be made to make the banks to sanction loans to the settlers who are interested in setting up business like small shops, (Bunks or Soda shops), tea stall, etc. Encouragement for self-employment schemes provides much-needed fillip to make them aware of their latent capacities in fields like business. (9) Steps should be taken to see the members of denotified tribes are not concentrated in one place. And also it is observed that the presence of habitual offenders and other hardened criminals in the DNT colonies is an impediment in the reform of the members. It is desirable to keep them in separate places.

IV

Conclusion

To sum up, certain bureaucratic procedures can be dispensed with forgiving due consideration to these neglected sections of people in our society. Since economic development is a continuous process, steps must also be taken to establish rural banks in the area for mobilising their savings to be used again for their benefit. The present oppressive and exploitative economic structure developed around the settlements should be dismantled. Stolen property dealers, corrupt police officials, investors in crime and greedy advocates started exploiting the situation and major share of booty was knocked away by them. The Report of the Backward Classes Commission stated: "The economic programme should go hand in hand with a dynamic and suitably oriented programme of social education so as to wean them away from socially undesirable tendencies."[25] The present system of education is not satisfactory. The entire gamut of reforming the ex-criminals here depends on how best educational facilities can be provided to them. Education is an effective weapon and instrument of social transformation. It is evident that in the quagmire of their poverty, they prefer immediate gains to long term benefits that accrue after a continuous schooling of 10 to 15 years. Therefore, need-based or job-oriented education is an effective alternative to the present monotonous and 'unproductive' education.

The feeling of the people when interviewed them, is that their children could not reach higher echelons of society because of the psychological barrier they suffer from. Restructuring the educational system for the denotified tribes requires a humanistic approach, which should give them self-confidence and guidance towards their becoming an integral part of the main stream of Hindu Society. [26]

The social experience of the denotified tribes still adds to their lurking fears dominated by the more vociferous strata of the society. Unless the society provides equal opportunities and treatment with others in every sphere of life, these people are not willing to come out of their shell. What we ought to do is to develop a sense of oneness with these people, a sense of unity and understanding. It necessarily involves a psychological approach. It should also be kept in mind that the rough treatment method shown to them by the police officials has a great bearing on their conduct. Experiencing stinking and miserable life in prisons, and the unsympathetic attitude of the police they develop a negative attitude, which in its turn, forces them to take the same activity.[27] Because of the colonial outlook or the system which we have inherited as a colonial handover has remained more or less the same and this has to be reorganised. Otherwise, it cannot work as a worthy instruments of change in a developing democratic society.

Another problem is that the DNTs cannot have emotional affinity with others as long as they are not free from fear of stigma and this cannot be wiped out as long as they do not wish to come out of their rut and narrow living and prove their integrity in society over a stretch of long period. By socialising them through social education and other rehabilitative measures they should be helped to break away from their psychological barrier. Mass adult education programmes, radio and library facilities, involvement of the youth of the DNT colonies in all these programmes, a coordinated approach in streamlining their life pattern, by providing basic infrastructural facilities such as electricity, communications and water supply will ensure their orderly progress and development.

NOTES

1. Clarence H.Patrick, 'The Criminal Tribes of India with Special Emphasis on the Mang Garudis', *Man in India Vol. 48, July-September 1965,* pp. 244-255.
2. Venogopala Rao S., *Indian Express dt.9.6.77.*
3. Haikerwal B. S., *Economic and Social Aspects of Crime in India,* George Allen and Unwin Ltd., London 1934, p. 166.
4. Boswell, *Nellore District Manual,* Madras, 1873, p. 147. And also see Frederick S Mullaly, *The Criminal Classes of Madras Presidency,* Madras, p. 8.
5. Letter from A.F.G. Mocardi, the then District Magistrate, Bellary addressed to the chief secretary to the government of Madras, dt. June 1914. Judicial proceedings, Archives of Nellore District Collectorate.
6. Fishman, A.T., *For This Purpose, New York, n.d.* p. 46. The Yerukala Industrial settlement at Kavali, a place of refuge and rehabilitation for those names by law as members of the 'CTs' was established. It did eventually, however, in two well-established agricultural colonies and active Christian churches and in the education of hundreds of the children of Criminals away from a life of crime and into useful, self-respecting service. Also see Government of Madras, *Gazeteer of the Nellore District upto 1938,* Madras, 1942, p. 84.
7. *Judicial Department, G.O. No. 910, May 10, 1913.* TNA.
8. Kapadia K M., "The Criminal Tribes of India" in *Sociological Bulletin Vol. I-II, 1952.* p. 106.
9. *History of Bitragunta Settlement,* the original document a Typed copy collected from Kapparala Tippa Police Station.
10. *Ibid.*
11. Harry William and William *Booth-Tucker, Booth's First Gentleman,* London, 1980, p. 184. Government of Andhra Pradesh, *The Report on the Tribes of Andhra Pradesh,* Tribal Cultural Research and Training Institute, Hyderabad, p. 12.
12. See Simhadri Y. C., "Criminal behaviour of an Ex-Criminal Tribe in An Indian Village", *Indian Criminology, Vol., 4, No. 1, January, 1976.*
13. In the field survey we found that the Sitanagaram settlement is divided into three parts, viz. Sainapuram where 19 families of settlers live, Kondapet where the other houses of settlers are situated and rifle range where the land belonging to the settlers is given to 3 political suffers by the government. *Judicial Department, G.O. No. 1161, 12.6.1913.*
14. Hemalatha Lavanam, *Mrutyorma Amrutangamaya, (Auto Biography),* Visalandra Book House, Hyderabad, 2004.

15. 'Raw deal to residents' of settlement colonies', *Indian Express,* June 16, 1984.
16. 'A change for the better, *The Hindu,* 19th June 1984.
17. 'Reform Process apace at Stuartpuram, *The Hindu,* March 13, 1999.
18. '25 hardcore dacoits of Guntur Surrender', *The New Indian Express,* Hyderabad, March 30, 1999.
19. Reformed criminals to take part in Meeting', *News Time,* 12-6-1984.
20. Bharal, G.P. "Denotified Communities and their problems of rehabilitation." Indian journal of social work, Vol. XXVIII, No. 4, January,1968, pp. 353-64.
21. Bowmic, P. K., 'Some Aspects of Indian Anthropology', Calcutta, 1980, p. 123.
22. Lalitha V., 'Report on The Rehabilitative measures for the ex-criminals of Bitragunta Reformatory Settlement and Kacherimitta', proceeding volume of *Andhrapradesh History Congress held at Nellore District, Kavali, 4.1.1971.*
23. Government of India, *Report of the Commissioner for Scheduled Castes and Tribes, op. cit.,* p. 103. "It is suggested that more persons should be encouraged to take up such business by giving them subsidies."
24. Lavanam, "Notes on Reflections on our Work in Rehabilitation of Ex-Criminal Tribes People in Settlements" Athiest Centre, Vijayawada.
25. *Report of the study Team on Social welfare and welfare of Backward Class Vol. I.,* New Delhi, 1959.
26. Basu, Minendranath, "Suggestions for the Educational plan of the aboriginal problems of India" in *Vanyajati,* Vol. 16, No. 3 July,1961, pp. 123-26.
27. *Ibid.*

6

Administration, Management and Control of Denotified Tribes

I

Introduction : History of Legislation to Deal with 'Criminal' Tribes

The report of the Indian Police Commission 1902-03 laid down the principle that it should be the aim of every police system to obtain the knowledge and secure the supervision of all persons addicted to crime. The Commission declared that the police should have more powers of control over CTs.[1] The Police Commission subsequently recommended certain amendments to the CTA in 1871. The Government of India considered the recommendations made by the Police Commission and found it necessary to repeal the Act of 1871. The Police Commission subsequently substituted in its place another Act in 1911. The 1911 Act was more comprehensive than the old one. One of the objectives of the 1911 Act was to enlarge the power of control by empowering the local governments.[2] The 1911 Act enabled the local governments : *(i)* Declare any tribe/class to be a 'criminal' tribe if the local government is satisfied that they are addicted to the systematic commission of non-bailable offences. *(ii)* Can order the registration of members of any 'criminal' tribe/class and take their finger impressions and *(iii)* Direct every registered member to report himself/herself at fixed intervals or notify his/her place of residence.[3] Another important feature of the 1911 Act was the local government was authorised to establish industrial, agricultural and reformatory schools and separate the children from their parents. The first thing done when the Act was passed was the framing of rules for the registration and supervision of the CTs.[4] In the provinces the control of CTs and 'criminal' settlements had been entrusted to officers on special duty. In Madras Presidency the work had been carried out by the district officers. The advantage was that it had given the responsibility of reforming the 'criminal' classes to the district officers. Gradually, the work had increased and the government directed the Inspector General of Police to use the services of the District Magistrates, Deputy Inspector-General of Police, Railways and CID Departments, District Superintendent of Police, Inspectors of Police, Reclamation Officers, Commissioners of Labour and the co-operative inspectors in the general supervision, control and administration of all the settlements.[5]

II

Advantages of Non-official Over Official Management

The CT settlements were managed by several Christian missionaries and philanthropic societies who worked for the moral upliftment of the CTs. About the management of the CT settlements, there was a debate in Madras Legislative Assembly. It was questioned as to why the Christian Missionaries alone should be given the management work of the CT settlements. It was pointed out that owing to the dedication and zeal of the Christian Missionaries, their interest in the reformation, rehabilitation of the depressed classes and in addition to that, their interest in evangelisation were responsible for handing over the CT settlements to these people.[6]

The primary object of a 'criminal' settlement is reformation but not segregation or confinement. Its management had fallen into the hands of the police. The police and the government officials had no training for the reclamation of 'criminals'. They could only inspire distrust in the 'criminal' classes. It was a hindrance to reclamation. In the non-governmental agencies the government would get the help of self-sacrificing men who are prepared to devote their lives to the reformatory work. Sometimes a Government officer who was keenly interested in the public service was transferred, then it was difficult to get a suitable substitute to carry on the work. It was noticed that the work of non-governmental agency for management had been successful.[7] Another consideration was its economy. The government could not get skilled service for the remuneration actually it paid to the non-official agencies. The manager of a settlement had full freedom to undertake the responsibility of reforming the CTs in his settlement. The non-official manager also enjoyed independence and prestige too. The Government of India remarked that : "The experiences gained in other provinces seems to indicate that, when organisations like the Salvation Army can be found to take up work and carry it through on proper lines, it is an economical arrangement to subsidise their undertakings, not only because less money is spent but also because better value is obtained for it."[8] The Government, therefore, decided to entrust the management of their settlements to non-official agency or missionaries. The missionaries also repeatedly declared their readiness to welcome the entry of Hindu and Muhammadan agencies in the field of social reform. But only the SA, the ABM and the London Mission had responded to the call of the Government.[9]

The Madras Government felt that agricultural and industrial settlements are the best sources for reformation work on these 'criminal' classes. In the cooli work, the labourers do little work. If a man is given a small plot of land he goes to the land early in the morning and works till dusk. Even if he has other works to perform, he will spare some time to work in his plot. Hence the Government made it compulsory in all settlements that agriculture should be the main industry. Each family was distributed a block of dry land and a piece of wet land to maintain themselves. If one is found to neglect his land he was given punishment with hard work such as breaking stones, digging earth and the land was taken away from him and given to another. The Government considered that in course of time, a patta for his land may be given to the settler who proves himself by continuous industry and good conduct.[10]

The Government also considered two conditions in the formation of the 'criminal' settlements: 1. There should be some professed religious or philanthropic agency attached to each settlement if not actually incharge of it and 2. In the settlements government should not involve in the removal of people beyond their own language area or to such a distance as may be rightly regarded as a foreign country. Thus seven 'criminal' settlements were established and administered by the missionaries and the government in Madras Presidency upto the end of the year 1915.[11]

III

Administration and Control of Siddhapuram Settlement

The settlement was kept under the charge of a sub-inspector of police assisted by a constable. The sub-inspector was the key person to manage the settlement. By the year 1917, it was upgraded and there was one inspector, one sub-inspector and two head constables and 25 constables in Siddhapuram. The constables used to watch the settlers and supervision was their responsibility. The settlers were given daily labour such as breaking clods, spreading earth, supply water to machinery, pushing empties and loading wagons at the site of *'Navvy'* (unskilled work), etc. They were found unsuitable on account of their inborn idleness and insubordination to the orders of the maistries under whom they were posted to work. It was not feasible to get the proper turn out of work from them. The maistries were threatened by the desperate employees. The next alternative was to employ them on piece-work system. Least skill was expected in certain work such as quarrying stones, building revetment, sectioning and sloping bund and gravel backing. They were employed only on earth work which required no skill [12].

The quantity of earth work to be done from them was 3,083 units during the year 1918. 120 coolies were engaged on the work. The recruitment of some of the Yerukulas would definitely affect the progress of work. This was a good solution to complete the work in a speedy manner. But, the Inspector General of Police, P.L. Moore informed on 27th August 1918, that the government approved his proposal to exclude the Yerukulas from the scheme. This was planned to provide employment to Waddars exclusively. P.L. Moore said, 'they were employed on irrigation works because the settlers were originally earth-workers by profession'.[13] A few Sugali families were given a grant of 20 acres of land within the settlement limits. They were supplied manure for their fields. Some Waddars lived in Piler Circle of Vayalpad Taluk, Chittoor District. They were brought into this settlement during the year 1929. The manager also brought new families from Hubli settlement. 25 members of Waddars came voluntarily in January 1930 from Betamcharla as a result of propaganda work by the manager. They were related to the old 'Donga' Waddars. They began to settle down in the settlement to become land owners. But their creditors in Betamcharla were against this proposal because they wanted to exploit their labour at cheap rates. 32 families of Tak-Waddars came in February 1931 from Pattikonda Taluk. Some were brought from Anantapur and Cuddapah districts.[14]

The District Superintendent of Police, Kurnool, transferred some Waddars to the reformatory settlement at Kavali. They were found incorrigible. The manager, Siddhapuram Settlement admitted some Waddars of Sitanagaram during the year 1933. They were sent to Konnur Settlement for employment as gang coolies in the railways. As they were found medically unfit there, they were sent to Siddhapuram Settlement on '0 I' passes.[15] The manager of Siddhapuram settlement transferred them to Bitragunta settlement. They did not show any signs of reformation and obtained their bread by pick-pocketing in shandies and fairs. They were a menace not only to the society, but to the co-settlers also. Some CT members of Stuartpuram were transferred to Siddhapuram on the ground they originally belonged to Atmakur of Kurnool district.

Twenty families of Kanjar Bhats were brought from Konnur settlement. They brought their own culture to the new settlement. Their intermingling with the settlers made them hardened 'criminals'. Some families of Yerukulas, Dasaries from various settlements were transferred to Siddhapuram settlement, during the year 1937. During the same year some members of Nawabpeta Korchas and Waddar tribes were transferred to Sitanagaram. They became out of view from 1.9.1937 without 'G' pass and got arrested on 16.1.1938 in the hills.[16] They were incorrigible criminals who led purposeless life. These criminals committed a number of burglaries in the surrounding areas. Some Boyas were transferred from Tanjore to Siddhapuram during the year 1938. They passed out of view in 1943 and committed serious house breakings and dacoities in Kurnool and Nandikotkur circles.

IV

Administration and Control of Stuartpuram Settlement

As already mentioned that this was an essentially an agricultural settlement started by the SA to be worked as an auxiliary and in conjunction with the Sitanagaram Settlement. The Yerukulas of Guntur district used to camp near the village of Bethapudi, Bapatla taluk, from December to August every year to carry grain from the ryots of the Ongole, Bapatla and Tenali taluks. From August to December, they grazed their cattle at Venukonda. During these sojourn years the Yerukulas were in the habit of committing crime. In 1913, with the police becoming more active and attentive, the Yerukulas took shelter under the wing of the SA on their own accord. Till September 1915, the settlement had not been declared to be a CT settlement. Consequently, the settlers were under nobody's control.

They could come and go as they pleased. To obviate this difficulty in October 1915, Bethapudi was declared to be a criminal settlement under Section 16 of the CT Act.[17]

In the beginning, a few of the well-conducted inmates were appointed as watchman in the settlement. They not only watched and gave information to the manager but they had also established the links between the manager and the settlers. The position of the watchman was looked upon a very honourable one by the settlers. This formed a valuable feature in the disciplinary machinery in the settlement[18]. During certain parts of the year the SA employed some agricultural maistries from old settlers. They used to supervise the fields and made provision for planting trees in the settlement. They used to instruct the new settlers on the techniques of cultivation. They neither had the inclination to cultivate the land nor the proficiency in doing it.[19] The settlers were placed in different groups under the incharge of a maistry. His duty was to bring his gang when the bell rings at 5.30 in the morning. He took them to work in the morning and brought them back in the evening. It was quite difficult to get these people to work in the beginning. Some settlers do not even know how to hold a basket or a salagapara. Some had to be instructed for two years and some for three years. Gradually the old settlers became a strong backbone to the settlement.[20]

In addition to agricultural maistries, a Karnam was appointed on full time basis to look after the land records, measurements, allotments and supervision of the cattle. It was stated that the only person in the settlement who had knowledge in cultivation was the settlement Karanam. He had to attend to the office from 8 a.m. till 5 p.m. every day. Later, the name of Karnam was changed as '*farm bailiff*' as his duties entailed much more than a Karnam.[21] The cases of escapes and overstayals of leave were more in the settlement. The district magistrate suggested that a majority of these cases should be left to the manager to deal with instead of taking them to the court. Marjori Banks, the SA official suggested the construction of a lock-up at the Settlement.[22]

During the year 1930, the settlers were sent on 'O' passes to the Kodanda Rama mica mines in the Rapur taluk of Nellore district for employment. During the year 1936, nearly 168 families were released on 'Q' passes and permitted to live in a newly formed colony near Chirala adjoining to the premises of the ILTD (Indian Leaf Tobacco

Department) Company where some other extra work had been provided for them.[23] In spite of the manager and local police, there used to be constant fights between the settlers. They became court birds. Maintenance of peace and order was a very big problem. The police used to apply security sections on these people. Those settlers who found themselves criminally active and uncontrollable were brought under restrictions and penalties under section 10 of the Madras Habitual Offenders Act 1948.[24]

V

Conclusion

The CT Acts were amended a number of times to control these people. Though the Act remained in force for about 80 years, it failed to achieve its purpose. The policy of the Government was to suppress the turbulent elements among the tribes and also to encourage them to settle on land and to provide them with means of earning an honest livelihood. But the conditions and the status of the settlers and the settlements were the same as before. The leaders and social reformers realised that the dubbing of a people as CTs was a blot on Indian society. *Jawaharlal Nehru* stated in a speech delivered at Nellore in October 1936 that "I am, aware of this monstrous provisions of CT Act which constitute a negation of civil liberty. Wide publicity should be given to its working and an attempt made to have the Act removed from the Statute book."[25] *Pattabhi Sitaramayya* angrily pointed out that, "cattle that are sold and brought in the market, wild animals that are hunted out of villages, worms that are trodden under the feet are not worse treated than the criminal tribes."[26] Criticizing the Criminal Tribes Act *Vennelacunti Raghavaiah,* a well-known social worker stated that "born amidst such strange and outrageous notions about caste system and the supposed heredity of crime, this act destroyed domestic peace, embittered human life and led to the most false of all theories, i.e. once a criminal, always a criminal."[27] *Thakkar Bapa,* Secretary, All India Harijan Sevak Sangh, remarked that 'Criminal Tribes Act is disgracing our Statute Book'. *Desabhaktha Konda Venkatapaiah Pantulu* observed that "It is the most inhuman statute that has outlived its purpose." *K.N. Katju* as Minister for Justice remarked that "It is an insult to God and humanity to treat innocent children of criminal tribes as born criminals." *V.V. Giri* said about the CTs that "Governments are actually aware of the inequalities in the country which become glaring when contrasted with the prosperity of some sections of the community. Change in social structure and the removal of the poverty are two aspects of the same question. One cannot be achieved without the other. To class therefore a whole tribe, indeed a sixtieth of the population of whole India as criminal is itself an act of criminality of which governments are guilty. *N.G. Ranga* strongly fought for the repeal or abolition of the CT Act and the upliftment of CTs in Madras Presidency. He said the CT Act was used to 'suppress political workers'.[28]

After Independence, the Indian Government appointed a Committee in 1949 to study the usefulness of the law. It expressed the view that the CT Act was against the spirit of the Constitution. The public also moved and as a result, the CT Act was repealed in 1952, and in its place the Habitual Offenders Act was enacted. With the repeal of the Act, about 2,268,348 persons in the country were legally set free. The Committee also recommended that suitable steps should be taken for the amelioration of the problem of CTs after the repeal of the Act.[29] The Government is now involved in initiating necessary steps to ameliorate the hardships of these groups of people. In spite of all the facilities provided by the Government of India, the social position of the CTs today remain the same as before. The stigma still haunts them. These people are unable to free themselves from social bondage. It is unfortunate to recall the whole tribe or a clan or family as criminals. There is no country in the world, to our knowledge, whose people practice crime as their occupation. To our surprise, even blind persons are registered as criminals.

To know the present conditions in Siddlapuram and Stuartpuram settlements interviews are conducted. They shared with us their present problems in the settlements. The Secretary of Ex-Criminal's Welfare Association (in Siddhapuram), K.R. Somanna demanded that the Government should include all the DNTs in the list of schedule tribes. He further lamented that whenever the police suspect a person he will immediately arrest the person and apply third degree methods. E.Lakshmayya said, "Every night the police are gathering information about our ex-settlement. Recently one of our youngsters was shot-dead by police when he was returning from a pilgrimage at Sri Sailam hill."[30] Whenever and wherever there is a crime the settlers of Siddhapuram will be under severe stress. Moreover, the settlement was situated in a forest area at the foot of the Nallamalai hills, and hence snakes, pythons and cheetas abound the area. There are no proper educational and health facilities for the settlers. The entire village is plagued by the evil of illicit liquor.

With regard to Stuartpuram settlement, after independence, Indian Government removed all the powers of the missionaries particularly the SA in Andhra Pradesh. The authority of the management of Stuartpuram Settlement was shifted to the Tribal Welfare Department. Presently the entire management, control and administration of the settlements are under the supervision of the Social Tribal Welfare Department, Government of Andhra Pradesh. But still the SA continues doing its work in stuartpuram settlement. A manager, his wife and the wardens are looking after the, church and the primary schools and upper primarys in the settlement (Colony).

NOTES

1. Government of Madras, *Madras Criminal Tribes Manual, Criminal Tribes Act VI of 1924, Brought upto 31st March 1927,* Superintending Government Press, Madras, 1927.
2. Government of India, *Report of the Criminal Tribes Enquiry Committee for the year 1947,* United Provinces of India, Superintending Govt. Press, Allahabad, 1948.
3. Government of Madras, *Note Showing the progress made in the Settlement of Criminal Tribes in Madras Presidency upto September 1916,* Government Press, Madras, 1917.
4. Government of Madras, *Note showing the progress made in the settlement of Criminal Tribes in the Madras Presidency upto January 1925,* Madras, 1926.
5. Government of India, *Home Department, File No. 88/2/1945 (Police), A Report on the work done for the Reclamation of Criminal Tribes in Madras Presidency,* Government Press, Madras 1948, Tamil Nadu Archives (Hereafter TNA). The Labour Commissioner Madras, used to carry the reclamation work in the settlements. He sued to sanction loans and opened the co-operative societies in the villages. The village munsif was the member of the village Panchayats. His main duty was to improve the conduct of the villagers. He also used to report the crimes committed by the offenders in the village to the police authorities. The Co-operative Inspectors main task was to see the repayment of small loans taken by the CTs for the Seasonal harvests, for the purchase of seeds, bulls etc. Heavy taxes and land revenue was levied on the poor tribals even if their crops were failed due to failure of manssons and floods. The installment of repayments of the loans taken by the tribals were decided by them. However, the co-opreative inspectors never issued receipts for the loan repayment amount m[illegible] the helpless tribals.

6. Government of Madras, *Judicial Department, G.O. No.1299, dated 30th June 1913.*
7. Rowland, L.E., *Report of the American Baptist Telugu Mission from May 1st to December 31st, 1928,* Orissa Mission Press, 1929.
8. Robert Sandal, *The History of the Salvation Army, Vol. III,* New York, 1955, p. 276.
9. Government of Madras, *Home Judicial Department, G.O. No. 1537,* dated 27.7.1917, Andhra Pradesh State Archieves.
10. Government of Madras, *Public Works (Labour) Department, G.O. No. 1147,* dated 26.5.1933 (APSA).
11. Government of Madras, *Madras Criminal Tribes manual brought upto 31st March 1927,* Madras, 1928, p. 3 (APSA). *The administration and management of the settlements included: (i)* Sanctioning of leave to the managers and assistant managers, *(ii)* Settlement population/men, women, children, old, infirm, destitute, lone women, released prisoners, new settlers transferred from the settlements etc. *(iii)* Providing employment opportunities such as agriculture, industries, weaving, match industry, carpentary, sandal making and other kinds of employement *(iv)* health *(v)* housing and sanitation *(vi)* education *(vii)* convictions *(viii)* abscondings *(ix)* discharges from the settlements *(x)* budget accounts *(xi)* cooperative stores *(xii)* profit and loss accounts *(xiii)* cattle wealth and settlement grants, etc.
12. Government of Madras, *Home Department, G.O. No. 2661, dated 25.10.1920,* p. 1. (APSA).
13. Government of Madras, *Public Works (Labour) Department, G.O. No. 1719, dated 9.8.1927* (APSA).
14. Government of Madras, *Public Works (Labour) Department, G.O. No. 2190, dated 28.8.1930* (TNA).
15. Government of Madras, *Public Works (Labour) Department, G.O. No. 2247, dated 17.10.1933* (TNA).
16. Government of Madras, *Home Department, G.O. No. 1217, dated 6.3.1939.*
17. Government of Madras, *Note showing the progress made in the settlement of Criminal Tribes in Madras Presidency upto September 1916,* Madras, 1917.
18. Government of Madras, *Home (Judicial) Department, G.O. No. 2074 dated 18.9.1916.*
19. Government of Madras, *Law (General) Department, G.O. No. 1714, dated 22.10.1921.* Also see *Law (General) Department, G.O. No. 3187, dated 14.11.1924.*
20. Government of Madras, *Home (Judicial) Department, G.O. No. 2074 dated 18.8.1916.*
21. See Government of Madras, *Law (General) Department, G.O. No. 748, dated 8.8.1925.*

22. Salvation Army monthly *The War Cry*, International Heritage Centre, London, April 1937. Also see Government of Madras, *Judicial Department, G.O. No. 1974,* dated 10.8.1920.
23. Government of Madras, *Public Works (Labour) Department, G.O. No. 2671 dated 6.12.1934.*
24. Government of Madras, *Administration Report on Habitual Offenders Settlements for the year 1949-50,* Government Central Press, Madras, 1951.
25. Raghavaiah, V., *The Problem of Criminal Tribes,* Bharatiya Adimjati Sevak Sangh, New Delhi, 1949, p. 6.
26. Lalitha, V., *The Making of Criminal Tribes, Patterns and Transition,* New Era Publications, Madras, 1995.
27. Raghavaiah, V., *1943 :17.*
28. *Ibid.*
29. Government of Madras, *Administration Report on Kallar, Koravar Reclamation for the year 1949-50,* Government Press, Madras, 1951. Also see, Simhadri, Y.C., *Denotified Tribes – A Sociological Analysis,* Classical Publishing Company, New Delhi, 1991.
30. Interview with *K.R.,Somanna and E., Lakshmayya,* Siddhapuram Settlement, dated 19.2.2006.

7

Financial Management of Denotified Tribe Settlements

I

Introduction

The CT settlements in Andhra Pradesh were not under the management of one single agency. The settlements worked in a circle. The cases of the CT settlements came up with confused conditions. The control of the CTs and their settlements were entrusted to the district officers in the Presidency. The government maintained records for the settlements. Since the government found it difficult to prescribe a uniform set of rules with regard to the financial management of the settlements, the government entrusted the work to the Christian Missionaries. The government sanctioned grants for the supervision of the settlements, old and infirm people, management of hospitals, schools, sanitation and plantation work. There was economic management problem at every quarter from the settlements. There was also mismanagement of funds sanctioned for the running of the settlements. Added to this, there was severe moral problem from the managers, settlers, police, district officers, missionaries and the police authorities. The present chapter deals with the various issues such as the grants provided to the missionaries for running the settlements, auditing of the settlement accounts, grants provided for the settlements which were under the deplection stage, financing of the CT settlements, deficit in the working of the Denotified Tribe Settlements, financial management and mismanagement of Kavali, Siddhapuram and Stuartpuram settlements in a historical perspective. Sitanagaram and Stuartpuram settlements were under the control of the Salvation

Army.[1] The SA agreed to follow the general principles laid down by the government. The government paid the SA an annual fixed amount for the administration and supervision of the settlements. The government paid the amount in four quarterly instalments in a year. The items of expenditure on the settlements were classified into service charges and industrial charges. The net surplus unspent balance in the grants of the government of the settlements in Andhra Pradesh on 31.3.1922 was Rs.25,635.[2]

II

Grants Provided to the Salvation Army for Running the Settlements

Most of the settlements in Andhra Pradesh worked on deficit and financial loss. The government recouped the SA by cancelling the loans to the extent of the deficits. The recurring grants provided to the settlements were increased. The government provided the non-recurring grants towards buildings, roads, agricultural development and industries. Booth Tucker said : "There was the loss on contracts. The quarries were worked on the contract system. There was the large deficit under quarries. The losses on contracts including quarries were due to the bad business methods of the managers."[3] The government sanctioned grants for the supervision of the settlements, for the supervision of old and infirm people, for the management of hospitals and schools and for the sanitation and tree plantation work, etc. The then district magistrate of Madras pointed out: "The settlements are expected to work more economically."[4] The recurring grants were increased by the government for the better working of the settlements. The finance department used to audit all the accounts and loans granted for the continuation of the settlements.

III

Grants Provided for Settlements

The missionaries submitted new proposals to the government for the release of fresh loans. The SA constructed new buildings in the settlements out of the fresh loans obtained from the government. All the buildings erected out of the government grants remained the property of the government.[5] For the sake of saving expenditure, the government wanted to close down some settlements. Agriculture and industries in the settlements worked out with heavy losses.

Some settlements were marked for their closure because of the bad management and high recurring expenses. The settlements were abandoned due to: 1. non-availability of land for the new settlers, 2. lack of hope for the industrial development, 3. the proximity of towns and 4. the government solely depending on the qualified managers to run the settlements, etc. The government provided with the construction of additional huts, subsistence allowances and the grant of medical relief for the new settlers.[6]

IV

Financing of the 'Criminal' Tribe settlements

E.A. Davis, the then District Magistrate of Guntur said: "Regular reports were called upon to know the future conditions of the 'criminal' settlements." He emphasised on 1. the grant of the lumpsum allowances on a liberal scale which was sufficient to finance all classes of expenditure and providing employment, 2. placing the settlements under the direct control of the district magistrates for effective control and to correspond with the missionary authorities. This procedure lead to the decentralization of the financial arrangement of the DNT settlements.[7]

V

Deficit in the Working of the Denotified Tribe Settlements

The cases of the 'criminal' settlements came up with confused conditions. The control of the CTs and their settlements were entrusted to the district officers in the Presidency. The Inspector General of Police, Madras, stated : "The Deputy Inspector-General Criminal Investigation Department might informally be constituted as an adviser to the Inspector-General of Police and the district magistrates on all matters connected with settlements."[8] The Deputy Inspector General of Police, Railways and the Criminal Investigation Department exercised the general control over the settlements for the purpose of organising and co-ordinating the work. The Deputy Inspector General of Police acted as a co-ordinating officer. Special officers were appointed by the government to make the industrial survey to discover the sources of employment for the settlers. Gillman wrote: "The reversion of the system is to continue until the circumstances permit of a special officer being appointed."[9]

The district magistrates faced the problem of supervising the settlements. Alexander Cardew, a district magistrate in Madras

Presidency suggested the abandonment of the settlements. Booth Tucker, the SA Officer objected the district magistrates control over the settlements. The district magistrate's correspondence with the settlement managers used to result in friction. The SA complained: "The government misunderstood the management of the criminal tribe settlements by the missionaries."[10] The government requested; the missionaries to avoid the friction between the district magistrates and the missionaries.

The government maintained the records for the settlements. The records consisted of the form of management in force, the nature of pecuniary assistance given by the government, stock file of grants, the expenses under various items, the civil budget estimate and the grants given by the government for specific purposes, etc. The grants given by the government and the expenditure incurred were classified under main heads. They were submitted to the government with specific recommendations.

Separate grants were provided with regard to the schooling facilities in the settlement. The government treated the schooling in the settlements as a separate unit. The then district magistrate of Madras said: "The cost of schooling was very high. The schools' perhaps may be allowed to earn the educational grant-in-aid. The grant for the medical relief was given by the District Boards."[11] The medical relief grants were undertaken by the government with the help of the private agencies. Duty allowances were paid to the sub-assistant surgeons who attended the medical relief work in the settlements. The missionaries spent a lot of expenditure on petty things. Loans and advances have been sanctioned for the maintenance of the settlements by the government. Separate advances were sanctioned for the cultivation of lands and for the payment of daily wages to the settlers. The 'incapables' in the settlements were 'managed' by the SA.

VI

Financial Management of Kavali Settlement

The Kavali settlement was under the management of the ABM (Telugu) Mission. The government used to bear the net cost for running of the settlement. The Baptist Mission only paid the Managers' salary. A fixed grant was being paid to the Manager at the beginning of every month. This system came into force during the year 1915. The monthly grant given by the government fluctuated every year due to the strength in the settlement. The amount sanctioned was not a fixed grant in the strict sense of the word. Additional grants have been paid to the mission to meet the deficits. Arthur Knapp the then British officer on the settlements said : "after a detailed analysis of the expenditure as compared with other settlements, Kavali settlement costed the government most. A large amount of expenditure was incurred for running of the settlement."[12]

The cause for the heavy expenditure of the Kavali settlement was due to the boarding school at Kavali. The school provided education for all the school going children in the settlement. The expenditure on education for the school going children during the year 1923 was Rs.22,533.39.[13] The school was doing excellent work. The money that had been spent was useful. The cost of the supervision work was also very high. The expenditure for the supervision work during the year 1924 was Rs. 15,523,03.[14] The other cause for the high expenditure of the settlement was due to the reason that the settlers were mainly belonging to 'habitual' classes. There was also the difficulty of finding work for the settlers. The settlers were sent out for long distances under the supervision of the police guards. It was noticed that the Salvation Army men were cheaper than the men employed by the American Baptist Mission.

The examiners of the local fund accounts used to audit the accounts of the DNT Settlements. The examiners of the local fund accounts often complained against the system of accounts maintained by the authorities in the settlements. To tide over the difficulty of want of remunerative work at the settlement, the settlers often had been transferred to Bitragunta and Allur. The Kavali Settlement was established as a Penal or Reformatory settlement. The missionaries maintained separate accounts for the reformatory settlements[15].

VII

Financial Management of Siddhapuram Settlement

Siddhapuram settlement was under the direct management of the government. The net cost of the settlement was borne by the government itself. The main items of the expenditure of the settlement were: 1. the maintenance of sick or incapable settlers, 2. medical charges for each settler, 3. fixed travelling allowances paid to the sub-assistant surgeons who visited the settlement periodically,

4. for the cost of the maintenance of the police staff and 5. for the education of the Waddar children. It was stated that: "No pupil of Siddhapuram settlement was sent up so far for higher education after they had completed their education in the settlement school. With a view to providing higher education for the children of Siddhapuram settlement, the manager of the settlement made the arrangements. They were admitted as free boarders in the Adi Andhra Free Boarding Home at Atmakur. They will be having their free education there. These pupils are ineligible for the award of scholarships as they exceeded the age limit of the scholarship notification. As these pupils are Waddars who are generally very backward and as some of the pupils are reported to be intelligent and fit for higher studies, the government is pleased to award the scholarships whenever necessary as a special case."[16] The cost for the maintenance of the police staff at Siddhapuram settlement consisting of one Inspector, two head constables and 14 constables were met from the government from the police budget. A temporary clerk on Rs. 50 had been sanctioned for the settlement.

VIII

Financial Management of Stuartpuram Settlement

The SA was provided with grants by the Government of Madras to transfer the families of the CTs from one settlement to another settlement. With more transfer of families into the settlements the government increased the police staff for the better supervision of the settlers in the colonies. The Accountant General placed the funds into the SA account in a Bank located at Madras. The charges to maintain the settlement expenses were met from the yearly sanctioned budget under the major head of the police.[17] Two important questions were raised by the government. One, with regard to the transfer of the families from one settlement to another settlement by the SA and the other why the sanctioning of the subsistence allowance should be made to the SA? The Salvation Army emphasised that the object of the subsistence allowance asked by the SA was to enable the settlers to maintain themselves and cultivate the land put at their disposal until the crops were grown.[18] Separate proposals were made by the Salvation Army to increase the settlers strength in Stuartpuram settlement. Booth Tucker wrote to Harold Stuart the then member in Council, Madras that: "I am rather nervous about having so large a settlement as Robilliard contemplates, but I will consult the Inspector-General of Police and the District Magistrate and see what can be done...."[19]

The SA asked the government for the provision of additional watchman for better supervision of the settlers. But the government raised objections to sanction more staff. The government asked the SA the question that why should not the families be made to do some wage earning work? The SA authorities reported that: "the case of the settlers is exactly the same as the case of the previous batches sent to the settlements. If the new settlers are put on wage-earning work they obviously cannot open up new land and this is the reason for asking more grants."[20] Captain Robilliard asked for one watchman for every 100 settlers whereas Mr.Bawden asked for one watchman for every 50 settlers. The government recognized the usefulness of the watchman. The Secretary of the then British government observed that: "The watchmen are doing good work and I should be loath to do anything to impair their usefulness.... They are really special constables."[21]

A total amount of Rs. 70,000 was sanctioned to the SA for the supervision of the settlers in 1916. The government had given to the SA authorities a monthly recurring grant of Rs. 300 per mensem for a period of 5 years for the cost of supervision and other expenses, an additional recurring grant of Rs. 75 per mensem for the payment of the Yerukula watchmen and an additional recurring grant of Rs. 100 per mensem to meet the increased supervision charges of the settlers. The government while sanctioning the amount asked the SA what steps were proposed to be taken to place additional 'crims' (settlers) in Stuartpuram, settlement. Who were to be sent to Stuartpuram settlement? The Salvation Army replied that since the Suramangalam settlement and Karuppur settlements were not started, it was intended to send the Rudrapad Korachas into the settlement. The financial department accepted the additional settlers proposed by the Salvation Army.[22]

The SA employed peons in the Settlement schools. They continued in the service at the rate of Rs. 8 per mensem. Mackenzie stated: The peons are not peons in the ordinary sense but their main duty is the collection of children from all parts of the scattered settlement. A certain amount of pressure has to be brought to bear to get the children to school."[23]

The managers of Stuartpuram and Sitanagaram settlements visited the other settlements in Madras, Bombay and Nizam dominions at the cost of the government for the exchange of ideas. Such visits were encouraged by the government. The places visited by the managers were from Bezwada to Lingala settlement, Secunderabad, Hotgi, Sholapur, Bijapur, Bagalkot, Gaddak, Gaddak Falls, Hubli, Trichinopoly, Madurai, Tinnevelly (Kulasekarapatnam settlement), Tanjore, Borstal Institute, Aziz Nagar, Pallavaram, Kavali, Bitragunta and Allur settlements. A sum of Rs. 250 was sanctioned by the government to visit other settlements for the purpose of studying different managements. The managers stated : "The direct railway fares for visiting the places amounts to second class (Rs. 112) and third class (Rs. 40.93). Other charges such as travelling by road to various other places, lodging would amount to about Rs. 75."[24] The managers were asked to travel in third class and thus the charges came to Rs. 125 for the whole trip. Mr.Ellis the then Collector of Madura had given his opinion to the effect that "studying the reclamative movements among the Kallars would be immensely useful and instructive."[25]

The SA appointed Assistant Managers to help the Managers in running of settlements. The pay of the Assistant Managers was very low. They were paid an amount of Rs. 180 per mensem. A European Assistant Manager was appointed in Stuartpuram Settlement during the year 1923. His pay was fixed at Rs. 1800 per annum. The SA reported that : "With regard to the European Assistant Managers, they had the same financial obligations in the shape of furlough, passage money, etc. as in the case of the managers in the settlement."[26] The industries carried on in the settlement were related to cattle, gardening and cultivation. The term "Industries" was apt to be misleading. The upkeep of the cattle was not much. The SA sold all the cattle as and when the opportunity occurred. The expenditure on account of the maintenance of cattle had fallen from Rs. 807.57 during the year 1925-26 to Rs. 495 during the year 1927-28.[27]

Stuartpuram settlement was the largest SA settlement in the Madras Presidency. The financial secretary reported that there was a deficit in the working of the settlement. The scheme for casuarinas plantation was first reported on 30.1.1920. The initial cost of the plantation scheme was prohibitive. The return was very slow. The extension of wet cultivation was suggested in the settlement. It was stated that: "The personality of Captain Robilliard who is a genius as a gardener, combining general skill with tremendous enthusiasm. His plantation of mango, rubber and other trees on the Bapatla sands are wonderful."[28] The fruit canning methods in Europe and the experienced people in the industry were called to these settlements. They suggested the tomato canning scheme. The Madras and local markets received the products. The casuarina plants developed by the settlers were felled when they were 8 years old. The settlers converted the trees into firewood. They transported the firewood to the markets and got income by the sale of firewood. 2/3 of the settlement villagers were accustomed to labour work. Daily labour was paid to the settlers at the rate of 4 annas a day. J.F. Hall the then Commissioner of Labour Madras stated that: "The territorial commanders in the Salvation Army with the help of the government maintained, lone women in the settlements. The government sanctioned the money required by the Salvation Army from the budget earmarked for the maintenance of the Criminal Tribe Settlements."[29]

T.G. Rutherford the then British Govt. official in the year 1936 said that there were a number of children in Stuartpuram settlement. The children were orphans. They were the children of destitute parents. They were not given adequate attention and care. Many of them were the children of widowed mothers who could not provide sufficient food. The children never attended the schools regularly. It was very difficult to compel the parents to send their children to school due to the circumstances which prevailed in the settlement. The Salvation Army requested the government that the children may be fed at the government expense at the rate of Rs. 3.84 per head per mensem. The expenditure was met from the savings anticipated in the yearly budget provision.[30] The SA often complained the settlers that for generations the settlers had lived by their wits which they preyed upon the society.[31] The financial and moral support from the government and the missionaries is aimed to change the settlers into self-respecting and law abiding citizens. These people by providing financial support, at first they were taught to work and regard a life of honest work as natural and normal. They were released from the restraints only under the condition that they were able to put the lessons to effect. They assured the managers to carry out work assigned to them. They promised that they will not be subjected to any temptation even when they will be driven to economic stress. The settlers used to promise the authorities that they will not revert to their old habits. The SA also had maintained its tactics. It contemplated not the gradual reduction and disappearance of the settlements. The Salvation Army's work was accomplished leaving as the crown of their endeavours. They thought their task will be completed as and when the men and women had regained their position as independent self-supporting and valuable members of the society.[32] Thus the missionaries had governed the history of the Settlements. The zeal, enthusiasm and the genius of its managers had accomplished their wonders and demonstrated this great potentialities and possibilities.

IX

Conclusion

If examined closely the activities and schemes provided by the government and the missionaries, they were more appropriate to the purpose of an enterprising development syndicate during its labour from the open market than to those by which alone the settlement can justify its existence. The settlers were the subserviant to the schemes instead of the schemes to the settlers. Their economic regeneration is yet far to seek even their daily subsistence is far from assured. The sources from which it has been drawn are largely unascertained but suspect.[33] The SA also perpetuated disadvantages to the existing system by converting the settlers into its fold. The settlements became an open market for the large scale demand of cheap labourers available from the settlements and free conversions of people to Christianity. The SA and the British Government offered little prospect of economic emancipation to the settlers. The financial prospects of the settlers under the financial control and management of the missionaries and the government if examined carefully, it will be clearly understood that they did not prosper instead the settlers became the source of economy to the government and the missionaries.

NOTES

1. Government of Madras, *Law (General) Department, G.O. No. 2454 dated 7.10.1922.*
2. Any small deficit in one settlement was not allowed to be met by savings in another. No reappropriation was permitted from the various heads of expenditure. Accounts were demanded in respect of the grants by the government. The supervision grant included all expenses of transfers, leave, acting allowances, travelling allowances for bringing

European Assistants and the headquarters supervision charges, etc. See Govt. of Madras, *Law (General) Department, G.O. No. 432 dated 9.2.1924.*

3. The service charges included items such as education, medical relief, buildings, maintenance of incapables and grants for the new settlers. The industrial charges included items such as the maintenance of various industries in the settlement. The accounts under industries were kept distinctly. The expenditure under services was governed by rules, such as vouchers, sanction, re-appropriation, surrenders, etc. The Managers of the settlements had no powers to sanction any establishment under the head of industries. The annual budget was provided for the expenditure under capital charges. The surplus after closing the accounts was credited to the government. See Government of Madras, *Home (Judicial) Department, G.O. No. 1225 dated 20.5.1918.*
4. Government of Madras, *Home (Judicial) Department, G.O. No. 22 dated 5.1.1920.*
5. Government of Madras, *Home (Judicial) Department, G.O. No. 2000 dated 3.12.1912.* The government sanctioned all the proposals submitted by the missionaries. The missionaries in turn suggested the government to cancel the Governments part of the loan. In return the missionaries lost the money which was advanced by them to the management authorities in the settlements.
6. Government of Madras, *Home (Judicial) Department, G.O. No. 22 dated 5.1.1920.*
7. Government of Madras, *Home (Judicial) Department, G.O. No. 573 dated 29.2.1916.* Also see, Dilip D'Souza, *Branded by Law: Looking at India's Denotified Tribes,* Penguin Books, New Delhi, 2001.
8. Government of Madras, *Home (Judicial) Department, G.O. No. 678 dated 13.3.1916.*
9. Government of Madras, *Home (Judicial) Department, GO. No. 818, dated 5.4.1918.* Also see, Politics of 'hereditary' crime, *The Hindu,* September 9, 2001.
10. Government of Madras, *Home (Judicial) Department, G.O. No. 625, dated 18.3.1918.*
11. Government of Madras, *Home (Judicial) Department, G.O. No. 1225 dated 20.5.1918.*
12. Government of Madras, *Home (Judicial) Department, G.O. No. 2233 dated 29.9.1919.*
13. Government of Madras, *Note showing the progress made in the Settlements of Criminal Tribes upto 1925,* Government Central Press, Madras, 1926.
14. *Ibid.*
15. Government of Madras, *Law (General) Department, G.O. No. 432 dt 9.2.1924.*

16. Government of Madras, *Public Works (Labour) Department, G.O. No. 1843 dated 25.8.1927.*
17. Government of Madras, *Home (Judicial) Department, G.O. No. 2615 dated 13.12.1917.*
18. Government of Madras, *Home (Judicial) Department, G.O. No. 2491, dated 12.10.1915.*
19. Government of Madras, *Home (Judicial) Department, G.O. No. 1275 dated 3.6.1914.*
20. Government of Madras, *Home (Judicial) Department, G.O. No. 716 dated 30.3.1917.*
21. Government of Madras, *Home (Judicial) Department, G.O. No. 2273 dated 20th September 1915.*
22. Government of Madras, *Home (Judicial) Department, G.O. No. 430 dated 17.2.1906.* Also see, Meena Radhakrishna, *Dishonoured by History: 'Criminal Tribes' and British Colonial Policy,* Orient Longman Limited, New Delhi, 2001.
23. Government of Madras, *Law (General) Department, G.O. No. 1771 dated 26.5.1926.*
24. Government of Madras, *Law (General) Department, G.O. No. 1098, (Mis) dated 1.4.1926.*
25. Government of Madras, *Law (General) Department, G.O. No. 950 dated 4.8.1926.*
26. Government of Madras, *Law (General) Department, G.O. No. 1786 dated 24.11.1926.*
27. Government of Madras, *Law (General) Department, G.O. No. 1098 (Mis) dated 1.4.1926.*
28. Government of Madras, *Home (Judicial) Department, G.O. No. 2907 dated 3.2.1920.*
29. Government of Madras, *Home (Judicial) Department, G.O. No. 22 dated 5.1.1920.*
30. Government of Madras, *Home (Judicial) Department, G.O. No. 958 dated 30.4.1919.*
31. Government of Madras, *Home (Judicial) Department, G.O. No. 2163 dated 23rd September 1918.*
32. Government of Madras, *Home (Judicial) Department, G.O. No. 829 dated 6.4.1918.*
33. *Home (Judicial) Department, G.O. No. 1449 dated 13.7.1917.* Also see, Viswanathan, S., "Suspects forever, Members of the "denotified tribes" continue to bear the brunt of police brutality, *Frontline, Vol. 19, Issue 12, June 8-21, 2002.*

8

Land Allotment

I

Introduction

The DNT settlements were covered with reserved forests. In the initial period, the forest department did not use the lands. This enabled the private owners to succeed in encroaching the lands. The private persons made profits out of the forest lands. Timber was cut in order to obtain quick profits. The private owners restricted the grazing rights of the poor tribal population. Meanwhile the rich people in the surrounding areas brought pressure on the government to reclaim the swamp lands. The Cooperative Societies Association used to appeal to the government to aid the association.

The government of Madras provided agricultural and Industrial settlements for the DNTs. The government assigned the land to the managing agencies on many conditions. The settlers were expected to earn an honest means of livelihood by tilling and cultivating the land.

The government deforested the lands in order to encourage the private enterprise. The government planted trees in the sandy tracts (loose sandy soil) and classified the tribal settlement lands under six major heads: *(i)* areas in which casuarina plants were already developed, *(ii)* area taken up for fresh plantation with casuarina plants, *(iii)* area planted with mango plants, *(iv)* open pastural area, *(v)* the area covered with scrub jungle and *(vi)* the area of unproductive salt parra (unproductive land).[1]

The area already with casuarina plants, the area under fresh plantation with casuarina and the area planted with mango plants were under the forest department. The district forest officers used to prepare regular working plans for the areas planted with casuarina plantations. The grazing needs of the cattle, buffaloes, sheep and goats of the tribal population were overlooked. The parra lands in the settlement areas were unproductive. The scrub jungle was thickly grown with prickly-pear shrubs, (cactus thorns.) The private owners occupied the scrub jungle areas free of cost. The forest department sold parts of the settlement lands at cheaper rates to private and wealthy persons to invest their capital and provide employment for the poor. The private persons made profits out of these forest lands. Timber was cut in order to obtain quick profits. The private owners restricted the grazing rights of the poor tribal population.[2]

II

Deforestation of Lands Reserved for Tribals

Thousands of acres of land was reserved by the British Government in order to plant the trees in the forests. The government planned to ensure rainfall and conserve the resources of the land. This was a wise and beneficial act done by the British government. People in their ignorance destroyed the forests. Hundreds of acres in the reserved forests remained vacant and unplanted by the forest department. There was a great demand for the firewood in the surrounding areas. The private land owners planted thousands of acres with Casuarina and other trees. Thus, the forest land owned by the private land holders was large in extent. The government sold the forest lands to the private enterprisers due to the following reasons : 1. The government wanted to increase the private enterprise in the tree plantation work. 2. The government wanted to increase money for other public utility services by selling the forest lands in auction. 3. The rich people did not want to invest their savings in mercantile ventures. The purchase of the forest lands from the government ensured them a safe and productive investment of their funds. 4. The annual assessment amount on the lands was paid by the private owners. Thus the deforested area greatly increased the revenue of the government. 5. The benefit for the general public was that: the forests offered the remunerative labour to thousands of coolies in the settlement areas.[3]

III

Demand for Swamp Lands

The rich people in the surrounding areas brought pressure on the government to reclaim the swamp land in the settlement areas. The tribal hamlets were impoverished by the swamp land cultivation by the landlords. Their crops were swept away by the floods. They could not secure more than three poor crops over a period of 10 years.[4] The Co-operative Societies' Associations used to appeal the government to aid the associations. The associations requested the government to appoint them as the agents of the government to sell the lands to worthy ryots in the association. By selling the lands to the rich people in the association they tried to enrich themselves at the expense of the poor cultivators.

The government gave the lands to the poor and the worthy ryots with the following terms and conditions: 1. The Public Works Department had fixed a price of Rs. 25 per acre on the swamp land. The government asked the associations to sell the lands at rates fixed by the govt. 2. In the waste lands only palmyra palms were allowed to grow. The palmyra palms produced only leaves. The cultivators who secured the swamp land were allowed to secure 10 cents of land free of cost. The cost of the trees in the waste land formed additional hamlets in the settlement areas. 3. The lands are inalienable until the cultivators got the right to sell from the district collectors. 4. A permanent revenue from the swamp lands and the house taxes from the settlement lands were assured to the govenment[5].

In order to prevent moneylenders from securing the swamp lands, building sites, etc. the local public petitioned the government not to allot the land to the co-operative societies. The request of the petitioners to the government was: 1. All reserved forests in the settlement areas should be deforested and sold to the private parties who sought to invest their capital. 2. The swamp lands should be given to the cooperative associations to distribute to its members.[6]

IV

Apportionment of Land Among 'Criminal' Tribes

The Government of Madras provided agricultural and industrial settlements for the CTs. Agricultural settlements were considered as a reward for the good behaviour of the settlers. It means those who behaved well in the industrial settlements were placed in agricultural settlements. The government reported : "It is proved by experience in all countries and with all classes, that so long as the cooli system is in force the labourer does as little work as possible, but as soon as a man is given a small plot of land he turns out at dawn and works till late; and even if he has other tasks to perform he will manage to find time to devote a certain amount of labour with his own plot."[7] The government decided on agriculture as the main industry in all the settlements and provided land for the settlers.

V

The Policy of the Government in Assigning Land for the Settlers

The government assigned land to the managing agencies on many conditions. The land was not given to the settlers directly. The government was the sole agent for assigning and taking away the land from the settlers. The practice of allotting land for the settlers varied from settlement to settlement. However, as a general principle, the government distributed among each family of the settlers a block of dry land and a piece of wet land. The settlers were made responsible for the cultivation of the lands. In order to prevent the settlers from the alienation of their lands, the settlers were made as tenants of the managing body of the settlements. The settlers were asked to pay rent for their lands. The government in course of time provided pattas for the settlers' lands who had proved their fitness to own land by their hard work and good conduct with continuous industry, and fitness to own the land.[8] Thus, the settlers were expected to earn an honest means of livelihood by tilling and cultivating their lands. Out of seven 'CT' settlements established under 'CT Act of 1911, upto the end of the year 1915, the lands in five settlements were managed by the SA. The land in Kavali Settlement was managed by the American Baptist Telugu Mission and the forest land in Siddhapuram Settlement was under the official management of the government.[9]

VI

Land Allotment for the Opening of Siddhapuram, Sitanagaram and Stuartpuram Settlements

(a) Siddhapuram Settlement

Siddhapuram settlement was a voluntary settlement. The boundaries of this settlement were as follows. In the north-southern boundary, there is Krishnapuram Agraharam. In the west-southern boundary, there is Velgode Reserve and Dornal-Atmakur Road. In the east, the boundary runs south-west along the sim's line to a point where it meets the Siddhapuram tank bund and in the south, the boundary runs to the south-east corner of Kandam. Likewise in the west, the boundary runs northwards of the Velgode reserve (terailine) to the starting point. The whole settlement was within 200 to 300 yards of the bund of the big tank. Between the bund and the village is a depression from which earth for the bund was excavated. Water stagnates throughout the year and there is a dense growth of bulrushes and other marsh-grass. Two hundred yards to the north of the village is a drainage depression in which water stagnates and bulrushes flourish.

The village is surrounded by ideal breeding grounds for anopheles. The forest humidity and water logging bred mosquitoes, and malaria claimed a heavy death toll. The main source of livelihood for the settlers was agriculture. 1066 acres of land was distributed to the settlers in the beginning. There was a great demand from outsiders for the settlement land which is a sign of its value. To develop the minds of the settlers with an idea that they are ryots and not 'criminals' the manager: 1. removed a few families' names from the registers who had done well 2. a headman was appointed to perform the duties of those of the ordinary village headman, 3. two talayaris were appointed to control the community and 4. temporary pattas were given for 5 years. Wet and dry lands were cultivated on behalf of the government partly to teach the settlers proper method of agriculture and partly to provide a certain amount of labour for them. The officers of the agricultural department visited the settlement frequently. The efforts of the agricultural maistries was very effective towards the improvement of agriculture.

(b) Sitanagaram Settlement

Sitanagaram Settlement was formed by the SA by placing some Yerukula women whose male relatives were in jail. An extent of 84.06 acres of land at Sitanagaram (relinquished by the Madras and Southern Mahratta Railway Company) was provided to the SA on free of cost. The government also entrusted the SA with the occupancy rights and free assessment rights on the lands. The settlement was the first of its kind. The settlement was actually opened in January 1913. Agriculture was made as the chief means of livelihood for the

Yerukulas. But, in the beginning, there was very little scope for the settlers to do agricultural work in the settlement.

(c) *Stuartpuram Settlement*

In Guntur district three settlements worked closely with each other. The different characteristic features made the settlements suited for co-operating with each other with an interchange of the tribal settlers. This was very conducive for the success of each settlement. All the settlements worked together under similar conditions.[10] Sitanagaram and Stuartpuram settlements were open settlements. The two settlements were reserved for 'would be goods'. The settlers, who settled there rarely absconded from the settlements. The speciality of the two settlements was such that even if any settler chose to abscond from the settled life, the nature of the other settlers made them not to abscond from the settlements. The nature and scope of the two settlements prevented the other settlers from absconding from their settled life. To some extent this was due to the allotment of land for the settlers in the DNT colonies.

Stuartpuram settlement was essentially an agricultural settlement.[11] The settlement was started by the SA as an auxiliary settlement. Some Yerukulas of Guntur district used to camp near Betapudi village, Bapatla taluk every year. They used to carry grain to the ryots of Ongole, Bapatla and Tenali taluks. They grazed their cattle at Venukonda. During the year 1913, the Yerukulas took shelter under the wings of the SA. As a result of this, the government in the year 1914 gave 1,860 acres of land to the SA to open a settlement for the Yerukulas. In the mean time, certain inhabitants of Bapatla and the neighbouring villages started an agitation protesting against the increase of crime in the locality and the grant of land for the purpose of the opening settlement. On careful enquiry the government was convinced that the Yerukulas were not responsible for crime and the agitation was set up by certain persons with unworthy and selfish motives. In October 1915, Bethapudi was declared to be a 'criminal' settlement under Section 16 of the CT Act 1911.[12]

Betapudi settlement flourished very well. This settlement got a good name among the neighbours. The settlers expressed their preference for agricultural work. The reserve forest was located on either side of the railway line. It was stretched from Mr. Powell's sugar farm located at the outskirts of Bapatla taluk to the village of

Ipurupalem. It was on the sandy ridge. The settlement lands had plenty of good water near the surface. It was suited for ragi, groundnut and other crops. Experts said that the land was excellent for mulberry plantation. It was reported that: "The government proposed to run the settlement along either side of the railway line on the Canadian system of long narrow strips with the huts facing the railway line on each side and a garden in front and the rest of their land at the back: thus each cottage would be on its own land and the whole thing would present a most picturesque appearance."[13] The swamp land in the settlement was very valuable but they had the problems of drainage, bunding and irrigation. A block of 1500 acres was earmarked for colonising the settlers. A small rent was fixed to serve the working expenses.[14]

Several of the waste lands were lying vacant and were very close to the Romperu swamp. Mackenzie, the SA Officer in the company along with the then Tahasildar of Bapatla, visited the lands and had carefully gone through the area and selected several pieces of land. The fields finally selected were situated in the villages of Betapudi, Murukondapadu and Ipurupalem villages. They were broadly classified under *Reserved Forests* and *Assessed Waste Lands.*[15] The then Conservator of Forests inspected the land and said: "The lands should not be deforested. The Board has recently called for proposals for deforesting the reserved forests in this district and the matter is under enquiry. Each forest has to be inspected jointly by the District Forest Officer and the Divisional Officer and it will be fully six months before the report can be drawn up. The question of assigning the Vedullapalli reserve to private individuals may lie over for the present, and Mr. Mackenzie has selected other lands in its place."[16]

The government approved the proposals made by the SA officer Commissioner Booth Tucker for opening a settlement for the CTs near Betapudi in Guntur district. A block of 360 acres of assessed waste dry land in Murukondapadu and Ipurupalem villages and another area of 1500 acres comprising within the areas of Romperu swamp lands were given to the SA to run the settlement. The orders for starting the settlement was given by the revenue department transferring the land to the SA imposing the conditions and making the SA the sole agent on the land.[17]

The SA obtained 13 acres of land in Bethapudi. Several members of the CID gang No.VIII were induced to settle there. Booth Tucker, the then SA Commissioner agreed to start a regular agricultural colony. Large extent of the waste land was available for the opening of the settlement. Booth Tucker inspected the land in person. The land was granted to the SA on 15th December 1913 without bothering about the interests of other ryots.[18]

VII

The Romperu Swamp Lands, and the Yerukulas

The swamp lands were located between Commamur canal on one side and the sandy ridge along with the railway lines on the other. It starts from Mulapalem near Bapatla and ends at Peda Ganjam. The Public Works Department was unable to supply the canal water regularly. The settlers depended on rain water and the drainage water from the surrounding area fields for irrigation. The Romperu swamp traversed the limits of 17 villages. It covered a total area of 20,000 acres. The excavation of the Perali drain and the construction of undersluices in the Nallamada drain tended to improve the matter of cultivation.[19] The Yerukulas who settled near Betapudi came on their own accord. They intended seriously to settle down as agriculturists. Supervisory methods were exercised over them. The movements of the settlers were restricted. Good conduct settlers only were allotted to possess lands permanently. No permanent pattas were sanctioned to them.[20]

The Board opined that the reserve forest near Betapudi was the best location for the initial settlement of the Yerukulas. The board assigned a total number of 360 acres for the purpose and assigned the land to the SA through Revenue Department. The Board also considered two blocks of land in *Survey No. 1B and 144 at Ipurupalem village* and reserved them for the occupation of the Yerukula settlers. The board also considered the application of the SA for allotment of lands in the tracts of Andhra Pradesh but their request was not granted for technical reasons.[21]

VIII

Irrigation Cultivation in the Swamp Lands

The swamp lands extended from Nallamada drain upto Pedaganjam and passed through 17 villages from Mulapalem to Pedagangam.[22] To improve the drainage system in the settlement, the Public Works Department made the channels for the East Swamp lands. Shutters were provided to the drainage channel. Its main objective was not to allow water to the Nallamada drain.[23] During the floods, water used to overflow the drainage channels. The water used to damage all the crops in the swamp lands in the villages of Mulapalem, Jammulapalem, etc. The water used to stagnate in the lands more than 10 days. The Government provided screw grazing shutters to shut out the water of the Nallamada drain during the floods.[24] The Perali drain was dug up during the year 1899-1900 and the same was repaired during the years 1909-10 by the Public Works Department. The Perali drain was not effective due to the reason that it was on a sandy track. To make the Romperu drain more effective the Perali drain was closed. The swamp lands in the four villages were not fit for cultivation.[25]

The Romperu drain in the western part of the settlement area passed upto the end of the swamp lands located at Chirala. The lands were fertile. The soil being black, cotton was grown in most of the year. But the lands provided for the settlers were unfit for cultivation. The lands were liable for submersion for a long period during the year. No facilities were provided by the government either from the irrigation department or the public works department to make the lands fit for cultivation. The Public Works Department only tried to deepen the Romperu and Perali drains. Though the swamp lands were useful for raising the dry crops, no drainage channels were properly provided for the settlers. The crops raised by the settlers were frequently affected by the floods. The yield was very poor. The irrigation was precarious. There was no source of income for the poor settlers. The fertility of the soil was very poor. The lands were saline. Consequently large number of Yerukulas escaped from the settlement.[26]

During certain parts of the year, the missionaries employed agricultural maistries from the old settlers. They used to instruct the new settlers on the techniques of cultivation. In addition to agricultural maistries, a Karnam (Village Officer) was appointed on full time basis to look after the land records and allotment of land. The Karnam was engaged with the duties such as collection of land cess, remeasurement of cultivation plots, settling disputes regarding lands and boundaries, repairs to channels and clearance of silt, to prepare estimates for the agricultural operations and for the maintenance of peace and tranquility from the land disputes in the settlement.[27] The settlers cultivated paddy, ragi, groundnut, curry leaf, tobacco, tomato, green gram, casuarinas, coconut and eucalyptus. Majority of the settlers were satisfied with their cultivation. Most of the settlers picked up the techniques of cultivation and understood the value of land and the favourable effects of cultivating it. The settlers cultivated the land without interruption. The agricultural activities yielded rich rewards to them. There was an increase in the settlers income every year. Cultivation was taken up with great enthusiasm by the settlers. They also developed lot of attachment towards their lands. Today the Yerukulas are giving a lot of value for their settlement lands.[28]

IX

The Condition of the Lands in DNT Colonies Today

When the land was given to the settlers on the basis of individual pattas, it became an eyesore to the rich people in the neighbouring villages. Even today, the adjoining ryots are fighting with the settlers to vacate their patta lands. But the settlers unitedly fought with the neighbouring people. They appealed that the lands were in nobody's possession. The rich people with a selfish motto of grabbing the land used to complain of the criminal activities of the Yerukulas. On careful enquiry, the government realised that the settlers were not responsible for the crime in the neighbourhood and the agitation was due to certain unworthy and selfish personal motives. With the object of giving protection to the inhabitants of Bapatla, the government sanctioned authority to the local police to watch and patrol the roads properly. Since the settlers were under nobody's control they could come and go as they pleased. To obviate this difficulty, in October 1916, Betapudi was declared to be a 'criminal' settlement under their section 16 of the CT Act. Even today the moneyed people belonging to Bapatla, Chirala, Karamchedu, Karlapalem, Ipurupalem began buying the settlers' land at cheap rates and rack-renting the actual cultivator whenever a crop could be raised.

X

Conclusion

Today, the DNTs are facing many problems with regard to the possession of their lands. The DNTs were not provided with permanent pattas. Due to this reason, the poor tribes cannot approach the banks to get loans for raising their crops. Added to this, the lands allotted to the denotified tribes are not provided with water facilities. The lands were left barren due to non-availability of water. Most of the DNTs left cultivation. The poor settlers in the colonies though requested the government to provide water for irrigation purposes, the government paid deaf ear for providing water for the lands. The settlers in all the DNT Colonies are unable to irrigate the additional area of land given to them by the government. Thus, the DNTs are becoming poorer and reverting to their age old profession. Further, the denotified tribe settlements are located in the thick forests (Siddhapuram and Lingala settlements). The only sources of water for the settlers is the rain. Though a tank was constructed for the irrigation purpose in Siddhapuram settlement, it is dysfunctional. It is not completely repaired by the government. The people of Siddhapuram feel that not only themselves but surrounding twenty villages will be benefited by the tank, if it is repaired. Today, the settlers of Siddhapuram, Lingala and other settlements are good cultivators and farmers. They are requesting the government to provide them with regular water supply along with latest technology tools in order to improve the quality of their lands. They are also pleading the government to provide with bank loans for raising different kinds of cash crops in the settlement lands. The poor settlers are also requesting the government for good market facilities and prices, storage facilities for the crops produced by them. Agriculture has become the main source for their development today. The settlers are also facing the problem of land tax payment for their lands. Unable to bear the land cess, some of the settlers left their lands and some settlers stopped cultivating their lands. The government should give up the land cess to help the settlers to continue agricultural activities in the settlements. Today it is the responsibility of the government to make the settlers' lands productive and cultivable by providing suitable help for them as a part of their social and economic rehabilitation programmes.

NOTES

1. *Revenue Department, G.O. No. 2971, dated 9.10.1913.*
2. *Board of Revenue, G.O. No. 365-Gt/13.-2 dated 22nd September 1913.*
3. *Board of Revenue, G.O. No. 5265/A/13-1 dated 12th November 1913.*
4. *Board of Revenue Proceedings, Forest No.7, dated 12.1.1914.*
5. Government of Madras, *Note showing the progress made in the Settlement of Criminal Tribes in the Madras Presidency upto September 1916,* Government Press, Madras, 1917.
6. The Collector of Guntur informed the petitioners that out of an extent

of 28,912 acres of reserve in Bapatla, a total number of 5,067 acres was worked out for the supply of fuel. A total number of 7,605 acres was worked out for pasture. The portion of the scrub jungle covering an area of 9,427 acres was handed over to the forest department to remove the prickly pear on the land. 1,564 acres of the assessed waste land in the Bapatla Taluk was allotted for Casuarina Plantation work. Under these circumstances, the Collector said : "The Board is not prepared to disafforest any portion of the reserved forest." *Home Department, G.O. No. 749 dated 18.3.1920, PWLD, G.O. No. 475 dated 19.2.1920 and Board of Revenue, G.O. No. 651 dated 10.2.1912.*

7. Government of Madras, *Note Showing the Progress made in the Settlement of Criminal Tribes in the Madras Presidency upto September 1916,* Government Central Press, Madras, 1917, TNA.
8. Government of Madras, *Note showing the progress made in the Settlement of Criminal Tribes in the Madras Presidency upto January 1925,* Govt. Central Press, Madras, 1927.
9. *Ibid.*
10. *Home (Judicial), G.O. No. 572 dated 8th March 1917.*
11. *Home (Judicial), G.O. No. 946, dated 27.4.1918.*
12. *Home Department, G.O. No. 2451 dated 3.6.1940.*
13. *Judicial Department, G.O. No. 2419, dated 12.10.1915.*
14. *Law (General) Department G.O. No. 1714, dated 22nd October 1921.*
15. *Law (General) Department G.O. No. 2267 dated 16.7.1925.*
16. *PWLD, G.O. No. 1551, L., dated 20th July 1927.*
17. *PWLD, G.O. No. 1654 L., dated 6th July 1928.*
18. *Home (Judicial) G.O. No. 1093 dated 16.5.1919.*
19. *PWLD, G.O. No. 1838 dated 30.8.1932.*
20. *PWLD, G.O. No. 3003, dated 3.12.1920.*
21. *PWLD, G.O. No. 2394 L., dated 23rd August 1929.* Also see *Revenue Department, G.O. No. 2971 dated 9.10.1913.*
22. *PWLD, G.O. No. 305, dated 7.2.1918.*
23. *PWLD, G.O. No. 1298, dated 6th September 1921.*
24. *PWLD, G.O. No. 357, dated 13.5.1921.*
25. *PWLD, G.O. No. 268 dated 5.2.1927.*
26. The poor income for the settlers was attributed to the various causes as detailed below : 1. The lands were virgin and newly reclaimed, 2. the transplantation was done very late, 3. the seedlings had to be purchased at a fairly high price, 4. a long duration paddy was raised in a portion of the lands, 5. no rotational crop was raised and the period of engagement of the pumping plant beneficially utilised, 6. lands were not well manured and properly prepared, 7. the cultivation was not done properly due to inexperience and laxity on the part of the settlers and 8. the full extent of land that could have been favourably brought under irrigation was not attempted. See,

Government of Madras, *PWLD, G.O. No. 2394 L., dated 23rd August 1929.*

27. Government of Madras, *Law (General) G.O. No. 748 dated 8th August 1925.* Also see *PWLD, G.O. No. 36 dated 4th January 1930,* p. 1.
28. Government of Madras, *PWLD, G.O. No. 1551 dated 20th July 1921.*

Table–4
Land Particulars in Stuartpuram Settlement
Ipurupalem Village

Land	*Survey*	*Area in Acres*	*Assessment*		
Assessed waste,	832-C	40.56	10	2	0
Dry land	832-E	38.02	9	8	0
	832-G	159.64	39	15	0
	833	4.25	1	1	0
	Total	242.27	60	1	0

9

Economic Profile of Denotified Tribe Settlements

I

Introduction

In the early part of the 20th century about 20 or 30 supernumeraries of Waddars wandered in Guntur, Kurnool districts and the Nizam dominions. The Waddars of Kurnool district i.e., Gang No. XIV became notorious for professional dacoities, robberies, house breaking and cases of a miscellaneous nature.[1] Under these circumstances, the government considered a proposal to establish a settlement at Siddhapuram, Kurnool district under Section 12 of the CTA of 1911 for Waddars and a section of Yerukulas.[2] The number of Waddars at Siddhapuram settlement on the 31st December 1914 was 112 consisting of 30 men, 40 women and 42 children. They are employed on Siddhapuram irrigation project.[3]

The old site was malarious. The whole settlement was within 200 to 300 yards of the bund of the big tank.[4] The village is surrounded by ideal breeding grounds for Anopheles mosquitoes.[5] The forest humidity, water logging, bred mosquitoes and malaria claimed a heavy death toll.[6] A new site was selected about 1½ miles from the old site. This was 1½ miles distance from Bhavanasi nullah.[7] The change of new site contributed to the health and comfort of the settlers. The site of the settlement was shifted to the present place in January 1927.[8]

II

Economic Profile of Siddhapuram

Apart from the subsidiary industries, the main source of livelihood for the settlers was agriculture. 1066 acres of land was distributed to the settlers in the beginning. They were provided with bullocks, rope making, basket making and mat weaving were done by the settlers for whom material was available.[9] Marketing facilities were also provided for them. About 173 acres of land was cultivated during the year 1920.[10] Horse gram and cholum were mainly cultivated and others included ragi, chillies and vegetables. Necessary agricultural implements were provided.[11] Men and women were employed on monthly wages. Rs. 8 for men and Rs.6 for women were given for looking after cattle and for watching fields.[12] The tamarind crop gave them encouragement to get more money. While doing hard work the settlers showed an inclination to take up agriculture in a big way. A vast improvement was affected during the year 1920. More land came under cultivation.[13]

The settlers earned money from various heads of the Public Works Department such as 1. construction work, 2. forest contract work, 3. cultivation, 4. spinning, 5. weaving, 6. petty shops, 7. clearance of jungles and 8. sale of cattle, etc.[14] The average monthly earnings per family from 1.4.1926 to 12.12.1926 was Rs. 11. The increase in harvests further added materially to their income.[15]

The settlers were provided capital in the form of bulls and carts to make them self-sufficient. This was to bring them into the main stream of life. In course of time these criminals transformed themselves into ryots.[16] Traces of healthy signs of development of village life were seen. The land under cultivation was virgin soil and yield was expected to be good. Temporary pattas (or D form pattas) were granted for a period of five years to the settled villagers. After five years, on satisfactory behaviour, permanent pattas were supposed to be provided.[17]

The total area of land cleared in the year 1927 was 210 acres of dry land belonging to the government directly. Ten acres of wet and 100 acres of dry land of settlers was brought under cultivation.[18] During the year 1930, they had cultivated 200 acres of land of which 40 acres was wet. They had a fairly good crop. They were more and more interested in cultivation. Agriculture supplied labour to many of the settlers and some of the neighbouring villagers had paid attention to it. Another receipt which goes under agriculture is the sale of fuel.[19]

The margin of profit in the case of agriculture was little and less in the case of inexperienced cultivators like the settlers. They found it difficult to make both ends meet after paying the heavy rates of land revenue and water rates.[20] The assessment of the land revenue was cheaper than the other land. The government wanted to make Siddhapuram settlement purely an agricultural settlement. The government supplied Ongole breeding bulls in 1932 to the settlers to improve the livestock. They were also provided more cows. Cows were given as gifts to the settlers who showed interest in agriculture. It was an incentive to other settlers to evince similar interest in agriculture. Cholum was the staple food of the settlers and it was grown on greater extent.[21]

In Siddhapuram settlement, an agricultural advance was sanctioned in the year 1932-33. In the first year of loan, they had to work on the land which they had cleared and get enough money to maintain themselves. In the second year, they could not save much. In the third year, crops were a failure for want of rains. Hence the manager recommended for three more years to repay the amount.[22] The *'black quarter'* broke out in July 1934 and timely inoculations carried on by the veterinary department which prevented death of the cattle.

The Commissioner of labour maintained a government farm in Siddhapuram settlement. As the bulk of the settlers were highly ignorant of farm practices, two farm servants in addition to the agricultural maistry were appointed at the cost of Rs. 7 per month.[23] The government farm provided labour work to the settlers who had no cultivation of their own land also to others when they did not have work on their fields.[24] Wet and dry lands were cultivated on behalf of the government partly to teach the settlers proper method of agriculture and partly to provide a certain amount of labour for them. In connection with the cultivation and for instruction of the settlers, two agricultural maistries, one on Rs.18 per month and the other on Rs.17 per month were employed.[25] A bonus annually to the maistries upto a limit of Rs. 100 per annum was given to the head maistry and the assistant maistry. During the year 1942, the total land brought under cultivation was 1,538 acres.[26]

It was during the year 1944, 1,538 acres of land were brought under cultivation. Dalwa paddy and groundnut yielded good results. The sinking of a few wells enabled them to save their paddy fields.[27] Tobacco seedlings were grown during the year 1948-49 and a profit of Rs. 6,000 they got from its sale. During the year 1949, the total extent of land cultivable was 2,150.45 acres and out of this, only 429 acres of wet and 158 acres of dry land were under cultivation. But the settlers lost their interest in cultivation as they were only tillers of the soil and not the real owners. On account of frequent transfers of the managers, there had been considerable dislocation of work. Loan applications for purchase of bulls, etc. left undisposed for months together.[28] During the year 1951, the government reserved 1,135.40 acres of land in Siddhapuram. The remaining lands distributed to political sufferers, landless poor and ex-service men. Conditional pattas were issued by Revenue Department to take steps to improve the land.

The reserve forest department had been complaining of the behaviour of the settlers. The District Forest Officer devised the means for prevention and prompt booking of offences. The settlers usually go deep into the forest and used to steal timber and other forest produce.[29] During the year 1954, about 1,300 settlers were employed during the tobacco season. The Siddhapuram tank is one of the biggest tanks in Kurnool district with a tank-bed of 504.06 acres. It has abundant facilities for fishing. During March and April, they were expected to make use of their rights in fishing in Siddhapuram tank. Fishing in the tank has been a supplementary occupation for the settlers in the past several years. It goes a long way to solve their food problem.[30]

During the summer, the settlers faced a hard life. There was no sufficient water for drinking purpose even.[31] During the year 1964, out of an extent of 1251.35 acres available land, an extent of 1,066.04 acres was distributed among the colonists, 96.94 acres to artisans and 62.75 acres were given to the model agricultural farm run by the Agricultural Department. An extent of 25.62 acres was vacant. The agricultural farms were managed by the manager of the colony, transferred to the agricultural department for running as State seed farms.[32] Due to lack of sufficient rainfall, cultivation is badly affected. The borewells and wells constructed in Siddhapuram settlement stopped working properly.

Till January 1942, Waddars maintained themselves by working as coolies taking up work such as: 1. road repairs, 2. improvements to schools and managers' quarters, 3. tank revetment, 4. repairs to the police lines, etc. The average earning of a male was annas 3 per day (9 paise) and a female annas 1½ per day (7 paise).[33] They had sufficient scope to earn a living working as coolies: 1. cultivation of their own lands and also of the ryots, 2. coolie work such as ploughing and weeding, 3. reploughing of land after harvest, clearing of lands over grown with *nutt* (*Nattu* in Telugu means bent grass). 4. cutting fuel and selling it in head loads, 5. cutting grass and selling it as fodder, 6. cutting tangedu wood and removing its bark, 7. coolie work and repairs of roads, etc.[34]

There was distress among them. Their conditions became worse. Mr.Turner of the Krishna Cement Works had kindly consented to provide work for some settlers in the lime stone quarries at Kaza. Thus, 10 families were sent to Kaza.[35] During the year 1960, the Siddhapuram Colony's Advisory Committee resolved to provide a match factory on cottage industries scale in the colony to provide subsidiary occupation.[36]

The settlers had a large airy wool shed with 12 looms and other accessories. The looms were all locally made under the supervision of the acting inspector and turned out very fair blankets. The settlers made 182 cumblies during the year 1920. They had the SA loom. One of the settlers was their weaving maistry. He got 281- annas a month and for extra work he was paid more. On the daily wages, the settlers were given 5 annas (15 paise) for men and 3 annas (9 paise) for women. On piece work, they earn from 5 to 9 annas for men and 3 to 5 annas for women a day.[37]

Sericulture programme was developed in the settlement but it also failed. The men at Siddhapuram drew a hill allowance at the rate of 3/10th of their pay. A cooperative society was formed in the settlement during the year 1925. Through the cooperative society all loans were advanced. The settlers had ploughing bulls, goats, cows and she-buffaloes. The cooperative society was organised by the settlers themselves and it was supervised by the manager. The savings of the settlers increased. The cooperative society was started to enable the settlers to obtain loans from the government. It was to be paid back without interest in instalments. The society had to be worked by the manager. Necessary registers were maintained in his office.

The weaving industry was vital to the success of the settlement during the year 1921. There was no demand for the cumblies produced here. Cumblies produced elsewhere in the district were cheaper. Mill made ones from Bangalore and other places were cheaper and finer too.[38] The weaving shed was blown off in June 1927. A sum of Rs. 4,800 was sanctioned for the construction of a pucca building.[39] There was steady demand for the better class cumblies costing Rs. 4 to Rs. 5. Difficulty was experienced in finding a market for the cheaper cumblies costing between Rs. 2 and Rs. 3.

Adi Andhras of Pedda Anantapuram and Atmakur were permitted to stay in the settlement during the year 1943. The manager stated these families were good weavers and agriculturists. They helped the settlers in teaching them weaving and in executing war supplies to Gauze cloth.[40] The weaving of gauze cloth for some of the government hospitals was also undertaken and their demands complied with. The manager reported that it was very difficult to run the industry at a profit or even on self-supporting lines.

Though weaving industry was started to provide supplementary income to setters, it failed because there was no proper interest evinced by them. As a result, this was closed on 31.10.1949. The manager reported that it was very difficult to run the industry at a profit due to the following reasons: 1. Because of unfavourable fluctuations in the yarn market, e.g. the price of yarn purchased in March 1949 was much higher than 1950 and as 15% of the price of the yarn and 10% of the weaving charges were to be added to the cost. 2. The cloth of finer counts was available in the market at a cheaper rate. There was difficulty in finding a market for the coarse cloth, manufactured in the settlement. 3. There was no scope for unlimited expenditure or production to balance possible losses, etc. The weavers could not weave finer counts. 4. The settlers were not evincing much interest in the industry because of low wages.[41]

The managers of the settlement reposed confidence in the settlers and made them understand that they were ryots and not criminals. The managers treated them as an independent village community. They removed the names of the settlers who proved to be good from the register. The labour commissioner, Mr. Moir, stated, "The success of this settlement was due to the efficient and tactful management of Mr. K. Subramania Ayyar, the then Inspector General of Police. He was associated with the settlement since its inception in 1913.[42] It was his main aim to make the settlement a full fledged village. He took real interest and invited Waddars from the neighbouring villages to reap the benefits of settled life. Charges of various types involving immorality, loss of articles, evidence, extraction of statements were dealt with by the manager of the settlement.

The State Government had taken various measures for their welfare such as: 1. provision of suitable land for cultivation, 2. starting handloom weaving centers as cottage industries, 3. setting up co-operative societies for supplying credit and other necessities of life, 4. construction of pucca houses for habitation and 5. imparting training for the inmates of industrial and agricultural settlements, etc. Apart from the government, social workers also helped the settlers to engage themselves in gainful occupations and thus lead a life of normal citizens.[43]

To know their present economic conditions in the Siddhapuram settlement, interviews were conducted. They shared with us their present problems in the settlement. The settlers were always ready to involve themselves in any employment. "We only feel that we should be paid according to the rates prevailing. Sometimes this is not so. For example, the forest ranger of Byrluti informed us that whatever amount the government earmarks for works of present nature, the same amount will be distributed in the settlement. However, the sanction of the government is always lower compared to the existing wage rates.[44] K.R. Somanna further explained elaborately the agony faced by the villagers. Even the Venkatapuram Panchayat in which their village is located is neglecting them. In spite of the drought conditions, to their misfortune Siddhapuram was not considered famine stricken area. At present the entire three villages are plagued by the evil of illicit liquor.[45] The local liquor barons encourage the settlers in this direction. Whenever the excise people unearth these activities, they are always at the receiving end and the real culprits escape punishment.[46] They amass huge wealth. While they are rolling in luxuries, the settlers are reeling in poverty. Lack of proper employment makes them lay their hand in it.[47]

"Avocations like mat-making and carpet making cannot sustain our families. If industries are established, thereby providing us some gainful employment, we are confident that we can lead a trouble-free life. In recent past, the government initiated sericulture programme and associated us with it. It is regretted that the programme did not succeed. Even to equip ourselves with ration cards, unless civil supplies officials are bribed we do not get our ration cards. We are in a dilemma as we cannot resume our criminal activities or to get ourselves away from the present scenario."[48]

III

Economic Profile of Stuartpuram

Stuartpuram settlement was purely an agricultural settlement managed by the SA.[49] The strength, in the beginning of the settlement, was 691 people consisting of 200 males, 196 females and 295 children. The manager was captain H. Robilliard, and he was assisted by his wife and the Indian assistant. Captain H. Robilliard managed the settlement effectively and won laurels for his praise worthy efforts. Gilleman says: "Captain Robilliard had done wonders and is to be heartily congratulated on the success."[50]

The Yerukulas in Stuartpuram were very poor and depended on forest produce. Harold stuart said: "They had been traders dealing in salt and grain carried by their pack animals hundred of miles interior. Adjustment to new conditions was difficult, they had the cattle, they had a wide field of operation and they continued their migrations. Cattle trading often became cattle stealing and the disposal of stolen property from other gangs who entrusted their booty to them and built up a combine of criminal organisation."[51]

The SA introduced agriculture to transform their lifestyle. In the beginning a block of 360 acres of dry land and 1500 acres in the Romperu Swamp were placed at the disposal of the SA in 1914. In his report on the working of the settlement Mackenzie stated: "The irrigation difficulty threatens to be a serious one. The settlement was not self-supporting".[52] During certain parts of the year, the SA employed agricultural maistries from old settlers. They used to supervise the fields and made provision for planting trees in the settlement. They used to instruct the new settlers on the techniques of cultivation. Gradually, the old settlers became a strong backbone to the settlement and exerted a reassuring influence on new arrivals. The settlers, however, cultivated paddy, ragi and ground nut on this land. They also got money from mats, ropes, baskets, curry leaf, tomato and green gram cultivation. In addition to agriculture, these settlers were also given road work, stone quarrying, drain digging and other works from the department of public works. The wages given to daily labourers and piece workers were four to five annas a day for men and three annas a day for women. Their income during the year 1915 from the above source was Rs. 19,520.[53]

The manager leased out lands to the settlers. The total extent of land leased out in 1916 was 420 acres. The SA collected Rs. 1126. At the opening of the settlement a loan was obtained from the government, amounting Rs. 10,000, with 6 per cent yearly interest. When Harold Stuart, in company with Marjori Banks, visited the settlement the question was brought up as what the settlers would pay for taxes. Harold Stuart stated: "The case of Stuartpuram Settlement is unfairly. This Settlement was the most successful having the best land. Its progress appeared fast."[54] The normal rainy season in the locality extended from July to middle of November. The rainfall varied from 21 inches to 50 inches per annum. The settlers started cultivation from the month of May. In May, seeds were sown in nurseries. They kept the seeds till July doing work such as watering and looking after the nurseries in general. The seedlings were kept for 50 days growth, before they were transplanted in the fields. A shallow pit was dug in the sand near by which supplies surface percolation water and the seedlings were pot watered three times a day. They transplant the seedlings during the first week of August.[55]

The Jail Committee opined some subsidiary industry was necessary at Stuartpuram, either casuarina plantation or tomato canning. Bazlulla, the agricultural officer, set up a scheme for casuarina and for tomato canning. Robilliard favoured planting coconut and eucalyptus. Robilliard had extreme success. The land was pure sand and heavily manured for successful cultivation. 160 acres of waste land in Murakondapadu was handed over to the settlers. It was a valuable gift worth rupees 1000 per acre in those days.

To overcome the problem of manure, they purchased some cattle and kept it under the control of the manager. Krishna canal water was allowed for the wet lands in the settlement.[56] In order to give a better supply of water to bring greater area under cultivation, a dam across the river Romperu was built in June 1919. Good behaviour was a sin rather than a profit for the settlers as there was no place for them to go. The SA, in 1921, realised, that when the good conduct settlers were exempted, these homeless poor would go back from where they were brought. The only alternative for them would be thieving i.e., going back again to their old profession. The SA found that the real success lay in colonizing these people.[57]

During the year 1924, the SA handed over some mango, cashewnut, coconut and other plantations to the settlers in order to boost up their incomes. The SA collected 'land revenue' for the 600 acres of land which was being kept under its control. The salaries of various SA officials were paid from this amount. The rest they used to spend on the maintenance of the village.[58]

There was an increase of the settlers income from Rs. 84,189,05 to Rs. 1,3,109,8 during the year 1924-25. Their total earnings from various sources from the year 1925 to 1930 were as follows.[59]

Table–5
Income Pattern of Stuartpuram Settlers (1925-1930)

Year	*Total Earning : Rs*
1925	1,25,741
1926	0,75,327
1927	1,47,522
1928	1,08,513
1929	1,83,981
1930	1,16,066

The settlement land was parly swamp and partly dry sandy soil. Every year the cultivation became a gamble. The settlers had little encouragement to venture their little capital in which there was no certainty. The government prepared to spend a very considerable out lay in reclaiming the land. During the year 1926. 335 acres of the settlement lands and 110 acres of block no. 600 were cultivated under paddy. 50 acres of groundnut and 50 acres of ragi were also cultivated.[60] George Paddison proposed to build a bund in order to protect the fields from submersion of water from the swamp. The object of the pumping installation was two fold: 1. To provide water for irrigation at times of scarce supply, at the beginning of the season (i.e. in the month of October), 2. To irrigate an additional area of land.

Cultivation was taken up with great enthusiasm from the year 1927. The cyclone in November 1927 ruined the whole crop of paddy. 63 acres of groundnut, 75 acres of Sazza, 75 cents of Zonna and 50 acres of ragi were cultivated. The plots of ragi and groundnut near their houses helped them as lucrative employment during the time when out side work was slack.[61] The settlers planted 609 acres of paddy during the year 1928. 158 acres of groundnut, 80 acres of ragi were cultivated. The total value of the crop was Rs. 29,557. Slater, the then commissioner of labour visited stuartpuram settlement in

July 1928. The settlers presented a petition to him requesting that they might be given permanent pattas.[62]

In a dry year, crop was wealthier and in a wet year they are liable to submersion. Robilliard, in his record of daily occupations, showed that some of the settlers resorted to begging in which case there was ample scope for stealing.[63] The deputy director of agriculture came to the settlement during the year 1930 and made suggestions for the improvement of the sandy soil by means of suitable measures. The executive engineer of Bezawda furnished suggestions for methods of irrigating various parts of the land based on a schedule.[64] During the year 1930, the settlers were sent on 'O' passes to the Kodanda Rama mica mines in the Rapur taluq of Nellor district for employment. The manager of the mines also offered employment to a certain number of Kavali settlers. The work in the mica mines was temporary. It was a partial solution to the problem. Another batch proceeded to Thummala Talpur, village in Rapur taluq (Nellore District), for employment.[65]

The tobacco company was completely closed from September 1930 to March 1931 due to lack of sufficient funds and hence unable to provide employment to the settlers. F.W. Stewart, the district magistrate made suggestions for vegetable growing during the year 1930. Some others worked on the village tank scheme at Parchoor 17 miles away from the settlement.[66]

Further these people were also provided small works in different places. The minor works included road construction, digging of pits, fencing, manuring, spraying and watering plants, etc. Referring to the unemployment during the year 1930-31, the Inspector General of Police, Madras said that: "the manager should be congratulated on successfully tiding over the crisis in the year 1930."[67] 449 acres of wet land and 70 acres of dry land were cultivated during the year 1931. Out of 174 candies of paddy, the settlers earned Rs. 14,711 45acres of ragi and 25 acres of ground nut brought Rs. 2,820 to the settlers.[68] During the year 1932, 654 acres of paddy yielded 328 candies. They got Rs. 16,400. The sale of straw was Rs. 1,640 and thus the total income was Rs. 18,040. The ragi crop yielded Rs. 1,325 on 43 acres. 200 acres of ground nut realized 82 candies at a price of Rs. 3,690. A number of settlers had given evidence that they became permanent settlers and regularly cultivating the pieces of land placed at their disposal for a number of years.[69]

The collector of Guntur issued permanent pattas to the settlers' lands of those who had been regularly cultivating for a considerable period. In connection with this subject, the Tahsildar of Bapatla visited the settlement. He suggested all those settlers who had been regularly cultivating for a period of 3 years and against whom there was no complaint of crime were given permanent pattas. The SA and the labour commissioner argeed to the suggestion. According to this proposal 262 families were found eligible for the issue of permanent pattas. In addition to agricultural maistries, a Karanam (village officer) was appointed on full time basis to look after the land records, measurements, allotments and supervision of the cattle. The date on which the Karanam joined duty was 1.10.1933. The Karanam was given the pay of Rs. 27 per month.[70] The post of Karanam was included in the miscellaneous staff in stuartpuram settlement. The government gave up land cess over the settlers' lands to encourage cultivation. Most of them, later on, picked up the techniques of cultivation and understood the value of land and the favourable effects of cultivating it. 1000 acres of dry land were cultivated by the settlers and the yield was 500 candies of paddy and 1000 bags of ragi during the year 1950. 700 families were allotted lands. A government official in high position, when visited the settlement said, "I noted specially the large amount of ragi cultivation in the sand by pot cultivation and individual settlers casuarina patches."[71]

There was gradual improvement in the cultivation of the settlers every year. The total extent of land available in the settlement during the year 1964 was 2007.71 acres of land and the extent of land cultivated by the settlers was 1772.58 acres.[72] The settlement worked under heavy economic difficulties during the year 1965. But, the Indian Leaf Tobacco development company at Perala somehow supported the settlers and saved the settlement from its financial difficulties. However, much difficulty had been experienced in finding sufficient employment for the people in the settlement. The settlers were unemployed for five months in ILTD Company. Cooli labour on the piece work system was supplied by ILTD factory upto an amount of Rs. 37,060 during the year 1966.[73] There were a number of absconders from the village during the year 1967-68. The abscondings in the settlement were chiefly due to the following reasons: 1. unemployment, 2. Domestic troubles, 3. Slackness of work, 4. The general spirit of unrest, 5. The policies of the government, 6. The harassment of the police and 7. Strict supervision etc.[74]

Though land was given to these people, agriculture was entirely foreign to them. Due to frequent occurrence of floods, cyclones, late supply of water and infertility of the soil, they were losing their crops. It was reported that 80 to 90 per cent of the convictions in Stuartpuram resulted from absconding. The number of absconders on the rolls, from the beginning of the settlement, upto the end of the year 1920-21, was 168, and the number of absconders, since then, upto the end of the year 1924, was 161. The following table shows the residential status of the settlers with 'criminal' behaviour in the village from 1921 to 1930.[75]

Table–6
Residential Status of Stuartpuram Settlers from 1921-30

Year	*Men*	*Women*	*Children*	*Total*
1921	546	500	561	1,607
1922	556	541	682	1,779
1923	539	526	718	1,783
1924	649	638	829	2,116
1925	666	657	881	2,204
1926	664	651	907	2,222
1927	699	640	890	2,229
1928	678	615	743	2,036
1929	679	601	775	2,055
1930	692	611	813	2,116

The development of seed buds cultivation, directly by the company, simplified the problem of employment. Mr. Whitted, the manager of ILTD, made experiments in the cultivation of tobacco on the sand. It was successful. Every year the tobacco cultivation expanded on the sandy area. A co-operative society was organised with 290 share holders before 1927. The share capital, amounted to Rs. 2947.70, was paid. Through this society, the settlers were able to help the people in improving their land, providing the irrigation facilities, etc.[76] The main purpose for which co-operative societies were organised were as follows: 1. Acquisition of house sites on the easy payment system, 2. Loans for agricultural purposes,

3. Cultivation and reclamation of land, 4. Discharge of loans borrowed at ruinous rates of interest from moneylenders, 5. Collective bargaining 6. Sale and trade and 6. Relief for persons affected by the floods.

George Paddison, the then commissioner of labour and , HMFM, Tyler, the then Deputy Registrar of Co-operative Societies visited the settlement during the year 1927 and had given the settlers their valuable suggestions. The financial condition of the cooperative society in the settlement from the year 1948 to 1950 was as follows[77]:

Table–7
Financial Condition of Co-operative Society in Stuartpuram Settlement-1948-50

Source	*Year 1948: Rs.*	*Year 1949: Rs.*	*Year 1950: Rs.*
Reserve Fund	454.00	454.00	501.00
Shares Collected	49.00	38.00	NA
Total Share Capital	2146.00	2156.00	2188.00
Assets	6008.00	6174.00	6424.00
Liabilities	5421.00	5529.00	5039.00
Loans paid out	350.00	350.00	450.00
Loans Collected	404.00	509.00	587.00

The cooperative society and stores in the settlement were wound up in July 1949 as they were running on a loss. However, the government sanctioned an amount of Rs. 5,000 to the tenants co-operative society of stuartpuram during the year 1961-62.[78] After the repeal of the CT Act in 1952, it was contemplated that all State Governments should undertake welfare schemes for these people. In order to supplement the efforts of the State Governments, to undertake the economic schemes, it was decided by the Central Government, for the first time, in 1953 to give grant Schemes for the Welfare of the DNTs. Dr. Rajendra Prasad said: "State Governments had played their part satisfactorily but much more remains to be done by them."[79]

Certain welfare schemes for denotified communities were undertaken by the concerned states as a part of their state sector programmes in the first five year plan. In the second five year plan, funds were sanctioned by the government for economic development. During the 3rd five year plan, a plan provision of Rs. 375.00 Lakhs was made for the purpose. An estimated expenditure of Rs. 55.36 Lakhs was incurred during 1962-63. Special steps were initiated in the 4th plan for a close study of the problems of these people. Economic, social and cultural aspects were taken into consideration. A sum of Rs. 43,900 Lakhs was incurred on these communities. From the fifth five year plan onwards no separate provisions has been made under centrally sponsored programmes for undertaking schemes for Denotified Communities.[80] For instance, in 1974, the State Government of Andhra Pradesh made a special effort as an experiment to reform the Ex-'Criminals' of Stuartpuram. About 135 acres of fertile land was assigned to 145 'criminals' or their families. Arrangements were made for the payment of wages, supply of seeds, fertilizers, pesticides, etc. The Girijan co-operative society gave rickshaws to some of the settlers on a loan-cum subsidy basis. Loans were given by the state government for the purchase of sewing machines, materials for making baskets, etc.[81]

Input supply programmes were implemented to help the agriculturists under economic support schemes. During the year 1974-75, trade loans to a tune of Rs. 12,200 were sanctioned to 62 tribal households. Agricultural implements worth Rs. 7250 were supplied to the tribal cultivators. Besides, 12 pairs of ploughing bullocks for ploughing were supplied to tribal cultivators in Stuartpuram. During the year 1976-77, milch cattle were supplied to 65 tribals under economic support progrmme. A scheme has been prepared and submitted to District Tribal Welfare Department by the Block Development Officer, Bapatla to supply short term inputs, land reclamation, etc. During the year 1980-81, under economic support programme, 29 identified households were supplied with milch cattle.[82]

During the years 1983-85, the Andhra Pradesh Government implemented a scheme to improve these settlers economically. T. Gopala Rao I.A.S., who worked as collector of Guntur district, helped the settlers in the form of loans, distribution of land and construction of houses. During the tenure of Chandrayya, as district collector, 136 acres of dry land and 146 acres of wet land were allotted to the ex-'criminals' of this settlement. Each family got 80 cents of land.

IV

Conclusion

The welfare measures initiated for Yerukulas, Yanadis and Sugalis, Woddars and other DNTs bear a resemblance to the efforts at squeezing oil from sand. The development of scheduled tribes is a real challenge to the present government. The utterances of the government on the welfare measures are making much noise emanating from empty vessels. Policy formulation and its execution, most often, fall apart. Tribal children are required to pay special fee at the time of admission, though they are exempted from other fees. Poor tribal students are not in a position even to pay this. Added to this, tribal welfare scholarships are generally delayed and released at the end of the year. As a result students are bound to face many problems. There is a lot of injustice being done to tribal people in the distribution of surplus lands. Their repeated memoranda to revenue officials are of no use.

In the sphere of employment too, tribal people are facing serious problems. Though the public advertisements earmark a number of vacancies to these people, they appear so with a clause saying that the posts would be filled by candidates of other castes in the absence of eligible tribal candidates. In such a situation the very policy of reservation loses its meaning and validity. It is suggested that the government should take appropriate measures to overcome these problems. The elected representatives from the tribal region should educate the government about the fundamental hardships of tribal people.[83]

The DNT colonies consists of a number of unemployed families. Only a few families are employed in government jobs, industrial establishments, agricultural operations and petty trade. But majority of the families are leading a miserable life due to poor economic conditions and due to lack of employment. Those people who have 'criminal' background also they are averse to committing crime. The reasons are obvious viz.; some of their kinsmen are killed by the police, they are unable to bear the ill treatment and harassment either by the police or from the public. Education has enabled them to realize their folly. They are interested in the future of their children and they want to lead a respectable life by joining the mainstream of life. Gradually they are taking to small jobs and business and changing their lifestyles. But there are not many opportunities either in the private or public sector to provide them with some meaningful occupations, even though the government is providing some succour in the shape of small loans, cattle, rickshaws, etc. It is needless to state such measures are inadequate.[84]

In view of the above analysis, few suggestions can be made to improve the economic conditions and for the welfare of denotified tribes of Andhra Pradesh.

1. The government has to conduct sample surveys to know about their present economic position, their present livelihood, state of literacy, housing and other activities.
2. Large share of the funds should be spent on their economic development by providing some kind of lawful employment as an alternative means of livelihood.
3. 'D' form pattas (Un-loanable pattas) are issued to them. They should be converted into loanable pattas in future. All those members of denotified tribes in various colonies who have real interest and aptitude for cultivation should be provided enough land, continuous water supply and other irrigational facilities.
4. Labour contact societies should be organised in consultation with members of these communities without any favouritism and nepotism.
5. Brick making, mat making, dress making centers and certain Jobs which require minimum technical skill and guidance should be established for them.
6. Self-employment schemes are very useful to their economic development. These are to be organised on the co-operative basis for which the government should provide financial assistance.
7. They should be provided with jobs which give them immediate remuneration and relief. Some of them who are minimum educated, may be recruited into the departments of police as constables, water boys and sweepers. Some of them are already appointed as watchman with good reputation.
8. Arrangements should be made with banks to sanction loans to the settlers who are interested in setting up in small business such as tea bunks, soda shops, etc.
9. The police killed some of the ex-'criminals' in the settlements.

Their children and family members are suffering with acute financial problems. This should be tackled immediately. Reformation of the Denotified Tribes is more on economic development rather than violent process.

10. A large number of industries (plantation industries) and factories can be established on the vacant lands availabe in the settlements. This can solve the unemployment problem in the DNT colonies.

NOTES

1. *Home Judicial Department, G.O. No. 1279, dt. 10th June 1915,* p. 2, TNA.
2. *Home Judicial Department, G.O. No. 1860, 5th September 1917,* p. 1. dt. Waddars are registered as 'criminal' tribes by the Criminal Investigation Department, Gang No. XIV, and Yerukulas Gang No. XIII.
3. The boundaries of this settlement were as follows. In the North-Southern boundary, there is Krishnapuram Agraharam. In the West-Southern boundary there is Velgode Reserve and Dornal-Atmakur Road. In the East, the boundary runs south-west along the Sims's line to a point where it meets the Siddhapuram tank bund and in the South, the boundary runs to the south-east corner of Kandam. Likewise in the west, the boundary runs northwards of the Velgode reserve (terailine) to the starting point. *Home Judicial Department, G.O. No. 1284, dated 27.3.1937,* p. 4.
4. The site of the settlement was shifted to the interior village in the forest area about 13 km east of Venkatapuram village on Atmakur Srisailam Road. It is in Atmakur police station limits and about 12 kms east of Atmakur town, *Home Judicial Department, G.O. No. 6170, dated 22.12.1938,* p. 3.
5. Between the bund and the village is a depression from which earth for the bund was excavated. Water stagnates throughout the year and there is a dense growth of bulrushes and other marsh-grasses. Two hundred yards to the north of the village is a drainage depression in which water stagnates and bulrushes flourish. Four to five hundred yards south and south-west of the village, the same conditions prevail along the course of the Bhavanasi Nullah for a distance of 2 to 3 furlongs. See Government of Madras, *Public Works Labour Department, (PWLD) G.O. No. 137 dated 19.1.1927,* p. 2.
6. These stagnant pools are largely the result of the building of the tank and are fed by sub-soil percolation. There are deep pits in the tank bed which hold water all the year round. During the south-west monsoon when malaria is most prevalent, the wind blows from the village, a probable source of infection. The Bhavanasi adjoining the new site is

clear of growth of weeds. *Public Works Labour Department, G.O. No. 1719, dated 9.8.1927,* p. 13.

7. *Public Works Labour Department, G.O. No. 2190 dated 28.7.1930,* p. 5, APSA.
8. Before coming to Siddhapuram settlement, the Waddars had a meager income. They led a hand-to-mouth existence in the surrounding areas. Even now their earnings from agricultural operations are insufficient to maintain their families. The Waddars of the Siddhapuram settlement mainly depended on agriculture. The British government constructed a huge water reservoir for the cultivation of the lands attached to the settlement. Since it is rain-fed and the rainfall in turn very scarce, the tank is most often empty. If it functions well, it is useful for 20 villages of surrounding areas. Every year the crop yield has been dismally low. Even the manual work does not fetch more than Rs.15 per day. *Public Works Labour Department, G.O. No. 1433, dated 31.3.1928,* p. 2.
9. *Public Works Labour Department, G.O. No. 2661 dated 25.10.1924,* p. 2, NAI.
10. Agricultural loans were granted to the settlers by the Labour Commissioner, Mr.Moir. The loans were used for purchase of cattle and carts. Instalments were regularly paid. Government of Madras, *Home Department, G.O. No. 2661 dated 25.10.1920,* p. 1. NAI.
11. *Home Department, G.O. No. 2661 dated 25.10.1920,* p. 1, NAI.
12. *Home Department, G.O. No. 2661 dated 25.10.1920,* p. 1. NAI
13. Implements were provided for repairs. People were given seeds for their crops. Fodder was supplied to the cattle of the settlers. Cow boys were employed. Maistries were appointed to instruct them about the value of land and the knowledge of the production of various crops. The land cultivated by settlers was different from government lands. The government used to extract work from the settlers, but the produce was stored by the government for its own administration. The whole process was supervised by the maistry. Government of Madras, *Home Department, G.O. No. 2661, dated 25.10.1920,* p. 1.
14. *PWLD, G.O. No. 2425 dated 12.11.1935,* p. 1, APSA.
15. The settlers were allowed to take water from the tank. The settlement land was not included in the regular ayacut of the tank. The tank had never received full supply of water. There was small extent of wet cultivation in the settlement. Government spent considerable amount on levelling the land and making it fit for wet cultivation. The position of tank is not changed even now. The inhabitants of the settlement are feeling unhappy about the negligence of government to make it fit for further cultivation. They also say that 19 villages of the surrounding areas depend upon this tank. *PWLD, G.O. No. 137 dated 9.8.1927,* p. 6, APSA.
16. *PWLD, G.O. No. 1719 dated 9.8.1927,* p. 6, APSA.

17. *PWLD, G.O. No. 2543, dated 5th September 1929*, p. 4, APSA.
18. *PWLD, G.O. No. 137 dated 19.1.1927*, p. 4, APSA.
19. *PWLD, G.O. No. 137 dated 19.1.1927*, p. 3, APSA.
20. Mr.Tyler another Labour Commissioner, appointed a headman on a pay of Rs. 8 per month to perform duties analogous to the village headman. The settlers were appointed as Talayaris on Rs. 6 per month to see the Welfare of the Settlement, *PWLD, G.O. No. 137, dated 19.1.1927*, p. 3.
21. The adult settlers in the settlement were allotted lands of one acre wet and five acres dry each for cultivation. The lands were reclaimed and kept in reserve for future entrants, i.e. 1. those who were released from jails and sent to the settlement, 2. transferred from other settlements and 3. settler youths who attained majority *PWLD, G.O. No. 2671 dated 6.12.1934*, p. 4.
22. *PWLD, G.O. No. 2671 dated 6.12.1934*, p. 5.
23. *PWLD, G.O. No. 2671 dated 6.12.1934*, p. 10.
24. *PWLD, G.O. No. 1782, dated 23.2.1935*, p. 1.
25. *Home Department, G.O. No. 568 dated 23.2.1944*, p. 5.
26. *Home Department, G.O. No. 2113, dated 13.7.1944*, p. 1
27. *Home Department, G.O. No. 568, dated 23.2.1944*, p. 1.
28. *Madras State Administration Report for the year 1950-51: Part I*, Government Press, Madras, *1954*, p. 42.
29. *Government of Andhra Pradesh, Andhra Pradesh State Administration Report, 1961-62 : Vol. I*, Government Press, Hyderabad, 1963, p. 111.
30. *Home Department, G.O. No. 1227 dated 24.3.1942*, p. 10.
31. *Home Department, G.O. No. 2063 dated 7.6.1952*, p. 1.
32. *Home Department, G.O. No. 1227 dated 24.3.1942*, p.10.
33. *Govt. of Andhra Pradesh, State Administration Report for the year 1964-65: Vol.I, Hyderabad, 1966*, p. 86.
34. *PWLD, G.O. No. 1425, dated 5.5.1944*, p. 1, APSA.
35. *PWLD, G.O. No. 2190 dated 28.7.1930*, pp. 2-3, APSA.
36. *PWLD, G.O. No. 1719 dated 9.8.1927*, pp. 5-6, APSA.
37. *Government of Andhra Pradesh, Andhra Pradesh State Administration Report, 1961-62, Vol. I*, Hyderabad, 1963, p. 112.
38. *PWLD, G.O. No. 1719 dated 9.8.1927*, p. 3
39. *Govt. of Madras, Note Showing the Progress Made in the Settlement of Criminal Tribes in the Madras Presidency upto January 1925*, Madras, 1926, pp. 29-30.
40. *Home Department, G.O. No. 1227 dated 24.3.1942*, p. 10.
41. *Government of Madras, Administration Report on Habitual Offenders' Settlements for 1949-50*, Madras, 1950, p. 19.
42. *Home Department, G.O. No. 3570 dated 27.1.1951*, p. 5.
43. *PWLD, G.O. No. 137 dated 19.19.1927*, p. 6.

44. The Madras Police Department of the colonial era prepared a report on their lifestyle. According to the report, Waddera, Korava, Kathera and Korcha tribes have been wandering tribes, getting involved in criminal offences. They married women from other tribes like Yanadi, Sugali, Chenchu, Yerukula, etc. Waddars claimed that they are the descendants of the foregoing tribes and demanded that they should be included in scheduled tribes. Siddhapuram was officially recognised by the government as an ex-'criminal' tribe settlement. Members of other settlements like Bitragunta and Golla Kuppam went to the court to get the status of Scheduled Tribes but still that is not sanctioned. Interview with K.R. Somanna, Siddhapuram, dated 24.11.2006
45. Interview with E. Lakshmayya, Siddhapuram dated 24.11.2006.
46. Interview with K.R. Somanna, Siddhapuram dated 24.11. 2006.
47. Interview with E. Lakshmayya, Siddhapuram, dated 22.11. 2006.
48. Interview with K.R. Somanna, Siddhapuram, dated 24.11. 2006.
49. *Government of Madras, Note Showing the progress made in the settlement of Criminal Tribes in the Madras Presidency upto September 1916,* Government Central Press, Madras 1917, p. 6. TNA.
50. *See Captain Robilliard of the Salvation Army, Manager of the Stuartpuram Criminal Tribes Settlement, Bapatla, Madras, A written statement on the work of Stuartpuram Settlement,* p. 64. Stuartpuram settlement was opened on the 1st June, 1914. Few families lived at No.8 division, known then as Ratnapuram in a few dilapidated huts.
51. Mildred Mackenzie, *The Mud Bank, The Story of Missionary Endeavour,* 226 North Lynn Bonlevard, Pennsyloania, 1959, p. 20.
52. See *Home Judicial Department, G.O. No. 2074, 18th August, 1916,* p. 4. TNA.
53. See *Note Showing the progress made in the settlement of Criminal Tribes in Madras Presidency, upto 1927,* Govt. Press, Madras, 1928, p. 7.
54. Marjori Banks proposed Rs. 7 per acre on each settler. But it was reduced to Rs. 5, some settlers were charged Rs. 3, Rs. 2 and Rs. 1 according to value of their crops. The SA issued 140 Pattas of 2 acres each during the year 1916. See Home *Judicial Department, G.O. No. 572, dt. 8th March 1917,* p. 12. TNA.
55. From August to September, ploughing, seedling and transplantation continued. The wives and children rendered help to their husbands during this time. From October to January, they used to do watering such as opening small terrace bunds and closing them daily, thus allowing the water to circulate among the fields. They attended to weeding in the same period. From January to March, the reaping and harvesting season used to start. People were kept employed all through the year under the efficient manager. See Home *Judicial Department, G.O. No. 572, 8th March 1917,* p. 2, TNA.
56. About 30 acres of land was used for coconut intermixed with Mulbaries

on an experimental basis. Gordon Brown, an instructor of the Federated Malay, who visited the settlement in 1918 states that 40 × 40 was considered as the correct planting. See Home *Judicial Department, G.O. No. 305, 7th February 1918,* p. 8. TNA.

57. Here we have to mention one fact that the settlers with good conduct was sent out by the SA manager during the year 1921. This was done without providing an alternative employment to them. The settlers worked on their lands for so many years. Hence it is quite natural for them to settle in the settlement. Moreover, if they leave the settlement, where can they go? What is their native place? This good behaviour was a real punishment for them. Again they came and settled side by side with the so-called settlers.This is what has happened in Sitanagaram also. See *The War Cry, Salvation Army monthly,* May 1937, p. 5.

58. The government, in the year 1917-18, had considered the question of establishing Casuarina Plantation in an adjacent forest reserve. The government passed a condition that the plantation remained their property. Booth Tucker reported that the condition laid by the government was not acceptable. He did not undertake the work. During the year 1918-19, the government asked Mr. Paddison, the then labour commissioner, to take up the work. However, the district magistrate, Gutur was against the proposal, since the proposal was a loss to the government. Later Mr. Moir, the next labour commissioner, condemned the proposal of establishing Casuarina Plantation. Instead of Casuarina Plantation, he suggested for purchasing of cattle for manure purpose. Then the government agreed with Mr. Moir. See *Note Showing the progress made in the settlement of Criminal Tribes in the Madras Presidency upto January 1925,* Government Central Press, Madras, *1926,* p. 9, TNA.

59. The table is based on Government Orders from the year 1925 to 1930. See *PWLD G.O. No. 1926, 2881, 1147, 1313, 1927, 2007, 967, 1551, of January, 1928, 2394 of 23rd August 1930 and 2338 of 1931.* These earnings were derived from various sources like paddy crop, groundnut, ragi, making of mats, ropes and baskets, hired labour , trading in cattle, sack sewing, wages from LTD Company and other domestic services etc. Their total income of the above sources at the end of the year 1949 was Rs. 65,31,88,73- Milk cattle were kept in the settlement and one milkman was appointed in the settlement. The amount gained by the sale of milk was Rs. 4 to Rs. 5 per mensem.

60. *PWLD, G.O. No. 1551, 1st July 1927,* p. 1. APSA.

61. *PWLD, G.O. No. 1654, 6st July 1928,* p. 1. APSA.

62. *PWLD, G.O. No. 1147, 26st May 1933,* p. 2. APSA.

63. The settlers' income was very poor. The following reasons caused for their poverty in the settlement. 1. The lands were virgin and newly reclaimed 2. The transplantation was done very late. 3. The seedlings

were purchased at a high price. 4. A long duration paddy was raised in a portion of the lands 5. No rotational crop was raised 6. Lands were not well manured and properly prepared due to the lack of new technology. 7. Cultivation was not done properly due to inexperience and laxity on the part of the settlers. 8. The full extent of land that had favourably brought under irrigation was not accepted. See *Home Judicial Department, G.O. No. 475, dated 19.2.1920,* p. 2, *TNA.*

64. *PWLD, G.O. No. 36, 4th January 1930,* p. 1. APSA.
65. *PWLD, G.O. No. 170, 21st January 1931,* p. 2. APSA.
66. *Administration Report of the Inspector General of Police for the year 1921,* Government Central Press, Madras 1922, p. 28.
67. *PWLD, G.O.No.1313, 17th June 1932,* p. 7. APSA.
68. To augment the water supply, the public works department authorities had fixed a 12' pipe sluice in Cammamur canal exclusively for the benefit of the settler's lands. The water from this sluice was carried through a drainage channel called sakki-kalva which ultimately empties itself into the Romperu drain. Shutters were also provided to the dam across the Romperu drain in connection with the irrigation of Stuartpuram settlement in order to save water and control floods by the public works department. See *PWLD, G.O. No. 1149, 28th October 1930,* p. 1. APSA.
69. *PWLD, G.O. No. 1996, 16th June 1933,* p. 4.
70. It was stated that the only person in the settlement who had knowledge in cultivation was the settlement Karanam. He had to attend to the office from 8 a.m. till 5 p.m. every day. During dry season he was occupied with duties such as, 1. Collection of all land cess. 2. Remeasurement of cultivation plots. 3. Settling disputes regarding lands and boundaries. 4. Repairs to channels and clearance of silt. 5. To prepare estimates for the ordinary settlement and annual repairs to the settlement buildings and, 6. Maintenance of peace and tranquility in the settlement. See *Law General Department, G.O. No. 748, 8th August 1925,* p. 1. APSA.
71. Government of Madras, *Administration Report on Habitual Offenders Settlements for the year 1949-50,* Madras 1951, p. 2.
72. Government of *Andhra Pradesh, Andhra Pradesh State Administration report for the year 1963-64, Vol. I,* Government Press, Hyderabad, 1965, p. III.
73. *Law (General) Department, G.O. No. 1974, 10th August 1920,* p. 6. TNA.
74. See *PWLD, G.O. No. 697, 1st July 1926,* p. 3 also See *PWLD, G.O. No. 1551, 20th July 1927,* p. 4. APSA.
75. See *PWLD, G.O. No. 697, 1st July 1926,* p. 3.
76. See *Administration Reports of the Inspector General of Police, Madras presidency from 1921 to 1931,* Government Central Press, Madras. Also see *Law (General) Department proceedings,* Madras presidency from 1921 to 1931 APSA.

77. See *PWLD, G.O. No. 1551, dated 20th July 1927,* p. 4., During the year 1927, the share capital amounted to Rs. 2947.70 was paid. Fixed deposits were to the extent of Rs. 345 made by the settlers. Shares and fixed deposits received amounted to Rs. 4360-90 Rs. 4282 were let out as loans to the settlers during the year 1927. A sum of Rs.3555-11-11 was received by the society. The voiceless settlers thanked the authorities for their better days than they were earlier. See *PWLD, G.O. No. 1654, dated 6th July 1928,* p. 2, APSA.
78. See *Administration Report on Kallar, Koravar and Yanadi Reclamation and Habitual Offenders settlements from 1948 to 1952,* Government Press, Government of Madras, TNA.
79. *See Andhra Pradesh State Administration Report, 1961-62, Vol. I,* Government of Andhra Pradesh, Hyderabad, 1963, p. 87.
80. See *Report of the Commissioner for Scheduled Castes and Scheduled Tribes for the year 1953, 3rd Report by L.M. Sreekant,* New Delhi, 1954, p. 200.
81. See *Report of the Commissioner for Scheduled Castes and Scheduled Tribes for the year 1962-1974. Also see Report of the 7th conference for Scheduled Tribes and Tribal Areas,* Guntur, 1964, p. 66.
82. See *Report of the Commissioner for Scheduled Castes and Scheduled Tribes 1973-74, 22nd Report,* New Delhi, 15th September 1975, p. 288.
83. See Chenchuraju, *Stuartpuram Girijan settlement, A Rehabilitation Centre for Ex-Convicts,* Govt. Press, Hyderabad, 1981 p. 2.
84. See *Adivasi (Telugu Monthly), Issue No. 10, No. 6,* Guntur, dt.15-9-1962. p. 2.

10

Education Scenario of Denotified Tribes

I

Introduction

Education of children of the DNT communities is a very important concern of our government. Although schools were provided in their colonies, attendance was made compulsory for the children of school-going age, the expenses on education were met by the governments, children were fed, yet desirable results have not been achieved in the standard of education. The educational problems concerning these DNT children should be tackled by the apex educational organisations as a part of their extension programmes. It is with this background that it has been decided to study the educational pattern available to these DNT children with a view to improving the achievement levels of DNT children in the present settlement schools. The main objective of the chapter is to study the academic/educational conditions of the children of the DNTs and to suggest the ways and means to improve their quality of education.

II

Profile of Education in Siddhapuram

For the education of the Waddar children, a school was established during the year 1915. Twenty-six boys and 26 girls were receiving instruction during the year 1916. Education was imparted in the 3Rs and no attempt had been made to give them industrial training. The attendance was fairly regular. The school was run by 2 masters and 1 mistress who were paid Rs.15 and Rs.12 and Rs.10 respectively.[1] Educational Department was inspecting the school now and then.

The average attendance during the year 1924 was 76.[2] The boys were made to learn agricultural work in the fields during the season. Carpentry, weaving tapes, masonry and brick-making work was taught. The girls were taught sewing. They had the proficiency in making their own jackets. Taylor the then Labour Commissioner, said: "the children look well cared for and show satisfactory knowledge of their subjects."[3] The settlement school was excellent in every way. Most of the boys used to read and write Telugu well. They were smart, clean and well drilled. The following table shows the classwise distribution of children during the year 1927.[4]

Table–8
The Strength of Siddhapuram School, 1927

Standard	*Boys*	*Girls*	*Total*
Infant	8	7	15
1st class	2	2	4
2nd Class	-	3	3
3rd Class	3	2	5
4th Class	5	-	5
5th Class	4	-	4

The scout troop of boys was started in 1923. The boys scouts were prepared for the inspection of officers. The officers were pleased with their smart turnout. The educated Waddar settlers were sent to teachers' training at Kurnool and were later appointed as teachers in the school. The school worked for 252 days in a year.[5] The school mistress, the wife of the compounder, took care of the girls in the lower classes. Elementary school boys were given practical lessons in agriculture on the government farm. The school was regularly inspected by the Deputy Inspector of Schools, the District Educational Officer and the Sub-Assistant Inspectors. Elderly boys were taught some agricultural theories in the class and then they were given manual work on the government farm. Some were sent to weaving. Some were trained as scouts. The best boys were presented with 8 goats as school prizes to promote interest in education.[6]

The Headmaster was a secondary grade trained teacher. He possessed good teaching ability and organising capacity. English was introduced as an additional subject in the IV and V standards during the year 1937, as suggested by the collectors. The headmaster was the only person who was competent to handle that language.[7] We can draw comparisons between Siddhapuram children to those students of advanced localities in the district. The Waddar children were brought under excellent discipline. They were trained to become self-reliant and useful members of society. The old boys of the school were encouraged to form into a drama troupe and enacted four street dramas. It served them as a diversion and moral instruction. "*The Animal Week*" was celebrated and the settlers were taught how to show sympathy towards their animals. Leaflets were read and explained to them. The supply of mid-day meals to the school children commenced in Siddhapuram from 13.3.1937.[8]

Sometimes the settlement manager used the innocent Waddars in scandals. Since the manager was the incharge of the school, tuition work was given to the grown-up girls. Elderly girls in the school used to visit delinquent's houses for preparing lessons and learnt Banjara songs. Brutal assaults were made on school girls. It was very sad to know that, "In a school, especially of criminal settlers, a strict standard of discipline was absolutely essential and any chastisement by the Headmaster in the exercise and maintenance of such a discipline should not be criticised. Exercise of discipline must be measured with a different standard."[9]

The school was developed into a first grade elementary school during the year 1938. Pupils who completed 5th standard joined in higher elementary school.[10] The government sanctioned, to open the sixth standard in the school at Siddhapuram during 1947-48 and to convert one of the higher elementary grade teachers' post into a secondary grade post. The students who passed the sixth standard were sent to Velgode for further studies in the Telugu lower secondary school. The settlers' girls who passed the sixth standard were sent for training in midwifery.[11] The students of elementary school and secondary grade school were too slow to understand lessons due to lack of proper motivation. The children in each classes were more in number. This was not an easy task for a teacher to coach up more than a reasonable number. The parents of the children did not appreciate the value of education. They were constantly goaded to send the children to the school. The strength of the school during the year 1948-49 was as follows.[12]

Table-9
The Strength of Siddhapuram School During the Year 1948-49

Standard	*Average Attendance Strength 1948-49*	
	Boys	*Girls*
1st Class	18	17
2nd Class	10	6
3rd Class	9	6
4th Class	10	2
5th Class	6	1
6th Class	4	11
Total	57	43

At present, the location and condition of the school at Siddhapuram is in a deplorable condition. A teacher with the secondary teacher training qualification (SGT) is running the school. It is not planned properly, since there is no syllabus or curricula prescribed for the school. The environment is not conducive for the children to study. There are only two graduates in the entire settlement and they too are still unemployed.

III

Profile of Education in Stuartpuram

The SA thought that education was compulsory for the Yerukulas of this settlement and therefore, started an elementary school in 1916. Elementary education was made compulsory and those not attending the school were strictly punished. Out of 481 children in the settlement, 250 children were school going during the year 1916. 74 children attended the school regularly. The children in the school were very bright. The Governor of Madras was delighted with the school and took a photograph of the boys.[13]

The school was run in a Palmyra shed of the size '60 × 20' which was leaky. In the elementary school, the children were taught three 'R's and general knowledge including rural science, gardening, nature study, English, physical training and the Bible. In the higher standards of the school, industrial education and moral training were introduced. Instruction in agriculture was made compulsory in school education. The school was a co-education school. There were 40 children in each section. Class books, maps, slates and slated pencils, pictures of animals and plants, a globe, Ananda Primer and Ananda Readers for Standards I, II and III, and garden implements for children were purchased by the manager. Night classes were conducted for adults. The teachers employed in the day school taught in the night schools also. The wives of the teachers evinced keen interest in girls' education. For this, the teachers were given extra salary of Rs. 8 to Headmaster and Rs. 5 for assistant teachers. The subjects taught in the night school were reading, writing and arithmetic.[14] The strength and attendance of students in the elementary school on 29th October 1917 was as follows.[15]

Table-10

Strength of Elementary School, Stuartpuram, 1917

Standards	*No. on Rolls*		*No. Present*		*Total*
	Boys	*Girls*	*Boys*	*Girls*	
Infants A	14	11	14	9	23
Infants B	22	14	13	11	24
Infants C	15	23	10	18	28
Infants D	30	34	25	27	52
1st Standard	8	3	6	2	8
2nd Standard	11	1	8	1	9
3rd Standard	7	3	7	3	10

The management of the school and the employment of teachers were left entirely to the SA. The government desired that the rules prevailing in the Educational Department should be adopted. An interesting feature of that time was that qualified teachers from the Yerukulas, both men and women, were appointed as teachers in the school.[16] This was done with the intention of creating an atmosphere in the settlement primarily to promote the self-confidence of the whole tribe and, secondly to prove that those who were committed to do any work they were asked to do seriously. To strengthen this, periodical inspections were arranged by the educational officers of high mental caliber.[17] The teachers were given better salaries and provided with free quarters in the settlement. *Ganji* (boiled rice water) was supplied at noon to the students who were present both in the morning and in the evening.[18] The following table describes the teachers in the school during the year 1918.[19]

Table–11
Position of Teachers in Stuartpuram Elementary School

Name of the Teacher	*Qualifications*	*Scale of Pay*
K. Jacob	L.S.P.T.C. of 1915	25
Ch. Joseph	S.S.L.C. of 1915	20
Santhoshammal	L.S.P.T.C. of 1915	15
Soubhagyammal	L.S.P.T.C. of 1915	15
P. Simon	Unpassed	12
Lyssammal	Passed 4th Std.	12
B. Solomon	Unpassed	12

The newly established boarding school helped the settlers in withering away of the crime atmosphere. The boarding school was established for the sake of: 1. orphan children, 2. children whose parents were in jail, 3. children of parents who were miserably poor, 4. children of parents just returned from jails, 5. children of parents from whom separation was made because of the bad character of parents or because of the suspected character of children and 6. children of absconding settlers.[20]

The boarding school was very well managed and in a report the manager stated that the school was an asset to the settlement. In order to improve the sleeping conditions of the children of the settlers, the Commissioner of Labour constructed separate dormitories for boys and girls. Two matrons were appointed separately to take care of them. Another classification was the young children and the older ones. A separate building was arranged for recreation purpose.

The meeting of parents and children either at the school or at home added to the disturbance of the children's minds. It was felt that reformation was impossible in an atmosphere where the crime culture was not forgotten. The SA dissuaded the parents from meeting their children. But the influence of the parents on their separated children was very severe. The new generation was made up of honest people. The SA visualised the hours of work as to make use of timings in such a way that no time was left for them to visit their parents and hence no perpetuation of crime among the youth.[21] Thus they segregated their children from their parents and arranged a boarding school in the settlement and permitted occasional visits of the parents.

The SA appointed peons for the reformation of the children of the ex-settlers. The peons for these schools were selected from the settlers themselves.[22] Their duty was to go round and collect the children for the school. At the age of 5 years, the settlers' children were sent to schools.[23] In the elementary school, instruction was given upto 5th standards. The headmaster was with a certificate of higher grade training.[24]

There was an increase in the number of children attending the school every year. During the year 1924 there were nearly 401 children on rolls and the average attendance was 261.[25] Furthermore, the outside influences were felt by the children. The SA authorities considered that the solution to the problem was in sending girls to Nellore and boys to Perambur (Near Madras city).[26] It would help them in reformatory process. Mackenzie, the SA official wanted to change the structure of the building to create a new atmosphere in the settlement. The availability of buildings at Nellore was a positive factor and this was congenial to the growth of children. The SA suddenly closed the boarding school in Stuartpuram and shifted some of the girls to Nellore girls school. But the closing down of the Stuartpuram Boarding School (1926) had a severe blow on the settler's children.[27]

A significant feature of the settlement school was that, the manager L.R. Gale, gave a Christian bias to the whole atmosphere of the school. When the first children batches of Yerukulas were brought into this settlement, school boys and girls were dirty looking and they involved in petty thefts and road robberies. It was not an easy task to teach CTs to be on the path of righteousness'. But much had been done towards this good end. The younger generation understood and responded well.[28] The SA constructed a church in the year 1915, ostensibly to reform the Yerukulas by giving Bible education and thereby making them disciplined. All the settlers were gathered and brought into the church.

S.H. Slater, the Labour Commissioner, bestowed attention on the school children. Some students got through the SSLC (Secondary School Leaving Certificate) examination. Those who failed were also given utmost care. They were admitted either in Paddison hostel or in the Industrial School, Perambur, Madras.[29] Some of the boys who passed through the five standards in the settlement school were admitted in the 4th and 6th forms of the high school at Bapatla.[30]

Dowson, the then Deputy Inspector General of Police, Madras, inspected the settlement school on 8.7.1931 and wrote "I knew this settlement in its earliest infancy. My visit today was peculiarly interesting. My first visit was in 1914. Today, i.e. 8.7.1931, it is possible to see that the settlement has completely filled the purpose for which it was instituted."[31] After inspecting the school, he said: "The kiddies looked fat and happy. Neither the manager nor the police had any controversies. The settlement is in a most flourishing condition."[32]

The SA opened a new girls' school for the development of women's education. During the year 1921, there were nearly 100 girls in it.[33] During the year 1926, few girls were transferred to Nellore Industrial School. Owing to the closure of the girls reformatory school at Nellore, a number of girls were sent back to their parents. There were no classes above 5th standard. The girls who studied at Nellore in the higher classes were again sent to the higher elementary boarding school at Kavali. Nursing and sewing training were given to the girls. The manager of Stuartpuram settlement selected some women who were familiar with three 'R's and talented with the art of conversation and possessed with the ability to describe, explain them completely to have an idea of such topics. In addition to that, they were also trained in the proper maintenance of the house or the working place by sweeping, dusting and cooking. For extracting talent from them, they were encouraged. For example, on 10th March 1928 a modal was done by a girl for essay writing on 'Home Sanitation' during *Health Week Competition.*[34]

The settlers had a brigade of scouts since 1923. Although the members were constantly changing owing to employment and other circumstances they had a creditable brigade. A small bugle band had been formed and equipment supplied. The Assistant Manager had taken a keen interest in the movement and himself went into camp with the scouts.[35] The scouting activities in the schools were conducted by the school teachers who were trained as scout masters.[36] All the adult-reformed settlers were expected to give importance to morality. Polygamy were prevalent and the traces of polyandry were rare among them. The SA thought that religious and moral instruction were the greatest factors for their improvement. They used to instruct the womenfolk of the settlement to take stern steps to control their crimes. But it happened to the contrary that even the wives were also involved in the culture of crime.[37]

The supply of mid-day meals was started at Stuartpuram for the first time only from December 1947. Other settlements' school children were also supplied with mid-day meals at the government cost of Rs. 3. The introduction of mid-day meals to the school children was to encourage the children to attend the school regularly and make them fit to receive instruction.[38] The school children were taken to excursions. The government authorities, the DIG of Police, CID and railways sanctioned the expenditure not exceeding Rs. 50 per year.[39]

It is striking to note that among the Yerukula community of Stuartpuram already some secured good employment both in central and state governments. At present, more than 150 members even received University Education. This is obviously to some extent due to the efforts of the SA and the awareness among the youth. Separate hostels are also being maintained by the SA for these children. Consequently, there are nearly 155 students in these hostels today. In the hostels there are 101 boys and 54 girls studying in class I to the S.S.C. (10th class). It is providing scholarships, food, hostel facilities and clothes to the students. The SA had requested the Secretary, Government of Madras, to sanction a general library for children outside the premises of the school and it was conceded.

In the year 1958, the SA combined with the Inspector General of Police, opened a new high school for the children of the settlers. The school comprised of mainly Yerukula children and some converted Christians together with the children of upper castes. Later, it was converted into a middle school from the academic year 1958-59. It was run by the Social Welfare Department.[40] The high school followed the syllabus prescribed by the Board of Secondary Education, Andhra Pradesh, Hyderabad. The strength of the high school as per the annual record of the year 2006 is 277. The division of boys and girls from class VI to X was as follows.[41]

Table-12

Strength of High School in Stuartpuram, 2005

Class	*Boys*	*Girls*	*Total*
VI	34	26	60
VII	29	18	47
VIII	26	17	43

(Contd.)

Class	*Boys*	*Girls*	*Total*
IX	34	28	62
X	41	24	65
Total			277

After the repeal of the CTA Act in 1952, it was contemplated that all state governments should undertake welfare schemes especially education. In the second five year plan, funds were sanctioned by the government for the education of these tribal children.[42] During the 3rd five year plan, a plan provision of Rs. 375.00 lakhs was made for the purpose. An estimated expenditure of Rs. 55.36 lakhs was incurred during 1962-63. In the fifth five year plan no separate provision has been made under centrally sponsored programmes for undertaking educational and other schemes for DNT communities.[43]

Various societies such as Bharatiya Adimjati Sevak Sangh (New Delhi), Andhra Rastra Adimjati Sevak Sangh and Andhra Rashtra Yerukula Maha Sangam came forward to reform these people.[44] The main aims and objectives of Andhra Rashtra Adimjati Sevak Sangh were: 1. Education, 2. Literature, 3. Liberation, 4. Sadachar work, etc.[45] Yerukulas, Yanadis and Banjaras were included in the list of Scheduled Tribes by the Parliament in 1956 owing to the efforts of the B.N. Datar, the then Minister of Home Affairs.[46] The first school for Scheduled Tribes was started by the Sangh in 1934. The first Harijan hostel was started in 1929. The first tribal hostel was started in 1939. Female education among tribals was taken up by the Sangh.[47] Various types of books, magazines and articles were published in Telugu and English. The best examples are Kallumunta, Rama Rajyam, Yekalavya which are ballads. *Adivasi, Dalit Marg, Girijana Jyoti, Yekalavya Patrika and Harijanoddharana* were other important newspapers published by Andhra Rashtra Adimjati Sevak Sangh.[48]

In addition to the SA and various social organizations, social workers namely Gora, Lavanam, Hemalatha Lavanam of Atheist centre Vijayawada and M.V.Thomas, the former Superintendent of Police, T. Gopala Rao, the former collector of Guntur district, endeavoured hard to reform these people, through education. During the year 1983, DNT students who secured highest marks in public examinations in VII and X standards in the school at

Stuartpuram were awarded prizes by Lavanam and Hemalatha Lavanam.

The welfare measures initiated for Yerukulas, Waddars, Yanadis and Sugalis bear a resemblance to the efforts to squeezing oil from sand. The development of scheduled tribes is a real challenge to the present government. The utterances of the government on the welfare measures are making much noise emanating from empty vessels. Policy formulation and its execution, most often, fall apart. Tribal children are required to pay special fee at the time of admission, though they are exempted from other fees. Poor tribal students are not in a position even to pay this. Added to this, tribal welfare scholarships are generally delayed and released at the end of the year. As a result, students are bound to face many problems. There is a lot of injustice being done to tribal children.

In the sphere of employment too, tribal children are facing serious problems. Though the public advertisements earmark a number of vacancies to these people, they appear so with a clause saying that the posts would be convertible to other castes in the absence of the eligible tribal candidates. In such a situation, the very policy of reservation loses its meaning and validity. It is suggested that the government takes appropriate measures to overcome these problems. The elected representatives from the tribal region should educate the government about these fundamental hardships of tribal children.

It is evident that in the quagmire of poverty, they prefer immediate gains to long term benefits that accrue to their children after a continuous schooling of ten to fifteen years. They are under the false impression that the schooling eats away their economic fruits. Therefore, need-based or job-oriented education is an effective alternative to the existing monotonous and unproductive education. In the interviews, we found from the settlers that their children could not reach higher echelons of society because of the psychological barriers they suffer from. For this, revamping the present school set up, on ashram or gurukula type, would make a considerable difference. Trained teachers and well-equipped schools would be a significant factor in moulding the personalities of children in these colonies. This is what we have observed in Siddhapuram settlement. There is no proper schooling for the children. Hence no advancement is found in that settlement.

There should be a major drive to eradicate illiteracy among these people. It goes without saying that any positive change in their attitude towards earning their livelihood, necessarily drives them towards a positive realisation of the important aspect like education. The aim of social education can best be achieved only when feelings of deprivation, discrimination and aloofness are erased from their minds. A dynamic group of young volunteers and social workers will have to shoulder the responsibility of disseminating enlightened ideas among these people.

Today, there is a strong objection raised regarding the pathetic conditions of education and educational institutions prevailing in the settlement schools. The status of Andhra Pradesh in respect of these tribes stands in unique contrast to the rest of the country. There are social and behavioural changes taking place among the members of the denotified tribal settlement areas in Andhra Pradesh. The denotified tribal settlements such as Stuartpuram, Seethanagaram (Guntur district), Kaparallatippa and Bitragunta (Nellore district), Siddhapuram (Kurnool district) and Lingala (Mahaboobnagar dist.) settlements constitutes a major segment of the total schedule tribe population in Andhra Pradesh. In all these settlement areas Yerukulas, Waddars, Katheras, Chenchus, Sugalis, Yanadis and other nomadic tribes form a major part of population. Some of the settlers are still having some serious problems of crime and illiteracy. On the whole, the scenario in Andhra Pradesh offers contrast on any comparison.

One of the main problems identified by the field experiences and the field survey is about the social treatment meted out to the families of these tribes. For generations together, the families and their members have been labelled as criminals suffered dishonour and social negligence. The reasons are not far to seek given the background of the socially despicable avocation as practiced by some of the people belonging to these tribes. The children and women, in particular, have suffered ignominy from mainstream society. The stigma of criminality is still one of the major impediments in the smooth run of educational progress of children and youth. Children often faced a kind of social alienation in most of the walks of social life. Social alienation particularly in young age hampers the growth of psycho-social faculties of the children. Social practices of the mainstream society have denied opportunities for the children coming from the so-called criminal families residing in the settlement areas. The approaches of the government often times remain impersonal and lack human element and eye on social cohesiveness, in its approach. However, there can be education without even the formal modes and methods of schooling. But mere efforts on mainstream socialisation do not open wide social canvas for the children because there is already a hostile attitude in the outside society. The school or the process of schooling in settlement areas or settlement schools may be used as instruments or tools to impart social culture, feelings of common fraternity, community approach, adjustment mentality, atmosphere of working and learning together and finally moral dynamics of social and cultural behaviour. The schools in settlement areas are to be treated or perceived from a different angle where they are expected to combine the role of an instructor, and change agent.

IV

Profiles of Schools (pen pictures of primary schools) in Settlements

The following is the situational analysis of Primary School facilities and educational needs of DNT settlement schools of Andhra Pradesh:

School 1 : Salvation Army Aided Primary School, Stuartpuram, Bapatla Taluk, Guntur Dist:

This school was established by a missionary group, viz. Salvation Army and later the Government of Andhra Pradesh provided aid and presently it is functioning as an aided primary school. It is a two teacher school. Both the teachers are not residing in the same school village but are residing in places upto a distance of 4 to 5 kilometres. The following are the details of roll of the school at present.

Table-13

Strength of Salvation Army Aided Primary School, Stuartpuram

	Boys	*Girl*	*Total*
I Class	10	10	20
II Class	10	05	15
III Class	11	06	16
IV Class	07	10	17
V Class	16	08	24
Total	54	39	93

The strength in each class is low, ranging from 15 to 24. On the whole, the number of male students is more than the number of female students except in class IV. Multigrade teaching is going on in the school and the head teacher is taking classes I to III and the assistant, teacher is taking classes IV and V. Instead of subject teacher system, class teacher system is adopted. Children are provided free textbooks and mid-day meals. No other incentives are enjoyed by the pupils. Except for teachers, there is no furniture for students. The school and classrooms do not possess the minimum equipment. Teacher grant and school grants are provided and from the school grant a radio was purchased and the students are exposed to the radio lessons. Daily school assembly is organised and news is read. The children need to be exposed to moral education stories, wise sayings, etc. Further there is need to organize activities which develop honesty among the children. The school is situated in a place having railway line on one side and road on the other side. It is not accessible to children in the sense that parents are afraid of sending their children to school for fear of accidents. The school is being run in a tiled building having 5 rooms. Only two rooms are under use and the other three are vacant and used only for using the school furniture. The roof is leaky and needs immediate repairs. Neither the aided management, nor the government which is providing aid are looking after the repairs of the building. Because of craze towards English medium education, many parents are sending their children to nearby towns wherein conveyance facility by school bus or auto or riksha are available. There is no compound wall to the school and no garden and no demarked playground. Only open space is used as playground. Socially useful productive work (SUPW) activities are also not given the required attention in the school.

Table–14

The Population Details of the Settlement (colony)

Population	:	661	688	1349
School age	:	139	143	282
Enrolled	:	54	39	93
Remaining	:	85	104	189

Some well to do family children are studying elsewhere and very few children whose parents are very poor, are left out and they are to be enrolled. Limited play material is available with schools like skipping ropes, rings, etc. Last year (2005-06) about 20 students who have completed class V were admitted into class VI in the High School situated in the same village. Some of the problems faced by the teachers are as follows: *(i)* Repairs to school building, *(ii)* Lack of equipment like furniture to students, aids, etc., *(iii)* Lack of learning aids and play materials, *(iv)* Lack of sanitation facilities and compound wall, *(v)* Absence of students for long because of their parental harassment by police. The students are psychologically depressed by this and are not able to concentrate in their studies and attend the school, *(vi)* Lack of facilities for organisation of SUPW activities, *(vii)* The social stigma is attached on the part of the community. Because of this, the educated children are neither employed nor able to have self-support. Due to this, there is danger of reverting to the old practice of thefts and robberies. and *(viii)* Early child care education centre, (ECE) is not in the school campus, etc.

In view of the present conditions of education prevailing in the colony the following are some of the suggestions that can be made to improve condition of the school : *(i)* to provide for close supervision facilities by the Dept. of Education/Tribal Welfare to the teachers. *(ii)* to provide facilities for the organisation of SUPW activities. *(iii)* to organise such activities which develop honesty among the students. *(iv)* arrange extension lecture by local educated youth and others who are employed. *(v)* In the broader interest of the village the solution lies with the voluntry organizations of the specific programmes. *(vi)* Formation of co-operatives for providing self-support to the settlers (villagers) such as milk cows, mushroom growth, autos, piggery, cashew plantation growth, etc. *(vii)* establishment of industries by inviting the interested industrialists which provide employment opportunities to the settlers in the settlement itself, *(viii)* some of the NGOs (Samskar) should think of these programmes in the interest of the settlers, *(ix)* convert these settlement schools as Ashram schools and introduce vocational courses, *(x)* provide incentive facilities more in number like uniforms, writing materials, etc. and finally. *(xi)* lack of safety to girl students. Therefore, security measures should be adopted for the welfare of the girl children also.

School 2 : Government Denotified Tribal Elementary School, Siddhapuram, Kurnool Dist.

This school was established by the British. Government during the year 1913 for the benifit of the DNT children and the following is the present strength of the school during the year 2006.

Table-15
Strength of the School in Siddhapuram

Class	*Boys*	*Girls*	*Total*
I	13	18	31
II	18	23	41
III	17	2	29
IV	16	06	22
V	10	10	20
Total	74	69	143

In lower classes, the strength of girls is more than that of the boys. The school age population (children 5 –11 age group) of the village is 168. Yet 25 pupils are to be enrolled in the school during the year 2006. The population of the village is 571 males and 564 females with the total of 1,135. The literacy rate of the village is 34%. This is a four teacher school. Class teacher system is followed in the school in place of subject teacher system. Only one teacher is incharge of multiple class teaching; he is handling classes III and IV. None of the teachers are residing in the school village. All are residing outside school village. Some are residing at a distance of 10 kms and some at a distance of 5 kms. The school is being run in three buildings (two RCC buildings and one tiled old building.) The tiled old building needs immediate repairs wherein class I is located. The two RCC buildings have a verandah and one room each in which two classes each are located. There is no furniture to pupils and it is available only to teachers. Playground is available to the school. No equipment is available to the school. Teacher grant and school grant are provided to the school. It is reported that the major occupation of the villagers is illegal preparation of arrack. Even the students are involved in the preparation and transportation of the same. The dire need of the village is to have an upper primary school. The girls are afraid of going to nearby upper primary schools because of eve teasing and lack of social security. The village needs area specific programmes. Some of the areas in which some industries can be established are sericulture, matchstick industry, weaving gauge clothes, honey collection and preservation, beedi leaf collection, Bamboo work, etc.

Some NGOs can come forward and help the local villagers in their development and self-support. S.U.P.W. scheme needs special care and attention in the school to train students to support themselves in life.

School 3 : Bitragunta Salvation Army Govt. Upper Primary School, Kaparallatippa, Bogole Mandal, Nellore District.

This is an upper primary school with seven classes as follows: The strength of the School during the year 2006 is:

Table–16
Strength of the School

Class	*Boys*	*Girls*	*Total*
I	22	27	49
II	16	16	32
III	08	13	21
IV	03	11	14
V	09	17	26
VI	04	12	16
VII	08	09	17
Total	70	125	175

The population of the village is 640 men and 660 women with a population 1300 people. There are about 10 children yet to be enrolled in the school. None of the teaching staff are residing in the school village. The HM and other teachers are coming from a distance of 20 km and others are residing at a distance of about 2 kms. The HM is incharge of classes VI and VII and the others are teaching one class each. Class teacher system is in vogue in the school. The school is being run in three buildings a tiled one, an asbestos roofed one and an RCC building) All the three buildings need repairs. Upto 5th class furniture is available for students. The school needs equipment and aids. Teacher grants and school grants are also received for the school. The following are the problems of the school. Lack of equipment and A.V. Aids, Upgradation as High School, Girls afraid of eve-teasing, and social security is needed to girls in the colony.

School 4: Government Upper Primary School, Sitanagaram Colony, Tadepalli Mandal, Guntur District :

The school was established by the erstwhile British Government during the year 1916. The Government of Andhra Pradesh provided the aid under Social Tribal Welfare Department. Presently the school is managed by Tribal Welfare Department, Govt. of Andhra Pradesh. The school has the strength of 9 teachers, viz. two B.Ed. qualified teachers, five secondary grade teachers and two pandits. The following is the details of the enrolment of DNT children of the Colony during the year 2006.

Table–17
Strengh of School Children

Class	*Boys*	*Girls*	*Total*
I	1	2	3
II	1	1	2
III	2	1	3
IV	2	2	4
V	1	3	4
VI	1	1	2
VII	0	0	0

Subject teacher system, class teacher system is going on. Children from other communities, viz. such as Christians, Muslims and Hindu caste groups are undergoing instruction simultaneously with the DNT group children. The DNT (Tribal) children are not provided free textbooks, uniforms, notebooks, scholarships, mid-day meals, etc. Other incentives are also not provided by the govt. to the school so far. The children are squatting on the floor. Furniture is not available to the students. The school building is collapsed and damaged very badly. The school does not possess the minimum equipment and aids. The settlement population are scattered in 3 areas-that is: Tadepalli 1st ward, Tadepalli 2nd ward and Annapurna Devi Nagar. The well-to-do family settlers' children are sending their children to the nearby English medium schools. Some elderly girls who dropped out of the school were provided tailoring work in the school. The headmaster is handling maths and science subjects for all classes. TLM grant though provided, still the grant is not utilised by the headmaster.

V

Conclusion

The social conditions, living standards, income and educational level of the tribal people living in these settlements are much below than the conditions of non-tribal people living in Andhra Pradesh. This fact remains as a grim reminder to the more privileged people in spite of the efforts and huge amount of money allocated and spent by the government. Over the years in spite of the efforts put in by missionary and non-governmental organisations such as Salvation Army, American Baptist Telugu Mission, Canadian Mission and other Christian missionary groups and also several voluntary organisations/NGOs, etc.

Lack of census data, absence of Policy-level discussions on DNTs, treatment of DNT issues seems outside the purview of Planning Commission estimates (always Primitive Tribal groups (PTG) other than DNTs are covered), weak community participation in the settlements or colonies and lack of need-based training (contextual) given to teachers teaching in settlement schools, are some of the gaps identified during the visit of the settlements which are seriously affecting the progress of the DNTs in their colonies.

A complete and comprehensive survey conducted in the five settlements hints at the establishment of separate schools with English as the medium of instruction. Many of the reformed parents in the selected settlements wish to send their wards to schools at a different places. For, they perceive English medium of instruction as one important tool of mainstream social integration. The NGOs working in the settlements look for a time bound tie-up between RIE/NCERT and wish to ground a separate school with an eye on social integration. NGOs also expressed their wish to shoulder the responsibility of land procurement, construction, recruitment, school infrastructure and admissions of students from settlements (also from non-settlement areas of the surrounding settlements). The NGOs are also looking at RIE/NCERT or similar apex educational bodies for help in training the teachers. The NGOs should be in a position to shoulder complete responsibility of the education of the DNT children. The future tie-up will be confined to teacher training and teaching aid support from RIE/NCERT or similar institution. A comprehensive census data collection may be undertaken in all the existing settlement areas by the NCERT as a part of educational survey reports, PAC/ ERIC programmes. To undertake advocacy campaign and networking meets with government departments and NCERT so that issues and problems of these tribes in transition will be put on the agenda of general discussion on tribal welfare.

In view of the above analysis, few suggestions can be made to improve the educational scenario of the denotified tribes of Andhra Pradesh.

1. The government has to conduct sample surveys to know about their present position pertaining to the present state of literacy achievement levels of the DNT children in primary schools.
2. They should be provided with jobs which give them immediate remuneration and relief. Some of them who are minimum educated, may be recruited into the departments of police as constables, water boys and sweepers.
3. Educational facilities as they exist today are not adequate. A few more schools may be established and all these schools should be provided with necessary infrastructural facilities.
4. Rigid enforcement of the provisions of the compulsory primary education Act is highly essential. The Government should issue strict orders to the various school boards to enforce primary education in schools situated in areas where the members of DNTs are residing in considerable number.
5. Free coaching centers should be opened in these colonies for educated unemployed youth. Coaching facilities should be provided for the students of both technical and general courses.
6. Best sports persons are available among these denotified tribe children. Physical education should be improved and special training facilities should be provided to make them national and state level players, etc.

NOTES

1. The teachers were supplied clothing, rations and all sorts of contingency grants. A special pay, unhealthy locality allowance of Rs. 5 per month was sanctioned to the assistant teachers in Siddhapuram elementary school. The higher elementary grade teachers were placed in the scale of Rs. 27-1-1-50 from 1.4.1932. Rs 10 were paid as unhealthy locality allowance from 1.4.1932. *See Public Works (Labour) Department, G.O. No. 1675 dated 9.8.1932,* pp. 1-2, APSA.

2. Of the 76 children at the settlement 23 boys and 17 girls attended the school. The average attendance was 19 for the whole year 1924. See Note *Showing The Progress Made in the Settlements of Criminal Tribes in the Madras Presidency upto January 1926, Madras,* 1927, p. 30, AP State Gazetteers Office, Hyderabad.
3. See *Public Works (Labour) Department, G.O. No. 137 dated 19.1.1927,* p. 5, APSA. The children are kept away from their parents. The younger children are sent home at night. Others sleep in the school building. Also See *Public Works (Labour) Department, G.O. No. 1719, dated 9.8.1927,* p. 2, APSA.

Table–18

The Strength of the School During the Year 1930

Standard	*Boys*	*Girls*	*Total*
I	24	26	50
II	2	1	3
III	2	2	4
IV	3	-	3
V	5	-	5
Total	36	29	65

4. See *Home Department, G.O. No. 3557 dated 6.9.1937,* pp. 1-3, National Archives of India (NAI).
5. See *Public Works (Labour) Department, G.O. No. 2190 dated 28.7.1930,* p. 7-13, (APSA)
6. See *Public Works (Labour) Department, G.O. No. 2671 dated 6.12.1934,* p.5, Andhra Pradesh State Archives.
7. See *Home Department, G.O. No. 6170 dated 22.12.1938,* p. 36, NAI.
8. See *Public Works Labour Department, G.O. No. 2671 dated 6.12.1934,* p. 6, Andhra Pradesh state Archives.
9. See *Home Department, G.O. No. 6170 dated 22.12.1938,* p. 3, NAI.
10. *Ibid*
11. See *Home Department, G.O. No. 149, dated 11.1.1947,* pp. 1-2, NAI.
12. The strength of the school was improved after the internment of Golla Kuppam Dasarees. After passing Vth Standard, the children were sent to Kurnool for studies. See *Administration Report on Kallar Reclamation, Korava Reclamation, Criminal Tribes Settlements and Yanadi Reclamation for the year 1947-48,* Madras, 1949, p. 13.
13. See *Home (Judicial) Department, G.O. No. 2074, 18th August 1916,* p. 4, Tamil Nadu State Archives.
14. See *Home (Judicial) Department, G.O. No. 1225, 20th May 1918,* p. 6, TNA.
15. *Op. Cit,* p. 6.

16. See, Mildred Mackenzie, *The Mud Bank,* Peensylvania, 1959, p. 12.
17. See, *Law (General) Department (Annual Report), G.O. No. 3187, 14th November 1924,* p. 3, APSA.
18. *Ibid.*
19. The two unpassed teachers were sent up for the sessional school. See *Home (Judicial) Department, G.O. No. 1225 dated 20th May 1918,* p. 6.
20. See *Law (General) Department, G.O. No. 1714, 22nd October 1921,* p. 4, APSA.
21. Settlers criticized that it was cruel to separate the children from their parents. The SA made the parents to understand that the separation was done to enable them to get in future an honest employment. The parents put forward no objections. However, we can note that both Mabe and Robilliard were strongly opposed to the separation of children from their parents. They did not object for the boarding schools in the settlement where the parents were allowed to see the children under supervision. See *Home (Judicial) Department, G.O. No. 1759, 5th August 1918,* p. 1, TNA.
22. See *Law (General) Department, G.O. No. 2267, 16th June 1925,* p. 2, APSA.
23. See *PWLD, G.O. No. 2338, dt.19th August 1930,* p. 2, APSA.
24. *Ibid.*
25. See *Law (General) Department, G.O. No. 3187, 14th November 1924,* p. 3, APSA.
26. See *Law (General) Department, G.O. No. 1907, 15th June 1925,* p. 1, APSA.
27. See, *Law (General) Department, G.O. No. 2267, 16th July 1925,* p. 2, APSA.
28. See *PWLD G.O. No. 1551, 20th July 1927,* p. 6, APSA.
29. See *PWLD G.O. No. 2061, dated 21.8.1928,* p. 1, APSA.
30. See, *PWLD G.O. No. 1926, dated 30.7.1931,* p. 2, APSA
31. See *PWLD G.O. No. 1313 dated 17.6.1932,* p. 7, APSA.
32. *Ibid*
33. Booth Tucker said that, "If a man wished to marry one of the girls in the settlement he had to come into the settlement and live there." Gillman pointed out that the proposed husband would in the majority of cases, be already a member of the tribe. See *Home (Judicial)* Department, *G.O. No. 1759, 5th August 1918,* pp. 13-17, APSA.
34. See *Home (Judicial) Department, G.O. No. 1639, 8th August 1917,* p. 2, TNA.
35. The Scouts went to the camp during the year 1931 for 5 days and enjoyed the outing. See *PWLD G.O. No. 1313, 17th June 1932,* p. 6, APSA.
36. See *Home Department, G.O. No. 1571, 21st April 1947,* p. 1, NAI.
37. See *Home Department, G.O. No. 1508, 21st March 1938,* p. 1, NAI.
38. See *Home Department, G.O. No. 1571, 21st April 1947,* p. 1, NAI.

39. See *Home Department, G.O. No. 1571, 21st April 1946,* p. 1, NAI.
40. Interview with the Headmistress, Stuartpuram High School dated 6.2.2006.
41. *Ibid.*
42. Interview with The Manager of Stuartpuram Settlement, Stuartpuram dated 2.2.2006.
43. See *Report of the Commissioner for Scheduled Castes and Scheduled Tribes for the year 1962-74.*
44. See L.M. Sreekant *Report of the Commissioner for Scheduled Castes and Scheduled Tribes for the year 1953,* 3rd Report, New Delhi, 1954, p. 200.
45. See L.M. Sreekant, *Report of the Commissioner for Scheduled castes and Scheduled Tribes for the year 1954,* 4th Report, New Delhi, 26th February 1955, p. 232.
46. See *Adivasi, Issue No. 9 and 10 dated 15.12.1962 and 15.1.1963,* p. 1.
47. See *Adivasi (Telugu monthly) Published by R. Nagaiah, Vol.10, Nos. 9 and 10, Guntur dated 15.12.1962* and *dated 15.1.1963,* p. 1.
48. *Kallumunta* is a ballad. The authors of the work are Ponna Koteswara Rao and Ponna Satyanarayana. It was published in 1950. *Rama Rajyam* is another ballad on Yerukulas by Ponna Koteswara Rao. It was published by Jayanti Publications, Vijayawada during the year 1960. These two sources, through valuable, are out of print today. The two important sources give detailed information of the culture of Yerukulas, how they perform their marriages. They also provide information on the general conditions in the settlements. *Adivasi Patrika* is a Telugu monthly published by Rameswaram Nagaiah from Guntur in 1943. Each issue was priced at 1 anna and the annual subscription rate was Rs.1. *Yerukula Patrika* was published by Kampa Punnaiah during the year 1943. *Dalit Marg* was another monthly by Ponna Koteswara Rao. Some other papers of the same kind were *Girijana Jyoti* and *Yekalavya.* Out of financial crisis, these publications were stopped from 1980 onwards.

11

Status of Health Among the Denotified Tribes

I

Introduction

The study of medical missionary enterprise in Andhra Pradesh has long been a neglected area of historical research. Missionaries in Andhra Pradesh performed the role of the 'change agents'. They undertook efforts to change the health standards and behavioural attitudes of the people in Telugu land with whom they came into contact. The missionaries frequently pointed out that undernourishment, overpopulation and lack of proper sanitation facilities were responsible for high incidence of diseases like tuberculosis, cholera and smallpox. They believed that prevalence of superstitions and unflinching faith in quick remedies led to heavy loss of lives.[1]

The missionaries carried their work in Andhra Pradesh in the areas with stories of mysteries, deaths and horrors. They carried out their work among the natives under colonial rule. They realised the implications of their "Care and Cure" policy vis-à-vis the complex process of Christianisation. In 1920 a European missionary observed, "For the continued preservation of Christianity to Hindus and Muslims, there is no more potent agency than the work of Medical Mission."[2]

The onset of famines and wide scale loss of human lives convinced the missionaries that medical missions needed to be recognised as powerful adjuncts of missionary work. The Canadian Baptist Telugu missionaries utilized medical missions to gain new followers in the coastal Telugu speaking districts. They treated diseases like influenza, cholera and leprosy. The leper asylum homes made them popular amongst the lower castes.[3] The American Baptist missionary activity in India paved the way for the contacts between the Canadian Baptists and the Telugu people. In 1830, Rev. Samuel Day of American Baptist Missionary Union laboured in the Southern part of the Telugu country. The 1897 famine followed by devastating epidemics of cholera and smallpox helped the missionaries to send their medical missionaries to boost the governments' relief programmes. The wide spread effect of the famine, afforded more opportunities to the Canadian Baptists for medical work.

It was at this stage that the Government realised that the successful work done by the missionaries such as the SA, the American Baptist Telugu Mission and other philanthropic agencies in providing great help to these people. The SA was the first organisation that stepped into the medical mission activities of the 'Criminal' tribes of the country. In 1895, the Salvation Army was very young. Commissioner Booth Tucker came to India in January 1901. Ensign Mackenzie was sent to the Telugu country. He was stationed, at 200 miles north of Madras. The Telugu speaking people in these places in 1902 numbered 26,000,000. The Salvation Army entered into several districts in Andhra Pradesh very soon.[4]

1920s witnessed the expansion of medical relief work. Both foreign and Indian funds were utilised to construct new buildings, acquire new instruments and promote advanced method in treatment. The SA took the help of Indian doctors to carry out leprosy mission campaigns and to establish outdoor dispensaries. The SA also attended long distance calls to provide medical relief to the distressed. The service provided by the SA to these people, proved to be one of the important factors of transformation in the social environment. The Salvation Army used advanced clinical techniques to cure patients suffering from chronic stomach ailments and diseases like leprosy. They described the change as 'revolution'. It was observed: "On one side of the tank are the Brahman priests, modern pirates, washing their hands in the sacred waters to get rid of their sins; on the other side is the Christian doctor, modern representative of the Great Physician, cleansing purefying sores, healing diseases and treating ills of all sorts, for all conditions of people, then pointing them to the Lamb of God, who takes away the sins of the world."[5]

In 1920, the involvement of the SA with the treatment of diseases like tuberculosis and leprosy became much more pronounced. The success enjoyed by the SA in the treatment of leprosy paved the way for the large scale conversion of untouchables to Christianity. Most of the leprosy infected patients who were diagnosed as 'burn-outs' preferred to accept Christianity to escape from social oppression. Many of the 'cured' embraced Christianity to secure a guaranteed livelihood. The cured became the missionary workers.

In 1930, the SA faced several problems due to economic depression. Typhoid was very much prevalent. The widespread effect of cholera epidemic also posed difficulties to the missionaries. The Indian assistant doctors were employed in the hospitals dealing with the cases of cholera and maternity. Despite many problems, the missionaries did commendable work in several spheres. A large number of Indian boys and girls were trained in nursing. House to house campaigns were arranged to eradicate leprosy and other forms of skin infection. But the missionaries were supported by the fellow missionaries involved in educational work, undertook propaganda work in the villages. They also took the help of Indian Pastors and Churchmen to implement decrees condemning the consumption of alcoholic drinks. In 1890, the Government of India had remarked that "The experiences gained in other provinces seems to indicate that, when organisations like Salvation Army can be found to take up this work and carry it through on proper lines, it is an economical arrangement to subsidise their undertakings, not only because less money is spent but also because better value is obtained for it."[6]

Therefore, the Government of Madras decided to entrust the medical issues of the settlers as far as possible, to non-official agency, missionary or otherwise, and they have repeatedly declared their readiness to welcome the entry of Hindu and Muhammadan agencies in the field of social reform and medical work. But it was only the SA, the American Baptist Mission and the London Mission that had responded to the call for the medical relief of poor and distressed people in the presidency. The Government had established under their management 10 settlements,[7] with schools and hospitals. The government had maintained great hope of these Settlements as a means of reducing crime and diseases of the jail population. The chief thing aimed at was to provide good health, proper education and to earn an honest living. The medical work done in many of the existing settlements was of high order. The government hoped that in course of time more persons and societies of a philanthropic disposition will come forward to assist the government in this valuable work.[8]

II

Role of the Christian Missionaries

The DNT settlements were established in thick forests. The sites where the houses constructed for their settlements were filled with malaria disease. The settlements were surrounded by ideal breeding grounds for Anopheles. The forest humidity and weather logging bred mosquitoes and malaria claimed a heavy death toll of the DNT tribes.[9] Death rate was high during the year 1915 in Madras presidency due to influenza. New hospitals were built by the government. The hospitals were only two furlongs from the nearest settlement areas where the DNT settlements are located. Generally hospitals were constructed on the right side of the main road, The death rate in the settlements were distinctly high largely owing to influenza. A sub-assistant surgeon was called bi-weekly from nearset places and medicines were supplied for diseases like dysentery, cholera, malaria, fever, smallpox, beriberi, boils, heart diseases, etc., The daily average attendance was not less than 200 in the settlements.[10]

In order to improve the health conditions of the settlers medical officer were appointed and all the sick settlers were treated by him. Malaria was common disease among the settlers. Registers were also opened in the settlements to record the names of persons found sick, name of disease and other remarks. A dispensary with a compounder was opened in the settlemets from April 1920s. The *"Health Week"* was celebrated every year in DNT settlements. Prizes were distributed as incentives to the settlers to keep their huts and surroundings clean and to devote more attention to the health of their babies.[11] The condition of the DNT villages at present is really pathetic. The hospitals established in 1920s became dysfunctional. Women die at the time of delivery. For medical help they have to rush to hospitals located in distant places. The settlers in all the DNT colonies pleaded for a regular hospital in their places.[12] At Stuartpuram settlement a hospital was established in the year 1914 by the SA. In order to improve the health conditions the SA constructed a hospital. The SA paid special attention in times of cyclones, drought and other natural calamities. Individual cases were given continuous treatment until they were cured. The medical issues were taken care of by V. Sitarama Ayyar, the sub-assistant surgeon. He took keen interest in the well-being of the Yerukulas. Cases of dysentery and eczema were frequent due to unsuitable diet of the people.[13] The destitute parents were not given adequate attention and care of their children. Many of them were children of widowed mothers who could not provide sufficient food. The children did not attend the school regularly as it was found difficult to compel them to do so in these circumstances. However, the present condition of the settlement is very poor.[14]

The SA was seriously involved in the efforts to establish more hospitals and dispensaries. The rise in the number of patients led to the construction of more wards. Training was also provided for para-medical personnel, for compounders and medical assistants. The compounders, who generally provided medical relief to the lower castes, were made to undergo a vigorous training programme in health care and sanitation.[15] The expansion of medical work, posed a few challenges to the SA. Their close connections with the depressed casts made them increasingly aware of the need to start strong campaigns in favour of temperance. The SA authorities believed that women medical missionaries alone could break down the caste Hindu opposition towards the treatment of leprosy patients. The efficient functioning of the surgical and outpatient department in the hospitals evoked a great deal of public support. The expertise displayed by the medical officers in diagnosing and treating various types of diseases led to the break down of popular superstitions and prejudices. The SA successfully encountered the challenges by 'Sorcerers' and traditional medical practitioners. The sincerity with which the SA served the patients from these communities influenced some of the families to turn to the Gospel for relief and support.[16] The old life of drinking, revelry, witch craft and demon worship with its existing horror prevailed in the settlements.

The hot season took its toll of energy and strength. People became languid and longed for rains. But before the rains start awful visitations occurred in the settlements. Cholera, the dread name is only mentioned with bated breath. It is believed to be a goddess and she is referred to as "Ammah" or "Mother". She is the mother of terror and must be appeased. The settlement Managers came forward with their rites to 'persuade' her to leave the village but the sickness spread from house to house. The dead and the dying laid side by side. The medical authorities went from house to house pouring medicine down the throats of all who had any hope of recovery. The dead were taken out for burial. In one grave, the manager reported 'buried thirty bodies'. The people were urged to abandon their homes and take to the open country until the disease subsided.[17]

The days before the cholera visitation, a notorious practice of devil possessing in women prevailed among the settlers to whom in fear all the settlers paid due respect. One woman settler in a DNT settlement said : "A man came upon me, an evil presence entered into my mind and being overpowered me."[18] During these times of possession, she falls into a stupor and then wakes up to utter strange and terrible words. Sometimes she would shriek and scream until people were terrified to hear her. People bring to her gifts and flowers believing that she was the mouthpiece of an evil spirit and she must be propitiated.[19]

The SA appointed an Indian doctor and an assistant in the leper colonies, to do their best. Some people were affected with ringworm disease. Even today the leper colonies are under the care of the SA with its own doctors. The SA made splendid additions and it had 250 houses for leper patients.[20]

In Madras presidency cholera swept the towns and its adjacent villages. The Boarding schools in DNT settlements consisted of many children. The SA strictly controlled their movements. No one was allowed to go out of the compound. Though every precaution was taken, some school boys were down with cholera. The students were isolated. The news was kept secret by the missionaries. Hot water fomentations and internal medicines were supplied. But the efforts made by the SA was invain. The boys who died were buried at once. But those who carried the bodies of the children were infected with cholera. Their rooms were limewashed and their garments were burnt.[21]

Discipline of the DNT settlers was a difficult task. But rules were made and enforced. The restraints of a settled life after the freedom of the open country were irksome. The SA did not allow alcoholic drink in the settlements. Sometimes it was smuggled into the settlements. Drinking resulted in fighting. Diversions such as games, competitions, entertainments were tried in all religious meetings.[22] The SA gathered the children who were not working in the fields or watching the village herds. The managers taught them the elementary rules of learning. Soon the boys and girls learnt to read.[23] one SA official said : "The very little children used to dance in the sunshine or bathing in the village tank or wayside canal, watching the village cattle grazing in the reserved areas. Small girls used to adorn each other's hair with oleander blossoms. Small boys used to play with home made kites. In the evening time, they come back home riding on the back of the buffalos taking their life for granted. But trouble, sickness and death always visited their homes. The Gods would not hear, even though lavish vows were made and sacrifices were offered, the Gods would not be appeased. There was black silence, no hope, no help, no light anywhere."[24]

III

Health and Hygiene in Siddhapuram Settlement

The health of the Waddar settlers was very poor in the beginning. The settlement site was malarial. The whole settlement was within 200 to 300 yards of the bund of the big tank. Between the bund and the village is a depression from which earth for the bund was excavated. Water stagnates throughout the year and there is a dense growth of bulrushes and other marsh-grasses. Two thousand yards to the north of the village is a drainage depression in which water stagnates and bulrushes flourish. Four to five hundred yards south and south-west of the village, the same conditions prevail along the course of the Bhavanasi *nullah* for a distance of 2 or 3 furlongs. The pits continued to act as a breeding place for mosquitoes. They were connected with each other by drains during rainy season. Other pits were located within a distance of about 2 furlongs from the settlement village site. The soil was very damp during rainy season. It was proposed to remove the settlement to the safe and convenient locality on 20.12.1926. [25]

The village is surrounded by ideal breeding grounds for Anopheles. These stagnant pools are largely the result of the building of the tank and are fed by sub-soil percolation. There are deep pits in the tank bed which hold water all the year round. During the south-west monsoon when malaria is most prevalent, the wind blow from the village and probable source of infection. The Bhavanasi adjoining the new site is clear of growth of weeds.[26] The forest humidity and water logging bred mosquitoes and malaria claimed a heavy death toll. A new site was selected about 1½ miles from the old site. The change of the new site contributed to the health and comfort of the settlers. The site of the settlement was shifted to the present place in January 1927.[27] A medical officer was appointed on Siddhapuram tank project and all the sick settlers were treated by him. Malaria was common disease among the settlers in Siddhapuram. High temperature was responsible for the deaths, particularly old people and children. A large number of settlers suffered from veneral diseases. All the interior forest areas are malaria prone areas even now.[28] A register had opened in the settlement to record the names of persons found sick, name of disease and other remarks. The sub-assistant surgeon of Atmakur used to visit the settlement monthly and got medicines from Atmakur hospital and handed over to the officer incharge of the Settlement. The sick had to be sent to Atmakur for better attention. A dispensary with a compoundary was opened in April 1929. The average daily attendance at the dispensary was 24. The common diseases treated in the settlement were bronchitis, rheumatic fever, malaria, pneumonia, dyspepsia, smallpox, common cold, digestive disorders, ear and throat complaints, ulcers and skin diseases and a few cases of influenza.[29]

The cause for low birth rate in the settlement was the loose character of both men and women. They change husbands frequently and suffer from syphilis and other veneral diseases. Neo-salvation injections were given for syphilis. For high mortality malaria was the chief cause. All these factors indicate the sympathetic and systematic approach adopted by the British administrators and how they bestowed interest on the settler's health problems. Even the minutest problems were taken care of. [30] The number of deaths increased during the year 1927. A large number of people suffered from veneral diseases. The district medical officer sent the settlers to the Guindy hospital for examination. Necessary steps were taken to eradicate the diseases. A weighing machine was purchased by the manager to enable the doctor to take the weight of the school children from time to time to watch their health. The manager encouraged small-hand- cinema. He could occasionally arrange for the cinema to visit the settlement. Magic lanterns were purchased for the entertainment of the settlers.[31]

It is an interesting factor that the manager of Siddhapuram settlement was instructed to keep a record of all the settlers living in the settlement with a brief note of their history, associations, avocations, movements, conduct, behaviour with a view to help the police as well as the management to have a proper control and watch over them. The subdivisional officers of police used to watch the settlement periodically and inspect them annually. Police constables and head constables from the police outpost in the settlement used to go round in the nights regularly and check the settlers to find out whether they go out in the nights for committing crimes.[32]

The 'Health Week' was celebrated every year in Siddhapuram settlement. The district medical officer and the Commissioner of Labour celebrated the *health week* from 20th October 1930 to 27th October 1930.[33] In connection with the celebration of the health week, the manager proposed to award prizes as follows :

Table-19
Prizes Awarded to Siddhapuram Settlers

Sl. No.	*Item*	*Prize*	*Rs.*
1.	For cleanest house	1st Prize	Rs. 6
2.	For cleanest house	2nd Prize	Rs. 4
3.	For healthiest baby	1st Prize	Rs. 2
4.	For healthiest baby	2nd Prize	Re. 1
		Total	*Rs. 13*

These prizes were an incentive to the settlers to keep their huts and surroundings clean and to devote more attention to the health of their babies. The amount of prizes raised from year to year. Thus, during the year 1934, for the cleanest baby Rs. 3 and for the cleanest hut Rs. 9 were given as first prizes.

Sometimes the settlement manager(s) used the innocent settlers in scandals. The manager was the incharge of the school. Tuition was given to the grown-up girls. Elderly girls in the school used to visit delinquent's houses for preparing lessons and learnt Banjara songs. Brutal assaults were made on school girls. It was sad to know that, "In a school, especially of criminal settlers, a strict standard of discipline was absolutely essential. Any chastisement by the headmaster in the exercise and maintenance of such a discipline should not be criticised. Exercise of discipline was measured with a different standard."[34]

To know their present conditions of health in Siddhapuram settlement, interviews are conducted. The Secretary of Denotified Tribe Welfare Association (in Siddhapuram), K.R. Somanna said, "The condition of the village at present is really pathetic. The only hospital established in 1929 became dysfunctional. Women die at the time of delivery. For medical help we have to rush to Atmakur. We are pleading for a hospital." The Settlement is situated in a forest area at the foot of the Nallamalai hills, and hence snakes and cheetas abound the area. The inhabitants found health and hygiene in Stuartpuram settlement unsafe to move about after sunset. It is, therefore, proposed to provide lights and good medical facilities in the settlement.[35]

IV

Health and Hygiene in Stuartpuram Settlement

Stuartpuram (Bethapudi) settlement is essentially an agricultural settlement started by SA to be worked as an auxiliary to and in conjunction with the Sitanagaram Settlement. Employment had been a troublesome problem at Sitanagaram and the SA founded the new settlement with the intention of placing in it the well-behaved members of the Sitanagaram settlement as a reward for good conduct. The manager was Captain Robilliard, a Guernsey man. He was an expert agriculturist trained in intensive gardening in his youth and with experience in rubber planting in the East. He had done excellent work. He developed the settlement on admirable lines. The government congratulated the SA on the useful work done in the settlement.[36]

The settlers on the whole kept good health. The birth rate during 1915 was 36 per mille. Early in 1915, the settlers complained of the excessive mortality of the settlement. On examination, it was found that the annual death rate was only 29 per mille and that the complaints were grossly exaggerated. The government had directed the sub-assistant surgeon at Bapatla to pay periodical visits to the settlement and have agreed to give him an extra allowance of Rs. 10 per mensem. The death rate during the year 1915 was 47 per mille. Special measures were taken to eliminate the "blacks courge" *(ankylostomiasis)* which was found to be somewhat prevalent amongst the settlers.[37]

During the year 1918, the Settlement had to face many difficulties, not the least important of them being influenza epidemic. As many as 600 settlers were down with the disease. But fortunately there was only twenty deaths (19 adults and one child). There was no hospital at the settlement, the wants of the sufferers attended to by the sub-assistant Surgeon, Bapatla, who visited Stuartpuram twice in a week. This arrangement did not prove particularly satisfactory during the influenza season. But as the conditions in 1918 were exceptional it was not thought necessary to provide a separate medical establishment at the settlement.[38]

The death rate at the settlement during the year 1918 was 30 per mille. It was not unduly high. It is hoped that the health of the settlers will improve on account of establishment of a dispensary, the provision of regular work and the curtailment of opportunities for drinking. In the year 1918, the settlement had faced two serious epidemics—cholera and smallpox. Unfortunately 70 per cent of the vaccinated cases developed smallpox subsequently. The result was that the settlers became intensely restless and began absconding in large numbers. The settlement officer, A.G. Cardew remarked: "I regret I cannot regard the working of the settlement as satisfactory. To improve the conditions the existing site of Stuartpuram improved by thinning out the existing village and extending it by building 30 new huts to the north of it with suitable arrangements for drainage."[39]

There was a severe epidemic of influenza during the year 1919. The Government sanctioned to the SA a grant of Rs. 500 for the equipment of the hospital. [40] The manager of Stuartpuram reported that the Settlement was in a state of famine on account of failure of rains. Rs. 2000 was sanctioned as a famine relief measure. The Surgeon General visited the settlement and opined that the pits should be filled up at once. He considered it as a source for malaria. This filling up further provided labour to the settlers. To avoid the calamity, the settlers forced to approach the government for famine relief work. Cooked food was distributed to the settlers upto September 30, 1919.[41] The settlement was without a doctor for many months. But fortunately, there were no epidemics and the health of the settlers was good in the year 1921. The sub-assistant surgeon, Mangalagiri visited the place twice a week and administered to the needs of the inmates.

A dispensary was established and the District Board, Guntur, contributed Rs. 25 per mensem to its maintenance. As regarding the medical relief, the Government discussed the question of constructing a separate hospital in the Settlement (G.O. No. 357, dated 13th May 1921) and on the advice of the Surgeon-General decided to drop the matter as they were of opinion that in practice the existing arrangements worked very well.

Death rate was high during the year 1923 due to influenza. A new hospital was built by the government. The hospital was two furlongs away from the nearest gang. It was on the right side of the main road. The small dispensary was watched by a qualified European nurse. Complicated cases were sent to Chirala and Bapatla, five miles away from the settlement. Hypodermic syringe, abscess knife probe, glass earthern and spatula were used. There were only a few deaths in the settlement during the year 1925.

A sub-assistant surgeon was called bi-weekly from Bapatla and medicines were supplied for diseases like dysentery, cholera, malaria, fever, smallpox, beriberi, boils, heart diseases, stomach ache. The daily average attendance was not less than 200. It was recorded that during the year 1925 the number of deaths were innumerable in the settlement. The consequence was that large number of Yerukulas absconded from the settlement.[42]

Stuartpuram is an extensive settlement but very scattered. Their houses were scattered over an area of two or three furlongs. The settlers lived outside their houses and camped all through the year sleeping outside. They use their little 'beehive-like' huts during rains or heavy dews. The visitors often questioned why the settlers were not provided with better houses? The main reason was that mud was too expensive.[43] The opinion of Deputy Inspector General of Police on the subject was worthy to note : "There is trouble over getting mud for hut building. This is caused by there being no road out to Ratnapuram, but above all, there being no level crossing over the railway line."[44]

On the settlement, there were a number of settlers who were very poor and some of them were very old. Whenever there was a cyclone, it had an enormous effect on their dilapidated huts. Pennik, the Salvation Army Officer, stated, "The roofs of all the huts have been blown away and that they needed reconstruction. It would be useless to rely on Palmyra leaves being available in the locality. The cyclone had struck not only the settlement but every hut in the neighbourhood."[45]

A grant of Rs. 4 was sanctioned for each damaged hut for reconstruction. Some of the government buildings had been badly damaged and need urgent repairs. The staff of the SA and number of the younger generation of the community responded to the emergency. They saved the lives and the safety of the people. The

Salvation Army purchased 50 bags of rice to supply food. Passes were not issued and all settlers were kept in the settlement. Rs. 3700 was spent by the SA in rebuilding the huts damaged by the cyclone, feeding the settlers as an emergency measure and for urgent repairs to the government buildings damaged by cyclone. It was stated that: "A most interesting feature of the settlement is the excellent houses which those settlers who have taken to agriculture have recently built for themselves, evidence that they do propose to make the settlement their native place."[46]

The SA paid special attention in times of cyclones, drought and other natural calamities. For the maintenance of huts, the Government of Madras used to sanction money from time to time on an average cost of Rs. 16 per hut to each family.[47] Individual cases were given continuous treatment until they were cured. During the year 1927, 10,650 cases had been attended in the dispensary. To our surprise, 'The National Health Week' was celebrated for the first time during the year 1927. Government sanctioned Rs. 250 towards *National Health Week* Celebrations. The Yerukula settlers responded well.[48] The medicines supplied to the supplement dispensary were inadequate to meet the needs of the people. Kondayya Naidu was appointed as a medical officer during the year 1927 and helped the settlers. A compounder was appointed in Stuartpuram dispensary during the year 1927. The scale of pay of the compounder was Rs. 30 — ½ - 35 ½ - 40. The SA appointed compounders who had the same qualification as the compounders in government hospitals.[49]

J. Grary, the Commissioner of Labour, Madras visited the settlement during the year 1929. He inspected the isolation ward of the hospital for cholera and infectious diseases. There was no one to attend to such patients except the compounder and the attending nurse. A ward boy was appointed on Rs. 10 per month to assist in looking after the patients.[50]

The medical issues were taken care of by V. Sitarama Ayyar, a sub-assistant surgeon, during the year 1930. He took a keen interest in the well-being of the settlers. He even allowed some of the settlers to be in his local hospital at Bapatla so as to have the benefit of his constant attention. G.R. Premayya, a non-official visitor, made the following remarks, "It is a great blessing to the settlers to have an experienced compounder and a midwife living in the settlement."[51] The hospital was very useful for the settlers. As regards the health of the settlers, they are happier in the hospital which was ventilated in a good fashion and also the government provided all facilities for the settlers to lead their life in a comfortable manner.[52] A maternity ward was opened in the settlement during the year 1930. The territorial Commander of SA stated that: The number of outpatients and the number of maternity cases had been steadily increasing. A full time medical officer was appointed in the place of the visiting medical officer in the Settlement."[53]

Cases of dysentery and eczema were frequent due to unsuitable diet of the people. The Yerukulas lived almost exclusively on broken rice and chilli powder. There were twenty four villages within a radius of four miles from Stuartpuram. People made frequent requests that the hospital be made open to the public. The hospital was untidy and it smelt unhealthy. The doctors were irregular. Some settlers were infected with leprosy during the year 1934. They were given treatment as outpatients in the SA Leper colony at Bapatla. Clothes, food and medicines were supplied. Records were maintained for the births and deaths in the settlement by the SA.[54]

The destitute parents were not given adequate attention and care of their children. Many of them were children of widowed mothers who could not provide sufficient food. The children did not attend the school regularly and it was found difficult to compel them to do so in these circumstances. The SA fed the children at government expense at the rate of Rs. 3 per head per mensem. The feeding of destitute children in Stuartpuram boarding school was subjected to the following conditions: *(i)* The expenditure on each child should not exceed Rs. 3 per month, *(ii)* the children should attend the school regularly, *(iii)* the feeding should be discontinued when any child ceased to be a destitute and in any case, *(iv)* feeding for the child should be discontinued after attaining the age of 16 years.[55]

There were lapses and fighting amongst the settlers. This was largely due to the sale of toddy in neighbouring villages like Betapudi, Gavinivaripalem, Ipurupalem and Vedullapalli. Whenever toddy was obtainable, there feuds were inevitable. The granting of license for the sale of liquor in the village of Epurupalem was indiscrete. Many settlers pass through the village (Epurupalem) twice a day from work at the ILTD Company. [56] During full seasonal time, 3500 people both men and women, were employed in ILTD factory. The free colony settlers regularly attended the factory work. The settlers walked 7 kms to work in the morning. The Commissioner of Labour stated: "The settlers were not incorrigibles and they were not confined behind barbed wires. No special police staff was employed to watch the settlers when they were working in tobacco factory."[57]

Old men and women received subsistence allowance under two main categories: 1. widows with children, and, 2. women whose husbands absconded or in jail. The money was misused in many directions. Getting good food was appreciated by all those in real need. An arrangement was made by a new system by which the food and clothes required by the incapables was supplied. The Administration report for the year 1933-34 stated : "One thing is obvious. The cash as given at present may be misused in many directions whereas the certainty of getting food would be appreciated by those in real need."[58] The compounder at Stuartpuram was discharged when the rural medical practitioner took charge from 4th January 1949. The midwives in the dispensary helped the maternity cases in the settlement. There was a serious attack of smallpox in Stuartpuram settlement during the year 1950. Timely action was taken by the health department to eradicate smallpox in the settlement.[59]

V

Conclusion

From 1945, the activities of the missionaries underwent a decline. With the war showing signs of coming to an end in Europe, many of the missionaries expressed their desire to return to their country. The missionaries and medical technologists in Andhra also expressed their return to their country. It was the huge financial drain caused by the war which impeded much of the humanitarian activities of the missionaries. It has become very difficult for the missionaries to provide medical relief free of cost. Subsequently, with the Government of India introducing special rural healthcare programmes, the missionary hospitals faced a challenge from Govt. run institutions. Thus, in order to survive, the missionaries preferred to amalgamate their hospitals and pool their resources in closer unity.[60] The activities of the missionaries reveal the importance of 'Medical Evangelism'. The literature of the missionaries, since the early decades of 1920s are replete with stories of medical mission work. There were frequent assertions that missionaries combining the rare elements of religion and medicine could be the most effective catalysts for mass conversions.[61]

However, it is doubtful whether the missionaries endowed with such double qualities could act as effective facilitator in the complex process of mass conversion. In India, the missionary work rarely succeeded in mass conversions. Their success by and large was confined to leprosy–infected patients who underwent treatment in their leper homes. The missionaries sent well qualified doctors, started medical training centres, established hospitals and dispensaries in the areas affected by contagious diseases like typhoid and cholera. They achieved success in the sphere of maternity and child care. The medical relief provided by the missionaries was smaller than that of the government institutions. Despite their limited scale of operation the outcome of their medical missionary work in terms of treatment and health and use of modern techniques and equipment is satisfactory.[62] The qualities of sympathy, motherliness and self-forgetting service of the missionaries accounted for the remarkable success in treating patients. The missionaries had toiled hard to gain social recognition for their work. The campaign launched by the upper caste priests often impeded their progress. The successful treatment of infectious diseases on the part of the missionaries countered the popular aversion. The sincerity and devotion displayed by the Salvation Army ABM, canadian and other missionaries attracted a section of the settlers. There were an increasing number of patients willing to undergo treatment in the settlement hospitals. The missionaries believed in soul service and in the universal brotherhood of man.

NOTES

1. Yuet-Wah Cheung, *Missionary Medicine in China: A Study of Two Protestant Missions*, Lanham, 1988, p. 3.
2. Mary Pauline Jeffrey, *Ida S. Scudder, of Vellore An Appreciation of Forty years of Service in India*, Mysore, 1939, pp. 13-17.
3. D. Clarke Willson, *The Story of Dr. Ida Scudder of Vellore*, London, 1959, pp. 83-87. The Canadian Baptist Missionaries in Andhra Pradesh devoted their energies towards medical relief. They found their followers in tribal localities. They organised churches, mission stations and annual conferences. They employed several women missionaries in preaching the Gospel, opening of schools, dispensaries and hospitals for the cure of the sick belonging to depressed classes.
4. *Home (Judicial) Department, G.O. No. 475, dated 9.2.1920*, p. 3, TNA. Also see Government of Madras, *Note Showing the Progress Made in the Settlement of Criminal Tribes in the Madras Presidency upto January 1925*, Madras, 1926, p. 8.

5. *PWLD, G.O. No. 2671, dated 6.12.1934,* p. 2, APSA.
6. *Ibid.*
7. *Note Showing the progress made in the Settlement of Criminal Tribes in the Madras presidency upto January 1925,* Madras, 1927, p. 10.
8. *Ibid.*
9. See *Home Department, G.O. No. 372, dated January* 28th 1937, p. 4.
10. See *PWLD, G.O. No. 379, dated 30th April, 1943.*
11. See *Home Department, G.O. No. 1625, dated 31st March 1941.*
12. See *Home Department, G.O. No. 140, dated 10th June 1941.*
13. See *Home Department, G.O. No. 372, dated January 28th 1937.*
14. *PWLD, G.O. No. 738, dated 27th May 1936.*
15. See *Home Department, G.O. No. 1284, dated 28th March 1937.*
16. See *Home Department, G.O. No. 2181, dated 7th June 1937.*
17. Mildred E. Mackenzie, *The Mud Bank,* Pensilvania, p. 30.
18. *Ibid.*
19. Booth Tucker, F., *Muktifouj or 40 years with the Salvation Army in India and Coylon.* Marshall Brothers, London, N.D., p. 40.
20. Booth Tucker, F., *Criminocurology or the Indian Crim and what to do with the him—A Report of the Salvation Army among the Criminal Tribes, Habituals and released prisoners in India,* London, n.d.
21. *Salvation Army, The War Cry,* World, International Heritze Centre, London, 1908-18.
22. *Salvation Army The War Cry,* International heritage Centre, London, 1909, p. 4.
23. *Salvation Army, The War Cry,* 1911 to 1919, International heritage Centre, London.
24. *Ibid.*
25. *PWLD G.O. No. 52, dated 6th January 1927,* p. 2, APSA.
26. *PWLD G.O. No. 137 dated 19.1.1927,* pp. 1-2, APSA.
27. *PWLD G.O. No. 2190 dated 28.7.1930,* p. 5, APSA.
28. *Home Department, G.O. No. 2661, dated 25.10.1920,* NAI, p. 3, Since September 1926, the Sub-assistant Surgeon of Atmakur paid four visits monthly. Also see *PWLD, G.O. No. 137, dated 19.1.1927,* p. 4, APSA.
29. *PWLD, G.O. No. 2190, dated 28.7.1930,* p. 6, APSA
30. *PWLD, G.O. No. 137, dated 19.1.1927,* p. 4, APSA.
31. Government of Madras, *Note Showing the progress made in the Settlements of Criminal Tribes in Madras Presidency,1916,* Government Central Press, 1917, p. 2. A midwife was appointed in Siddhapuram settlement at the cost of Rs. 25 per month. There was a steady increase in the number of deaths due to fever and smallpox. It was prevented by timely vaccination. *Home Department, G.O. No. 2113 dated 13.7.1944,* pp. 1-8, NAI, Also See *PWLD, G.O. No. 2190 and 2671 of 1930 and 1934,* pp. 12 & 13.

32. *PWLD G.O. No. 2671, dated 6.12.1934,* p. 4, APSA.
33. *PWLD, G.O. No. 2970, dated 8.1.1934,* p. 3, APSA.
34. *Home Department, G.O. No. 149 dated 8.1,1934,* p. 3, APSA.
35. Interview with K.R.Somanna, President of the Denotified Tribe Association in Siddhapuram Settlement dated 24.11.2006.
36. *Home Judicial Department, G.O. No. 475, 2074, dated 18th August 1916,* p. 4, TNA.
37. *PWLD, G.O. No. 1974, 10th August 1920,* pp. 27-29, APSA. Also *See Home Judicial Department, G.O. No. 878, at 22nd March 1920,* p. 1, TNA.
38. During the year 1918, the death rate was distinctly high largely owing to influenza. Giffard, the medical supervisor disliked to attend the hospital in the settlement. At Chirala, Vetapalem and Bapatla malaria affected severely. Hence, there was a great effect of Malaria in Stuartpuram. The Roman Catholic priests abandoned their mission owing to malaria. The district medical and sanitary officer recommended the following anti-malarial measures : 1. The filling in of the drain, 2. Destruction of all rubbish, 3. Filling in all pits, 4. Burying all broken pots and empty tins found near dwelling houses and 5. Use of pyrethrum and kerosene in closing up pits where mosquitoes breed. The salvation army took the responsibility.
39. *Home Department, G.O. No. 1974, 10th August 1920,* p. 4. NAI.
40. *Law (General) Department, G.O. No. 1714, at 22nd October 1921,* p. 6, APSA.
41. *Law (General) Department, G.O. No. 732, dt. 8th August 1925,* p. 1, APSA.
42. *PWLD, G.O. No. 1996, dt. 16th January 1939,* pp. 5-6, APSA.
43. *PWLD, G.O. No. 3064 dated 5.11.1936,* p. 1, APSA.
44. There were all together 14 buildings in Stuartpuram during the year 1934. Building No. 1 & 6, was occupied by the manager. Building No. 2 was by Assistant Manager, Building No. 3, 4, 5, 6, 7, 8 and 14 were occupied by teachers. Building No. 10 was by nurses. Building No. 11 by compounder. Building No. 13 was store room. Building No. 9 was post office, Building No. 13 was occupied by the Manger's cook, PWLD *G.O. No.* 1757, dated 6.8.1935, p. 1, APSA.
45. *The War Cry,* Salvation Army Monthly, April 1937, p. 3.
46. *PWLD G.O. No. 1996 dated 16th January 1933,* pp. 5-6. Also *See Law (General) Department Proceedings, G.O. No. 748, dt. 15th September 1925,* p. 3, APSA.
47. *PWLD G.O. No. 1551, dated 20th July 1927,* p. 4, APSA.
48. *PWLD G.O. No. 1654, dated 6th July 1928,* p. 3, APSA.
49. *PWLD G.O. No. 973, dated 3rd April 1928,* pp. 1-7, APSA.
50. *PWLD G.O. No. 3260, dated 18th November 1930,* p. 1, APSA.
51. *PWLD G.O. No. 156, dated 30th July 1931,* pp. 2-3, APSA.
52. *PWLD G.O. No. 2007, dated 11th September 1934,* p. 6, APSA.

53. *PWLD G.O. No. 1298 dated 4th June 1935*, p. 1, APSA.
54. *PWLD G.O. No. 543, dated 1st March 1935*, p. 5, APSA.
55. *PWLD G.O. No. 1925, 25th September 1936*, p. 10, APSA.
56. *Home Department, G.O. No. 5701, dated 30.10.1939*, p. 22, NAI.
57. *PWLD G.O. No. 1313, dated 17.6.1932*, p. 1, APSA.
58. The following table shows under which circumstances the settlers received the subsistence allowance.

Table–20
Subsistence Allowance

Sl. No.	*Circumstances*	*Amount Paid per month*
1.	Widow with two young children	Rs. 4.00
2.	Husband in jail, one son in school	Rs. 4.00
3.	Abandoned woman with 2 children	Rs. 4.00
4.	Widow with two young children	Rs. 4.00
5.	Husband in jail, with 3 children	Rs. 4.00
6.	Husband in jail	Rs. 3.00
7.	Husband in jail, one young child	Rs. 4.00

59. Rosemary Fitzgerald, ***'Clinical Christianity : The Emergence of Medical work as a Missionary strategy in colonial India, 1800-1914'*** in Biswamy Pati and Mark Harrison (eds), *Health, Medicine and Empire : Perspectives on Colonial India*, Hyderabad, 2001, p. 89.
60. *PWLD G.O. No. 2671, dated 6.12.1934*, p. 4, APSA.
61. The missionaries developed Christianity where diverse cultures and faiths prevailed. Dr. Ernest F. Neve, *A Crusader in Kashmir : The Life of Dr. Arthur Neve, with an account of the Medical Missionary work of Two Brothers and its later developments down to the present day*, London, 1928, p. 14.
62. *Report of the Canadian Baptist Mission in India, 27th Annual Conference*, p. 16. *Also see*
    1. *Mission Handbook, Baptist Foreign Missionary Society*, Toronto, 1895, p. 13.
    2. Orville E., Daniel, *Rising tides in India (A profile of the past and present), The Calcutta Christian Observer*, Vol. V, 1836, p. 362.
    3. Rev. M.L. Orchard, and K.S. Mclaurin, *The Enterprise, The Juilee strory of the Canadian Baptist Mission in India 1874–1924*, Toronto, 1924, p. 32.
    4. Rev. M.L. Orchard, *Canadian Baptists at work in India*, Toronto, 1922, Report of the Canadian Baptist Telugu Missions for 1899 (23rd Annual conference held in Coconada, 12-16 January 1900) Madras, 1900 p. 38.
    5. Marys McLavrin, *25 years*, p. 100.

12

Denotified Communities After Independence

I

Introduction

The CT Act was passed by the colonial government as early as 1871, arbitrarily and unjustly against some of the aboriginal tribes, castes and even a section of the Muslims of our country. This Act was enacted by the colonial government with a view to control some turbulent and criminally proclaimed sections of our population. By gradual modifications, this Act was consolidated in the year 1924 : The Madras Presidency repealed the CT Act in 1947 and Bombay in 1949. The All India CTs Enquiry Committee in 1949 evaluated the problems of criminal tribes and recommended for repealing the Act. Henceforth, people belonging to these 'criminal' groups were recognised as 'Denotified Communities'.

To check the 'criminal' tendencies of these CTs, the British government started several settlements and entrusted the task of management of them to some voluntary agencies like the SA, ABM, Chief Khalsa Diwan, Deo Samaj, Arya Samaj etc. In addition to these, Adimajati Sevak Sangh was also put incharge of the management of some settlements. These were assisting the Government in the moral uplift of the CTs. After the repeal of the CTA, many such, so-called 'criminals' were freed from the stigma of criminality. The Backward Class Enquiry Commission (1995) appointed by the Government of India suggested ameliorative measures to enable them to turn over a new leaf and make them good citizens.

The social experience of the DNTs still add to their lurking fears of being dominated by the more vociferous strata of the society. Unless the society provides equal opportunities and treatment with others in every sphere of life, these people are not willing to come out of their shell. What we ought to do, is to develop a sense of oneness with these people, a sense of unity and understanding. It necessarily involves a psychological approach.[1]

II

Change in Statusquo: Forest Laws, Land Ownership and Agriculture

Tribal communities are considered as early settlers or indigenous groups of people; it is at the same time true that they are also non-static or itinerant groups owing to many compelling circumstances. For thousands of years, these tribes lived in their sylvan setting without having any intercourse with the outside world. During 19th and 20th centuries communication facilities, such as railways and roads, were carried through the hills and forests and the land hungry peasants of upper castes invaded the sparsely populated tribal regions of central and south India. Moneylenders, contractors and land-grabbing landlords encroached upon the tribal lands and the tribals were kept in perpetual indebtedness. Formerly, the tribals depended upon forests for their living. But the forests were fast denuded by landholders and the government. The non-tribals on the one hand and the forest laws framed by colonial administration on the other made the tribals to migrate from place to place for their bare living.[2] As Bhowmick said, "This economic and territorial displacement under a new setting affected very seriously the old patterns of economic life and upset the equilibrium of the whole society."[3] As one hill man succinctly put it, "The forests have belonged to us from time immemorial, our ancestors planted them and protected them, now they have become of value, government steps in and robs us of them."[4] For example, the Chenchus, a primitive tribe was affected by the forest laws. Their hunting activity was considered to be illegal. They were denied the rights over the forest produce. In desperation they turned into bandits.

III

Crime and the Social Components

The problem of crime in society has been a gigantic and complex phenomenon. In recent times, crime rate, as a whole is increasing very rapidly all over the world. Crime thrives wherever economic deprivations, social disruptions and radical discriminations prevail. Inequality, economic exploitation, unhealthy greed for possessing material goods and rapid change in the standard of morality in society constitute the breeding ground of crime in society. Criminality is not hereditary and the criminal propensity of many castes and tribes is due to the disintegration of their social moorings under economic and territorial displacements from time to time. The most important cause of their deprivation is the loss of their traditional means of livelihood. No man is a criminal by birth.

The term 'criminal' tribe is a misnomer, because category of both tribe and caste and also number of communities are classified under the 'CTs in India. Some of them would be found to be the members of scheduled caste or the other Backward class communities. In Srikakulam district, Rellis are considered to be a 'criminal' tribe. Even now they live only in two small villages (known as Pullota and Thallota) and carry agriculture or coolie labour work as their occupation. Kapotipalem Malas of Nellore district and Malas of Anneboyinipalli a of Prakasam district are also wage labourers.[5] Sher Singh Sher said, "The system is destroyed, the profession is ruined; the guild is scattered, never again to be associated into a great corporate body. The craft and the mystery of thugee will be no longer handed down from father to son."[6]

The CTs are distributed in almost all states of India. They are still leading a primitive style of living, some still retaining the food gathering or hunting or pastoral stages. In 1937, the CT committee headed by Tiwari opined that : "Criminal Tribes were a legacy of unhealthy social environments and wrong methods pursued through many centuries in dealing with them. They are not the sinners, they have been sinned against." The so called CTs of north India are: Bawarias, Bhantu, Kanjar, Nat, Karwal, Meena, Pakhiwara, Tagu, Sansiya and Lodhas. Likewise, Lambadis, Koravas, Dommaras, Waddars, Kallars, Pariahs are some of the CTs of south India and in Eastern India the Lodhas and the Kherias were classified as CTs.[7] Bowmick said, "Criminal Tribe has been a label, a straight jacket to mark a few groups as 'habitual' rather natural offenders."[8]

IV

Committees and Commissions

After the repeal of the CTA, a large number of committees were appointed to study the existing conditions of the DNT settlements. With the help of these recommendations many of the CTs were freed from the stigma of criminality. The *Backward Class Enquiry Commission* (1955) appointed by the Government of India suggested ameliorative measures to enable them to turn over a new leaf and make them good citizens. Those are : 1. CTs should be called DNT communities or Vimuktajatis', 2. These communities should be included in the categories of scheduled castes, tribes and backward classes, 3. They should be resettled in batches and gradually integrated them with the larger society, 4. Proper education should be imparted to them for making them free and responsible citizens of independent India, 5. Reformatory activities should be undertaken, 6. Distinction should be made between the persons who take collective 'criminal' activities and those who take it up individually, 7. Proper type of education and employment for their children should be provided, 8. Economic rehabilitation should be ensured simultaneously.[10] These suggestions, if implemented, will pave the way to settling the DNTs surely in the society.

If we analyse these ameliorative measures we will come to understand the fact that how far the implementation has been taking place in our society. In this context, the conditions of the Doms of U.P. (for whom the first CT Settlement in India was opened in the year 1908) and Sansis of Punjab and the Meenas of Gujarat and Rajasthan are important to note. The Doms are the Scheduled caste like Dombs of Orissa. They are still coming under the category of untouchables. Sansis are still like the Yerukulas of Andhra Pradesh and not much serious rehabilitative work was done by the respective Punjab government. Some of the members of the Marvaras of Tamil Nadu and Meenas of Rajasthan have become rich and they are no more called as DNT communities."

It is wrong to call all of them as 'DNTs.' What is the big change whether we call them as 'criminal' or 'ex-criminal' or 'denotified communities? All these words should be removed completely and make them as free citizens of this country. Why should they be called as beggars, pickpocketers ? These communities though be included in the categories of scheduled castes, tribes and backward class communities, by their inclusion they are not benefited much excepting a very few of them. The rest of them are leading a life of almost nomadism. It is the responsibility of the nation to absorb them slowly into social fold and make them believe that they are a very important the segment of the society. After 60 years of independence, they are not rehabilitated properly and how can we expect them to integrate themselves with the larger society. In this context, we have to say that Siddhapuram, Sitanagaram, Stuartpuram, Kaparallatippa and Lingala settlers are crippled with regard to education and employment. Still they are under the surveillance of the police. These settlers who are segregated from the society developed hostile attitude towards the government and people. They have lost self-confidence and developed an attitude of resignation and distance even towards their own kith and kin. They are of the opinion that they are let down by the society. In this environment their children are brought out. As. J.J. Panakkal said, "No reformation of the denotified communities is complete until the society accepts them into their fold without distinction."[11]

The prime reason for their living at the subsistence level is their unstable occupations with uncertain income and disproportionate expenditure. They realised the fact that their children should not lead the same life. They are very much worried about the future of their children. Opportunity should be given to them to intermix socially with the children of higher castes. As Sikka Krishnalal rightly pointed out that, "Family is the spring board of the child's social and personal growth."[12] Education is an effective weapon and instrument of social change. It plays a significant role in changing the fortune and lifestyle of these children. So the entire gamut of reforming these communities depends on how best educational facilities can be provided to these children. Education helps to channelise their energies into productive purposes. Their economic plight and environmental influence have their impact on their education.

Comparing them to the rest of the society, they are bound to suffer from an inferiority complex and the parents are afraid that their children could not reach higher echelons of society because of the psychological barrier they suffer from. The children may be educated in a healthy and proper environment free from oppression, fear, harassment and suspicion. As Lavanam said in this context, "Transformation is taking place from the culture of crime to the culture of sociability. From anti-social means to social means of livelihood, from eternal complex to cooperative spirit and from harsh behaviour to reason and understanding."[13]

The vital aspect of the entire question is how to wean them away from crime and make them an integral part of the mainstream of society. In spite of their innumerable depredations, the settlers are still in the clutches of poverty. The fruits of their hard work are being snatched by a section of people like the rich landlords, merchants, moneylenders, politicians, lawyers and corrupt police officers.[14] That means the ex-settlements have become a vicious circle in which stolen property dealers, corrupt police officials, investors in crime and greedy criminal lawyers form a part and parcel of exploitative situation.[15]

The welfare measures initiated for Yerukulas, Yanadis and Sugalis and all the DNT tribes bear a resemblance to the efforts at squeezing oil from sand. The utterances of the government on the welfare schemes are making much noise emanating from empty vessels. It is evident that in the quagmire of poverty, they prefer immediate gains to long term benefits that accrue to their children after continuous schooling of ten to fifteen years. Therefore, need-based or job-oriented education is effective to the existing monotonous and unproductive education.[15]

V

The Present Situation

In the DNT colonies waste land is abundantly available. The land is under the control of the government. Irrigational facilities were not adequately provided. The lands cannot be sold or mortigaged by the DNTs. All the settlers are daily wage workers. Those who joined in the public employment were bringing white money from their jobs in order to keep their families going without any interruption. There is thus more clamour for public placement. So emphasis is more on education of the children in the DNT colonies. Without good education how can the DNT children would get selected in government jobs? Because the DNTs belong to ST category, the government provided them free boarding, lodging, fees, books, etc. These facilities continue to the level of postgraduation. Today, there are several educated persons including matriculates, graduates and even postgraduates from the reformed DNT families in some settlements.

Crime is a cobweb. Along with the criminal, the stolen property dealers, the investors in crime, criminal lawyers and corrupt officials used to share the booty of crime. Very often the criminal is left with a meagre amount for his antisocial labour, the major share of his booty being cornerned by ' white collar' people out side. As long as the cirminals were committing crime, there was an assurance for the investors in crime that they would get back their investment. So they were ready to finance for criminal families, the loan amount often being used for household consumption. Once the criminal stops crime, there was no readiness on the part of the investors as there could not be an assurance on repayment. Stoppage of crime means an impending poverty for the criminals. Hence it became very difficult for the changed criminals to get even small amount of loan from others including their own relatives.

The biggest problem in the reformation work is how to get some work for these people to ekeout a small livelihood in a respectable manner. Hard pressed to meet the basic needs, the DNTs some times indulge in petty thefts like pickpocket, etc. Therefore, it is a moral dilemma for any social reformer whether to find fault with them or not. The saying goes, ' all property is nothing but theft'. The members of out side society always look upon the DNTs as dangerous elements. There were incidents where some DNT family members committed suicide in order to escape from the illtreatement of the public.

The DNT colonies are filled with some people with the habit of drinking alcohol and gambling. Whenever anyone stepped into these colonies one can see at least some families male factors involved in severe beating of elders, children and womenfolk. Men who involved in gambling sometime loose money in the gambling. In order to maintain the family they commit petty offences. Role plays, banning of gambling, wine shops will bring a desired change among them. The greatest problem here is the DNTs even after psychological rehabilitation, they are frequently involved in this type of offences.

In the culture of crime among the DNTs mutual distrust, harshness in personal and social relations and dealings are glaringly visible. As criminals the male members of the families are always haunted by the fear of being caught by the police. Even though they are at home sometimes they cannot afford to live in peace. Neither they can spend time with their families happily when they are at large and when they are away from their family, they are again aloof from their family members. When in jails, they cannot meet every one and talk to them. Thus the lack of familial love and intimate human bondage made the DNTs very harsh. The DNTs suffer from the harshness of feelings and actions through the major part of their life.

The state government should appoint a new committee (Many committees have been appointed to study the conditions of DNTs in the colonies) in view of the changed circumstances of the lives of the DNTs to look into the problems and prospects of the DNT colonies in Andhra Pradesh. Road, electricity, communication facilities hospitals and improvement of sanitation and education facilities are the important necessities in DNT colonies today. Criminal reformation is a there dimensional process. The reformation work involves different kinds of actors and characters. 1. The criminals themselves. 2. The state machinery (including police and other officials) and 3. The society at large.

The DNTs are ready to change themselves. In fact they have changed. Support mechanism from the state, from all the departments and NGO's should be actively involved or come forward to provide social and economic rehabilitation. In view of the above analysis, a few important programmes that needs urgent attention is:

1. Designing of a common minimum programmes for the people of the DNT colonies.
2. An integrated approach to all the programmes designed for the DNTs where the benefits would be shared by all the DNT colony population.
3. Youth exposure programmes where the participants would be drawn form the community.
4. Employing all available opportunities and possibilities of providing regular work for the youth in the DNT colonies.
5. Grounding of common health and education programmes.
6. Organisation of women groups.
7. Development of agro-based industrial programmes.
8. Shaping of a research and reference institute with emphasis on documentation, preservation, preparation of training modules for reformation work among the DNTs. Also exploring the possibilities of involvement of government in the process.
9. Conduct of periodic awareness programmes and workshops

on human rights with emphasis on interface interaction among the reformed families, public officials, social activists and academicians.

10. Organisation and strengthening of the central and state DNT commissions and empowering the commission to work for the development of DNTs in the state, etc.

VI

Reformation and Rehabilitaion : Constraints and Progress

The ultimate aim is to resocialise the DNTs, to readjust them to the society and to rehabilitate and change them. The rehabilitative programmes concerning these people be entrusted either to educational institutions or to hand over to reputed social service organisations who can evince real interest in them. The growing apprehension among them is the future of their children. They should be dispelled and their responsiveness be channelised into purposive activities for their own betterment. The whole issue of rehabilitation hinges totally on the complex process of convincing them and transforming them into people who can eke out their livelihood through the sweat of their brows. Since their problems originate on the social and economic basis, the main thrust of rehabilitation should be socio-economic in nature. Tempered rehabilitation has to be with a human approach to the entire question. These problems can be solved in phased manner. The following suggestions are made with a view to bring about an improvement in the programme for the welfare of DNTs of Andhra Pradesh. 1. The government has to conduct sample surveys to know about their present position pertaining to their livelihood, state of literacy, housing and other activities. Guntur District has already done this type of survey and sent an Action Plan for the government, 2. Large share of expenditure should be spent on their economic development. Some kind of lawful employment should be provided for them as an alternative means of livelihood, 3. 'D' form pattas, issued to them should be converted into loanable pattas. And also those members of DNTs in various ex-settlements who have real interest and aptitude for cultivation should be provided land and other facilities, 4. A number of DNTs work as labourers in construction and road works; extracting stones from quarries, etc. like in Sitanagaram settlement. Labour contract societies should be organised in consultation with members of these communities, lest favourism, nepotism should prevail, 5. Brick-making, mat-weaving, nawara-making, dress-making centres or the cottage industries which require least technical skill and guidance should be provided, 6. Dairy farming, piggery, poultry and horticulture are very useful in the economic development. They should be given priority. These are to be organised on the cooperative basis for which the government should provide financial assistance on loan-cum-subsidy basis, 7. As the members of DNTs prefer jobs which give them immediate remuneration. Industrial employment absorbing them should be created for them in large-scale and this will give them satisfaction. (For example in Sitanagaram settlement, many of them are provided with jobs and crime has been reduced to the minimum.) They may be recruited into the department of police as constables, waterboys, sweepers in forest departments', etc. Some of them are already employed as watchmen with good reputation, 8. Arrangements should be made to make the banks to sanction loans to the settlers who are interested in setting up business like small shops (bunks or soda shop), tea stalls, etc. Encouragement for self-employment schemes provides much needed fillip to make them aware of their latent capacities in fields like business.

VII

Conclusion

The rapid transformation of country towards liberalisation, privitisation and globalisation has added some more problems to the poorer sections and especially to the DNT communities. By means of liberalization, the womenfolk of these communities are over-burdened in the work, both in domestic front and workplace. The inevitability of the situation is that they have to work and get less benefits. Moreover, it is difficult for these communities to send their children to private schools which they cannot afford. Above all these circumstances, globalisation is taking place in a speedy manner. The multinationals have encroached the forest land and creating serious threat to their daily life. India as a developing nation is committed to welfare state; now our question is if everything is privatised including education, banking, industry and communications, then how are we going to provide opportunity to the marginalised sections of society? In this context, the only alternative left to the country is whithering away of the administration.

To sum up, certain bureaucratic procedures can be dispensed with for giving due consideration to these neglected sections of people in our society. Since economic development is a continuous process, steps must also be taken to establish a rural bank in the area for mobilising their savings to be used again for their benefit. The present oppressive and exploitative economic structure developed around the settlements should be dismantled. The Report of the Backward Classes Commission stated : "The economic programme should go hand in hand with a dynamic and suitably oriented programme of social education so as to wean them away from socially undesirable tendencies." The present system of education is not satisfactory. The entire gamut of reforming the DNTs here depends on how best educational facilities can be provided to them. Education is an effective weapon and instrument of social change. The feeling of the people in our interviews is that their children could not reach higher echelons of society because of the psychological barrier they suffer from. Restructuring the educational system for the DNTs required a humanistic approach which should give them self-confidence and guidance towards their becoming an integral part of the mainstream of our society. The social experience of the DNTs still adds to their lurking fears of being dominated by the more vociferous strata of the society, unless the society provides equal opportunities and treatment with others in every sphere of life, these people are not willing to come out of their shell. What we ought to do is to develop a sense of oneness with these people, a sense of unity and understanding. It necessarily involves a psychological approach.

It should also be kept in mind that the rough treatment method shown to them by the police officials has a great bearing on their conduct. Experiencing stinking and miserable life in prisons and the unsympathetic attitude of the police they develop a negative attitude, which, in its turn, forces them to take up the same activity. Because of the colonial outlook of the system which we have inherited as a colonial hangover has remained more or less the same and this has to be reorganised. Otherwise it cannot work as a worthy instrument of change in a developing democratic society.[16] Another problem is that the DNTs cannot have emotional affinity with others as long as they are not free from fear of 'stigma' and this cannot be wiped out as long as they do not wish to come out of their rut and narrow living and prove their integrity in society over a stretch of long period. By socialising them through social education and other rehabilitative measures they should be helped to break away from their psychological barrier.[17] Mass adult educational programmes, through electronic media and library facilities, involvement of the youth of the settlements in all these programmes, a coordinated approach in streamlining their life pattern, by providing basic infrastructural facilities such as electricity, communication and water supply and medical facilities will ensure their orderly progress and development.

NOTES

1. Arnold, David, 'Dacoity and Rural Crime in Madras, 1860-1940', *Journal of Peasant Societies,* January, 1979.
2. Bhargava, B.S., *The Criminal Tribes of India,* Lucknow, 1949.
3. Bhowmick, P.K., *The Lodhas of West Bengal,* Calcutta, 1963.
4. Ramachandra Guha and Madhav Gadgil 'State Forestry and Social Conflict in British India', – *Past and present, No. 122-123, Feb. 1989.*
5. Gandhi, Malli, A. Historical Survey of Ex-Criminal Tribes Settlements in Andhra: A Case Study of Siddhapuram and Stuartpuram Settlements, 1913-90. Unpublished Ph.D., Thesis, Department of History, University of Hyderabad 1996. These tribes are as follows: Telaga pamulas, Dandasis, Konda Doras, Rellis, Paids, Kintil, Kalinga, Nakkalas, Piriki Mukkalas, Donga Yathas, Vedurupaka malas, Boyas,Netti Kothalas, Reddikas, Yanadis, Dommaras, Anipi Malas, Vaddi Upparas, Buda bukkalas, Lombadas, Waddars, Kemparis, Pamulas, Reddy Yanadis, Jarugumalli Madigas, Donga Dasari, Mondi Banda, Jogula, Nawabpeta Korcha, Amagunta Palegars, Paraya, Thota Naiks, Bhatyu, Turaka, Pedda Boya, Dabbala Vagula, *Nirshikari, Iranis, Kanjar Bhatt, Jatur mixed gang* all are dubbed as CTs. Cited from the *Files of the Superintendent of Police, Crime Branch, Hyderabad, vide No.1185/CIB/58 dated 27.2.1958.*
6. Sher Singh 'Sher', *The Sansis of Punjab : A Gypsy and Denotified tribe of Rajput Origin,* Munshiram Monoharlal, Delhi, 1965, p. 80.
7. Government of Madras, *Home Department Proceedings, 1937 to 1952.*
8. Bhowmick 1963: 48.
9. Lalitha, V. *Denotified Tribes of Andhra Pradesh : Some Problems of Rehabilitation Andhra Pradesh, Proceedings of the AP History Congress 6th Session,* Hyderabad, 1982.
10. Lalitha, V., *The Making of Criminal Tribes : Patterns and Transition,* Madras, 1995.
11. Panakall J.J., An Agenda for Criminology, *Indian Journal of Criminology,* Modras 1973.
12. Lalitha, V., *Socio-Economic and Administrative Aspects of an ex-Criminal Tribe* an unpublished M.Phil. thesis Tirupati University, 1973.
13. Haikerwal, B.S., *Economic and Social Aspects of Crime in India,* London 1934. Lavanam and Hemaltaha Lavanam, 'Problem of Denotified Tribes–An Experiment on Stuartpuram'. Atheist Centre, Vijayawada, 1984.

14. Jaspal Singh, *Crime in India*, London, 1924 & *Reformation of Ex-criminals*, 1976.
15. Meena Radha Krishna, 'Surveillance and settlement under the Criminal tribes Act in Madras', *Indian Economic and Social History Review, Vol. XXIV, No. 2, April-June*, 1992.
16. Nigam, Sanjay, *Disciplining and Policing the Criminals by Birth part I & II, Indian Economic and Social History Review*, New Delhi 27, 2, (1990).
17. Satyanarayana, Chalavadi, *Yerukalas, An Ex-Criminal Tribe of Andhra in its settlement (Stuartpuram)*, M.A. Dissertation, Sagar University, Agra, 1959-60.

APPENDIX-I
List of 'Criminal Tribe' Settlements

Name of the Settlement and District.	*Nearest Railway Station*	*Nearest Police Station*	*Postal Address*	*Subdivisional Magistrate or other Officer in whose jurisdiction the settlement lies.*
1. Sitanagaram, Guntur district	Tadepalli	Mangalagiri	Tadepalli Post	Subdivisional Magistrate, Guntur
2. Stuartpuram, Guntur district	Stuartpuram	Bapatla	Bapatla Post Office	Subdivisional Magistrate, Ongole
3. Siddhapuram Kurnool district	Nandyal (40 miles from settlement)	Atmakur	Siddhapuram (via) Atmakur	Subdivisional Magistrate, Nandyal
4. Pallavaram Chingleput district	Pallavaram	Pallavaram	Pallavaram	Subdivisional Magistrate, Saidapet
5. Perambur Madras district	Perambur	Perambur Barracks G-3 Police Station	Cook's Road, Otary, Perambur Barracks Post Office	Commissioner of Police, Madras
6. Kavali (Including Allur & Bitragunta), Nellore district	Kavali Town	Kavali	Kavali	Subdivisional Magistrate, Kavali
7. Aziznagar South Arcot district	Oomangalam	Oomangalam	Aziznagar, U Mangalam Post Office.	Subdivisional Magistrate, Chidambaram

(*Source : Madras 'Criminal Tribes' Manual, Government Press, Madras, 1927*)

APPENDIX-II

List of Settlements in which 'Criminal Tribes' Were Placed

Name of the Settlement and District	*Agency by Which Managed*	*Amount of Supervision Grant paid by Govt. Rs.*	*No. of Settlers on 1st April 1924*	*Tribe or Tribes in the Settlement*	*Occupation*	*Names of Non-Official*
1	2	3	4	5	6	7
Sitangaram, Guntur District	Salvation Army	5,218	1,031	Donga Yerukulas and Nawabpeta Korachas	Agricultural and Industrial (Weaving, Carpet-making & stone dressing)	Khan Sahib Mohammad Abdur Rahman Sahib Bahadur, Guntur Mr. S. Vepa, Barat Law Guntur
Stuartpuram Guntur District	Salvation Army	7,300	1,958	Donga Yerukulas and Nawabpeta Korachas	Agricultural and Industrial (mat, and basket making gardening)	M.R. Ry. J. Kuppuswami Choudari Jagarlamudi Mr. P. S. Thalpasaye, Bar at Law, Bapatla
Kavali, (Allur and Bitragunta) Nellore District	American Baptist Mission	16,800	2,055	Donga Yerukulas, Donga Dasaris, Dommaras and Katheras	The main occupation of the settlers at Allur and Bitragunta is agriculture. At Kavali the settlers are employed in oil-pressing and weaving	M.R. Ry. A.S. Krishna Rao Pantulu B.A., B.L., M.R. Ry. S. Ramayya Pantulu Retired Deputy Collector M.R. Ry. B. Ramachandra Reddy B.A., Buchireddipalem
Perambur, MadrasDistrict	Salvation Army	4,000	284	Veppur Adi-Dravidas	Employment is provided for settlers in the cotton and ginning mills and weaving	Mr. P. Holt & M/s P. Holt & Company Ltd., Madras. M.R.Ry. J.R. Sivasubrahmanyam Avargal Retired Engineer Swarna San Thome High Road, Mylapore

(Contd.)

1	2	3	4	5	6	7
						Khan Bahadur Abdul Kareem Sahib Farukh retired Deputy Superintendent of Police
Pallavram, Chingleput District	–do–	4100	204	–do–	Industrial (leather work, quarry work, carpet making and gardening)	Mr. C.A. Parkhumt, Pallavaram; M.R.Ry. R. Nagasundarma Ayyar, Retd. Deputy Collector, Adamabakkam, St. Thomas Mount.
Aziznagar, South Arcot District	Government	..	1,052	–do–	Agricultural and Weaving	M.R.Y. M.G. Parthasrathy Mudaliar Avaragal; President Taluk Board, Vriddhachalam; M.R.Ry. C.V. Srinivasa Acharya, Municipal Chairman, Chidambaram
Siddhapuram, do Kurnool District	–do–	...	200	Donga Waddars	Agricultural and Industrial (Cumbli Weaving & road work)	None have been appointed.
Kulasek-harapatam, Tinnevelley District	Agent, East India Distilleries & Sugar Factories (M/s Purry & Co. Ltd.)	1,320	265	Uppu Koravas of Koil pattu and Anavara Danallur and certain other Koravas of the Tinnevelly District	Employment found for the settlers in the sugar factory	The Rev. A.P. Randle Priest, S.P.G. Nazarath M.R. Ry. S.K. Subba Ayyar avargal, B.A., B.L., Sri Vilkumatam.

(*Source:* Government of Madars, Note Showing the Progress made in the Settlement of Criminal Tribes in the Madras presidency upto January 1925, Madras, 1927).

Appendix-III

Stigma—'Criminal Tribes' registered Under Sections 3 and 10 of the Criminal Tribes Act

District	*Name of the Criminal tribe*	*Government Order Applying Sections 3 and 10(b), Criminal Tribes Act.*	*Government Order Applying Section 10 (a), Criminal Tribes Act*	*Remarks*
Ganjam	Telaga Pamulas	160, Home (Judl.), 23rd January, 1917.	160, Home (Judl.) 23rd January, 1917	Registration restricted to know criminal males and their relatives and associates.
	Dandasis	116, Judl, (Police), 13th March, 1923.	116, Judicial (Police), 13 March, 1923.	
Vizagapatnam	Konda Doras	1583, Home (Judl.), 21st July 1914	1579, Home (Judl.), 1st Aug. 1917.	
	Rellis	965, Judl. 4 May 1915	-do-	
	Padis	1891, Judl., 27 July 1910	-do-	
	Telaga Pamulas	160, Home (Judl.), 23rd January, 1917.	160, Home (Judl.), 23rd Jan. 1917.	
	Kintali Kalingas	473, Home (Judl.), 4th March 1921.	473, Home (Judl.), 4th March 1921.	
Godavari Agency	Oriya Dombs	439, Home Judl., 16th February 1920.	439, Home (Judl.), 16th February 1920	
	Nakkalas	2120, Judl., 21st October 1913. (Sec 3) and 1128, Judl, 21 May 1915 (Sec, 10(b))	1579, Home (Judl.), 1st August 1917.	
	Telaga Pamulas	160, Home (Judl.), 23rd January 1917	160, Home (Judl.) 23 Jan 1917.	
	Anippai Malas	48, Home (Judl.), 7th January 1920	48, Home (Judl.) 7th January 1920.	
	Donga Dasaris	924, Judl., 10th May 1913*		* The members were removed to the Kavali Settlement, Nellore Dist.

(Contd.)

Krishna	Donga Yerukalas	917, Judl., 10th May 1913	816, Judl., 31st October 1921	
	Donga Waddars	1161, Judl., 12th June 1913 and 1279, Judl., 10th June 1910	-do-	
	Telaga Pamulas	160, Home (Judl.), 23 Jan 1917	160, Home (Judl.), 23 Jan. 1917	
Guntur	Donga Yerukalas	917, Judl., 10th May 1913	1579, Judl., 1st Aug. 1917	
	Donga Waddars	1161, Judl., 12th June 1913	349, Judl., 14th March 1922	
	Telaga Pamulas	160, Home (Judl.), 23rd Jan.1917	160, Home (Judl.), 23rd Jan. 1917	Restricted to Kavali settlement
	Gundlapad Woddars	450, Judl., (Police), 30 August 1923	450, Judl., (Pol.) 30 August 1923	
	Jarugupalli Madigas	585, Judl., (Pol) 2nd Nov. 1923	585, Judl., (Pol.) 2 Nov. 1923	
	Chakala & Pamula, Budabukkalas	656, Judl., (Pol) 18 December 1923	656, Judl., (Pol.) 18 Dec. 1923	
Nellore	Donga Dasaris	924, Judl., 10th May 1913	–	–
	Donga Yerakala	917,Judl., 10th May 1913	1937, Home (Judl.) 13 Sept. 1917	
	Dommaras	1639, Judl., 13th August 1913	1619, Judl., 19th July 1919	
	Vayalpad or Nawabpeta Korachas	918, Judl., 10th May 1913 and 1796 Judl, 5th September 1913.	1619, Judl., 19th July 1919	
	Jogulas (Jogis)	109, Judl., 19th January 1915 and 461, Judl., 21st February 1914.	1937, Home (Judl.), 3 Sept. 1917	
	Telaga Pamulas	160 Home (Judl.), 28 January 1917	160,Home (Judl.) 23 Jan. 1917	

	Donga Waddars	1161, Judl., 12th June 1913 and 2859, Judl., 27th December 1918	1937, Home (Judl.,) 13 Sept. 1917	
Kurnool	Donga Yerakalas	917, Judl., 10th May 1913	1579, Home (Judl.), 1st Aug. 1917	
	Donga Waddars	1461, Judl., 12th June 1913	-Do-	
	Boyas (1)	1120, Home (Judl.), 13 May 1918	1120, Home (Judl.) 13 May 1918	
	Boyas (2)	824, Judl., 3 July 1922	824 Judl., 3rd July 1922	
	Nirshikaris	1245, Judl., 7 November 1922	1245, Judl., 7th November 1922	
	Sugalis	623, Judl., (Pol.) 28th Nov. 1923	623, Judl., (Pol.) 28th Nov.1923	
	Madigas and Malas (Nagireddipalli village)	344, Judl., (Pol.) 27th June 1924	344, Judl., (Pol.) 27th June 1924	
Bellary	Rudrapad Korachas	1369, Judl., 5th July 1913	1579, Judl., 1st August 1917	Removed to Sitanagaram Settlement
	Donga Yerakalas	917, Judl., 10th May 1913 and 1714, Judl., 4th July 1916	–	
	Donga Dasaris	681, Home (Judl.), 26th Mar. 1917	681, Home (Judl), 26th Mar. 1917	Removed to Hubli settlement
	Nirshikaris	1245, Judl., 7th November 1922	1245, Judl., 7th November 1922	
	Sugalis	240, Judl., (Pol.) 21st May 1923 and 582, Judl., (Pol.) 30th Oct. 1925	240, Judl., (Pol.) 21st May 1923 and 582, Judl., (Pol.) 30 Oct. 1923	
	DO (Siddhapuram Taluk)	343, Judl., (Pol.), 27th June 1924	313, Judl., (Pol.) 27 June 1924	

Anantapur	Donga Waddars	1161, Judl., 12th June 1913	1140, Home (Judl.), 1st May 1920.	
	Vayalpad or Nawabpeta Korachas	918, Judl., 10th May 1913 and 1796, Judl., 5th September 1913	1649, Home (Judl.), 19th July 1919 & 2197, Home (Judl.), 29th Oct. 1919	
	Donga Dasaris	681, Home (Judl.), 26th March 1917 & 2293, Home (Judl.), 7th Oct. 1919.	681, Home (Judl.), 26th March 1917 and 2293, Home (Judl.), 7 Oct 1919.	
	Donga yerakalas	110, Judl., 27th April 1921	110, Judl., 27th April 1921	
	Jatur Mixed Gang	161, Judl., 12th May 1921	161, Judl., 12th May 1921	
	Donga Urkorachas*	52, Judl., 31 June 1923	52, Judl., 31 January 1923	*Applied to Donga Urkorachas living within the limits of Kambadur Police Station of Kalyan-durg circle.
	Sugalis	241, Judl. (Pol.), 21st May 1923	241, Judl., (Pol.) 21st May 1923	
	Donga Urkorachas	62, Judl., (Pol.), 1st February1924	62, Judl., (Pol.) 1st February 1924	
	* Donga Urkorachas (within the limits of Kalyandurg and Banaganapalli police stations)	396, Judl., (Pol.) 21 July 1924	396, Judl., (Pol.) 21st July 1924	
	Donga Urkorachas	566, Judl., (Pol.) 11th November 1924	566, Judl., (Pol.) 11th November 1924. *Applied to men residing in the limits of Patnam Palakonda, and Machavaram Police stations.	*Applied to Donga Urkorachas which resides in the limits of Anantapur and Singanamala stations of the Anantapur taluk and of Tadimarri station of Dharma-varam taluk.

Cuddapah	Donga Woddars	1161, Judl., 12th June 1913	
	Thogamalai Kora-vars or Kepmaris	1193, Judl., 18th June 1923	
	Hired Assassins	700, Judl., 21st March 1914	
	Donga Dasaris	681, Home (Judl.) 26th Mar. 1917	681, Home (Judl.), 26th Mar. 1917
	Vayalpad or Nawabpeta Korachas	918, Judl., 10th May 1913, 1796, Judl., 5 Sept 1913 and 414, Home (Judl.), 20th February 1918	–
	Donga Yerukulas	917, Judl., 10th May 1913 and 1635, Judl., 15th July 1913	–
	Jatur Mixed gang	161, Judl., 12th May 1921	161, Judl., 12th May 1921
	Donga Waddars	918, Judl., 10th May 1913	243, Judl., 3rd May 1921
		918, Judl., 10th May 1913	1649, Home (Judl.), 19th July 1919 and 2497, Home (Judl.), 29th October 1919.
Chittoor	Vayalpad or Naw-abpeta Korachas	918, Judl., 14th February 1914	1579, Home (Judl.), 1st Aug. 1917
	Jogis	461, Judl., 21st February 1914	–
	Donga Dasaris	681, Home (Judl.), 26th Mar. 1917	681, Home (Judl.), 26th Mar. 1917
	Nattam Korachas	390, Home (Judl.), 18th Feb 1918	390, Home (Judl.), 18th Feb. 1918
	Amagunta Paligars	640, Judl., 21st September 1921	640, Judl., 21st September 1921

	Dommaras	266, Judl., 11th June 1921	266, Judl., 11th June 1921
	Bhattu Turkas	51, Judl., 31st January 1923	51, Judl., 31st January 1923
	Sugalis	71, Judl., 17th February 1923	71, Judl., 17th February 1923
	Yanadis or Irulars (Vayalpad Taluk & the Sadam station limits)	227, Judl., (Pol.) 21st April 1924	227, Judl., (Pol.) 21 April 1924
	Boyas	272 (Judl.) (Pol.) 23rd May 1924	272, Judl (Pol.) 23rd May 1921
North Arcot	Thogamalai Koravars or Kepmaris	1193, Judl., 18th June 1913	1579, Home (Judl.), 1stAugust 1917
	Salem Molurnad Koravars	1645, Judl., 14th August 1913 (Sec 3) and 872, Judl, 27th April 1917, Sec 10b)	1390, Home (Judl.), 23rd August 1919
	Venganur Parayas	381, Judl., 14th February 1914	1579, Home (Judl.), 1st Aug.1917
	Jogis	461, Judl., 21st February 1914	-Do-
	Sakkarattamadal Koravars	101, Home (Judl.), 15th January 1917	1142, Judl., 12th October 1922
	Thottia Naiks	616, Judl., 13th May 1922	616, Judl., 13th May 1922
	Dommaras	1141, Judl., 12th October 1922	1141, Judl., 12th October 1922
Chinglepet	Togamalai Koravas or Kepmaris	1193, Judl., 18th June 1913	1579, Home (Judl.), 1st Aug. 1917
	Jogis	461, Judl., 21st February 1914	-Do-

	Kaloddars	396, Judl., (Pol.) 8th August 1923	896, Judl., (Pol.), 8th Aug. 1923	
	Veppur Parayas	1098, Judl., 4th June 1913	*2258, Home (Judl.), 2nd Oct. 1919	* To those not placed in settlement
South Arcot	Thogamalai Koravas or Kepmaris	1193, Judl., 18th June 1918	665, Home (Judl.) 21st Mar.1918	
	Atturkilaud Koravars	2066, Judl., 13th Oct. 1918 (Sec 3) & 872, Judl., 27th April 1917 (Sec 10b)	1930, Home (Judl.) 28th Aug. 1919	
	Jogis	461, Judl., 21st February 1914		
	Vellayankuppam Padayachis	2490, Judl., 14th November 1914	70 Judl (Pol.) 17th February 1923	
	Sakkarattamudaikoravas	1089, Home (Judl.), 26th Apr. 1920	1089, Home (Judl.), 26th Apr. 1920.	
	GuduDasaris	616, Judl., 13th May 1922	616, Judl, 13th May 1922	
	Thotta Naicks	-Do-	-Do-	
Tanjore	Guandarvakottal Koravars	2554, Judl., 9th Dec 1913 (Sec 3) and 2357, Home (Judl.), 14 Nov. 1917 (Sec 10b)	2357, Home (Judl.), 14th Nov. 1917	
	Thotta Naicks	616, Judl., 13th May 1922	616, Judl, 13th May 1922	
	Koottappa Kallars	26, Judl., 6th January 1915	1519, Home (Judl.), 1st Aug.1917	
	Melurnad Koravars	450, Judl., (Pol), 29th Aug. 1924	450, Judl., (Pol.), 29th August 1924	
	Uraligoundans	811, Judl., 19th April 1917	811, Judl., 19th April 1917	
	Thogamalai Koravars	1193, Judl., 18th June 1913	665, Judl., 21st March 1918	

	Salem Melurnad Koravars	1645, Judl, 14th August 1913 (Sec 3), and 872, Judl, 27th April 1917 Sec 10-b	1930, Home (Judl.) 28th Aug. 1919
	Attur Kilnad Koravars	2066, Judl, 13th October 1913 (Sec 3) and 872, Judl, 27th April 1917 (Sec 10b)	-Do-
Trichinapoly	Kottappal Kallars	26, Judl., 6th January 1915	1579, Home (Judl.), 1st Aug. 1917
	Thottai Naicks	616, Judl., 13th May 1922	616, Judl. 13th May 1922
	Varaganori Koravars	117, Judicial (Pol.) 13th Mar.1923	117, Judl. (Pol.) 13th March 1923
	Ambalagars in Kulitt alai taluk & in the village of Suriyanur	226, Judl., (Pol.), 21st April 1924	226, Judl. (Pol.), 21st April 1924
	Vethiva Goundans	226, Judl., (Pol.),21st April 1924	226, Judl. (Pol.), 21st April 1924
Madras	Vaduvarpatti Koravars	1890, Judl., 20th July 1916	1579, Home (Judl.), 1st Aug.1917
	Piramdai Kallars	1331, Home (Judl.), 5th June 1918	1331, Home (Judl.) 5th June 1918
	Salem Melurnad Koravars	470, Home (Judl.), 4th March 1921	470, Home (Judl.), 4th Mar.1921.
	Thottai Naicks	616, Judl. 13th May 1922	616, Judl., 13th May 1922
	Valayars	499, Judl. (Pol.), 18th Sept. 1923	499, Judl., (Pol.), 18th Sept. 1923
Ramnad	Chettinad Valayas	919, Judl.,1 May 1915	1579, Home (Judl.), 1st Aug 1917
	Vaduvarpatti Koravars	1890, Judl., 27th July 1916	-Do-
	Thotia Naicks	616, Judl., 18th May 1922	616, Judl., 18th May 1922

	Piramalai Kallars	1172, Judl., 18th Oct, 1922	1172, Judl., 18th October 1922	
	Karumbaravas	53, Judl., 31st January 1923	53, Judl., 31st January 1923	Restricted to the settlement at Kulasekharapatnam
	Sombanad Maravars	72, Judl., 17th February 1923	72, Judl., 17th February 1923	-Do-
	Uppu Koravars (Anavaradanallur and Koupatti)	2494, Judl., 12th October 1915	.....	-Do-
	Koravars (Mela Eral, etc)	1834, Home (Judl.), 1 Sept. 1917	.....	-Do-
Tinnevelly	Koravars of Vaduvar Patti (Ramnad District) (1)	1890, Home (Judl.), 27th July 1916	1579, Home (Judl.), 1 Aug. 1917	-Do-
	Koravars of Vadu-varpatti (Ramnad District) (2)	553, Judl., 28th April 1922	553, Judl., 28th April 1922	-Do-
	Maravars of Poolam	405, Home (Judl.), 18th Feb. 1919	405, Home (Judl.), 18th Feb. 1919	Sec 10-b only has been put in force.
	Thottia Naicks	616, Judl., 13th May 1922	616, Judl., 13th May 1922	
Salem	Salem Molurnad Koravars	1645, Judl., 14 Aug. 1913 (Sec 3), and 872, Judl., 27th April 1917 [Sec 10(b)]	2009, Judl., 5th September 1918	
	Atturkilnad Koravars	2066, Judl., 13th Oct. 1913 (Sec 3), and 872, Judl., 27th April 1917 [Sec 10(b)]	1579, Judl., 1st August 1917	
	Thalli Koravars (Hosur taluk)	1817, Judl., 9th August 1918	1817, Judl., 9th August 1918	

Pennagaram Perum babai koravars	Attur Malnad Koravars	805, Judl., 28th October 1921	805, Judl., 28 Oct., 1921 812, Judl., 31st October 1921
	Uppu Koravars	581, Judl., (Pol.), 30th Oct. 1923	581, Judl., (Pol.), 30th Oct. 1923
	Uppu Koravars (Krishnagiri Taluk)	31, Judl., (Pol.), 12th Jan. 1924	31, Judl., (Pol.), 12th January 1924
	Sarangapalli Koravars (Hosur Taluk)	282, Judl. (Pol.), 28th May 1024	282, Judl., (Pol.), 28th May 1924
	Monda Koravars (Dharmapuri Taluk)	342, Judl. (Pol.), 27th June 1924	342, Judl., (Pol.), 27th June 1924
Coimbatore	Salem Melurnad Koravars	1645, Judl., 14th Aug. 1913 (Sec 8), 872, Judl., 27th April 1917 [Sec 10 b]	1203, Home (Judl.), 18th May 1918
	Valayars 1	1385, Judl., 26th May 1916	1579, Home (Judl.), 1st Aug 1917
	Valayars 2	404, Home (Judl.), 19th Feb. 1917	624, Home (Judl.), 18th March 1918
	Valayars 3	405, Home (Judl.), 19th Feb. 1917	624, Home (Judl.), 18th March 1918
	Valayars 4	2026, Home (Judl.), 28th Sept. 1917	2038, Home (Judl.), 28th September 1917
	Valayars 5	2027, Home (Judl.) 28th Sept. 1917	2027, Home (Judl.), 28th Sept. 1917
	Valayars 6	18, Home (Judl.), 4th Jan. 1918	18, Home (Judl.), 4th Jan. 1918
	Valayars 7	147, Home (Judl.), 18th Jan. 1918	147, Home (Judl.), 18th Jan. 1918

Valayars 8	232, Home (Judl.), 28th Jan. 1918	232, Home (Judl.), 28th Jan. 1918
Valayars 9	233, Home (Judl.), 28th Jan. 1918	233, Home (Judl.), 28th Jan. 1918
Valayars 10	482, Home (Judl.), 25th Feb. 1918	482, Home (Judl.), 25th Feb. 1918
Valayars 11	714, Home (Judl.), 25th March 1918	714, Home (Judl.), 25th March 1918
Valayars 12	1820, Home (Judl.), 4th June 1918	1820, Home (Judl.), 4th June 1918
Valayars 13	1593, Home (Judl.), 6th July 1918	1593, Home (Judl.), 6th July 1918
Valayars 14	1618, Home (Judl.), 12th July 1918	1618, Home (Judl.),12th July 1918
Valayars 15	184, Home (Judl.), 24th Jan. 1919	184, Home (Judl.), 24th Jan. 1919
Valayars 16	186, Home (Judl.), 24th Jan. 1919	186, Home (Judl.), 24th Jan. 1919
Valayars 17	1035, Home (Judl.), 9th May 1919	1035, Home (Judl.), 9th May 1919
Valayars 18	1850, Home (Judl.), 13th June 1919	1850, Home (Judl.), 13th June 1919
Valayars 19	1514, Home (Judl.), 4th July 1919	1514, Home (Judl.), 4th July 1919
Valayars 20	2246, Home (Judl.), 1st Oct. 1919	2246, Home (Judl.), 1st Oct. 1919
Valayars 21	377, Judl. (Pol.), 26th July 1923	377, Judl., (Police), 20th July 1922
Valayars 22	397, Judl. (Pol.), 3rd Aug. 1923	397, Judl., (Pol.), 3rd Aug. 1923
Valayars 23	655, Judl. (Pol.), 18th Dec. 1923	655, Judl. (Pol.), 18th Dec. 1923
Thottia Naicks	616, Judicial, 13th May 1922	616, Judl., 13th May 1922
Gudu Dasaris	616, Judl., 13th May 1922	616, Judl., 13th May 1922
Valayars (residing in certain villages of Coimbatore taluk)	549, Judl., (Police), 31st Oct. 1924	549, Judl., (Pol.) 31st October 1924

Madras City	*Koravars*	*367, Judicial Police 4th July 1924*	*540, Judicial (Police)29th Oct. 1924*	*Movements resticted to the area comprised within the limits of Madras City.*
Whole Presidency	Kanjar Bhats Iranis	148, Judl. (Police), 13th March 1924 506, Judl. (Police), 7th October 1924	148, Judl. (Police, 13th March 1924 506, Judicial (Police), 7th Oct. 1924	506, Judl. (Police), 7th Oct. 1924
Anatapur	Dommaras	658, Judl. (Police) 15th Dec. 1924	658, Judical (Police), 15th Dec. 1924	
Anatapur	Pedda boyas	9, Judicial (Police), 8th January 1925	9 Judicial (Police), 8th January 1925	
Nellore	Donga Yanadis	678, Judicial (Police), 27th Dec. 1924	678, Judicial (Police), 27th Dec. 1924	
Nellore	Malas	676, Judicial (Police), 23rd Dec. 1924	676, Judicial (Police), 23rd Dec. 1924	
Chingleput	Nokkars	645, Judicial (Police), 10th Dec. 1924	676, Judicial (Police), 23rd Dec. 1924	
Salem	Uppu-DeKoravars	646, Judicial (Police), 10th Dec.1924	646, Judicial (Police), 23rd Dec. 1924	
South Arcot	Irulars	54, Judicial (Police), 2nd Feb. 1925	54, Judicial (police), 2nd February 1925	
Tanjore	Jambuvanodai Mixed gang	96, Judicial (Police), 24th Feb. 1925	96, Judicial (Police), 24th February 1925	
Chinglepet	Koravars	8 Judicial (Police) 8th Jan. 1925	8 Judicial (Police) Jan. 1925	The total number of persons registered under the act at the close of the year 1923 was 3795.

(*Source:* Government of Madras, Note Showing the Progress Made in the Settlement of Criminal Tribes in the Madras presidency upto January 1925, Madras, 1927.

Appendix–IV
Opening, Management, Employment Conditions and the Assistance Given by the Government to the CT Settlements Under Main Heads

Name of the Settlement with district	*Opening of the settlement during the year*	*Managed by the authority*	*Population in the settlement at the end of the year 1917*	*Nature of employment in the settlement*	*Details of charges Particulars*	*Budget Estimate during the year 1919-1920*	*Revised Estimates during the year 1918-1919*	*Budget Estimates 1918-1919*	*Accounts 1917-1918*
Sitanagaram Settlement, Guntur District	January 1913	Salvation Army	989	Stone quarrying, earth work, contracts, agriculture, sericulture, silk and cotton weaving. The settlement was divided into two parts. There were two supervising European officers.	Recurring: 1. Supervision: Recurring grant @ Rs.400/- per month	4,800	4,800	4,800	4,800
					2. Maintenance of old and infirm people @ Rs.10/- per month.	840	840	840	840
					Non-Recurring. Miscellaneous charges	----	18	---	295
					Total	5,640	5,658	5,640	5,935

Sitanagaram Settlement, Guntur District	1914	Salvation Army	1223	Agriculture, experimental gardenting, sericulture, trand in cattle, coolie work, making of mats, baskets and ropes. There was a European married Assistant in addition to the manager in the settlement	Recurring: Supervision: Recurring grant @ Rs.500/- per month Grant for payment to watchmen @ Rs. 96/- per month.	6,000	5,800	4,800	4,800
					Pony allowance for the manager @ Rs. 15/-	1,152	1,152	1,152	955
					Grant for pony,	180	55	----	----
					Education grant,	----	300	----	----
					School funiture Allowance allowance of	2,000	1,400	----	771
					sub-assistant surgeon, Bapatla	300	800	700	----
						180	180	720	90
								900	
					Non-recurring Purchase of hospital Insturments Maintenance of hospital				
					Total	9,887	9,687	8,272	6,616

Bhumanna gadda Settlement Chittoor Dist	January 1914	Salvation Army	513	Agriculture, Sericulture weaving, making of mats, baskets ropes, cultivation of mangoes, coconuts and tabacco.	I. Recurring: Supervision: @ Rs.280/-	3,360	2,880	2,400	2,400
					Setters wages @ Rs. 300/-	2,736	3,600	4,800	6,000
					2. Education capitation grant@ Rs. 3/- per month per boy for 100 boys.	3,600	---	---	---
					3. Medical Relief : Fees for American Arcot Mission	360	360	360	90
					II. Non recurring Boarding School	7,600	---	---	---
					Inspection Bungalow	4,700	---	---	---
					Water Supply Scheme	950	3,000	---	---
					Miscellaneous	730	---	---	---
					Total	24,036	9,840	7,840	8,490

Siddhapuram Settlement, Kurnool Dist.	1913	Official Management (Govt.)	128	Relamation and Cultivation of land, cumbly weaving and road work	Recurring : Education including rations, Medical charges Weaving establishment	944 50 1,590	784 2,060	754 150	
					Non-recurring : petty construction and repairs	600	600	600	
					Total	3,184	3,184	3,184	600
Reformatory Settement Guntur	Formerly Prisoners Home Nov. 1913	Salvation Army	31	Work in jute mill, weaving, carpentry. gardent work in the settlement, road work, petty contracts	Recurring : Supervision Repair of Building, Municipal tax, medical Relief Dutty allowance for Sub-Asst Surgeon, Guntur Non-recurring Travelling	3,600 250 304 120 200 200	3,600 250 304 120 300 200	3,600 250 304 120 300 300	3,600 250 302 60 140 140
					Total	4,674	4,774	4,874	4,432

Kavali Settlement Nellore District	1917 Sub-Settlements at Allur and Bitragunta	American Baptist Mission. The services of the Manager was given free by the Mission	1393	Contracts, agriculture carpentry, weaving, limekiln, coolie work, stone quarry, fire wood cutting	I. Recurring : Settlement Maintenance including supervision charges@	33,000	39,000	45,000	29,868
					Rs. 1200/- Medical relief allowance to local medical Officer	120	120	120	120
					Contribution to Taluk Board for medicines	250	373	---	---
					II. Non-recurring Contingencies and Miscellaneous	2,350	---	200	1,549
					Total	35,720	39,493	45,320	31,537
Salvation Army Girls School Nellore	1915	Salvation Army	Crim children were being education since 1915 total strength was 48 girls	Needle work, domestic duties, General Education	Recurring : Monthly stipend @ Rs. 4/- for 60 girls	2,880	2,400	2,400	2,248
					Non-recurring Initial grant Construction of a building for crim children	50	4,894	---	
					Total	2,930	7,294	2,400	2,248

Source : See, Government of Madras, Home (Judicial) Department, G.O.NO.2491 dated12.10.1915

Bibliography

PRIMARY SOURCES

Archival Sources, Reports, Gazetteers, District Records, Missionary Sources and Manuals

Government orders from various departments like Judicial, Public Works (Labour) Department, Law (General) Department, Home, Home (Judicial) Department, were collected from Tamil Nadu State Archives, Egmore, Chennai; Andhra Pradesh State Archives and Research Institute, Tarnaka, Hyderabad and National Archives, New Delhi.

HOME DEPTT.,

Home Deptt., Government Order No. 48, dated January 7, 1920.
Home Deptt., Government Order No. 22, dated January 26, 1920.
Home Deptt., Government Order No. 451, dated February 17, 1920.
Home Deptt., Government Order No. 475, dated February 19, 1920.
Home Deptt., Government Order No. 503, dated February 23, 1920.
Home Deptt., Government Order No. 596, dated March 3, 1920.
Home Deptt., Government Order No. 637, dated March 6, 1920.
Home Deptt., Government Order No. 725, dated March 16, 1920.
Home Deptt., Government Order No. 1269, dated May 19, 1920.
Home Deptt., Government Order No. 1339, dated May 31, 1920.
Home Deptt., Government Order No. 1356, dated June 1, 1920.
Home Deptt., Government Order No. 1389, dated June 4, 1920.
Home Deptt., Government Order No. 1390, dated June 4, 1920.
Home Deptt., Government Order No. 1407, dated June 8, 1920.
Home Deptt., Government Order No. 1469, dated June 14, 1920.
Home Deptt., Government Order No. 1555, dated June 24, 1920.
Home Deptt., Government Order No. 1560, dated June 25, 1920.
Home Deptt., Government Order No. 1867, dated July 30, 1920.
Home Deptt., Government Order No. 3070, dated December 9, 1920.
Home Deptt., Government Order No. 2005, dated August 11, 1920.
Home Deptt., Government Order No. 1979, dated August 11, 1920.
Home Deptt., Government Order No. 1985, dated August 11, 1920.

Home Deptt., Government Order No. 2008, dated August 13, 1920.
Home Deptt., Government Order No. 2052, dated August 18, 1920.
Home Deptt., Government Order No. 2075, dated August 20, 1920.
Home Deptt., Government Order No. 2124, dated August 25, 1920.
Home Deptt., Government Order No.2247, dated September 9, 1920.
Home Deptt., Government Order No. 2349, dated September 21, 1920.
Home Deptt., Government Order No. 2468, dated October 4, 1920.
Home Deptt., Government Order No. 2482, dated October 5, 1920.
Home Deptt., Government Order No. 2661, dated October 25, 1920.
Home Deptt., Government Order No. 2679, dated October 27, 1920.
Home Deptt., Government Order No. 2904, dated November 20, 1920.
Home Deptt., Government Order No. 2948, dated November 25, 1920.
Home Deptt., Government Order No. 1855, dated October 4, 1921.
Home Deptt., Government Order No. 1912, dated October 12, 1921.
Home Deptt., Government Order No. 2332, dated December 20, 1921.
Home Deptt., Government Order No. 277, dated February 2, 1925.
Home Deptt., Government Order No. 227, dated February 12, 1925.
Home Deptt., Government Order No. 243, dated February 13, 1925.
Home Deptt., Government Order No. 244, dated February 13, 1925.
Home Deptt., Government Order No. 292, dated February 25, 1925.
Home Deptt., Government Order No. 267, dated March 25, 1925.
Home Deptt., Government Order No. 497, dated April 2, 1925.
Home Deptt., Government Order No. 716, dated May 14, 1925.
Home Deptt., Government Order No. 71, dated January 18, 1927.
Home Deptt., Government Order No. 12, dated January 4, 1927.
Home Deptt., Government Order No. 194, dated February 10, 1927.
Home Deptt., Government Order No. 314, dated March 4, 1927.
Home Deptt., Government Order No. 852, dated March 12, 1927.
Home Deptt., Government Order No. 587, dated April 26, 1927.
Home Deptt., Government Order No. 1790, dated June 2, 1927.
Home Deptt., Government Order No. 1834, dated June 17, 1927.
Home Deptt., Government Order No. 1087, dated July 15, 1927.
Home Deptt., Government Order No. 1087, dated July 15, 1927.
Home Deptt., Government Order No. 1869, dated July 30, 1927.
Home Deptt., Government Order No. 2479, dated August 4, 1927.
Home Deptt., Government Order No. 2087, dated December 3, 1927.
Home Deptt., Government Order No. 4079, dated December 20, 1927.
Home Deptt., Government Order No. 4091, dated December 21, 1927.
Home Deptt., Government Order No. 423, dated March 8, 1928.
Home Deptt., Government Order No. 821, dated May 4, 1928.
Home Deptt., Government Order No. 1813, dated October 25, 1928.
Home Deptt., Government Order No. 1816, dated October 25, 1928.
Home Deptt., Government Order No. 1820, dated October 25, 1928.
Home Deptt., Government Order No. 1828, dated October 27, 1928.

Home Deptt., Government Order No. 1704, dated October 8, 1928.
Home Deptt., Government Order No. 27, dated January 5, 1929.
Home Deptt., Government Order No. 172, dated January 28, 1929.
Home Deptt., Government Order No. 231, dated February 6, 1929.
Home Deptt., Government Order No. 234, dated February 7, 1929.
Home Deptt., Government Order No. 268, dated February 13, 1929.
Home Deptt., Government Order No. 385, dated March 5, 1929.
Home Deptt., Government Order No. 1971, dated November 11, 1929.
Home Deptt., Government Order No.1962, dated November 11, 1929.
Home Deptt., Government Order No. 2034, dated November 19, 1929.
Home Deptt., Government Order No. 2143, dated December 2, 1929.
Home Deptt., Government Order No. 525, dated April 8, 1931.
Home Deptt., Government Order No. 560, dated April 15, 1931.
Home Deptt., Government Order No. 905, dated June 17, 1931.
Home Deptt., Government Order No. 984, dated July 4, 1931.
Home Deptt., Government Order No. 1283, dated August 28, 1931.
Home Deptt., Government Order No. 1426, dated September 29, 1931.
Home Deptt., Government Order No. 1614, dated November 7, 1931.
Home Deptt., Government Order No. 505, dated April 12, 1932.
Home Deptt., Government Order No. 1849, dated October 15, 1932.
Home Deptt., Government Order No. 892, dated May 19, 1933.
Home Deptt., Government Order No. 154, dated November 24, 1933.
Home Deptt., Government Order No. 195-196, dated, December 1933.
Home Deptt., Government Order No. 291, dated February 28, 1934.
Home Deptt., Government Order No. 472, dated April 9, 1934.
Home Deptt., Government Order No. 622, dated May 8, 1934.
Home Deptt., Government Order No. 713, dated May 31, 1934.
Home Deptt., Government Order No. 855, dated June 28, 1934.
Home Deptt., Government Order No. 1358, dated September 25, 1934.
Home Deptt., Government Order No. 1472, dated October 11, 1934.
Home Deptt., Government Order No. 1652, dated December 5, 1934.
Home Deptt., Government Order No. 785, dated June 1, 1935.
Home Deptt., Government Order No. 1066, dated August 1, 1935.
Home Deptt., Government Order No. 1573, dated November 9, 1935.
Home Deptt., Government Order No. 114, dated January 16, 1936.
Home Deptt., Government Order No. 178, dated January 25, 1936.
Home Deptt., Government Order No. 645, dated March 9, 1936.
Home Deptt., Government Order No. 662, dated March 10, 1936.
Home Deptt., Government Order No. 731, dated March 21, 1936.
Home Deptt., Government Order No. 454, dated March 21, 1936.
Home Deptt., Government Order No. 782, dated March 26, 1936.
Home Deptt., Government Order No. 802, dated March 28, 1936.
Home Deptt., Government Order No. 807, dated March 28, 1936.
Home Deptt., Government Order No. 850, dated March 31, 1936.

Home Deptt., Government Order No. 583, dated April 8, 1936.
Home Deptt., Government Order No. 602, dated April 15, 1936.
Home Deptt., Government Order No. 927, dated June 8,1936.
Home Deptt., Government Order No. 998, dated June 19,1936.
Home Deptt., Government Order No. 1097, dated July 6, 1936.
Home Deptt., Government Order No. 1376, dated August 17, 1936.
Home Deptt., Government Order No. 1470, dated August 27, 1936.
Home Deptt., Government Order No. 1480, dated August 28, 1936.
Home Deptt., Government Order No. 1581, dated September 14, 1936.
Home Deptt., Government Order No. 1624, dated September 14, 1936.
Home Deptt., Government Order No. 1577, dated September 14, 1936.
Home Deptt., Government Order No. 1766, dated October 8,1936.
Home Deptt., Government Order No. 1859, dated October 21,1936.
Home Deptt., Government Order No. 827, dated November 12,1936.
Home Deptt., Government Order No. 1981, dated November 5,1936.
Home Deptt., Government Order No. 2241, dated December 10,1936.
Home Deptt., Government Order No. 169 dated January 15, 1937.
Home Deptt., Government Order No. 207, dated January 16, 1937.
Home Deptt., Government Order No. 223, dated January 19, 1937.
Home Deptt., Government Order No. 372, dated January 28, 1937.
Home Deptt., Government Order No. 372, dated January 28, 1937.
Home Deptt., Government Order No. 373, dated January 28, 1937.
Home Deptt., Government Order No. 979, dated January 29, 1937.
Home Deptt., Government Order No. 373, dated January 29, 1937.
Home Deptt., Government Order No. 1284, dated March 28, 1937.
Home Deptt., Government Order No. 1573, dated April 20, 1937.
Home Deptt., Government Order No. 1787, dated May 6, 1937.
Home Deptt., Government Order No. 1885, dated May 15, 1937.
Home Deptt., Government Order No. 2181, dated June 7, 1937.
Home Deptt., Government Order No. 2230, dated June 10, 1937.
Home Deptt., Government Order No. 2309, dated June 14, 1937.
Home Deptt., Government Order No. 2411, dated June 24, 1937.
Home Deptt., Government Order No. 2506, dated July 2, 1937.
Home Deptt., Government Order No. 2732, dated July 17, 1937.
Home Deptt., Government Order No. 2848, dated July 26, 1937.
Home Deptt., Government Order No. 2732, dated July 27, 1937.
Home Deptt., Government Order No. 2977, dated July 30, 1937.
Home Deptt., Government Order No. 3114, dated August 9, 1937.
Home Deptt., Government Order No. 2411, dated August 27, 1937.
Home Deptt., Government Order No. 3541, dated September 4, 1937.
Home Deptt., Government Order No. 3610, dated September 11, 1937.
Home Deptt., Government Order No. 3686, dated September 16, 1937.
Home Deptt., Government Order No. 28, dated September 28, 1937.
Home Deptt., Government Order No. 4125, dated October 15, 1937.

Home Deptt., Government Order No. 4448, dated November 6, 1937.
Home Deptt., Government Order No. 4479, dated November 9, 1937.
Home Deptt., Government Order No. 4557, dated November 11, 1937.
Home Deptt., Government Order No. 4717, dated November 23, 1937.
Home Deptt., Government Order No. 4863, dated December 1, 1937.
Home Deptt., Government Order No. 5112, dated December 16, 1937.
Home Deptt., Government Order No. 32, dated January 3, 1938.
Home Deptt., Government Order No. 37, dated January 3, 1938.
Home Deptt., Government Order No. 373, dated January 21, 1938.
Home Deptt., Government Order No. 501, dated January 29, 1938.
Home Deptt., Government Order No. 710, dated February 11, 1938.
Home Deptt., Government Order No. 714, dated February 11, 1938.
Home Deptt., Government Order No. 767, dated February 14, 1938.
Home Deptt., Government Order No. 790, dated February 15, 1938.
Home Deptt., Government Order No. 820, dated February 17, 1938.
Home Deptt., Government Order No. 1316, dated March 11, 1938.
Home Deptt., Government Order No. 1448, dated March 19, 1938.
Home Deptt., Government Order No. 1489, dated March 19, 1938.
Home Deptt., Government Order No. 1200, dated March, 1938.
Home Deptt., Government Order No. 1519, dated March 22, 1938.
Home Deptt., Government Order No. 1839, dated March 31, 1938.
Home Deptt., Government Order No. 1796, dated April 4, 1938.
Home Deptt., Government Order No. 2370, dated May 6, 1938.
Home Deptt., Government Order No. 2748, dated May 14, 1938.
Home Deptt., Government Order No. 2520, dated May 6, 1938.
Home Deptt., Government Order No. 2445, dated May 11, 1938.
Home Deptt., Government Order No. 2509, dated May 16, 1938.
Home Deptt., Government Order No. 2510, dated May 16, 1938.
Home Deptt., Government Order No. 2575, dated May 20, 1938.
Home Deptt., Government Order No. 2594, dated May 23, 1938.
Home Deptt., Government Order No. 2694, dated May 27, 1938.
Home Deptt., Government Order No. 2846, dated June 3, 1938.
Home Deptt., Government Order No. 3055, dated June 16, 1938.
Home Deptt., Government Order No. 3880, dated August 9, 1938.
Home Deptt., Government Order No. 3285, dated July 4, 1938.
Home Deptt., Government Order No. 3492 dated June 26, 1938.
Home Deptt., Government Order No. 3973, dated August 15, 1938.
Home Deptt., Government Order No. 3380, dated July 9, 1938.
Home Deptt., Government Order No. 4087, dated August 24, 1938.
Home Deptt., Government Order No. 4271, dated September 3, 1938.
Home Deptt., Government Order No. 4826 dated September 9, 1938.
Home Deptt., Government Order No. 4519, dated September 18, 1938.
Home Deptt., Government Order No. 3842, dated September 28, 1938.
Home Deptt., Government Order No. 4721, dated September 29, 1938.

Home Deptt., Government Order No. 4719, dated September 29, 1938.
Home Deptt., Government Order No. 4823, dated October 5, 1938.
Home Deptt., Government Order No. 5219, dated October 27, 1938.
Home Deptt., Government Order No. 5273, dated October 31, 1938.
Home Deptt., Government Order No. 5275, dated October 31, 1938.
Home Deptt., Government Order No. 5394, dated November 8, 1938.
Home Deptt., Government Order No. 5395, dated November 8, 1938.
Home Deptt., Government Order No. 5535, dated November 16, 1938.
Home Deptt., Government Order No. 5536, dated November 16,1938.
Home Deptt., Government Order No. 5595, dated November 21,1938.
Home Deptt., Government Order No. 5747, dated December 1, 1938.
Home Deptt., Government Order No. 786, dated December 3, 1938.
Home Deptt., Government Order No. 5787, dated December 3, 1938.
Home Deptt., Government Order No. 5890, dated December 6, 1938.
Home Deptt., Government Order No. 5902, dated December 8, 1938.
Home Deptt., Government Order No. 50, dated January 5, 1939.
Home Deptt., Government Order No. 185, dated January 11, 1939.
Home Deptt., Government Order No. 235, dated January 16, 1939.
Home Deptt., Government Order No. 236, dated January 16, 1939.
Home Deptt., Government Order No. 2295, dated January 20, 1939.
Home Deptt., Government Order No. 299, dated February 4, 1939.
Home Deptt., Government Order No. 597, dated February 6, 1939.
Home Deptt., Government Order No. 609, dated February 6, 1939.
Home Deptt., Government Order No. 331, dated February 7, 1939.
Home Deptt., Government Order No. 348, dated February 8, 1939.
Home Deptt., Government Order No. 701, dated February 10, 1939.
Home Deptt., Government Order No. 734, dated February 13, 1939.
Home Deptt., Government Order No. 1083, dated February 27, 1939.
Home Deptt., Government Order No. 446, dated February 22, 1939.
Home Deptt., Government Order No. 1084, dated February 27, 1939.
Home Deptt., Government Order No. 1126, March 1,1939.
Home Deptt., Government Order No. 1369, March 11,1939.
Home Deptt., Government Order No. 1596, dated March 23,1939.
Home Deptt., Government Order No. 1792, dated March 30, 1939.
Home Deptt., Government Order No. 763, dated March 28, 1939.
Home Deptt., Government Order No. 304, dated March 31, 1939.
Home Deptt., Government Order No. 810, dated March 31, 1939.
Home Deptt., Government Order No. 957, dated April 15, 1939.
Home Deptt., Government Order No. 2138, dated April 18, , 1939.
Home Deptt., Government Order No. 2191, dated April 15, 1939.
Home Deptt., Government Order No. 2168, dated April 19, 1939.
Home Deptt., Government Order No. 2138, dated April 18, 1939.
Home Deptt., Government Order No. 2143, April 19, 1939.
Home Deptt., Government Order No. 2217,dated April 21,1939.

Home Deptt., Government Order No. 2940, dated May 27, 1939.
Home Deptt., Government Order No. 2456, dated May 4, 1939.
Home Deptt., Government Order No. 2551, dated May 8, 1939.
Home Deptt., Government Order No. 3092, dated June 5, 1939.
Home Deptt., Government Order No. 3210, dated June 12, 1939.
Home Deptt., Government Order No. 3533, June 29, 1939.
Home Deptt., Government Order No. 3624, dated July 4, 1939.
Home Deptt., Government Order No. 3673, July 6, 1939.
Home Deptt., Government Order No. 4363, dated August 14, 1939.
Home Deptt., Government Order No. 3981, dated July 21, 1939.
Home Deptt., Government Order No. 4044, dated July 25, 1939.
Home Deptt., Government Order No. 4443, dated August 18, 1939.
Home Deptt., Government Order No. 4567, dated August 25, 1939.
Home Deptt., Government Order No. 4772, dated September 6, 1939.
Home Deptt., Government Order No. 4849, dated September 11, 1939.
Home Deptt., Government Order No. 4863, dated September 12, 1939.
Home Deptt., Government Order No. 4932, dated September 15, 1939.
Home Deptt., Government Order No. 2295, dated September 20, 1939.
Home Deptt., Government Order No. 5037, dated September 21, 1939.
Home Deptt., Government Order No. 5216, dated October 2, 1939.
Home Deptt., Government Order No. 540, dated October13, 1939.
Home Deptt., Government Order No. 5415, dated October 14, 1939.
Home Deptt., Government Order No. 5461, dated October 17,1939.
Home Deptt., Government Order No. 5614, dated October 26, 1939.
Home Deptt., Government Order No. 5670, dated October 28, 1939.
Home Deptt., Government Order No. 5701, dated October 30, 1939.
Home Deptt., Government Order No. 2731, dated November 8, 1939.
Home Deptt., Government Order No. 2795, dated November 16, 1939.
Home Deptt., Government Order No. 2952, dated December 5, 1939.
Home Deptt., Government Order No. 6290, dated December 6, 1939.
Home Deptt., Government Order No. 6328, dated December 7, 1939.
Home Deptt., Government Order No. 6449, December 15, 1939.
Home Deptt., Government Order No. 56, dated January 5, 1940.
Home Deptt., Government Order No. 304, dated January 17, 1940.
Home Deptt., Government Order No. 492, dated January 31, 1940.
Home Deptt., Government Order No. 777, dated February 15, 1940.
Home Deptt., Government Order No. 1075, dated March 2, 1940.
Home Deptt., Government Order No. 1528, dated March 30, 1940.
Home Deptt., Government Order No. 1701, dated April 10, 1940.
Home Deptt., Government Order No. 1846, dated April 22, 1940.
Home Deptt., Government Order No. 2048, dated May 4, 1940.
Home Deptt., Government Order No. 83, dated May 29, 1940.
Home Deptt., Government Order No. 2413, dated May 29, 1940.
Home Deptt., Government Order No. 2685, dated June 21, 1940.

Home Deptt., Government Order No. 2797, dated July 2, 1940.
Home Deptt., Government Order No. 3035, dated July 19, 1940.
Home Deptt., Government Order No. 2904, dated July 10, 1940.
Home Deptt., Government Order No. 3016, dated July 18, 1940.
Home Deptt., Government Order No. 3048, dated July 22, 1940.
Home Deptt., Government Order No. 3583, dated August 31, 1940.
Home Deptt., Government Order No. 3793, dated September 14, 1940.
Home Deptt., Government Order No. 4249, dated October 21, 1940.
Home Deptt., Government Order No. 4474, dated November 7, 1940.
Home Deptt., Government Order No. 4027, dated September 30, 1940.
Home Deptt., Government Order No. 4604, dated November 16, 1940.
Home Deptt., Government Order No. 4714, dated November 22, 1940.
Home Deptt., Government Order No. 4828, dated November 30, 1940.
Home Deptt., Government Order No. 5085, dated December 14, 1940.
Home Deptt., Government Order No. 5281, dated December 23, 1940.
Home Deptt., Government Order No. 5303, dated December 31, 1940.
Home Deptt., Government Order No. 140, dated January 10, 1941.
Home Deptt., Government Order No. 238, dated January 17, 1941.
Home Deptt., Government Order No. 558, dated February 1, 1941.
Home Deptt., Government Order No. 733, dated February 12, 1941.
Home Deptt., Government Order No. 941, dated February 25, 1941.
Home Deptt., Government Order No. 948, dated February 25, 1941.
Home Deptt., Government Order No. 965, dated February 26, 1941.
Home Deptt., Government Order No. 1330, dated March 15, 1941.
Home Deptt., Government Order No. 1328, dated March 15, 1941.
Home Deptt., Government Order No. 1330, dated March 15, 1941.
Home Judicial Deptt., Government Order No. 1551, dated March 3, 1941.
Home Deptt., Government Order No. 1620, dated March 31, 1941.
Home Deptt., Government Order No. 1625, dated March 31, 1941.
Home Deptt., Government Order No. 1862, dated April 16, 1941.
Home Deptt., Government Order No. 1683, dated April 2, 1941.
Home Deptt., Government Order No. 1723, dated April 4, 1941.
Home Deptt., Government Order No. 2396, dated May 19, 1941.
Home Deptt., Government Order No. 2532, dated May 28, 1941.
Home Deptt., Government Order No. 2544, dated May 29, 1941.
Home Deptt., Government Order No. 140, dated June 10, 1941.
Home Deptt., Government Order No. 2811, dated June 16, 1941.
Home Deptt., Government Order No. 2863, dated June 19, 1941.
Home Deptt., Government Order No. 2671, dated June 19, 1941.
Home Deptt., Government Order No. 2894, dated June 23, 1941.
Home Deptt., Government Order No. 3275, dated July 23, 1941.
Home Deptt., Government Order No. 354, dated August 8, 1941.
Home Deptt., Government Order No. 39, dated August 30, 1941.
Home Deptt., Government Order No. 3944, dated September 2, 1941.

Home Deptt., Government Order No. 4080, dated September 10, 1941.
Home Deptt., Government Order No. 4137, dated September 13, 1941.
Home Deptt., Government Order No. 4171, dated September 16, 1941.
Home Deptt., Government Order No. 4134, dated September 13, 1941.
Home Deptt., Government Order No. 4142, dated September 13, 1941.
Home Deptt., Government Order No. 4817, dated November 1, 1941.
Home Deptt., Government Order No. 428, dated September 25, 1941.
Home Deptt., Government Order No. 5150, dated November 26, 1941.
Home Deptt., Government Order No. 4235, dated September 23, 1941.
Home Deptt., Government Order No. 2046, dated October 20, 1941.
Home Deptt., Government Order No. 461, dated October 20, 1941.
Home Deptt., Government Order No. 4224, dated September 25, 1941.
Home Deptt., Government Order No. 5896, dated December 4, 1941.
Home Deptt., Government Order No. 5867, dated December 2, 1941.
Home Deptt., Government Order No. 5929, dated December 5, 1941.
Home Deptt., Government Order No. 315, dated January 26, 1942.
Home Deptt., Government Order No. 605, dated February 12, 1942.
Home Deptt., Government Order No. 797, dated February 27, 1942.
Home Deptt., Government Order No. 862, dated March 3, 1942.
Home Deptt., Government Order No. 956, dated March 7, 1942.
Home Deptt., Government Order No. 1056, dated March 13, 1942.
Home Deptt., Government Order No. 1195, dated March 21, 1942.
Home Deptt., Government Order No. 900, dated March 6, 1942.
Home Deptt., Government Order No. 1156, dated March 19, 1942.
Home Deptt., Government Order No. 1321, dated March 27, 1942.
Home Deptt., Government Order No. 1188, dated March 21, 1942.
Home Deptt., Government Order No. 1266, dated March 24, 1942.
Home Deptt., Government Order No. 829, dated March 2, 1942.
Home Deptt., Government Order No. 2129, dated June 10, 1942.
Home Deptt., Government Order No. 1969, dated May 30, 1942.
Home Deptt., Government Order No. 2161, dated June 13, 1942.
Home Deptt., Government Order No. 2218, dated June 18, 1942.
Home Deptt., Government Order No. 2620, dated July 20, 1942.
Home Deptt., Government Order No. 2746, dated July 30, 1942.
Home Deptt., Government Order No. 2385, dated July 1, 1942.
Home Deptt., Government Order No. 2553, dated July 14, 1942.
Home Deptt., Government Order No. 2671, dated July 24, 1942.
Home Deptt., Government Order No. 3328, dated September 11, 1942.
Home Deptt., Government Order No. 3342, dated September 11, 1942.
Home Deptt., Government Order No. 3431, dated September 19, 1942.
Home Deptt., Government Order No. 3438, dated September 19, 1942.
Home Deptt., Government Order No. 3505, dated September 25, 1942.
Home Deptt., Government Order No. 3601, dated October 3, 1942.
Home Deptt., Government Order No. 4079, dated November 2 , 1942.

Home Deptt., Government Order No. 4292, dated November 18, 1942.
Home Deptt., Government Order No. 406, dated December 28, 1942.
Home Deptt., Government Order No. 1154, dated January 2, 1943.
Home Deptt., Government Order No. 5108, dated January 15, 1943.
Home Deptt., Government Order No. 5195, dated January 30, 1943.
Home Deptt., Government Order No. 5196, dated January 30, 1943.
Home Deptt., Government Order No. 5276, dated February 12, 1943.
Home Deptt., Government Order No. 294, dated February 15, 1943.
Home Deptt., Government Order No. 3247, dated February 15, 1943.
Home Deptt., Government Order No. 5396, dated March 6, 1943.
Home Deptt., Government Order No. 5448, dated March 15, 1943.
Home Deptt., Government Order No. 5532, dated March 30, 1943.
Home Deptt., Government Order No. 5560, dated April 5, 1943.
Home Deptt., Government Order No. 5711, dated May 3, 1943.
Home Deptt., Government Order No. 5794, dated May 17, 1943.
Home Deptt., Government Order No. 5801, dated May 19, 1943.
Home Deptt., Government Order No. 5810, dated May 22, 1943.
Home Deptt., Government Order No. 1342, dated June 8, 1943.
Home Deptt., Government Order No. 1274, dated June 28, 1943.
Home Deptt., Government Order No. 1542, dated July 6, 1943.
Home Deptt., Government Order No. 1620, dated July 13, 1943.
Home Deptt., Government Order No. 1633, dated July 14, 1943.
Home Deptt., Government Order No. 1735, dated July 24, 1943.
Home Deptt., Government Order No. 2117, dated August 30, 1943.
Home Deptt., Government Order No. 2119, dated August 30, 1943.
Home Deptt., Government Order No. 2797, dated September 24, 1943.
Home Deptt., Government Order No. 2410, dated September 25, 1943.
Home Deptt., Government Order No. 2545, dated October 5, 1943.
Home Deptt., Government Order No. 2574, dated October 6, 1943.
Home Deptt., Government Order No. 2673, dated October 18, 1943.
Home Deptt., Government Order No. 2713, dated October 20, 1943.
Home Deptt., Government Order No. 2841, dated November 1, 1943.
Home Deptt., Government Order No. 2862, dated November 2, 1943.
Home Deptt., Government Order No. 2890, dated November 5, 1943.
Home Deptt., Government Order No. 3805, dated November 24, 1943.
Home Deptt., Government Order No. 3310, dated December 16, 1943.
Home Deptt., Government Order No. 3424, dated December 28, 1943.
Home Deptt., Government Order No. 3425, dated December 28, 1943.
Home Deptt., Government Order No. 65, dated January 10, 1944.
Home Deptt., Government Order No. 87, dated January 12, 1944.
Home Deptt., Government Order No. 231, dated January 26, 1944.
Home Deptt., Government Order No. 323, dated February 4, 1944.
Home Deptt., Government Order No. 360, dated February 7, 1944.
Home Deptt., Government Order No. 418, dated February 10, 1944.

Home Deptt., Government Order No. 504, dated February 17, 1944.
Home Deptt., Government Order No. 578, dated February 23, 1944.
Home Deptt., Government Order No. 583, dated February 23, 1944.
Home Deptt., Government Order No. 628, dated February 28, 1944.
Home Deptt., Government Order No. 785, dated March 13, 1944.
Home Deptt., Government Order No. 785, dated March 13, 1944.
Home Deptt., Government Order No. 1944, dated March 24, 1944.
Home Deptt., Government Order No. 981, dated March 28, 1944.
Home Deptt., Government Order No. 992, dated March 28, 1944.
Home Deptt., Government Order No. 1287, dated April 21, 1944.
Home Deptt., Government Order No. 1324, dated April 25, 1944.
Home Deptt., Government Order No. 1837, dated June 13, 1944.
Home Deptt., Government Order No. 1992, dated June 29, 1944.
Home Deptt., Government Order No. 1991, dated June 29, 1944.
Home Deptt., Government Order No. 2151, dated July 6, 1944.
Home Deptt., Government Order No. 2184, dated July 21, 1944.
Home Deptt., Government Order No. 2266, dated July 31, 1944.
Home Deptt., Government Order No. 2397, dated August 11, 1944.
Home Deptt., Government Order No. 2445, dated August 16, 1944.
Home Deptt., Government Order No. 2555, dated August 26, 1944.
Home Deptt., Government Order No. 2684, dated September 8, 1944.
Home Deptt., Government Order No. 2971, dated October 6, 1944.
Home Deptt., Government Order No. 3005, dated October 11, 1944.
Home Deptt., Government Order No. 3092, dated October 20, 1944.
Home Deptt., Government Order No. 3243, dated November 3, 1944.
Home Deptt., Government Order No. 3336, dated November 13, 1944.
Home Deptt., Government Order No. 3603, dated December 12, 1944.
Home Deptt., Government Order No. 3606, dated December 13, 1944.
Home Deptt., Government Order No. 3649, dated December 18, 1944.
Home Deptt., Government Order No. 3743, dated December 29, 1944.
Home Deptt., Government Order No. 53, dated January 6, 1945.
Home Deptt., Government Order No. 73, dated January 10, 1945.
Home Deptt., Government Order No. 350 dated February 1, 1945.
Home Deptt., Government Order No. 363, dated February 2, 1945.
Home Deptt., Government Order No. 413, dated February 7, 1945.
Home Deptt., Government Order No. 457, dated February 12, 1945.
Home Deptt., Government Order No. 557, dated February 20, 1945.
Home Deptt., Government Order No. 639, dated February 27, 1945.
Home Deptt., Government Order No. 1134 dated April 10, 1945.
Home Deptt., Government Order No. 1136, dated April 10, 1945.
Home Deptt., Government Order No. 1523, dated May 12, 1945.
Home Deptt., Government Order No. 1551, dated May 17, 1945.
Home Deptt., Government Order No. 1859, dated June 12, 1945.
Home Deptt., Government Order No. 1927, dated June 19, 1945.

Home Deptt., Government Order No. 2231, dated July 9, 1945.
Home Deptt., Government Order No. 2271, dated July 11, 1945.
Home Deptt., Government Order No. 2382, dated July 19, 1945.
Home Deptt., Government Order No. 2427, dated July 23, 1945.
Home Deptt., Government Order No. 2843, dated August 21, 1945.
Home Deptt., Government Order No. 2862, dated August 21, 1945.
Home Deptt., Government Order No. 2880 dated August 22,1945.
Home Deptt., Government Order No. 3505, dated October 1, 1945.
Home Deptt., Government Order No. 3831, dated October 23,1945.
Home Deptt., Government Order No. 3983, dated November 1, 1945.
Home Deptt., Government Order No. 4133, dated November 14, 1945.
Home Deptt., Government Order No. 4205, dated November 22, 1945.
Home Deptt., Government Order No. 4235, dated November 24, 1945.
Home Deptt., Government Order No. 4568, dated December 24, 1945.
Home Deptt., Government Order No. 7, dated January 2, 1946.
Home Deptt., Government Order No. 46, dated January 3, 1946.
Home Deptt., Government Order No. 56, dated January 14, 1946.
Home Deptt., Government Order No. 225, dated January 15, 1946.
Home Deptt., Government Order No. 183, dated January 18, 1946.
Home Deptt., Government Order No. 312, dated January 29, 1946.
Home Deptt., Government Order No. 527, dated February 5, 1946.
Home Deptt., Government Order No. 435, dated February 11, 1946.
Home Deptt., Government Order No. 493, dated February 14, 1946.
Home Deptt., Government Order No. 740, dated February 18, 1946.
Home Deptt., Government Order No. 1645, dated February 21, 1946.
Home Deptt., Government Order No. 570, dated February 22, 1946.
Home Deptt., Government Order No. 589, dated February 23, 1946.
Home Deptt., Government Order No. 911, dated February 27, 1946.
Home Deptt., Government Order No. 699, dated March 6, 1946.
Home Deptt., Government Order No. 1146, dated March 9, 1946.
Home Deptt., Government Order No. 1052, dated March 12, 1946.
Home Deptt., Government Order No. 836, dated March 19, 1946.
Home Deptt., Government Order No. 1162, dated March 19, 1946.
Home Deptt., Government Order No. 950, dated March 29, 1946.
Home Deptt., Government Order No. 1023, dated April 4, 1946.
Home Deptt., Government Order No. 1117, dated April 11, 1946.
Home Deptt., Government Order No. 1153, dated April 15, 1946.
Home Deptt., Government Order No. 1645, dated April 24, 1946.
Home Deptt., Government Order No. 1376, dated May 3, 1946.
Home Deptt., Government Order No. 1434, dated May 8, 1946.
Home Deptt., Government Order No. 1927, dated May 14, 1946.
Home Deptt., Government Order No. 1563, dated May 20, 1946.
Home Deptt., Government Order No. 1744, dated June 10, 1946.
Home Deptt., Government Order No. 2459, dated, June 24, 1946.

Home Deptt., Government Order No. 2531, dated June 28, 1946.
Home Deptt., Government Order No. 2536, dated June 28, 1946.
Home Deptt., Government Order No. 2357, dated August 10, 1946.
Home Deptt., Government Order No. 2931, dated July 30, 1946.
Home Deptt., Government Order No. 2537, dated August 28, 1946.
Home Deptt., Government Order No. 2550, dated August 31, 1946.
Home Deptt., Government Order No. 3183, dated August 19, 1946.
Home Deptt., Government Order No. 2612, dated September 4, 1946.
Home Deptt., Government Order No. 3394, dated, September 4, 1946.
Home Deptt., Government Order No. 3411, dated October 20, 1946.
Home Deptt., Government Order No. 3494, dated September 12, 1946.
Home Deptt., Government Order No. 3594, dated September 20, 1946.
Home Deptt., Government Order No. 4214, dated November 12, 1946.
Home Deptt., Government Order No.355, dated November 14, 1946.
Home Deptt., Government Order No.4297, dated November 20, 1946.
Home Deptt., Government Order No. 4511, dated December 6, 1946.
Home Deptt., Government Order No. 3858, dated December 6, 1946.
Home Deptt., Government Order No. 3935, dated December 11, 1946.
Home Deptt., Government Order No. 357, dated January 27, 1947.
Home Deptt., Government Order No. 739, dated February 24, 1947.
Home Deptt., Government Order No. 878, dated March 6, 1947.
Home Deptt., Government Order No. 1126, dated, March 20, 1947.
Home Deptt., Government Order No. 2956, dated, July 28, 1947.
Home Deptt., Government Order No. 3488, dated September 10, 1947.
Home Deptt., Government Order No. 762, dated February 28, 1948.
Home Deptt., Government Order No. 1050, dated March 20, 1948.
Home Deptt., Government Order No. 1669, dated April 5, 1948.
Home Deptt., Government Order No. 2088, dated April 26, 1948.
Home Deptt., Government Order No. 2136, dated April 28, 1948.
Home Deptt., Government Order No. 1614, dated May 1, 1948.
Home Deptt., Government Order No. 1615, dated May 1, 1948.
Home Deptt., Government Order No. 1682, dated May 5, 1948.
Home Deptt., Government Order No. 1755, dated May 8, 1948.
Home Deptt., Government Order No. 3413, dated June 25, 1948.
Home Deptt., Government Order No. 2803, dated July 21, 1948.
Home Deptt., Government Order No. 2809, dated July 22, 1948.
Home Deptt., Government Order No. 2969, dated August 3, 1948.
Home Deptt., Government Order No. 3493, dated September 17, 1948.
Home Deptt., Government Order No. 3956, dated October 26, 1948.
Home Deptt., Government Order No. 4041, dated October 29, 1948.
Home Deptt., Government Order No. 4288, dated November 22, 1948.
Home Deptt., Government Order No. 4440, dated December 2, 1948.
Home Deptt., Government Order No. 223, dated January 19, 1949.
Home Deptt., Government Order No. 275, dated January 24, 1949.

Home Deptt., Government Order No. 295, dated January 26, 1949.
Home Deptt., Government Order No. 1485, dated March 21, 1949.
Home Deptt., Government Order No. 2347, dated May 2, 1949.
Home Deptt., Government Order No. 2355, dated May 3, 1949.
Home Deptt., Government Order No. 3115, dated June 10, 1949.
Home Deptt., Government Order No. 4227, dated August 16, 1949.
Home Deptt., Government Order No. 4277, dated August 19, 1949.
Home Deptt., Government Order No. 37, dated January 4, 1950.
Home Deptt., Government Order No. 42, dated January 5, 1950.
Home Deptt., Government Order No. 103, dated January 7, 1950.
Home Deptt., Government Order No. 371, dated January 28, 1950.
Home Deptt., Government Order No. 580, dated February 13, 1950.
Home Deptt., Government Order No. 708, dated February 22, 1950.
Home Deptt., Government Order No. 737, dated February 24, 1950.
Home Deptt., Government Order No. 756, dated February 25, 1950.
Home Deptt., Government Order No. 870, dated March 2, 1950.
Home Deptt., Government Order No. 1155, dated March 21, 1950.
Home Deptt., Government Order No. 1234, dated March 27, 1950.
Home Deptt., Government Order No. 1305, dated March 25, 1950
Home Deptt., Government Order No. 1344, dated March 28, 1950.
Home Deptt., Government Order No. 1434, dated April 11, 1950.
Home Deptt., Government Order No. 1632, dated April 24, 1950.
Home Deptt., Government Order No. 1834, dated May 5, 1950.
Home Deptt., Government Order No. 2237, dated May 13, 1950.
Home Deptt., Government Order No. 2210, dated May 12, 1950.
Home Deptt., Government Order No. 2205, dated June 1, 1950.
Home Deptt., Government Order No. 2595, dated June 30, 1950.
Home Deptt., Government Order No. 3201, dated August 16, 1950.
Home Deptt., Government Order No. 3396, dated August 29, 950.
Home Deptt., Government Order No. 3907, dated September 5, 1950.
Home Deptt., Government Order No. 4932, dated December 4, 1950.
Home Deptt., Government Order No. 5266, dated December 11, 1950.
Home Deptt., Government Order No. 938, dated March 9, 1951.
Home Deptt., Government Order No. 3085, dated August 2, 1951.
Home Deptt., Government Order No. 3377, dated August 24, 1951.
Home Deptt., Government Order No. 4119, dated October 25, 1951.
Home Deptt., Government Order No. 707, dated February 22, 1952.
Home Deptt., Government Order No. 2489, dated July 10, 1952 .
Home Deptt., Government Order No. 2900, dated August 8, 1952.
Home Deptt., Government Order No. 28, dated January 3, 1951.
Home Deptt., Government Order No. 305, dated January 22, 1951.
Home Deptt., Government Order No. 417, dated January 27, 1951.
Home Deptt., Government Order No. 459, dated January 30, 1951.
Home Deptt., Government Order No. 750, dated February 19, 1951.

Home Deptt., Government Order No. 751, dated February 19, 1951.
Home Deptt., Government Order No. 1003, dated March 9, 1951.
Home Deptt., Government Order No. 1449, dated March 31, 1951.
Home Deptt., Government Order No. 1659, dated April 12, 1951.
Home Deptt., Government Order No. 2047, dated May 7, 1951.
Home Deptt., Government Order No. 3977, dated September 4, 1951.
Home Deptt., Government Order No. 4327, dated September 28, 1951.
Home Deptt., Government Order No. 4504, dated October 11, 1951.
Home Deptt., Government Order No. 4569, dated October 17, 1951.
Home Deptt., Government Order No. 4655, dated October 22, 1951.
Home Deptt., Government Order No. 4780, dated October 27, 1951.
Home Deptt., Government Order No. 613, dated February 9, 1953.
Home Deptt., Government Order No. 815, dated February 23, 1953.
Home Deptt., Government Order No. 816, dated February 23, 1953.
Home Deptt., Government Order No. 955, dated March 2, 1953.
Home Deptt., Government Order No. 977, dated March 3, 1953.
Home Deptt., Government Order No. 1438, dated March 27, 1953.
Home Deptt., Government Order No. 1453, dated March 28, 1953.
Home Deptt., Government Order No. 2544, dated May 30, 1953.
Home Deptt., Government Order No. 2770, dated June 15, 1953.
Home Deptt., Government Order No. 1985, dated August 11, 1953
Home Deptt., Government Order No. 2008, dated August 13, 1953
Home Deptt., Government Order No. 1503, dated August 1953.
Home Deptt., Government Order No. 2124, dated August 25, 1953.
Home Deptt., Government Order No. 5576, dated December 31, 1953.

Judicial Deptt.,

Judicial Deptt., Government Order No.178-179, dated March 16, 1869.
Judicial Deptt., Government Order No. 1-2, dated April 3, 1871.
Judicial Deptt., Government Order No. 2930, dated July 4, 1871.
Judicial Deptt., Government Order No. 84-85, dated April 18, 1871.
Judicial Deptt., Government Order No. 162-163, dated June 27, 1871.
Judicial Deptt., Government Order No. 216-217, dated August 21, 1871.
Judicial Deptt., Government Order No. 181-182, dated April 22, 1872.
Judicial Deptt., Government Order No. 73-76, dated August 17, 1872.
Judicial Deptt., Government Order No. 54-66, dated October 18, 1872.
Judicial Deptt., Government Order No. 61, dated February 5, 1874.
Judicial Deptt., Government Order No. 94-96, dated April 17, 1874.
Judicial Deptt., Government Order No. 84-85, dated April 18, 1874.
Judicial Deptt., Government Order No. 89-92, dated May 17, 1874.
Judicial Deptt., Government Order No. 57, dated June 11, 1874.
Judicial Deptt., Government Order No. 183-184, dated June 27, 1874.
Judicial Deptt., Government Order No. 107-109, dated June 28, 1874.
Judicial Deptt., Government Order No. 119-120, dated August 22, 1874.
Judicial Deptt., Government Order No. 14-15, dated September 5, 1874.

Judicial Deptt., Government Order No. 63-65, dated September 9, 1874.
Judicial Deptt., Government Order No. 99-100, dated September 14, 1874.
Judicial Deptt., Government Order No. 84-86, dated September 20, 1874.
Judicial Deptt., Government Order No. 127-130, dated September 21, 1874.
Judicial Deptt., Government Order No. 73-74, dated November 19, 1874.
Judicial Deptt., Government Order No. 24, dated December 2, 1874.
Judicial Deptt., Government Order No. 142-165, dated December 19, 1874.
Judicial Deptt., Government Order No. 235-241, dated June 24, 1879.
Judicial Deptt., Government Order No. 136-137, dated September 16, 1879.
Judicial Deptt., Government Order No. 75-76, dated October 10, 1879.
Judicial Deptt., Government Order No. 1506-1507, dated June 17, 1883.
Judicial Deptt., Government Order No. 13, dated January 6, 1891.
Judicial Deptt., Government Order No. 630, dated June 15, 1891.
Judicial Deptt., Government Order No. 1334, dated June 30, 1891.
Judicial Deptt., Government Order No. 141, dated January 19, 1893.
Judicial Deptt., Government Order No. 1271, dated January 19, 1893.
Judicial Deptt., Government Order No. 1302, dated April 6, 1893.
Judicial Deptt., Government Order No. 1718, dated April 6, 1893.
Judicial Deptt., Government Order No. 743, dated April 10, 1893.
Judicial Deptt., Government Order No. 900-901, dated June 11, 1893.
Judicial Deptt., Government Order No. 969-970, dated June 23, 1893.
Judicial Deptt., Government Order No. 1581, dated August 9, 1893.
Judicial Deptt., Government Order No. 2109, dated October 10, 1893.
Judicial Deptt., Government Order No. 554, dated April 3, 1905.
Judicial Deptt., Government Order No. 2000-01 dated, 3.12.1912.
Judicial Deptt., Government Order No. 896, dated 8.5.1913.
Judicial Deptt., Government Order No. 1897, dated 15.9.1914.
Judicial Deptt., Government Order No. 526, dated 25.2.1916.
Judicial Deptt., Government Order No. 637, dated March 6, 1916.
Judicial Deptt., Government Order No. 629, dated 8.3.1916.
Judicial Deptt., Government Order No. 1313, dated May 20, 1916.
Judicial Deptt., Government Order No. 1569, dated 17.6.1916.
Judicial Deptt., Government Order No. 2764, dated 23.11.1916.
Judicial Deptt., Government Order No. 513, dated March 10, 1918.
Judicial Deptt., Government Order No. 1588, dated July 27, 1919.
Judicial Deptt., Government Order No. 2294, dated October 7, 1919.
Judicial Deptt., Government Order No. 21, dated January 4, 1919.
Judicial Deptt., Government Order No. 166, dated February 10, 1919.
Judicial Deptt., Government Order No. 2775, dated November 29, 1919.
Judicial Deptt., Government Order No. 2996, dated December 20, 1919.
Judicial Deptt., Government Order No. 376, dated February 13, 1919.
Judicial Deptt., Government Order No. 448, dated February 24, 1919.
Judicial Deptt., Government Order No. 474, dated February 27, 1919.
Judicial Deptt., Government Order No. 518, dated March 6, 1919.

Judicial Deptt., Government Order No. 197, dated January 28, 1919.
Judicial Deptt., Government Order No. 546, dated March 11, 1919
Judicial Deptt., Government Order No. 730, dated March 31, 1919.
Judicial Deptt., Government Order No. 565, dated March 11, 1919.
Judicial Deptt., Government Order No. 667, dated March 24, 1919.
Judicial Deptt., Government Order No. 594, dated March 13, 1919.
Judicial Deptt., Government Order No. 377, dated February13, 1919.
Judicial Deptt., Government Order No. 759, dated April 3, 1919.
Judicial Deptt., Government Order No. 2607, dated November 10, 1919.
Judicial Deptt., Government Order No. 1085, dated May 15, 1919.
Judicial Deptt., Government Order No. 1022, dated May 8, 1919.
Judicial Deptt., Government Order No. 1168, dated May 22, 1919.
Judicial Deptt., Government Order No. 898, dated April 24, 1919.
Judicial Deptt., Government Order No. 1468, dated June 27, 1919.
Judicial Deptt., Government Order No. 1610, dated June 16, 1919.
Judicial Deptt., Government Order No. 1147, dated March 22, 1919.
Judicial Deptt., Government Order No. 1337, dated June 11, 1919.
Judicial Deptt., Government Order No. 1093, dated May 16, 1919.
Judicial Deptt., Government Order No. 1640, dated, June 20, 1919
Judicial Deptt., Government Order No. 1314, dated June 12, 1919.
Judicial Deptt., Government Order No. 1427, dated June 21, 1919.
Judicial Deptt., Government Order No. 195, dated February 14, 1919.
Judicial Deptt., Government Order No. 1651, dated July 19, 1919.
Judicial Deptt., Government Order No. 1798, dated August 9, 1919.
Judicial Deptt., Government Order No. 1649, dated July 19, 1919.
Judicial Deptt., Government Order No. 1930, dated August 25, 1919.
Judicial Deptt., Government Order No. 2025, dated September 6, 1919.
Judicial Deptt., Government Order No. 1567, dated July 11, 1919.
Judicial Deptt., Government Order No. 1804, dated August 16, 1919.
Judicial Deptt., Government Order No. 2370, dated October 20, 1919.
Judicial Deptt., Government Order No. 2402, dated October 21, 1919.
Judicial Deptt., Government Order No. 1766, dated August 5, 1919.
Judicial Deptt., Government Order No. 2293, dated October 7, 1919.
Judicial Deptt., Government Order No. 2443, dated October 24, 1919.
Judicial Deptt., Government Order No. 2497, dated October 29, 1919.
Judicial Deptt., Government Order No. 2695, dated November 21, 1919.
Judicial Deptt., Government Order No. 2774, dated November 29, 1919.
Judicial Deptt., Government Order No. 2493, dated October 29, 1919.
Judicial (Police) Deptt., Government Order No. 51, dated January 31, 1923.
Judicial (Police) Deptt., Government Order No. 52, dated January 31, 1923.
Judicial (Police) Deptt., Government Order No. 70, dated February 17, 1923.
Judicial (Police) Deptt., Government Order No. 71, dated February 17, 1923.
Judicial (Police) Deptt., Government Order No. 72, dated February 17, 1923.
Judicial (Police) Deptt., Government Order No. 95, dated February 27, 1923.

Judicial (Police) Deptt., Government Order No. 656, dated March 13, 1923.
Judicial (Police) Deptt., Government Order No. 117, dated March 13, 1923.
Judicial (Police) Deptt., Government Order No. 121-122, dated March 24, 1923.
Judicial (Police)Deptt., Government Order No. 131-32, dated March 26, 1923.
Judicial (Police) Deptt., Government Order No. 142, dated April 2, 1923.
Judicial (Police) Deptt., Government Order No. 24, dated May 21, 1923.
Judicial (Police) Deptt., Government Order No. 344, dated July 12, 1923.
Judicial (Police) Deptt., Government Order No. 357, dated July 17, 1923.
Judicial (Police) Deptt., Government Order No. 377, dated July 26, 1923.
Judicial (Police) Deptt., Government Order No. 379, dated August 3, 923.
Judicial (Police) Deptt., Government Order No. 396, dated August 3, 1923.
Judicial (Police) Deptt., Government Order No. 334, dated August 8, 1923.
Judicial (Police) Deptt., Government Order No.450, dated August 30, 1923.
Judicial (Police) Deptt., Government Order No. 499, dated September 18, 1923.
Judicial (Police) Deptt., Government Order No. 407, dated October 2, 1923.
Judicial (Police) Deptt., Government Order No. 409, dated October 3, 1923.
Judicial (Police) Deptt., Government Order No. 126, dated October 14, 1923.
Judicial (Police) Deptt., Government Order No. 448, dated October 29, 1923.
Judicial (Police) Deptt., Government Order No. 581, dated October 30, 1923.
Judicial (Police) Deptt., Government Order No. 582, dated October 30, 1923.
Judicial (Police) Deptt., Government Order No. 585, dated November 2, 1923.
Judicial (Police) Deptt., Government Order No. 623, dated November 28, 1923.
Judicial (Police) Deptt., Government Order No. 499, dated December 4, 1923.
Judicial (Police) Deptt., Government Order No. 665, dated December 18, 1923.
Judicial Deptt., Government Order No. 63, dated January 12, 1928.
Judicial Deptt., Government Order No. 218-219, dated January 26, 1928.
Judicial Deptt., Government Order No. 81, dated February 13, 1928.
Judicial Deptt., Government Order No. 398-399, dated February 13, 1928.
Judicial Deptt., Government Order No. 662 dated March 7, 1928.
Judicial Deptt., Government Order No. 248, dated March 13, 1928.
Judicial Deptt., Government Order No. 1455 dated June 2, 1928.
Judicial Deptt., Government Order No. 307, dated June 14, 1928.
Judicial Deptt., Government Order No. 346, dated July 7, 1928.
Judicial Deptt., Government Order No. 2126 dated August 13, 1928.
Judicial Deptt., Government Order No. 2326, dated August 31, 1928.
Judicial Deptt., Government Order No. 467, dated September 25, 1928.
Judicial Deptt., Government Order No. 1523, dated July 30, 1928.
Judicial Deptt., Government Order No. 517, dated October 22, 1928.
Judicial Deptt., Government Order No. 167, dated April 1, 1929.
Judicial Deptt., Government Order No. 200, dated April 1, 1929.
Judicial Deptt., Government Order No. 193, dated April 12, 1929.
Judicial Deptt., Government Order No. 203-04, dated April 8, 1929.
Judicial Deptt., Government Order No. 410, dated August 4, 1929.
Judicial Deptt., Government Order No. 500, dated September 2, 1929.

Judicial Deptt., Government Order No. 562, dated October 23, 1929.
Judicial Deptt., Government Order No. 46, dated January 27, 1934.
Judicial Deptt., Government Order No. 165, dated April 5, 1934.
Judicial Deptt., Government Order No. 285, dated June 14, 1934.
Judicial Deptt., Government Order No. 329, dated July 10, 1934.
Judicial Deptt., Government Order No. 432-433, dated September 1934.
Judicial Deptt., Government Order No. 501, dated October 16, 1934.
Judicial Deptt., Government Order No. 506, dated October 22, 1934.
Judicial Deptt., Government Order No. 170, dated March 23, 1935.
Judicial Deptt., Government Order No. 242, dated April 27, 1935.
Judicial Deptt., Government Order No. 265, dated May 1, 1935.
Judicial Deptt., Government Order No. 304, dated May 31, 1935.
Judicial Deptt., Government Order No. 267-268, dated June 10, 1935.
Judicial Deptt., Government Order No. 339, dated June 24, 1935.
Judicial Deptt., Government Order No. 349, dated June 27, 1935.
Judicial Deptt., Government Order No. 478, dated September 6, 1935.
Judicial Deptt., Government Order No. 479, dated September 6, 1935.
Judicial Deptt., Government Order No. 505, dated September 19, 1935.
Judicial Deptt., Government Order No. 643, dated November 28, 1935.
Judicial Deptt., Government Order No. 163, dated December 23, 1935.
Judicial Deptt., Government Order No. 694, dated December 23, 1935.

PUBLIC WORKS (LABOUR) DEPTT.,

Public Works (Labour) Deptt., Govt. Order No. 64-65, dated January 11, 1929.
Public Works (Labour) Deptt., Govt. Order No. 144, dated January 21, 1929.
Public Works (Labour) Deptt., Govt. Order No. 196, dated January 24, 1929.
Public Works (Labour) Deptt., Govt. Order No. 856, dated March 5, 1929.
Public Works (Labour) Deptt., Govt. Order No. 778, dated March 5, 1929.
Public Works (Labour) Deptt., Govt. Order No. 970, dated March 21, 1929.
Public Works (Labour) Deptt., Govt. Order No. 1106, dated April 5, 1929.
Public Works (Labour) Deptt., Govt.Order No. 1184, dated April 12, 1929.
Public Works (Labour) Deptt., Govt. Order No. 1313, dated April 29, 1929.
Public Works (Labour) Deptt., Govt. Order No. 1373, dated May 3, 1929.
Public Works (Labour) Deptt., Govt. Order No. 1648, dated June 5, 1929.
Public Works (Labour) Deptt., Govt. Order No. 1831-32, dated June 19, 1929.
Public Works (Labour) Deptt., Govt. Order No. 1856, dated June 25, 1929.
Public Works (Labour) Deptt., Govt. Order No. 225, dated June 26, 1929.
Public Works (Labour) Deptt., Govt. Order No. 1925, dated July 4, 1929.
Public Works (Labour) Deptt., Govt. Order No. 1975-76, dated July 10, 1929.
Public Works (Labour) Deptt., Govt. Order No. 1997, dated July 10, 1929.
Public Works (Labour) Deptt., Govt. Order No. 2038, dated July 22, 1929.
Public Works (Labour) Deptt., Govt. Order No. 2142, dated July 31, 1929.
Public Works (Labour) Deptt., Govt. Order No. 2395, dated August 22, 1929.
Public Works (Labour) Deptt., Govt. Order No. 2542, dated Sept. 5, 1929.

Public Works (Labour) Deptt., Govt. Order No. 2394, dated August 23, 1929.
Public Works (Labour) Deptt., Govt. Order No. 2543, dated Sept. 5, 1929.
Public Works (Labour)Deptt., Govt. Order No. 2541, dated September 5, 1929.
Public Works (Labour) Deptt., Govt. Order No. 2531, dated September 5, 1929.
Public Works (Labour) Deptt., Govt. Order No. 2627, dated Sept.16, 1929.
Public Works(Labour) Deptt., Govt. Order No. 144, dated September 21, 1929.
Public Works (Labour) Deptt., Govt. Order No. 2782, dated October 4, 1929.
Public Works (Labour) Deptt., Govt. Order No. 2717, dated Sept. 26, 1929.
Public Works (Labour) Deptt., Govt. Order No. 2841, dated October 8, 1929.
Public Works (Labour) Deptt., Govt. Order No. 2864, dated October 10, 1929.
Public Works (Labour) Deptt., Govt. Order No. 3132, dated Nov. 2, 1929.
Public Works (Labour) Deptt., Govt. Order No. 3139, dated Nov. 2, 1929.
Public Works (Labour) Deptt., Govt. Order No. 3281, dated Nov. 13, 1929.
Public Works (Labour) Deptt., Govt. Order No. 3499, dated Nov. 30, 1929.
Public Works (Labour) Deptt., Govt. Order No. 3675, dated Dec. 19, 1929.
Public Works (Labour) Deptt., Govt. Order No. 94, dated January 10, 1930.
Public Works (Labour) Deptt., Govt. Order No. 208, dated January 24, 1930.
Public Works (Labour) Deptt., Govt. Order No. 323, dated February 1, 1930.
Public Works (Labour) Deptt., Govt. Order No. 670, dated February 24, 1930.
Public Works (Labour) Deptt., Govt. Order No. 837-38, dated March 13, 1930.
Public Works (Labour) Deptt., Govt. Order No. 868, dated March 15, 1930.
Public Works (Labour) Deptt., Govt. Order No. 1112, dated April 3, 1930.
Public Works (Labour)Deptt., Govt.Order No. 1115, dated April 4, 1930.
Public Works (Labour) Deptt., Govt. Order No. 1264, dated April 23, 1930.
Public Works (Labour) Deptt., Govt. Order No. 1524, dated May 22, 1930.
Public Works (Labour) Deptt., Govt. Order No. 1708, dated June 9, 1930.
Public Works (Labour) Deptt., Govt. Order No. 2001, dated July 9, 1930.
Public Works (Labour) Deptt., Govt. Order No. 2000, dated July 9, 1930.
Public Works (Labour) Deptt., Govt. Order No. 2076, dated July 17, 1930.
Public Works (Labour) Deptt., Govt. Order No. 2169, dated July 25, 1930.
Public Works (Labour) Deptt., Govt. Order No. 2307, dated August 13, 1930.
Public Works (Labour) Deptt., Govt. Order No. 2830, dated October 6, 1930
Public Works (Labour) Deptt., Govt. Order No. 2886, dated October 11, 1930.
Public Works (Labour) Deptt., Govt. Order No. 1099, dated October 28, 1930.
Public Works (Labour) Deptt., Govt. Order No. 3410, dated December 3, 1930.
Public Works (Labour) Deptt., Govt. Order No. 3433, dated December 8, 1930.
Public Works (Labour) Deptt., Govt. Order No. 557, dated March 12, 1940.
Public Works (Labour) Deptt., Govt. Order No. 631, dated May 27, 1940.
Public Works Deptt., Govt. Order No. 1826, dated September 14, 1940.
Public Works Deptt., Government Order No. 246, dated April 23, 1943
Public Works Deptt., Government Order No. 379, dated April 30, 1943
Public Works Deptt., Government Order No. 369, dated May 1, 1943.
Public Works Deptt., Government Order No. 734, dated May 27, 1943.
Public Works Deptt., Government Order No. 738, dated May 27, 1936.

Public Works Deptt., Government Order No. 919, dated June 10, 1943.
Public Works Deptt., Government Order No. 2034, dated July 21, 1943
Public Works Deptt., Government Order No. 2157, dated September 7, 1943.
Public Works Deptt., Government Order No. 2493, dated September 30, 1943.
Public Works Deptt., Government Order No. 2494, dated September 30, 1943.
Public Works Deptt., Government Order No. 2547, dated October 3, 1943.
Public Works Deptt., Government Order No. 2882, dated October 26, 1943.
Public Works Deptt., Government Order No. 3615, dated December 12, 1943.

SECONDARY SOURCES

Achariar, M.C. Tiruvenkata, *History of the Aziznagar Settlement*, Dass Press, Viriddhachalam, 1926.

Agarwal, B.C., *Yanadi : Response to Change*, Concept Publishing Company, New Delhi, 1985.

Aiyappan, A., *Report on the Socio-Economic Conditions of the Aboriginal Tribes of the Province of Madras*, Government Press, Madras, 1948.

Aiyappan, A., "Beggary in India: An Experiment in the Rehabilitation of a Beggar caste", in *International Journal of Asian Studies, Vol. I*, 1981.

Aiyar, K.B., "Tribal Welfare in Andhra Pradesh", *Kurukshetra*, 1914, 1 :12, 1970.

Aiyar, C.P., Ramasami, *District Problems, Home Rule Series No. 17*, Commonwealth Office, Adayar, Madras, 1916.

Khan, S. Akbar, "Power, Police and Public", *Kurukshetra, 1983*.

Alexander, R.R., Prasad, M.P., Jahangirdar, *Tribals' Rehabilitation and Development*, Jaipur, 1991.

Ambedkar, B.R., *'What Congress and Gandhi have done to the Untouchables'*, Bombay, 1946.

Ambedkar, B.R., *Annihilation of Caste*, Bombay, 1936.

Ambedkar, B.R., *Mr. Gandhi and the Emancipation of Untouchables*, Bombay, 1943.

Ambedkar, B.R., *The Untouchables – Who were they and why they became untouchables*, Amrit Book Company, New Delhi, 1948.

Ambedkar, B.R., *Who Were the Sudras - how they came to be Fourth Varna in the Indo-Aryan Society*, Thacker and Company, Bombay, 1946.

Ambirajan, S., 'Political Economy and Indian Famines', *South Asian Studies, No. 1*, August 1971.

Ambirajan, S., 'Laissez Faire in Madras, *Indian Economic and Social History Review, Vol. II, No. 3, July 1966*.

Ambrose, Stephen E., *Undaunted Courage*, Touchstone, New York, 1997.

Anderson, G.A., *Administration Report of Hyderabad District Police for the year ending 1946*, Government Press, Hyderabad, 1947.

Anderson, J.D., *People of India*, Cambridge, 1913.

Andhra Rashtra Adimjati Sevak Sangh, 'Karu Chikatilo Kanti Rekha: Mana Sangham', (Telugu Pamphlet) Vijayawada, 1985.

Ansari, M.A., *Tribals in Criminal Web*, Publication Scheme, Jaipur, 1987.

Anthrolikar, K.B., *Report of the Ex-Criminal Tribes Rehabilitation Committee*, November, 1950, Government Central Press, Bombay, 1951.

Apte, J.S., 'Talwada Ashram School - An Experiment in Tribal Education', *Vanyajati, Vol. VIII, No.2, 1960.*

Arbuthnot, A.J. (ed), *Sir Thomas Munro, Governor of Madras: Selections from his minutes and other Official Writings*, Vol. II, London, 1881.

Arensberg, Conrad, 'The Community Study Methods', *American Journal of Sociology*, September, 1954.

Arnold, David, 'European Orphans and Vagrants in India in the Nineteenth Century', The *Journal of Imperial and Commonwealth History*, Vol. VII, 1979.

Arnold, David., 'Industrial Violence in Colonial India', *Comprehensive Studies in Society and History*, Vol. XXII, 1980.

Arnold, David., 'Labour Relations in a South Indian Sugar Factory, 1937-39', *Social Scientist*, Vol. 65, 1997.

Arnold, David., Looting - Grain Riots and Government policy in South India, 1918', *Past and Present*, Vol. 84, 1979.

Arnold, David, 'Rebellious Hillmen: The Gudem-Rampa Risings, 1839-1924', in Ranajit Guha (ed) *Subaltern Studies*, Vol. I, Delhi, 1984.

Arnold, David, 'The Armed Police and Colonial Rule in South India, 1914-47', *Modern Asian Studies*, Vol. XI, 1977.

Arnold, David, 'Dacoity and Rural Crime in Madras, 1860-1940', *The Journal of Peasant Studies*, Vol. 6, No. 2, January 1979.

Arnold, David, '*Femine: Social Crisis and Historical Change*', Oxford, Basil Blackwell, 1988.

Arnold, David, *Police Power and Colonial Rule*, Madras 1859-1947, Oxford University, Press, Delhi, 1986.

Arnold, David, 'Bureaucratic Recruitment and Subordination in Colonial India: The Madras Constabulary 1859-1947,' in Ranajit Guha (ed) *Subaltern Studies Vol. IV: Writing on South Asian History and Society*, OUP, Delhi, 1985.

Arthur, T.C., *Reminiscences of an Indian Official*, London, 1891.

Asad, Talal, 'The Beduin as a Military Force: Notes on some aspects of power relations between nomads and sedentaries in historical perspective' in Cynthia Nelson (ed), *The Desert and the Sown: Nomads in the Wider Society*, Berkeley: Institute of International Studies, U.C. Berkeley, 1973.

Avanesov, F.G., *The Principles of Criminology*, Moscow, 1981.

Azeez Sahed, S.A., and Ghousia Begum, S. "Struggle Against Starvation: A Study of the Yanadi Food Getting Techniques', *Man in India*, Vol. 70, No. 2, 169 : 84.

Bailey, F.G., *Caste and Economic Frontier*, Manchestor: Manchestor University Press, 1957.

Bailey, F.G., *Tribe, Caste and Nation*, Manchester: University of Manchester, 1960.

Bailey, F.G., *Tribe and Caste in India, Contributions to Indian Sociology*, The Hague, 1961.

Bailey, F.G., *Closed Stratification in India, European Journal of Social Science*, 1(3) : 107-24.

Bailey, V., 'Salvation Army riots, the "Skeleton Army" and Legal Authority in the Provincial Town' in A.P. Donajgrodziki (ed.), *Social Control in Nineteenth Century Britain*, Croom Helm, 1977.

Baines, A., *Ethnography (Tribes and Castes)*, Strass Barg, 1912.

Baird, W., Bramwell, *The Call of the Jackals, Salvation Army Archives*, London, n.d.

Baker, C.J., *An Indian Rural Economy, 1880-1955: The Tamilnadu Countryside*, Oxford University Press, New Delhi, 1984.

Baker, C.J., and Washbrook, D. (eds), *South India: Political Institutions and Political Change, 1880-1940*, Delhi, 1975.

Baker, C.J., 'Madras Headmen', in K.N., Chaudhuri and C.J., Dewey (eds), *Economy and Society: Essays in Indian Economic and Social History*, OUP, Delhi, 1979.

Baldev, Raj Nayar, *Violence and Crime in India*, Delhi, 1975.

Baldwin, john. D., *Prehistoric Nations*, New York, 1869.

Barnes and Teeters, *New Horizons in Criminology*, Prentice Hall, U.S.A., 1951.

Barth, Frederick, *Nomads of South Persia-the Basseri Tribe of Khamesh Confederacy*, Oslo University Press, Oslo, 1961.

Barth Fredrik,"Ecologic relationship of ethnic groups in Swat, North Pakistan", in '*Man in Adaptation*', ed. by Cohen, A., Yehudi, Aldine Publishing company, Chicago, 1968.

Basak, Radha Govinda, "The Hindu Concept of The Natural World", in 'The religion of Hindu', ed. by Morgan, W. Kenneth, The Ronald Press, New York, 1953.

Beteille, Andre, *The Definition of a Tribe, Caste and Religion*. (ed), Romesh Thaper, Meerut, 1977.

Beteille, Andre, *Caste, Class and Power, Changing patterns of stratification in a Tanjore village*, Los Angeles, University of California Press, 1965.

Beteile, Andre, *Castes, Old and New, Essays in Social Structure and Social Stratification*, New York, 1969.

Beteille, Andre, 'The Indian Village: Past and Present', in E.J. Hobsbawm et al. (eds), *Peasants in History*, Calcutta, 1980.

Beteille, Andre, *Inequality and Social Change*, Oxford University Press, New Delhi, 1972.

Beteille, Andre and Madan, T.N., Encounter and Experience, Vikas Publishing House, New Delhi, 1975.

Beteille, Andre, *The backward classes and the new social order*, OUP, 1981.

Baugh, Commr *The Criminal Tribes Work in India : an Economic Experiment,* Salvation Army Archives, International Heritage Centre, London, 1930.

Bawden, S.D., Yerukula Industrial Settlement, Kavali, 1919-1920, *Indian Jails Committee, Vol. 2 and 3,* written statement (TNA).

Baxi, U., *The Crisis of the Indian Legal System,* New Delhi, 1982.

Bayley, D.H., *The Police and Political Development in India,* Princeton, University Press, 1969.

Beaglehole, T.H., *Thomas Munro and the Development of Administrative Policy in Madras, 1792-1818: The origins of the Munro System,* Cambridge, 1966.

Bearce, G.D., *British Attitude Towards India,* 1784-1858, London, 1967.

Beattie, John, 'The Pattern of Crime in England 1600-1800', *Past and Present, No. 72, 1974.*

Begbie, Harold, *Twice-Born Men, A Clinic in Regeneration,* New York, n.d.

Begbie, Harold, *Other Sheep, A Study of the people of India with particular reference to collision between Christianity and Hinduism,* London, 1909.

Beier, A.L., 'Vagrants and the Social Order in Elizabethan England', *Past and Present, 64, 1974.*

Benedict, Ruth, *Race and Racism,* London, 1951.

Bensman, Vidich and Stein (ed), *Reflections on Community Studies,* New York, John Wiley and Sons, Inc., 1964.

Betham, G.K., *The Story of Dacoity and Lolapur Week,* London, 1893.

Bhupendra Singh and Bhandari, J.S., *The Tribal World and Its Transformation,* New Delhi, 1980.

Bhartiya Adimjati Sevak Sangh, 'Origin of Sansis', The Report of the 5th Conference for Tribes and Tribal Areas, held at Boadi, *Bombay, January 1959, BASS, Delhi, 1960.*

Bhartiya Adimjati Sevak Sangh (BASS), *Monthly Letters of Bharatiya Adimjati Sevak Sangh,* New Delhi, 1949.

Bhartiya Adimjati Sevak Sangh (BASS), *Report on the work of the Sangh and its Affiliated Institutions during the period, October 1948 to October 1949,* Bhartiya Adimjati Sevak Sangh, New Delhi, 1950.

Bhartiya Adimjati Sevak Sangh, 'A Plea for Gypsy and Denotified Tribes', *Tribal Souvenir,* December 1963, New Delhi.

Bharatiya Adimjati Sevak Sangh (BASS), *Tour in Hyerabad, Pamphlet No. 11,* Adimjati Sevak Sangh, New Delhi, 1950.

Bhardwaj, R.K., *Urban Development in India,* Delhi, 1974.

Bhargava, B.S., *The Criminal Tribes: A Social and Economic Study of the Principal Criminal Tribes and Castes in North India,* Ethnographic and Folk Culture Society, Lucknow, 1949.

Bhattacharya, Sabyasachi, 'Laissez Faire in India', *Indian Economic and Social History Review, Vol. II, No. 1,* January 1965.

Bhattacharya, Subhas, Social Banditry in the Bengal Presidency, 1765-1813, *Marxist Miscellany, No. 10,* New Delhi, 1977.

Bhawani Shankar Bhargawa, *The Criminal Tribes,* Lucknow, 1949.

Bhowmick, P.K., '*Chenchus of the Forests and Plateau' – A hunting gathering tribe in Transition,* Calcutta, 1992, ISRAA (Institute of Social Research and Applied Anthropology).

Bhowmick, P.K., '*Crime and the Criminals among the Lodhas of West Bengal', Vanyajathi,* Delhi, 1961.

Bhowmick, P.K., 'Economic Life of the Lodhas', *Eastern Anthropologist,* Lucknow, 1960.

Bhowmick, P.K., *Essential Primary Considerations for Rehabilitation Schemes,* Calcutta, 1980.

Bhowmick, P.K., 'Religious Ideas of the Lodhas', *Vanyajati,* Delhi, 1957.

Bhowmick, P.K., *Some Aspects of Indian Anthropology,* Calcutta, 1980.

Bhowmick, P.K., The Lodhas and their Folksongs, *Vanyajati,* Delhi, 1957.

Bhowmick, P.K., *The Lodhas of West Bengal,* Calcutta, Puntipustak, 1963.

Bhowmick, K.L., *Tribal India,* Calcutta, 1971.

Bianco, L., Peasants and Revolution: The Case of China, *Journal of Peasant Studies, No. II, 1975.*

Bickers, Robert A., and Seton, Rosemary (eds), *Missionary Encounters: Sources and Issues,* Curzon Press, Great Britain, 1996.

Biddulph, J., *Tribes of Hindoo Koosh,* Calcutta, 1880.

Biddulph, J., The *Pirates of Malabar,* London, 1907.

Bidney, David., *Theoretical Anthropology,* New York, 1958.

Bimala, Charanhaw, *Some Kshatriya Tribes of Ancient India,* Calcutta, University of Calcutta, 1924.

Bishan Kapoor, *Bad Men of Bad Lands,* Agra, 1959.

Biswas, P.C., *The Ex-Criminal Tribes of Delhi State,* Unpublished Ph.D. thesis, University of Delhi, 1960.

Blackburn, Stuart H., 'The Kallars: A Tamil "Criminal Tribe" Reconsidered', *Journal of South Asian Studies, New Series, Vol. 1, No.1,* March 1978.

Blok, A., 'The Peasant and the Brigand: Social Banditry Reconsidered', *Comparative Studies in Society and History, Vol. XIV, 1972.*

Blumer, Herbert, *Symbolic Interactionism: Perspective, Method and Englewood Cliffs,* New Jersey, Prentice-Hall, Inc., 1969.

Boas, Franz., *Aryans and Non-Aryans,* New York, 1958.

Boden Kloss, C., *In the Andaman and Nichobars,* John Murray, London, 1930.

Bombay Presidency Gazette, Volume XVIII, Part III: Poona, Bombay, 1885.

Bombay Presidency Gazette, Volume XX: Sholapur, Bombay, 1884.

Bonarjee, P.D., *Handbook of the Fighting Races of India,* Delhi, 1975.

Booth, Tucker, Frederick, *Criminolcurology or the Indian Crim and What to do with him, A report of the work of Salvation Army, among the Criminal Tribes, Habituals and Released Prisoners in India,* London, 1912.

Booth Tucker, Frederick, *Jean Gold, Servant of India,* London, 1964.

Booth Tucker, Frederick, *Mukti Fauj or 40 years with the Salvation Army in India and Ceylon,* Marshall Brothers, London, 1910.

Booth, William, *In Darkest England and the way out: A Study of Poverty and Vice in England and a Scheme by the Salvation Army for Reclamation of Criminals and Prevention of Crime,* Salvation Army, Landon, 1890.

Bose, Ambicacharan, *A Hand Book of Criminology,* Calcutta, 1960.

Bose, N.K., *Tribal Life in India,* New Delhi, 1971.

Boswell, John, A.E., *Manual of the Nellore District,* Madras, 1873.

Boulger, Demetrius, C., *Lord William Bentinck,* Rulers of India Series, London, 1897.

Bovet, L., *Psychiatric Aspects of Juvenile Delinquency,* W.H.O., Geneva, 1951.

Bower, Rev. H., *An Essay on Hindu Caste,* Calcutta, 1851.

Boyd, W.C., *Genetics and Races of Man, An Introduction to Physical Anthropology,* Boston, 1950.

Brackenbury, C.F., *Madras District Gazetteers, Cuddapah,* Madras, 1915.

Brain Vesey Fitzgerald, *Gypsies of Britain, An Introduction to their History,* London, 1944.

Brewer, John and Styles, John (eds), *An Ungovernable People: The English and Their Law in the Seventeenth and Eighteenth Centuries,* Hutchinson, London, 1980.

Briggs, A., 'The Salvation Army in Sussex 1883-1892', in M.J. Kitch (ed), *Studies in Sussex Church History,* Leopard's Head Press, 1981.

Briggs, G.W., *The Chamars,* Oxford University Press, 1920.

Broeker, G., *Disorder and Police Reform in Ireland, 1812-36,* London, 1970.

Brown, H., *Parry's of Madras: A Story of British Enterprise in India,* Madras 1954.

Bruce, George, *The Stranglers, The Cult of Thuggee and Its Over throw in British India,* New York, Harcourt, Brace and World Inc., 1968.

Bruyn, Severryn, *The Human Perspective in Sociology: The Method of Participant Observation,* Englewood Cliffs, New Jersey: Prentice-Hall, Inc., 1960.

Buckly, Walter, *Sociology and Modern System Theory,* New Jersey: Prentice-Hall, Inc., 1967.

Budhan, the DNT-RAG Newsletter, *'Criminal Tribes Settlements: A Report (1924)',* Baroda, February-March, 1999.

Budhan, the DNT-RAG Newsletter, *'Interim Relief for Victims of Custodial Death'* (Pinya Kale case), Baroda, February- March 1999.

Budhan, the DNT-RAG Newsletter, *'The Criminal Tribes Act, 1871 Act XXVII of 1871',* Baroda, August-September 1998.

Budhan, the *DNT-RAG Newsletter, 'The Judgment by Honourable Justice Ruma J. Pal',* Baroda, 7 July 1998.

Burgess, Robert L., 'A Differential Association Reinforcement Theory of Criminal Behaviour', *Social Problems, XVI, No. II,* Fall, 1966.

Burman, Roy, 'Meaning and Process of Tribal Integration in a Democratic Society', *Sociologcal Bulletin, No. X,* March, 1961.

Byragi Brahmachari, *Nunsavatu Jivala Niak Sanmana Sanchika* (Autobiography in Telugu), Piduguralla, Gundur District, 1969.

Caldwell Robert, G., *Criminology,* New York, The Roland Press, 1965.

Caldwell, R., A *Political and General History of the District of Tinnevelly,* Madras, 1881.

Carstairs, G.M., *The Tribe Born,* London, Hogarth Press, 1957.

Cavan, Ruth Shonle, and Cavan, J. J., *Delinquency and Crime: Cross-cultural Perspectives,* Philadelphia, J.B., Lippincott Company, 1968.

Census of India, 1961, Andhra Pradesh, Vol. II, V – B, No. 8, *Ethnographic notes on Yerukula/Koracha, Boya, Nirshikari, Pardhis and Balasanthosha,* Manager of Publications, New Delhi, 1970.

Chaman Lal, Gypsies, *Forgotten Children of India,* Publications Division, New Delhi, 1962.

Chandavarkar, Rajnarayan, *Imperial Power and Popular Politics: Class, Resistance and the State in India, 1850-1950,* Cambridge University Press, Cambridge, 1998.

Chandrasekhar Bhat, *Ethnicity and Mobility, Emerging Ethnic Identity and Social Mobility among Waddars of South India,* New Delhi, 1984.

Chang Daeh, *Criminology, A cross-cultural perspective, Vols. I and II,* Bombay, 1976

Chapman, Denis, *Sociology and the Stereotype of the Criminal,* Tavistock Publications, 1968.

Chapman, Terry, 'Crime in Eighteenth Century England: EP Thompson and the Conflict Theory of Crime', *Criminal Justice History, Vol. 1,* 1980.

Charles, B., Devenport, *Anthropometry and Anthropology,* New York, 1926.

Chatterjee, B., The Darogah and the Countryside: The Imposition of Police Control in Bengal and its impact, 1793-1837, *Indian Economic and Social History Review, XVIII,* 1981.

Chatterjee, Partha and Gyanendra pandey, (eds), Subaltern studies, Vol. VII, Oxford University Press, New Delhi, 1992.

Chaturvedi, B. S., *Face to Face with Criminals,* Delhi, 1920.

Chaudhuri, N.C., "The Martial Races of India", *Modern History Review XL VIII, XLIX, 1930- 1931.*

Chaudhuri, Shashi Bhushan, *Ethnic Settlements in Ancient India,* Calcutta, 1955.

Chenchu, Raju, *Stuartpuram Girijan Settltment, A Rehabilitation Center for Ex-convicts,* Government Press, Hyderabad, 1981.

Chevalier, L., *Labouring Classes and Dangerous Classes in Paris during the First Half of the Nineteenth Century,* London, 1973.

Clifford, James, *The Predicament of Culture: 20th Century Ethnogrophy, Literature and art,* Harvard Universicy Press, Combridge, 1988.

Clifford, James, and George E., Maucus, (ed), *Writing Culture-The Poeties and Polities of Ethnography,* Oxford University Press, New Delhi, 1990.

Clifford, Kew, W., *The Salvation Army Christian Denomination Series,* Great Britain, 1977.

Clinard, Marshall B., *Anomic and Deviant Behaviour,* The Free Press, New York: 1968.

Cobb, Richard, *The Police and the People: French Popular Protest 1789-1820,* OUP, 1970.

Cockburn, J.S. (ed), *Crime in England 1550-1800,* Methuen, 1977.

Cohen, Albert, K., *Delinquent Boys: A Culture of the Gang,* New York: The Free Press of Glencoe, Illinois, 1955.

Cohen, A. Yehudi (ed). *'Culture as adaptation', 'Man in Adaptation',* Aldine Publishing Company, Chicago, 1968.

Cohn, B.S., 'Notes on the Study of Indian Society and Culture', in M. Singer and Cohn B.S. (ed), *Structure and Change in Indian Society,* Chicago, 1968.

Comaroff, Jean and Comaroff John, Of *Revelation and Revolution: Christianity, Colonialism and Consciousness in South Africa Vol. 1,* The University of Chicago Press, Chicago, 1991.

Confino, A., 'Collective Memory and Cultural History: Problems of Method'. *American Historical Review, 102,* 5 December 1997.

Copley, A.R.H., The Governor and his Premier: A Study in Indo-British Relationships, 1937-39, *Indo-British Review, IV and V 1973.*

Coutu, Walter, 'Role Play vs. Role Taking: An Appeal for Classification', *American Sociological Review,* 16 April, 1951.

Cox, Edmund, C., *Police and Crime in India,* London: Stanley Paul S. Co., 1946.

Cressy, Donald R., 'Application and Verification of the Differential Association Theory', *Journal of Criminal Law, Criminology and Political Science, Vol.* LIII, 63, 1955.

Cressy, Paul, 'The Criminal Tribes of India', *Sociology and Social Research, July-September, Vol. 73,* 1936.

Crooke, W., *The Tribes and Castes of North Western Provinces and Oudh,* (4 Vols.) Calcutta, 1896.

Cunningham, J.M., *Cholera: What can the State do to prevent It?* Calcutta, 1884.

Curry, J.C., *The Indian Police,* London, 1932.

Dalit Marg, *Telugu Fortnightly, 1979 to 1982,* Vijayawada.

Dale, S.F., The Mappila Outbreaks: Ideology and Social Conflict in Nineteenth-Century Kerala, *Journal of Asian Studies, No. XXXV,* 1975.

Dalton, E., *Descriptive Ethnology of Bengal,* Calcutta, 1872.

Dalton, E.T., *Tribal History of Eastern India, Office of the Superintendent of Government Printing,* Calcutta, 1872, Cosmo Publications, Delhi, 1973.

Dalton, George, 'Economic Anthropology and Development', New York, Basic Books, 1971.

Darrow Clarence, 'Crime: Its Causes and Treatment', London1934.

Darwin Charles, *Descent of Man,* London, 1905.

Darwin Charles, *Origin of Species,* London, 1906.

Dasgupta, Uma, 'Crime, Law and the Police in India', *1870-1880, The Indian Economic and Social History Review*, No. X, 1973.

Dale, S.F., *Islamic Society on the South Asian Frontier: The Mappilas of Malabar*, Oxford, 1980.

Davies, C.S.L., 'Slavery and Protector Somerset: the Vagrancy Act of 1547', *Economic and Social History Review, second series*, 19, 1996.

Demographic Study of Sansis', *Vanyajati*, Vol. X, No. 4. October 1962.

Demography of Sikligars', *Vanyajati, Vol. XI, No.* 2. April 1963, Delhi.

Dena, Lal, *Christian Missions and Colonialism*, Vendrame Institute, Shillong, 1988.

Deniker, J., *The Races of Man*, New York, 1990.

Desai, A.R., (ed) *Peasant Struggles in India*, Bombay, 1979.

Desai, A.R., *Rural Sociology in India*, Bombay, 1978.

Desai, A.R., *Tribe, Caste and Religion*, Romesh Thapar, in *Tribes in Transition*, Macmillan Camp, Ltd., of India, 1977.

Desai, Darshan, 'For Desar Villagers, Robbery is the main Occupation', *Indian Express, Bombay*, 8 December 1999.

Deutscher, Irwin, 'Buchenward, Mai Lai and Charles Van Doren: Social Psychology as an Explanation', *Sociological Quarterly*, 1970.

Deutscher, Irwin, 'Looking Backward: Case Studies on the Progress of Methodology in Sociological Research', the *American Sociologist, 4: 34-42, 1970.*

Deutscher, Irwin (ed), *Among the People*, New York: Basic Books, Inc., 1966.

Devy, G.N., *A Nomad called Thief, Reflections on Adivasi Silence*, Orient Longman, Hyderabad, 2006.

Dewey, C., and Hopkins A.G., *The Imperial Impact: Studies in the Economic History of Africa and India*, London, 1978.

Dhanagare, D.N., *'Agrarian Conflict, Religion and Politics: The Moplah Rebellions in Malabar in the Nineteenth and Early Twentieth Centuries' Past and Present, 74, 1977.*

Dhananje Keer, *Dr. Ambedkar, Life and Mission*, Bombay, 1954.

Dhebar, V.N., For a United Integrated and Contended India, *Tribal Souvenir* n.d.,

Dobriner, William M., *Social Structure and Systems: A Sociological overview Pacific Palisades*, California, Goodyear, 1969.

Donovan, Bill, M., 'Changing Perceptions of Social Deviance: Gypsies in Early Modern Portugal and Brazil', *Journal of Social History, Vol. 26, No. 1, Fall, 1992.*

Downie, David, *The Lone Star, A History of the Telugu Mission of the American Baptist, Foreign Mission Society*, Chicago, 1924.

Dube, S.C., *'Approaches to the Tribal problems in Indian'*, in *'Applied Anthropology in India'*, ed. By Vidyarthi, L.P., Kitab Mahal, Allahabad, 1968.

Dube, S.C., 'India's Changing Village', Routledge and Kengan Paul, London, 1960.

Dube, S.C., (ed.) *'Tribal Heritage of India (ethnicity, identity and interaction)'*, Vikas Publishing House, New Delhi, 1977.

Dube, S.K., and Mathur, F., *A Study of the Tribal People in the Areas of Madhya Pradesh,* Tribal Research and Development Institute, Bhopal, 1967.

Dubois, J.A., *Hindu Manners, Customs and Ceremonies,* Oxford University Press, London, 1936.

Dumont, L., and Pocock, D. (ed), *Contributions to Indian Sociology,* The Hague: Paris Mouton and Company, 1961.

Dutt, Bahari, *'The forgotten people'* -- Bawarias of Rajasthan, Proceedings of the Public Hearing, Muktidhara, Rajasthan, 2003.

Elwin, Verrier, *The Tribal World (an autobiography of Verrier Elwin),* Oxford University Press, New Delhi, 1964.

Elwin, Verrier, *'The Religion of an Indian Tribe,'* Oxford University Press, Bombay, 1955.

Elwin, Verrier, *Leaves from the Jungle: Life in a Gond Village,* Delhi : Oxford University Press, 1992.

Elwin, Verrier, *Muria Murder and Suicide,* London, 1950.

Elwin, Verrier, *The Aboriginals, Oxford Pamphlets on Indian Affairs, No. 14,* Oxford University Press, Humphrey Milford, London, 1943.

Emsley, Clive, *Crime and Society in England 1750-1880,* Orient Longman, London and New York, 1987.

Engels, Dagmar and Marks Shula (ed), *Contesting Colonial Hegemony, State and Society in Africa and India,* British Academy Press, London, 1994.

Enthroven, R.E., *The Tribes and Castes of Bombay,* Asian Education services, 3 Vols. Bombay, 1922.

Edwardes, S.M., *Crime in India,* OUP, London, 1924.

Edwardes, S.M., *Criminal Tribes at Hubli,* West Minister, 1931.

Eissler, K.R., (ed), *Searchlights on Delinquency,* New York: International University Press, Inc., 1949.

Ellis, Havelock, *The Criminal,* London, 1980.

Epstein, A.L., (ed). "The Case Method in the Field of Law", in the craft of *Social Anthropology,* Tavi Stock Publishers, London, 1967.

Erlanger, Steven, 'Across a New Europe, a People Deemed unfit for Tolerance', *The New York Times,* New York, 2 April, 2000.

Erskine, *'Madras and the New Constitution', Asiatic Review No. 37,* 1941.

Forbes, Geraldine, 'Managing midwifery in India', in Dagmar Engels and Shula Marks (ed), *Contesting Colonial Hegemony- State and Society in Africa and India,* British Academy Press, Landon, 1994.

Fabian, J., *Time and the Other: How Anthropology Makes Its Object,* Columbia University Press, New York, 1983.

Filstead, W.J., (ed), *Qualitative Methodology:* Markians Publishing Company, Chicago, 1970.

Fisher, R.J., and Austria, *Nomadic Groups in Caste System in India, Vol. 61, No. 1,* March 1981.

Fishman, Alvin, T., *Culture Change and the Underprivileged – A Study of Madigas in South India under Christian guidance,* Madras, 1941.

Fishman, Alvin, T., *For the Purpose,* New York, 1893.

Forde, Daryll, 'Primitive economics', in *'Man, Culture and Society'*, ed. by Harry L., Shapiro, Oxford University Press, New York, 1960.

Foucault, M., *Discipline and Punish: The Birth of the Prison,* Harmondsworth, 1979.

Foucault, M., *Power, Knowledge: Selected interviews and Other Writings, 1927-1977,* Brighton, 1980.

Francis, W., *Madras District Gazetteers: The Nilgiris,* Government Press, Madras, 1908.

Francis, W., *Madras District Gazetteers: Vizagapatam,* Government Press, Madras, 1907.

Francis, W., *Census of India, Vol. XV, Part I,* Government Press, Madras, 1902.

Frazer, J.G., *Toteoism and Exogamy, A Treatise on Certain Early Forms of Superstition and Society,* OUP, Delhi, 1910.

Freitag, Sandra. B., *'Sansiahs and the State: The changing nature of 'crime' and 'justice; in 19th century British India', Introduction.* Unpublished SOAS/Nehru Memorial Museum and Library, conference paper, March, 1994.

Freitag, Sandia B., *'Crime in the Social Order of Colonial North India', Modern Asian Studies, 25:2, 1991.*

Freeitag, Sandra, B., Collective Action and community : Public Areas and The Emergence of Communalism in North India, Oxford University Press, New Delhi, 1990.

Foucult, Michel, *Power, Knowledge, Pantheon,* New York, 1980.

Fuchs, Stephen, *Rebellious Prophets: A Study of Messianic Movements in Indian Religions,* London, 1965.

Fuchs, Stephen, *The Aboriginal Tribes of India,* Macmillan, New Delhi, 1973.

Furer Haimendorf, Christopher, Von, *Tribal Population of Hyderabad, Yesterday and Today,* Census of India, Vol. XXI, Part I, Report of Mazhar Hussain, Government Printing Press, Hyderabad, 1945.

Furer Haimendorf, Christopher, Von, *Tribes of India,* OUP, Delhi, 1982.

Furer Haimendorf, Christopher, Von., (ed), *Caste and Kin in Nepal, India and Ceylon,* Asia Publishing House, Delhi, 1966.

Furer Haimendorf, Christopher, Von, *Tribal Population and Cultures of Indian Sub-continent,* Netherlands, 1985.

Furer Haimendorf, Christopher Von, *Tribes of India: The Struggle for Survival,* OUP, New Delhi, 1985.

Furer Haimendorf, Christopher Von, *The Aboriginal Tribes of Hyderabad*, Vol. I, (the Chenchus), London, 1943.

Furer Haimendorf, Christoph, Von, *The Aboriginal Problem in Mulug and Narsaraopet Taluqs, A Tour Diary*, Hyderabad, Macmillan, 1947.

Furer Haimendorf, Christoph, Von, *The Tribal Hyderabad*, Azam Steam Press, Hyderabad, 1945.

Furer Haimendorf, Christoph, Von, *The Gonds of Andhra Pradesh: Tradition and Change in an Indian Tribe*, Vikas Publishing House, New Delhi, 1979.

Gafoor, Syed Khaja, Abdul, *Social Service Among the Tribes and backward Classes in Hyderabad*, Government Printing Press, Hyderabad, 1952 a.

Gafoor Syed Khaja, Abdul , *Tribes and Tribal Welfare in Hyderabad*, Government Printing Press, Hyderabad, 1952b.

Gadgil, Madhav and Ramachandra Guha, *This Fissured Land : An Ecological History of India*, Oxford University Press, New Delhi, 1992.

Geertz, Cliffored, Works and lives, *The Anthropologist as Author*, Stanford University Press, Stanfored, 1988.

Goodland, Robert, *Tribal Peoples and Economic Development, the man Ecologic considerations*, World Bank, Washington, 1982.

Government of Madras, *Board of Revenue, (Land Revenue Forests), Proceedings*, Forest No. 48, 25th April 1917, Government Press, Madras.

Government of Bombay, *Bombay Presidency Gazettee*, Volume XII: Khandesh, Bombay, 1880.

Government of Madras, *A Collection of Papers Relating to the Inam Settlement in Madras Presidency*, Madras, 1906.

Ghani, Muhammad, Abdul, *Notes on the Criminal Tribes of the Madras Presidency*, Minerva Press, Madras, 1915.

Government of Andhra Pradesh, *Guntur District Gazetteer*, The Government Publication, Hyderabad, 1977.

Gopal Singh, 'Adivasis' A plea for Better Understanding', *Journal of National Integration of India*, October-November, New Delhi, 1962,

Government of Madras, *Administration Report of Police of the Madras Province, 1904 -1940*, Government Press, Madras, 1941, Tamil Nadu Archives.

Government of Andhra Pradesh, *Census Handbook, Guntur District*, Government Press, Madras, 1953.

Government of India, *Census of India* "Scheduled Castes and Scheduled Tribes", *Series* I, 1971.

Government of Andhra Pradesh, *Census of India 1961, Vol. II, Andhra Pradesh, Part V-B (8), Ethnographic Notes on Yerukulas or Koravas, Boyas, Nirshikaris and Pardhis and Balasanthoos*, Office of the Director of Census Operations, Andhra Pradesh, Hyderabad, *Census of India, 1921: XIII: Madras, Part II, Madras, 1922.*

Government of India, *Census of India*, 1961, *Inquiries into the Spoken Languages of India*, Office of the Registrar General, India, 1962.

Government of India, *Census Report of Punjab and N.W.F.P.*, conducted by Sir Donald McLeod, Governament Press, Punjab, 1856.

Government of India, *Census Report of Punjab, 1868*, Conducted by A. Roberts, Government Press, Punjab, 1869.

Government of India, *Census Report of Punjab, 1881*, Conducted by Jelf Ibbetson, Government of Punjab, 1886.

Government of India, *Census Report of Punjab, 1891*, Conducted by E.D. MacLagan, Government of Punjab, 1892.

Government of India, *Census Report of Punjab, 1911*, Conducted by Pandit Hari Krishna Kual, Government of Punjab, 1912.

Government of India, *Census Report of Punjab, 1921*, Conducted by L. Middleton, Government of Punjab, 1922.

Government of India, *Census Report of Punjab, 1931*, Conducted by Khan Ahmad Hassan Khan, Government of Punjab, 1932.

Government of India, *Census Report of Punjab, 1941*, Conducted by Sheikh Fazal-I-Lahi, Government of Punjab, 1942.

Government of India, *Census Report of Punjab, 1951*, Conducted by Pandit Laxmi Chandra Vashista, Government of Punjab, 1952.

Government of India, Chakrabarti, S.S., *Criminals that hit the Headlines*, Calcutta, 1964.

Government of India, Chaman Lal, *Gypsies, Forgotten Children of India*, Publication Division, 1962.

Gadgil, D.R., *The Industrial Evolution of India in Recent Times 1860-1939*, OUP, Delhi, 1971.

Gaikwad, Laxman, *The Branded (Translated from the Marathi Original, 1988)*, Orient Longman, Bombay, 1998.

Gaitskell, Deborah, At Home with Hegemony? In Dagmar Engels and Shula Marks (ed), Contesting Colonial Hegemony – *State and Society in Africa and India*, British Academy Press, London, 1994.

Gall, Carlotta, ' Kosovo War over, Gypsies are Left Adim Vengeful Neighbours', *The New York Times*, New York, 11 July 1999.

Gall, Carlotta, 'Gypsies and others said to Draw Kosovar Fury; *The New York Times*, New York, 5 November 1999.

Gardiner, A.G., *Prophets, Priests and Kings*, J.M. Dent and Sons Ltd., London, 1914.

Gatrell, V.A.C., 'Crime Authority and the Policeman State 1750-1950' in Thompson F.M.L, (ed), *The Cambridge Social History of Britain 1750-1950*, Cambridge University Press, Cambridge, 1990.

Gatrell, V.A.C., *et al.*, (eds), 'Crime and Law: The Social History of Crime in Western Europe Since 1500', Europe Publications, 1980.

Gatrell, V.A.C., *Hanging Tree: Execution and the English People 1700-1868*, OUP, New York, 1994.

Gauri, Shankar, *Born Criminals*, Kishore Vidya Niketan, Varanasi, 1979.
Gayer G.W., *The Detection of Burglary in India*, Calcutta, 1908.
Gayer, G.W., *Lectures on Some Criminal Tribes of India and Religious Mendicants*, 2nd ed., Principal Police Training School, Central Province, 1910.
Government of Madras, Gazetteer of Nellore District, Brought up to 1938, Madras, 1942.
Government of Bombay, Gazetteers of Bombay State, Dharwad District, XXI, 1884, Bombay.
George B., Vold, *Theoretical Criminology*, New York.
George Macmunn, *The Underworld of India*, London.
Gerth, H.H., and Mills, C.W., From Max Weber: *Essays in Sociology*, (London, 1948).
Ghani, Mohammad Abdul, *Notes on the Criminal Tribes*, Provincial Police Training School, Vellore, 1915.
Ghosh, *Law Breakers and Keepers of Peace*, Calcutta, 1969.
Ghurye G.S., *Caste and Class in India*, Bombay, 1962.
Ghurye, G.S., "*The Aboriginal–So-Called and Their Future*, Popular Book Depot, Bombay, 1949.
Ghurye, G.S., *The Scheduled Tribes*, Popular Prakashan, Bombay, 1963.
Ghurye, G.S., *Caste and Class in India*, Bombay: Popular Book Depot, 1957.
Giallombardo, Rose (ed), *Juvenile Delinquency: A Book of Readings*, John Wiley and Sons, Inc., New York , 1966.
Gillen, *Criminology and Penology*, New York, 1945.
Gillin and Gillin, *Cultural Sociology*, New York, 1948.
Gillin, John Lewis, *Taming the Criminal*, New York: The Mcmillan Company, 1931.
Giri, V.V., *My Life and Times* (Telugu), Delhi, 1976.
Girijana Jyothi, Fortnightly, Vijayawada, 1972 to 1973.
Glaser, B.G., and Strauss, A.L., *The Discovery of Grounded Theory*, Chicago: Chicago Publishing Company, 1967.
Goffman, Erwin, Stigma: Notes on the Management of Spoiled Identity, Englewood Cliffs, Prentice-Hall, Inc., New Jersey, 1963.
Goldenweiser, A., *Anthropology*, London, 1937.
Gopal, S., *The Viceroyalty of Lord Irwin*, 1926-1931, London, 1957.
Gordon, Stewart N., *Bhils and the Idea of Criminal Tribes in Nineteenth Century India* in Anand A. Yang (ed), *Crime and Criminality in British India*, The University of Arizona Press, Arizona, 1985.
Gough, K., Caste in a Tanjore Village, in E.R. Leach (ed). *Aspects of Caste in South India*, Ceylon and North-West Pakistan, Cambridge, 1960.
Gough, K., Harijans in Thanavur in K. Gough and H.P. Sharma (ed), *Imperialism and Revolution in South Asia*, New York, 1973.
Gough, K., *Rural Society in South East India*, Cambridge, 1912.
Gould, Jean, *Servant of India*, The Campfield Press, St. Albans, Britain, 1964.

Gould, Stephen Jay, *The Mismeasure of Man,* W.W., Norton and Company, New York, 1981.

Gouldsbury, C.E., *Life of the Indian Police,* London, 1912.

Government of Andhra Pradesh, *Administration Report 1953 to 1977,* Government Press, Hyderabad.

Government of Andhra Pradesh, *Administration Report of the Harijan Welfare Deptt., for the year 1954-55,* Government Press, Kurnool, 1956.

Government of Andhra Pradesh, *Administration Report of the Harijan Welfare Deptt., of the Work Done for the Amelioration of the Condition of the Eligible Communities for the year 1952-53,* Government Press, Hyderabad.

Government of Andhra Pradesh, *Andhra Pradesh State Administration Report, 1953 to 1977,* Government Press, Hyderabad.

Government of Andhra Pradesh, *Andhra Pradesh State Administration Report, 1961-1965, Vol. I,* Government Press, Hyderabad, 1963.

Government of Andhra Pradesh, *Proceedings of the Chief Conservator of Forests,* Proceedings No. 321 (Press), 15th July 1932, Andhra Pradesh Gazetteers Office, Hydrebad.

Government of Andhra Pradesh, *Proceedings of the Chief Conservator of Forests, 1932,* Hyderabad, 1933.

Government of Andhra Pradesh, *Report of the 7th Conference for Scheduled Tribes and Tribal Areas, 1964, Guntur,* Government Press, Hyderabad, 1965.

Government of Andhra Pradesh, *Report on the Administration of the Hyderabad District Police for the year 1947,* Government Press, Hyderabad, 1948.

Government of Andhra Pradesh, *Report on the Administration of the Police of the Nizam's Government for the year 6th October 1916 to 5th October 1917,* Government Press, Madras, 1918.

Government of Andhra Pradesh, *The Koyas of Andhra Pradesh,* Government Press, Hyderabad, 1966.

Government of Andhra Pradesh, *The Report on the Tribes of Andhra Pradesh,* Tribal Cultural Research and Training Institute, 1958, Government Press, Hyderabad, 1964.

Government of Andhra Pradesh, *The Scheduled Tribes in Andhra Pradesh,* Government Press, Hyderabad, 1963.

Government of Andhra Pradesh, *The Scheduled Tribes, Welfare of Chenchus–Kurnool District,* Material Condition, Progress for 1959-60, Report submitted, Kurnool, 1961, Government Press, Hyderabad, 1962.

Government of Bombay, *Report of the Criminal Tribes Act Enquiry Committee, 1943,* Government Press, Bombay, 1943.

Government of Bombay, *Report of the Criminal Tribes Act Enquiry Committee,* Government Central Press, Bombay, 1939.

Government of India, *Legislature Deptt., Proceedings, March 1911: The Criminal Tribes Law Act III of 1911.*

Government of India, *A Collection of Acts of the Indian Legislature and the Governor General for the Year 1924, (Act No. VI of 1924),* Government Press, New Delhi, 1925.

Government of India, *A Collection of the Acts Passed by the Governor General of India in Council in the Year 1911,* Superintendent, Government Printing, Calcutta, 1912.

Government of India, *Abstract of the Proceedings of the Governor General of India in Council Assembled for the purpose of making Laws and Regulations, Vol. IX,* 3.10.1870, Government Press, Simla.

Government of India, *Census of India, 1961, Andhra Pradesh, Vol. 2, Part V, B.8, Ethnographic Notes on Yerukula, Koravas, Boya, Nirsikaris and Pardhis,* Government Press, Hyderabad.

Government of India, *Census of India, 1981, Special Tables for STs, Series 2,* Government Press, New Delhi.

Government of India, *Constituent Assembly of India, Legislative Debates, 1948 to 1949, Part 2, Vol. 3 to 6, No. 4 to 12,* Government Press, Delhi.

Government of India, *Criminal Classes in the Bombay Presidency, 1908,* Central Press, Bombay.

Government of India, *Jail Reports from 1900 to 1920,* Government Press, Simla.

Government of India, *Report of the Backward Classes Commission, 1955, Vol. 1,* Government Press, Simla.

Government of India, *Report of the Commissioner Appointed to Enquire into and Report upon the manufacture and sale and tax upon salt in British India,* Calcutta, 1856, Government Press, Calcutta 1857.

Government of India, *Report of the Commissioner for Scheduled Castes and Scheduled Tribes from 1953 to 1980,* Government Press, New Delhi.

Government of India, *Report of the Criminal Tribes Enquiry Committee,* 1948, United Provinces of India, Government Central Press, Allahabad, 1949.

Government of India, *Report of the Indian Famine Commission, 1878, Parts I, II and III, Vol. I,* Calcutta.

Government of India, *Report of the Indian Jails Committee, 1919-20, Vol. 1, Report and Appendices,* Government Central Press, Simla, 1920, Chapter XXII.

Government of India, *Report of the Indian Police Commission, 1902-1903,* Government Central Press, Simla, 1904.

Government of India, *Report of the Study Team on Social Welfare and Welfare of Backward Classes 1959, Vol. I,* Government Press, New Delhi.

Government of India, *Report on Inter-Provincial Crime, 1904, United Provinces, Bengal and Assam,* Madras, Government Press, Delhi.

Government of India, *Report on the Census of India, 1891, Vol. XIII,* Calcutta, 1892.

Government of India, *The Gazetteer of India, Volume IV* (Administration and Public Welfare), Ministry of Education and Social Welfare, New Delhi, 1978.

Government of India, Yeats, M.W.M., 1931, *Census of India, Vol. XVI, Parts I,* Government Central Press, Madras.

Government of Madras, *Report of the Administration of the Deptt., of Salt Revenue in the Madras Presidency and Orissa,* Madras, 1894-95.

Government of Madras, *A Selection of Papers from the Old Records of the Nellore District,* Government Press, Nellore, 1915.

Government of Madras, *Administration Report for the Criminal Tribe Settlement and Kallars, Koravar and Yanadis Reclamation for 1940,* Madras.

Government of Madras, *Administration Report of the Chief Conservator of Forest Deptt., Madras Presidency 1889-90,* Government Press Madras, 1981.

Government of Madras, *Administration Report of the Forest Deptt., (Southern and Northern Circles),* Madras Presidency for 1889-90, Madras.

Government of Madras, *Administration Report of the Inspector General of Police, 1904 to 1950,* Government Press, Madras.

Government of Madras, *Administration Report of the Labour Deptt., 1924-35,* Madras.

Government of Madras, *Administration Report of the Stuartpuram Settlement, 1915-28,* Madras.

Government of Madras, *Administration Report on Habitual Offenders Settlement from 1950-1955,* Government Press, Madras.

Government of Madras, *Administration Report on Kallar Reclamation, Koravar Reclamation, Criminal Tribes Settlement, Yanadi and Sugali Reclamation from 1947-1952,* Government Press, Madras, 1953.

Government of Madras, *Administration Report on Reclamation of Kallars, Koravars, Yanadis and Sugalis, 1950 to 1955,* Government Press, Madras.

Government of Madras, *Annual Administration Report of Nellore Girls School for the year 1925 to 1930,* Government Press, Madras.

Government of Madras, *Appendix to the Police Government Report 1863, Government Press,* Madras, 1964.

Government of Madras, *Development Deptt., Proceedings,* 1912, Government Press, Madras.

Government of Madras, *Home (Judicial) Deptt., Proceedings, 1920 to 1941,* Government Central Press, Madras.

Government of Madras, *Home (Miscellaneous) Deptt., Proceedings, 1919 to 1925,* Government Press, Madras.

Government of Madras, *Home Deptt., Proceedings, 1937 to 1952,* Government Press, Madras.

Government of Madras, *Judicial Deptt., (Confidential) Proceedings, 1920 to 1940,* Government Central Press, Madras.

Government of Madras, *Judicial Deptt., (Police Branch) Proceedings, 1923 to 1928,* Government Press, Madras.

Government of Madras, *Judicial Deptt., Proceedings, 1921 to 1929, Government Press,* Madras.

Government of Madras, *Law (General) Deptt., Proceedings, 1921 to 1936,* Government Press, Madras.

Government of Madras, *Madras Administration Reports from 1920 to 1965,* Government Press, Madras.

Government of Madras, *Madras Criminal Tribes Manual, 1927 Criminal Tribes Act VI of 1924, brought upto 31st March 1927,* Government Press, Madras.

Government of Madras, *Madras Government Bulletin, 1930, Vol. V, No. 1, Anthropology: Vision of the Uralis and Sholagas, More Marriage Customs in South India, Hookswinging, Paliyans,* Government Press, Madras.

Government of Madras, *Madras Government Museum Bulletin, 1903, Vol. IV and Vol. V, Nos. 1 and 3, Anthropology,* Government Press, Madras.

Government of Madras, *Madras Government Museum Bulletin, Anthropology, Vol. IV, No. 2,* Government Press, Madras, 1904.

Government of Madras, *Madras Police Administration Reports, 1877 to 1900,* Government Superintendent Press, Madras.

Government of Madras, *Manual of Jail Administration, 1889, Vol. I, Part II,* (Mended), Government Press, Madras.

Government of Madras, *Manual of the Administration of the Madras Presidency, Illustration of the Records of Government and the yearly Administration Reports, 1885, Vol. I,* Government Press, Madras.

Government of Madras, *Manual of the Administration of the Madras Presidency, Illustration of the Records of Government and the yearly Administration Reports, 1886, Articles on Geography, Ethnology and History,* Government Press, Madras.

Government of Madras, *Nellore District Manual, Vol. II, Madras, 1868.*

Government of Madras, *Note Showing the Progress Made in the Settlement of Criminal Tribes in the Madras Presidency upto September 1916,* Government Press, Madras, 1916.

Government of Madras, *Note Showing the Progress made in the Settlement of Criminal Tribes in the Madras Presidency upto January, 1926,* Government Press, Madras, 1927.

Government of Madras, *Proceedings of Madras Government, Judicial Deptt., 1859 to 1872* Government Press, Madras.

Government of Madras, *Public Works (Labours) Deptt., Proceedings, 1926 to 1935,* Government Press, Madras.

Government of Madras, *Report of the Chief Conservator of Forest Deptt.,* Government Press, Madras, 1932.

Government of Madras, *Report of the Forest Committee,* Vol. II, Madras, 1912.

Government of Madras, *Report of the Madras Salt Commission, 1856, 1876,* Madras.

Government of Madras, *Report of the Salt Commission 1876*, Government Press, Madras, 1877.

Government of Madras, *Report on the Administration of Inspector General of Police of the Madras Presidency from 1914 to 1950*, Government Press, Madras.

Government of Madras, *Report on the Administration of the District Police of the Nizam's Government, 1905, 1914 to 1916 and 1933*, Government Press, Hyderabad (1327 Fasli), APSA.

Government of Madras, *Report on the Census of the Madras Presidency, 1871, Vol. I*, Madras, 1874.

Government of Madras, *Revenue (Special) Deptt., Proceedings, 1918 to 1919*, Government Press, Madras.

Government of Madras, *Revenue Deptt., (Land Revenue and Forests) Proceedings 1917*, Government Press, Madras.

Government of Madras, *The Chenchus and the Madras Police, 1921, Parts I and II, From Publicity Bureau*, Superintendent Government Press, Madras.

Government of Madras, *Madras Administration Reports from 1871 to* 1951, *Madras Presidency*, Government Press, Madras. Tamil Nadu Archives.

Government of Madras, *Madras District Gazetteers*, Cuddapah District, Government Press, Madras, 1930.

Government of Madras, *Madras Legislative Assembly Debates, 1937-39, 1946-48*, Government Press, Madras, Tamil Nadu Archives.

Government of Madras, *Madras Legislative Council Proceedings*, 1920-36, Government Press, Madras, Tamil Nadu Archives.

Government of Madras, *Madras Mahajana Sabha, Report of the Non-Official Enquiry on Police Excesses in Madras on the 22nd, 25th and 27th April 1930*, Government Press, Madras, 1930.

Government of Madras, *Madras Police Administration Reports, 1865-1949*, Govt. Central Press, Madras, Tamil Nadu.

Government of Madras, *State Administration Report 1930 to 1965*, Government Superintendent Press, Madras, Tamil Nadu.

Government of Madras, *Madura District Records, Vol. No. 4680*, Collector of Madura to Bangalore 18.11.1832, Government Press, Madras, Tamil Nadu.

Government of Madras, *Nellore District Gazetteer*, Madras, 1938, Government Press, Madras, 1939.

Government of India, *Report of the Commissioner for Scheduled Castes and Scheduled Tribes for the year 1961-62 (Eleventh Report), Part II, Appendix XXXVII*, Government of India, New Delhi, 1963.

Government of India, *Report of the Commissioner for Scheduled Castes and Scheduled Tribes 1986-87*, Government of India, New Delhi, 1988.

Government of Madras, *Report of the Commissioners for the Investigation of Alleged Cases of Torture in the Madras Presidency*, Madras, 1855.

Government of India, *Report of the Conference of Police Officers held at New Delhi, January 19th to 24th 1931: Part II*, Government Press, Simla, 1931.

Government of India, *Report of the Criminal Tribes Act Amendment Committee, Bihar, 1950*, Government Press, Bihar, 1951.

Government of India, *Report of the Criminal Tribes Act Enquiry Committee*, Government Central Press, Madras, 1939.

Government of India, *Report of the Criminal Tribes Act Enquiry committee, 1949-50*, Government Press, New Delhi, 1951.

Government of Bombay, *Report of the Criminal Tribes Act Enquiry Committee*, Government Central Press, Bombay, 1939.

Government of India, *Report of the Criminal Tribes Act Enquiry Committee, U.P., 1947*, Allahabad, 1948.

Government of Andhra Pradesh, *Report of the Director of Tribal Welfare*, Sri Gopala Rao, I.A.S., R.C.D. 1-301/79, dated 14-5-1979, available in the District Collector's Office, Guntur.

Government of India, *Report of the Indian Jail Enquiry Committee, 1919–1920*, Government Press, Simla, 1921.

Government of India, *Report of the Indian Police Commission, 1902-03*, Government Central Press, Simla, 1904.

Government of India, *Report of the Railway Police Committee, 1921*, Government Central Press, Simla, 1921.

Government of India, *Report of the study Team on Social Welfare and welfare of Backward Classes*, Vol. I, New Delhi, 1959.

Government of India, *Report of the Third Conference for Tribes and Tribal Areas Kakasaheb Kalelkar*, Jagadlpur, 1915.

Government of India, *Report on Canonization and settlement (India), Parliamentary Papers 1857-58*, VII. Part I.

Government of Madras, *Report on the Census of the Madras Presidency, with Appendix 1871*, Vol.1, Madras 1874.

Government of India, *Report on the Tribes of Andhra Pradesh, Tribal Cultural Research and Training Institute*, Hyderabad, 1970.

Government of India, *Report on the Working of the C.T Act. XXXVII of 1871*, Government Central Press, Simla 1905.

Government of Bombay, *Report on the Working of the Criminal Tribes Act in the Bombay Presidency, 1918*, Government Press, Bombay, 1919.

Government of Madras, *Statement of the Police Committee on the Administration of the District in the Madras Presidency*, Madras, 1902.

Government of Madras, *Statistical Abstract, India 1951-52*, New Series No. 3, Government of India Publication, Calcutta, 1954.

Government of Andhra Pradesh, *The History of Andhra Pradesh Police, 1861-1961*, Government Press, Hyderadad, 1961.

Government of Madras, *The History of Madras Police*, 1859-1959, *Government Press, Madras, 1959.*

Government of India, *The Indian Penal Code, 1860, Act XLX of 1860*, Government Press, New Delhi, 1861.

Government of Madras, *The Madras Criminal Tribes Manual,* Government Press, Madras, 1924.

Government of India, *The Report of the Criminal Tribes Act Enquiry Committee,* Government Press, Bombay, 1930.

Government of India, *The Report of the Criminal Tribes Act Enquiry Committee*, Government Press, Punjab, 1914.

Government of India, *The Report of the Criminal Tribes Act Enquiry Committee*, Government Press, U.P., 1928.

Government of India, *The United Provinces Criminal Intelligence Gazette,* Government Press, Ist August 1906.

Gramsci, A., *Selection From Prison Note books, eds and translations, Q., Hoare and smith* G., Orient Longman, Hyderabad, 1996.

Griffith, P., *My People: The History of the Indian Police,* London, 1971.

Griffith, P., *The History of the Indian Tea Industry,* London, 1967.

Grigson, W.V., *The Aboriginal Problem in the Central Provinces and Berar,* Nagpur, 1994.

Grigson, W.V., *The Challenge of Backwardness,* Hyderabad, 1947.

Guenter, Lewy, 'Himmler and the "Racially Pure Gypsies", *Journal of Contemporary History, Vol. 34, No.* 2, April 1999.

Guha, B.S., *Racial Affinities of People of India, Census Report of India, Vol. 1. 1935.*

Guha, R., *Elementary Aspects of Peasant Insurgency in Colonial India,* Delhi, 1983.

Guha, Ranajit (ed), *Subaltern Studies: Writings on South Asian History and Society*, Oxford University Press, Vol. I-VII.

Gunthrope, E.J., *Notes on Criminal Tribes*, Times of Steam Press, Bombay, 1882.

Guntur Patrika (Telugu), 6th February 1923.

Gupta, A., *Crime and Police in India up to 1861,* Agra, 1974.

Gupta, A., *The Police in British India, 1861-1947,* Delhi, 1979.

Gupta, G.P., *Agricultural, Economic and Social Aspects of Crime in India,* London, 1992.

Gupta, J.P., *Rehabilitation Work among Ex-Criminal Tribes in India,* New York, 1955.

Gupta, M.K.D., *The problem of Tribal Education and the Santhals,* New Delhi, 1963.

Gupta, R.K., "Implementation of Tribal Welfare Project" (Bidisa- A case study), *Man and Life, Journal of Institute of Social Research and Applied Anthropology,* Calcutta, 1980.

Gurr, T.R., *Rogues, Rebels and Reformers: A Political History of Crime and Conflict*, Sage, Beverly hills, California, 1976.

Gwynn, C., *Imperial Policing,* (2nd edn), London, 1939.

Hal Foster, *the Anti-Aesthitic, Essays on Post Modern Culture,* Bay Press, Port Townesend, 1983.

Hankin, A.C., *Inspector-General of Police and Prisons,* Nizam's Dominion, 1893, Hyderabad.

Hardiman, David, *The Coming of the Devi-Adivasi Assertion in Western India*, OUP, New Delhi, 1987.

Hackenberg, Robert A., "The Parameters of an Ethnic Group: A method for studying the Total Tribes", *American Anthropologist, 69*, 5 October 1967.

Haddon, A.C., *The Races of Man and Their Distribution*, New York, 1925.

Haikerwal, B.S., *Economic and social Aspects of crime in India*, George Allen and Unwin Ltd., London, 1934.

Haikerwal, B.S., *A Comparative Study of Penology*, Allahabad,(n.d).

Haldane, J.B.S., *Heredity and Politics*., London, 1943.

Hanawalt, Barbara, A., 'Fur Collar Crime: the Pattern of Crime Among the Fourteenth Century English Nobility', *Journal of Social History*, 8, 1975.

Bharal, G.P., *Denotified Community and their problems of Rehabilitation, The Indian Journal of Social Work, Vol. XXXVIII, 1968.*

Hardgrave, R.L., *The Nadars of Tamilnad: The Political Culture of a Community in Charge*, Berkeley, 1969.

Harris, Marvin, *Culture, People, Nature: An Introduction to General Anthropology*, (2nd Ed.), New York, 1971.

Harris, Marvin, *Tribal Demography in India*, Bombay, 1949.

Hartland, Edwin Sidney, *Primitive Society: The Beginning of the Family*, London, 1921.

Harvey, H., *Cameos of Indian Crime*, Stanley Paul and Company, London, n.d.

Hastings, James, *Encyclopedia of Religion*, New York, 1958.

Hatch, W.J., *The Land Pirates of India*, Seeley Service and Co., London, 1928.

Hauser, Philip, M., and Otis Dubley, *The Study of Population*, Chicago, 1959.

Hay, Douglas, Linebaugh, Peter, Thompson, E.P. (ed), Albion's Fatal Tree: *Crime and Society in Eighteenth Century England*, Allen Lane, London, 1975.

Hay, Douglas, *War, Dearth and Theft in Eighteenth Century: The Record of the English Courts, Past and Present, 95, 1982.*

Heade, Walter, Emigration, *Migration and Nomadism*, edited by F.H.A. Marshall, New Delhi, 1931.

Hefner, Robert, W., (ed) *Conversion to Christianity: Historical and Anthropological Perspectives on a Great Transportation*, Berkeley, and University of California Press, 1993.

Hemalatha, Lavanam, *Jeevana Prabhatam*, (Telugu), Vijayawada, 1984.

Hemalatha Lavanam, *Nerastula Samskarana*, (Reform of Criminals Telugu), Vijayawada, 1985.

Hemalatha Lavanam, *Nerastula Vinnapamu*, (Telugu) Atheist Center, Vijayawada, 1983.

Hemalatha Lavanam, *The Problems of Denotified Tribes – An Experiment on Stuartpuram*, Vijayawada, 1975.

Hemalatha Lavanam, *Mrutyorma Amrutangamaya (Autobiography), Telugu*, Visalandra Book House, Hyderabad, 2004.

Hemalatha Lavanam and Lavanam, *Notes and Reflections on our work in Rehabilitation, Ex-Criminal Tribes*, Gandhi Peace Foundation, Vijayawada, 1976.

Hemalatha Lavanam and Lavanam,*Our Experiences in Stuartpuram*, Vijayawada, 1976.

Hemalatha Lavanam and Lavanam, *The Problem of Denotified Tribes – An Experiment on Stuartpuram*, Vijayawada, 1975.

Hemingway, F.R., *Madras District Gazetters: Godavari*, Madras, 1915.

Hemingway, F.R., *Madras District Gazetteers, Tanjore*, Madras, 1906.

Henry, E.R., *Classification and Uses of Fingerprints*, London, 1900.

Herbert, A., *Block and Gilbert Geis, Man, Crime and Society*, New York 1962.

Heredia, Rudolf, C., "Ethinicity, Class and Nation : Interrelationships, in a Multi-cultural state," *Economic and Political weekly, Vol. 33, No. 19*, 10th May, 1997.

Heredia, Rudolf, C., "Teaching as a subversive Activity, Pedagogies for Change", *New Frontiers' in Edcuation, Vol. 26, No. 3*, July-September, 1996.

Herschel, W.R., *The Origin of Fingerprinting*, London, 1916.

Hervey, *Report on Robbers of India and The Operations of Thugee and Dacoity Deptt.,s*, 1861.

Heward, S. Becker and Blanche Geer, "Participant observation and Interviewing", *A comparison in Human Organization*, New Delhi, 1957.

Hicks, J.R., *The Social Frame Work: An Introduction to Economics*", Oxford University Press, London, 1960.

Himes, Joseph, S., *The Study of Sociology, Glenview, III*: Scott, Foresman and Company, 1969.

History of Madhya Pradesh Police, Published by the Inspector General of Police, Bhopal, 1965.

Hitchcock, R.H., *A History of Malabar Rebellion, 1921*, Madras, 1925.

Hobsbawm, E.J., *Bandits*, London, 1969.

Hobsbawm, E.J., *The Primitive Rebels*, Manchester University Press, London. 1959.

Hollins, S.T., *The Criminal Tribes of the United Provinces*, Allahabad, n.d.

Homans, G.C., *Handbook of Modern Sociology*, III: Rand McNally S.Co., Chicago, 1904,

Honingmann, John J., *Understanding Culture*, New York, 1963.

Hooten, Earnest Albert, *Bandits*, Great Britain, 1939.

Hooten, Earnest Albert, *Crime and the Man*, Harward University, U.S.A. 1939.

Hooton, E.A., *Up from the Ape,* New York, 1958.

Hukumnamas and Papers relating to Sriharikota Yanadis, Vol. I, A Selection of Papers from the Old Records of Nellore District, Nellore, 1915.

Hunter, F., *Community Power Structure,* North Carolina: Chapel Hill, North Carolina Press, 1953.

Hunter, W.W., *England's Work in India,* Smith, Elder and Company, London, 1881.

Hunter, W.W., *Annals of Rural Bengal,* London, 1897.

Hutton, J., *A Popular Account of Thuggs and Dacoits, Hereditary Garrotters and Gang Robbers of India,* Delhi, 1856.

Hutton, J.H., *Caste in India, its Nature, Function and Origin,* (4th Ed.), OUP, London, 1963 (First Published in 1946).

Hindustan Times, Nats and Bazigars, *June 26, 1960, Nehru Memorial Library,* New Delhi.

Ignatieff, Michael, *A Just Measure of Pain: The Penitentiary in the Industrial Revolution 1750-1850,* Macmillan, London, 1978.

Irons, William, 'Nomadism as a Political Adaptation: The Case of the Yomut Turkmen', American Ethnologist, No. 1.

Irshick, Eugene, F., *Politics and Social Conflict in South India: A Study of The Non-Brahmin Movement and Tamil Separatism,* 1916-1929, University of California Press, Berkeley, Los Angeles, USA, 1938.

Issacs, Harold R., *India's Ex-Untouchables,* John Day Company, New York, 1965.

Iyer, L.K.A., *The Mysore Tribes and Castes, Vol. 1,* The Mysore University Press, Mysore, 1935.

James, Alter, *The Problems of Denotified Tribes – An Experiment in Missionary Preparation,* National Christian Council View, Vol. 74, No. 7, 1954.

Jaspal, Singh, *Reformation of Ex-Criminal Tribes,* Hyderabad, 1976.

Jaya Singh, Visuvathas, *'Social and Economic Aspects of Theft',* India Journal of Criminology, Vol 9. No. 1. January 1989.

Jean Gould, *Bharata Desa Sainya Sevakudu,* (Telugu) Madras, nd.

Jeffery, C.R., *"Criminal Behavior and Learning Theory",* Journal of Criminal Law, Criminology and political Science, *LVI, No. III September, 1965.*

Jeffries, C., *The Colonial Police,* London, 1952.

Johnson, Elmer, H., *Crime, Correction and Society,* The Dorsey Press, Homewood, 1964.

Johnstone, F.A., *Class Race and Gold, A study of Class Relations and Racial Discrimination in South Africa,* London, 1976.

Jolly, Asit, *'Pardhi Tribals Strike Terror With Spate of Violent Robberies in Punjab',* Asian Age, New Delhi, 7 September 1998.

Jones, David, Crime, Protest, Community and Police in nineteenth century Britain, *Routledge and Kegan Paul, London, 1982.*

Joseph, A., *'Yerukula Traditional Justice',* Tribal World, Vol. 4, Hyderabad, 1967.

Judges, P.V., *The Elizabethan Underworld*, London, 1930.
Kadhrirvel, S., *A History of the Maravas, 1700-1802*, Madurai, 1977.
Kale, Chandrasena, and Others, 'Criminal Writ Petition against State of Maharashtra, *Deputy Superintendent of Police, Baramati and Deputy Collector, Baramati'*, High Court of Mumbai, 1998.
Kamala Manohar Rao, P., Bulletin of the Tribal Cultural Research and Training Institute, Vol. I, Hyderabad, 1963.
Kamat, A.R, *Education and Social Change*, Economic and Political Weekly, 1982.
Kamladvi Chattopadhyaya, *Tribalism in India*, 1978.
Kamte, N.M., *From Them to Us*, Pune, 1981.
Kanetkar, V.G., 'Our Police Need Drastic Reform', *Indian Journal of Public Administration, XXIV 1978.*
Kapadia, K.M., The Criminal Tribes of India, *Sociological Bulletin, I, II*, 24 March, 1952.
Karan, Vijay, *'India's Police: The Dilmamas of an Aberrated System', in Shankardass, Rani Dhavan (ed)*, Punishment and the Prison: India and International Perspectives, Sage Publications, New Delhi, 2000.
Kareve, Dr. Irawati, 'Maharashtra: Land and its People', *Maharashtra State Gazetteer*, General Series, Bombay, 1968.
Kawashima, Koji, *Missionaries and a Hindu State: Travancore 1858-1936*, OUP, Delhi, 1998.
Keane, A.H., *Ethnology*, London, 1910.
Kelkar, Ashok, R., *Language Study in the Integration of Tribal Population in India*, Vivekanandakendra Patrika, 1972.
Kennedy, M., *The Criminal Classes in India*, New Delhi, 1909.
Kerawalla, Perim, C., *A Study in India Crime*, Bombay, Popular Book Depot, 1959.
Kerewalla Perim, C., *A Study in Indian Crime*, Bombay, 1959.
Khazanvon, A.M., *Nomads and the Outside World*, Cambridge, 1983.
Khodarkovsky, Michael, *Not by World Alone: Missionary Polices and Religious Conversion in Early Modern Russia, Comparative Studies in Society and History*, Vol. 38, No. 2 April 1996.
Kitts, E.J., *A Compendium of Tribes and Castes found in India*, Bombay, 1885.
Kloss, C., Boden, *In the Andaman and Nicobars, John Murray*, London, 1903.
Kluckohn Clyde, *Mirror of Man*, New York, 1949.
Knapp, S., *Collective Memory and the Actual Past*, Representations, 26, Spring, 1989.
Kosambi, D.D., *An Introduction to the Study of Indian History*, Popular Prakashan, Bombay, 1990.
Kramer, Judith, R., *The America Minority Community*, New York: Thomas Y. Crowell Company, 1834.
Krirk, E., Unveiled—*A Study of the Salvation Army from within*, London, 1915.
Krishna Iyer, *V.R., The Criminal Process and Legal Aid*, Indian Journal of Criminology, 1973.

Krishnaswami Ayyar, K.N., *Madras District Gazetteers, Statistical Appendix for Malbar District,* Madras, 1933.

Krishnaswami Ayyar, K.N., *Statistical Appendix and Supplement to the Revised District Manual for Coimbatore District,* Madras, 1933.

Kroeber L., Alfred, *"Relations of Environmental and Cultural factors", in* 'Environment and Cultural Behavior', *ed. by Andrew P., Vaedya,* University of Texas Press, London, 1969.

Kuper, Leo (ed), *Race, Science and Society,* The Unesco Press, Paris, 1975.

Lakshminarayana, Unnava, *Malapalli (Telugu),* Machilipatnam, 1922.

Lalitha, V., *"Denotified Communities of Andhra Pradesh – Some Problems of Rehabilitation",* Proceedings of A.P, History Congress, 1981.

Lalitha, V., "Historical Background of Kapparallatippa Settlement", *Proceedings of A.P. History Congress,* 1978.

Lalitha, V., "Socio-Economic and Administrative Aspects of an Ex-Criminal Tribe" *Unpublished M.Phil. Thesis,* Tirupathi University, 1977.

Lalitha, V., The Making of Criminal Tribes: Patterns and Transition, *New Era Publications,* Madras, 1995.

Latham, R.G., *Ethnology of British Colonies and Dependencies,* London, 1851.

Latham, R.G., *Ethnology of India,* London, 1859.

Law, B.C., *Tribes of Ancient India,* Poona, 1947.

Lawson, James, Gilchrist, *Deeper Experiences of Famous Christians,* Herald Publishing House, Ohio, 1911 (reprinted by Pyramid Books, New York, 1970).

Laxmanna M., 'Roots of Delinquency', *Social Welfare,* Vol. XXXIX, 1982.

Le Goff, J., *History and Memory,* Trans, S. Rendall and E. Claman, Columbia University Press, New York, 1992.

Le Goff, Jacques and Nora, P., *Constructing the Past: Essays in Historical Methodology, Cambridge, OUP, 1985.*

Leiner, G.W., *Detailed Analysis of Criminal Tribes in Punjab,* Punjab, 1880.

Lemmarchand, A.E.M., *Guide to the Criminal Tribes,* Nagpur, 1915.

Lensky, G.E., *Power and Privileged,* McGraw-Hill, New York, 1969.

Lewis, John, Gillean, *Taming a Criminal,* London, 1931.

Lewis, Oscar, *Village Life in North India,* Alfred A. Knopf, Inc., and Random House, Inc., New York, 1965.

Lodhi, Abdul and Tilly, Charles, "Urbanization, Crime and Collective Violence in Nineteenth Century France", *American Journal of Sociology, No. 79, 1973.*

Loomis, Charles P., and Beagle, A.J., *Rural Sociology: the Strategy of Change,* New Jersey: Prentice- Hall, Inc., 1957.

Low, D.A., *Civil Martial Law, Congress and the Raj: Facets of the Indian Struggle, 1917-47,* London, 1977.

Low, D.A., *The Government of India and the First Non-Co-operation Movement, 1920-22,* Journal of Asian Studies, No. XXV 1966.

Lowiew, Robert, *Primitive Religion,* London, 1936.

Lowiew, Robert, *Primitive Society*, London, 1921.

Lowiew, Robert, *Social Organization*, London, 1956.

Ludden, D., *Who Really Ruled Madras Presidency?* The Indian Economic and Social History Review, *XV, 4, 1978.*

Murali, Atlury, "Alluri Sitaram Raju and the Manyam Rebellion of 1922-1924", *Social Scientist, No. 131, 1984.*

Macritchie, David, *Account of the Gypsies of India*, New Society Publications, New Delhi, 1976.

Malakondaiah, Sri Rama, *Kurru Charitra* (Telugu) The History of the Yerukulas, Nayagara Paper Products (P) Ltd., Hyderabad, 2000.

Macfarlane, Alan, *Reconstructing Historical Communities*, Cambridge University Press, Cambridge, 1977.

Mackenzie, Mildred, *The Mud Bank, A Story of Missionary Endeavor*, Pennsylvania, 1959.

Mac Lean, C.D., *Glossary of the Madras Presidency*, New Delhi, 1982.

Macleane, C.D., *Manual of the Administration of the Madras Presidency, Vol. I & II*, Madras, I, II, 1885.

MacMunn, Lt. Gen. Sir George, 'Criminal Tribes and Classes' (Chapter VIII), in The Underworld of India, Jarrolds, London, 1932.

Madan, Gurumukh Ram, *Indian Social Problems, Social Disorganization*, Vol. 1, Bombay, 1940.

Mahalingam, T.V., *Administration and Social Life under Vijayanagar*, Madras, 1940.

Mahasweta Devi, 'Time is Running Out', in *Budhan, the DNT-RAG Newsletter*, Baroda, April 1998.

Mahboob Husain, Syed Khaja, *Social Services and Tribal Welfare*, Hyderabad, 1950.

Major P.R.T., Gordon, The Khasis, *Cosmo Publications*, Delhi, 1975.

Majumdar, D.N., and Madan, T.N., "An Introduction to Social Anthropology", Asia Publishing House, Bombay, 1970.

Majumdar, D.N., *Races and Cultures of India*, Asia Publishing House, Bombay 1961.

Majumdar, D.N., *The Fortunes of Primitive Tribes*, The Universal Publishers, Lucknow, 1944.

Majumdar, D.N., *Penal Settlement in Andamans*, New Delhi, 1975.

Majumdar, D.N., *The Affairs of a Tribe: A Study in Tribal Dynamics*, Universal Publishers Ltd., Lucknow, 1961.

Majumdar, R.C. (ed), *The History and Culture of the Indian people: The Age of Imperial Unity*, Bharatiya Vidyabhavan, Bombay, 1968.

Malcolm, John, *A Memoir of Central India*, 2 Vols. London, 1823.

Malcolm, John, *Report on the Province of Malwa and Adjoining Districts*, Calcutta, 1822.

Mamoria, C.B., *The Tribal Demography in India*, Allahabad, 1957

Mamoria, C.B., *Social Problems and Social Disorganization in India,* Allahabad: Kitab Mahal, 1960.

Mandelbaum, David G., *'Society in Indian',* Popular Prakashan, Bombay, 1970.

Mane, Lakshman, *Vimuktayan (Marathi),* Yashwantrao Chavan Pratishthan, Bombay, 1997.

Mane, Lakshman, Upara, *An Outsider, Autobiography (Marathi),* Sahitya Akademy, New Delhi, 1997.

Mangat Rai, E.N., *Patterns of Administrative Development in Independent India,* London, 1976.

Manganaro, Mare, (ed), *Moderist Anthropology: From Field Work to Text,* Prenceton University Press, Princetion New Jercy, 1990.

Manis, J.G., and Meltzer, B.L., (ed), *Symbolic Interaction: A Reader in Social Psychology,* Allyn and Bacon, Boston, 1968.

Marvin Harris, *Culture, People, Nature,* New York, 1971.

Mason, Phillip, *Call the Next Witness,* London, 1945.

Mason, P., *A Matter of Honour: An Account of the Indian Army, Its Officers and Men,* London, 1974.

Mayall, David, *Gypsy Travellers in Nineteenth Century,* Cambridge University Press, Cambridge, 1988.

Mayaram, Shail, 'Criminal or Community? Alternative Constructions of the Mev Narrative of Darya Kahn', *Contributions to Indian Sociology, 25, 1, 1991.*

Mayhew, Henry and Binny, John, *The Criminal Prisons of London and Scenes of Prison Life,* Griffin, Bohn and Company, London, 1862.

Megill, Allan, "History, Memory, Identity", *History of the Human Sciences,* Vol. II., No. 3 August, 1998.

Mehta B.H., Tribal Development Since Independence, *Tribal Souvenir.* (n.d).

Mehta, B.H., *Ex-Criminal Groups in India,* Indian Journal of Social Work, 1955-56.

Melossi, Dorio and Pavarini, Massimo, *The Prison and the Factory: Origins of the Penitentiary System,* Macmillan, 1981.

Memoria, C.B., *Social Problems and Social Disorganization,* Allahabad, 1960.

Memoria, C.B., *Tribal Demography in India,* Bombay, 1957.

Merton, Robert.K., *Social Theory and Social Structure,* The Free Press, New York, 1967.

Mendelsohn, Oliver and Uppendra Bzxi, *The Rights of Subordinated People,* Oxford Universicy Press, New Delhi, 1994.

Mills, C.W., *The Sociological Imagination,* New York: Grove Press, Inc., 1961.

Miner, David.W., *The Concept of Community,* Scott, S.Green Company, Chigaco, 1969.

Misra, P. K., "Indian Nomads", Unpublished paper, *Anthropological Survey of India, Southern Regional Office,* Mysore, 1979.

Misra, P. K., "Jenu Kuruba", *Bulletin Anthropological Survey of India, Vol. XVIII, No. 3, 1969.*

Misra, P. K., "Patterns of Inter Tribal Relations", in *'Tribal Heritage of India'*, ed. by S.C. Dube, Vikas Publishing House, New Delhi, 1977.

Misra, P. K., "Sex Relations, Law and Society", Article Presented in the *Seminar on Tribal customary Law', November 16 to 18, Anthropological Survey of India,* Calcutta, 1978.

Mithilesh, Gupta, "Rehabilitation of Criminal Tribes", *The Eastern Anthropologist,* Vol. XVII, No.1, Jan-April 1964.

Mohindar, Singh, *The Depressed Classes, Their Economic and Social Conditions*, Bombay, 1947.

Moore, B., *Social Origins of Dictatorship and Democracy: Lord and Peasant in Making of the Modern World,* Harmondsworth, 1969.

Moore, W.E., *Social Change*, Englewood Cliffs, Prentice-Hall, Inc., New Jersey, 1963.

Moreland, W.H., *India at the Death of Akbar,* London, 1920.

Morris, H., *A Descriptive and Historical Account of the Godavari District,* London, 1878.

Morris, Norval, *The Habitual Criminal,* Longman's Company, New York, 1951.

Morrison Willing, *Douglas, Crime and Its Causes,* London, 1985.

Mouat, G.E.D., *Handbooks for the Indian Army: Madras Classes,* Revised (edn) Delhi, 1938.

Mourant, A.F., *The Distribution of Human Blood Groups,* Black-well Scientific Publications, Oxford, 1954.

Mukherjee, Anima, Aboriginal Crime, *Man In India, Vol. 29, Nos. 3 and 4,* July December, 1949.

Mukherjee, N., *The Ryotwari System in Madras,* 1792-1827, Delhi, 1938.

Mukherjee, S.K., *Crime Statistics in India, A Commentary,* Indian Journal of Criminology, Vol. II, No. 2, 1974.

Mukhopadhyay, Chandidas, *Kharia: The Victim of Social Stigma,* K.P. Bagchi and Copmnay, Calcutta, 1998.

Mulki Raj, Policy for Freedom from Crime, *The Hindu,* quotation from U.S Law commission, 1975.

Mullaly, Fredrick, S., *Note on Criminal Classes of the Madras Province,* Madras, 1912.

Mullens Claud, *Why Crime?,* London, 1945.

Murdoch, Norman H., 'Salvation Army Disturbances in Liverpool, England, 1879-1887', *Journal of Social History, Vol. 25, No. 3, 1991.*

Nagabushanacharyulu, Chirravuri, *Adima Vasulu,* (Telugu), Tenali, 1949.

Nagabushanacharyulu, Chirravuri, *Sanchara Jatulu* (Telugu), Narasaraopet, 1977.

Naidu, M., and Paupa Rao, *The Criminal Tribes of India, No. II, A History of Korawars, Erukulas or Kaikaries,* Madras, 1905.

Naidu, M. and Paupa Rao, *The Criminal Tribes of India, No III: The History of Bauris, Sansis, Chapperbends, Cabulees and Iranies*, Higginbotham, Madras, 1907.

Nandy, Ashish, *The Intimate Enemy: Loss and Recovery of self Under Colonialism,* Oxford University Press, New Delhi, 1983.

Narayan, Abanindar, *The Korava Tribe, Their Society and Economy,* New Delhi, 1990.

Natarajan, Nalini, *The Missionary Among the Khasis,* Sterling Publishers, New Delhi, 1977.

Newsell, W.H., "The Development of the Tribes and Dialect Group From Social System to Social Category", *Sociological Bulletin,* No. IX (March, 1960).

Niak,T.B., "What is tribe: conflicting definitions", in '*Applied Anthropology in India',* ed. by L.P. Vidyarthi, Kitab Mahal, Allahabad, 1968.

Nicholas, W., Ralph, "Ecology and village structure in deltaic West Bengal", in *The Economic Weekly,* 15: 1185-1196, 1963.

Nigam, Sanjay, "Disciplining and Policing the Criminals by Birth, Part II", *The Indian Economic and Social History Review, Vol. 27, No. 2, 1995.*

Oddie, G.A., 'Protestant Missionaries, Caste and Social Change in India, 1850-1914, *The Indian Economic and Social History Review,* Vol. VI, No. 3. 1963.

Okley, Judith, 'The Traveller-Gypsies', Cambridge University Press, Cambridge, 1983.

Oppert, Gustav, *On the Original Inhabitants of Bharatavarsha or India,* Oriental Publishers, New York, 1893, (Reprint 1978).

Panakal, J.J., 'An Agenda for Criminology', *Indian Journal of Criminology,* Madras, 1973.

Panakal, J.J., and Punekar, V.B., *Welfare of Denotified Communities,* Bombay, 1975.

Paripurnanand, Varma, *Crime, Criminal, Convict,* Agra, 1963.

Parthasarthy, Jakka, "The kapu or Reddy – a dominant agricultural caste of Andhra Pradesh", *M.A. Dissertation,* Ravishankar University, Raipur (Unpublished), 1973.

Parthasarthy, Jakka., "Yerukula and their customary law", Unpublished Report, *Anthropological Survey of India, Mysore,* 1978.

Parthasarathy, Jakka, *Notes on Criminal Tribes,* (n.d).

Parthsarathy, Jakka, *The Yerukula: An Ethnographic Study,* Anthropological Survey of India, Calcutta, 1988.

Parthasarathy, Jakka, 'The marriage system of the Yerukula, In: B.B. Goswami, *Sarkar J., and Danda D., (eds.), Marriage in India,* Anthropological Survey of India, Calcutta.

Parulekar, Godavari, *Adivasis Revolt: The Story of Warli Peasant in Struggle,* Calcutta, 1975.

Panikkar, K. N., *Communalism in India: History, Politics and Culture,* Manohar, New Delhi.

Passerini, Lusia (ed), Memory and Totalitarianism, *International Yearbook of Oral History and Life Stories,* Volume I, OUP, Oxford, 1992.

Pati, R.N., and Jena, B. (Eds), *Tribal Development in India*, New Delhi, 1989.

Patrick, Clarence, H., "The Criminal Tribes of India with Special Emphasis on the Mang Garudi: A preliminary Report", *Man in India, Vol. 48: 3*, July-September, 1968.

Pearson, Geoffrey, *Hooligan: A History of Respectable Fears*, Macmillan, London 1983.

Peel, J.D.Y., 'For who hath despised the day of small things? Missionary Narratives and Historical Anthropology', *Comparative Studies in Society and History, Vol. 37, No. 3, July 1995.*

Perine, Kerawalla, *A Study in Indian Crime*, Bombay, 1958.

Perks, Robert and Thomson, Alistair (eds), *The Oral History Reader*, Routledge, London and New York, 1998.

Perlez, Jane, 'Czech Gypsies Face Bias from Beyond the Wall', New York Times, New York, 2 July 1999.

Perry, E.J., Rebels and Revolutionaries in North China, 1845-1945, Stanford, 1980.

Philips, David, *Crime and Authority in Victorian England: The Black Country 1835-1860*, Croom Helm, London, 1977.

Pickering, Charles, *The Races of Man*, London, 1863.

Pickett Waskom, J., *Christian Mass Movements in India*, Chicago, 1933.

Pratap, D.R., Festivals of Banjara, Tribal Cultural Research and Training Institute, Hyderabad, 1972.

Plosky, Ned, *Hustlers, Beats and Others*, Chicago: Aldrine Publishing Co., 1967.

Ponaldshan, *India – A Bird's Eye View*, Constable and Company Ltd., London, 1922.

Ponna Koteswara Rao, *Dalit Marg (Telugu)*, Vijayawada, 1940.

Ponna Koteswara Rao, *Rama Rajyam*, (Telugu Ballad), Vijayawada, 1960.

Ponna Satyanarayana and Ponna Koteswara Rao, *Kallumunta Telugu (Toddypot, Ballad)*, Vijayawada, 1950.

Portelli, Alessandro, 'The Peculiarities of Oral History', *History Workshop Journal*, issue 12, Autumn, 1981.

Potter, D.C., *Manpower Shortage and the End of Colonialism: The Case of the Indian Civil Service*, Modern Asian Studies, Vol. VII, 1973.

Pouchepdass, Jacques, "The Criminal Tribes of British India: A Repressive Concept in Theory and Practice", *International Journal of Asian Studies, Vol. 2, No. 2. 1982.*

Prabhat Kumar Sen, *Land and People of the Andamans*, Calcutta, 1962.

Pratap, D., Rabinandan, *Tribes of Andhra Pradesh*, World Telugu Conference, Hyderabad, 1975,

Pratap, D.R., *Andhra Pradesh Adimajathulu*, (Telugu) Tribal Cultural Research and Training Institute, Hyderabad, Andhra Pradesh, 1975.

Proctor, Tammy M., 'Uniforming Youth: Girl Guides and Boy Scouts in Britain, 1908-39', *History Workshop Journal*, No. 45, Spring 1998.

Pual Chowdary, D., *A Hand Book on Social Welfare*, Institute of Social Sciences, Agra University, Delhi.

Radhakrishna, Meena, 'Criminal Tribes Act in Madras', in *Budhan, the DNT-RAG Newsletter*, Baroda, December 1998-January 1999.

RadhaKrishna, Meena, 'From Tribal Community to Working Class Consciousness: Case of Yerukala women', *Review of Women's Studies, Economic and Political Weekly, April 29, 1989.*

Radhakrishna, Meena, 'Missionaries and Myth Making: Salvation Army and Itinerant Communities in Madras Presidency', *Research-in-progress Paper in History and Society*, Centre for Contemporary Studies, Nehru Memorial Museum and Library, New Delhi, 1997.

RadhaKrishna, Meena, 'The Criminal Tribes Act in Madras presidency: Implications for Itinerant Trading Communities', *The Indian Economic and Social History Review, Vol. 26, No. 3. 1989.*

Radhakrishna, Meena, "From Itinerant Communities to Wage Workers—The Criminal Tribies of Madras Presidency, 1910-1947", *Paper Presented at the first Annual Conference of Association of India Labour Historians (AILH) in March, 1998.* Research-in-progress paper, History and Society, Third series, No. LVII, March 2000, Nehru Memorial Museum and Library, New Delhi.

Radhakrishna, Meena, 'Colonial Construction of a Criminal Tribe: The Itinerant Trading Communities of Madras Presidency' in Neera Chandhoke (ed). *Historical Trajectory: Essays in Honour of Ravinder Kumar, Tulika, New Delhi, 2000. Also in Economic and Political Weekly, Vol. XXXV, No. 28, 29,* 15 July 2000.

Radhakrishna, Meena, 'Colonialism, Evolutionism and Anthropology - A Critique of the History of Ideas 1850-1930', *Research-in-Progress Papers, History and Society*, Nehru Memorial Museum and Library, New Delhi, June 1997.

Radhakrishna, Meena, 'Surveillance and Settlements under the Criminal Tribes Act in Madras', *The Indian Economic and Social History Review*, Vol. 29, No. 2, 1992.

Rafael, Vicentre L., *Contracting Colonialism: Translation and Christian Conversion in Tagalog Society under Early Spanish Rule*, Cornell University Press, Ithaca, 1988.

Raghavaiah, V., *The Problems of Criminal Tribes*, Akhila Bharatiya Adimjati Sevak Sangh (BASS), New Delhi. n.d.

Raghavaiah, V., *Tribes in India*, Andhra Rastra Adimjati Sevak Sangh, Nellore: (n.d).

Raghavaiah, V., *Muriyalu (Muriya Tribe)*, Nellore, 1951.

Raghavaiah, V., *Nomads*, Bharatiya Adimjati Sevak Sangh, New Delhi, 1968.

Raghavaiah, V., *The Yanadis*, A tribe of Andhra Pradesh, Bharatiya Adimjati Sevak Sangh. New Delhi, 1952.

Raghavaiah, V., *Tribal Justice,* Andhra Rashtra Adimjati Sevak Sangh, The Jupiter Press Private Ltd., Madras, 1977.

Raghavaiah, V., *Tribal Revolts,* Andhra Rastra Adimjati Sevak Sangh, Nellore, 1971.

Raghavaiah, V., *Tribes of India,* BASS, New Delhi, 1969.

Raghavaiah, V., *The Enadi,* Man in India, Vol. 24, No. 170, 1944.

Raja Rao, G.P., *The History of the Salvation Army in Andhra Pradesh,* Madras, 1993.

Rajayyan, K., *Rise and Fall of the Poligars of Tamil Nadu,* Madras, 1974.

Rajendra Prasad, *President of India and Prime Minister of India,* Speeches delivered at the Scheduled Tribe Conference in Delhi, on 7th June 1952, NMML, New Delhi, 1952.

Ram, Ahuja, "Religion of the Bhils: A Sociological Analysis", *Sociological Bulletin,* Vol. XIV, No. 21, March, 1965.

Ramachandra Sastri, E., *Neramulu Cheyu Jatala Charitamulu (Telugu History of Thieving Communities),* Vijayawada, 1930.

Raja Reddy, K., *Family and Kinship Among the Yerukulas of Rayalaseema,* Unpublished Ph.D. Thesis, S.V.University, Tirupati, 1995.

Ramakrishna, V., *Social Reform in Andhra,* New Delhi, 1983.

Ramanujam, T., *Prevention and Detection of Crime,* Madras, 1972.

Ramaswami, P.N., *Magisterial and Police Guide,* Vols. I and II, Madras, 1951.

Ramaswamy, B., Goud, J.D. and Salem, J.D., *Distribution of some genetic markers among two scheduled caste groups of Andhra Pradesh (South India),* Acta Anthropogenetica, 3 : 13-8, 1979.

Ramesan, "A Tribe in Andhra", in *The Hindu,* daily newspaper dated 31-1-1960.

Ranga, N.G., Revolutionary Peasant, Delhi, 1949.

Rangaiah, Desabhatla, 'Yerukulas', *Tribes in India,* Delhi, 1950.

Rangarao, K., "The Dynamics of Power and Conflict in an Indian village: "A Case Study", Ph.D. thesis submitted to Michigan State University, East Lansing, Michigan, 1969.

Rao, C.V.H., (ed) *Social Welfare in India,* Government of India Publication, New Delhi, 1955.

Rao, M.S.A., ed., *Social Movements in India,* New Delhi, 1979.

Rao, S., Venugopal, *Facts of Crime in India,* Allied Publishers, New Delhi, 1982.

Ray Sripati, *'Custom and Customary Law in British India',* Thare Press, Calcutta, 1911.

Ray, P.C., *The Tribal World and its Transformation, (ed).,* Bhupinder Singh and Bhandar, J.S., New Delhi, 1980.

Reith, C., *The Police Idea: Its History and Evolutionary in England in the Eighteenth Century and After,* London, 1938.

Reiwald, Paul., Society and Its Criminal, International University Press, Inc., New York, 1950.

Religious Beliefs and Practices of the Sansis of Punjab, Journal of Social

Research, Vol. IV, Nos. 1-2, March to September 1961. Prof. Majumdar Memorial Vol., Aspects of Religion in India Society.

Report of the Select Committee on East India Company's Affairs, Parliamentary Papers, 1813-32, XI (735-III).

Richards, J.F., *Madras District Gazetteers:* Salem Madras, 1918,

Richards, J.F. and Rao, V.N., 'Banditry in Mugal India: Historical and Folk Perception', *The Indian Economic and Social History Review*, Vol. XVII No. 3, 1980.

Ripendrachandrapal, N., *Crime-Cause and Cure*, West Bengal, 1963.

Risely, Sir Herbert, *The People of India*, Calcutta: Thacker, Sprink and Company, Calcutta, 1908.

Risely, H.H., *The People of India*, 2nd Edn., London, 1915.

Risley, H.H., *Census of India, Vol. I, India, Ethnographic Appendices*, Delhi, 1901.

Riwald Paul, *Society and its Criminal*, New York, 1950.

Rodriguez, E.A., *The Hindu Castes*, Madras, 1846.

Rose, H.A.(ed), *A Glossary of the Tribes and Castes of the Punjab and North West frontier Province*, Punjab: Superintendent, Government Printing, Punjab, 1918.

Rowland, L.E., *Report of the American Baptist Telugu Mission, from May Ist to December 31st, 1928*, Orissa Mission Press, Orissa, 1929.

Roy, Burman, B.K., *Integrated Area Approach to the Problems of the Hill Tribes of North-East India, Tribal Situation in India*, Proceedings of a Seminar, Indian Institute of Advanced Study, Simla, 1972.

Ruhela, Satya Pal, *The Children of Indian Nomads*, Sterling Publishers, New Delhi, 1984.

Russel, E.P., and Rigby, *The Making of the Criminal*, London, 1906.

Russell, R.V., and Hira Lal, *The Tribes and Castes of the Central Provinces of India*, Asian Education Service, New Delhi, 1933.

Russell, R.V., and Rai Bahadur Hiralal, *Tribes and Castes of the Central Provinces of India*, Vols. 3 and 4, New Delhi, 1975.

Satyanarayana, Chalavadi, *Yerukulas*, An Ex-Criminal Tribe of Andhra and its Settlement (Stuartpuram), Unpublished M.A. Dissertation, Sagar University, 1959-1960.

Sachchidananda., *Profile of Tribal Culture in Bihar*, Calcutta, 1965.

Sachidananda and Prasad, P.R., *Encyclopaedic Profile of Indian Tribes*, Vol.1-4, Discovery Publishing House, New Delhi, 1966.

Saha H.A., *How to Combat Crime*, Calcutta, 1958.

Salvation Army, *Some Aspects of Salvation Army Social Work*, Papers read at the International Social Council, London conducted by the Founder, 1911, The Salvation Army Printing Works, 1917.

Salvation Army, *The War Cry*, International Heritage Center, London, 1909-19.

Samuelson, James, *India, Past and Present*, London, 1890.

Sandal, Robert, *The History of the Salvation Army,* Third Volume on Social Reform and welfare work, Thomas Nelson and Sons, Ltd., New York, 1955.

Sanjana, J.E., *Caste and Outcaste,* Bombay, 1946.

Nigam, Sanjay, "Disciplining and Policing the Criminals by Birth", *Indian Economic and Social history Review,* Vol.27, No.2, New Delhi 1990.

Sarada Raju, A., *Economic Conditions of Madras Presidency 1800-1850,* University of Madras, 1941.

Sarma, Marla, Samskar, *A Profile, Gandhi Peace Society,* Heidelberg, Germany, 1992.

Sastri, Ramachandra, E., *History of Criminal Tribes in Madras Presidency,* Madras, 1929.

Saunders, Albert J., "Reclaiming Criminals in Sholapur, India", *Sociology and Social Research,* I Vol. XII, No.1 (September- October, 1927), 61.

Saxena, K.M.L., *The Military System of India 1850-1900,* Delhi, 1974.

Sayena, N.S., *Main Reasons for Increase in Crime in India in Recent Years,* The Indian Journal of Public Administration, 1975.

Schermerhorn, Richard, "Minorities and National Integration", *Journal of Social Research,* Vol. XII, No. I, 1970: 32.

Schermerhorn, R., *Comparative Ethnic Relations, A Framework for Theory and Research,* New York, Random House, 1970.

Selection of Papers from the Records at the East India Company Relating to the Revenue, Police Civil and Criminal Justice under the Company's Government of India, London, 1820, Vol.II, September 1916, Madras, 1917.

Sethana, M.J., *Society and the Criminal,* Leader's Press, Ltd., Bombay, 1952.

Shah, A.M., *The Household Dimension of the Family in India,* Orient Longman, New Delhi, 1973.

Shaprio, Harry, L., Man, *Culture and Society (edited),* New York, 1956.

Sharma, A.N., *Man and Crime, Mankind,* Hyderabad, 1958.

Sharma, B.D., 'Effectives of Police', *Indian Journal of Public Administration, Vol. XXIV, 1978.*

Sharma, B.D., *Indian Police: A Development Approach,* Delhi, 1977.

Sharma, Ramnath and Sharma, R.K., *Social Anthropology and Indian Tribes,* Bombay, 1986.

Sharpe, J.A., *Crime in Early Modern England 1550-1750,* Longman, New York, 1984.

Shastri, Rajaram and Goyal, C.P., *Social Organization Attitudes and Denotified Communities in U.P,* Institute of Social Sciences, Varanasi, 1969.

Shaw, Bernard, 'Major Barbara', *The Complete Prefaces of Bernard Shaw,* Paul Hamlyn, London, 1965.

Sher Singh 'Sher', Ex-Criminal Tribes of Northern India need Re-Classification on more Authentic and Scientific Grounds', *Journal of Social Research,* Vol. III, No.2. Ranchi, 1960.

Sher Singh, 'Sher', *The Sansis of Punjab: A Gypsy and Denotified tribe of Rajput Origin,* Munshiram Manohar Lal, New Delhi, 1965.

Sherring, M.A., *Hindu Tribes and Castes,* Vol. III, Delhi, 1974.

Sherring, M.A., *'Tribes and Castes of Madras Presidency',* Delhi, Cosmo Publishers, 1975.

Sikka, K.D., *After- care programme for Juniveniles,* Where does it stand today? *The Indian Journal of Social Work,* Tata Institute of Social Work, Bombay (unpublished M.Phil Thesis), 1981.

Silver, A., *The Demand for Order in Civil Society,* in D.J. Bordua (ed). The Police: Six Sociological Essays, New York, 1967.

Simhadri, Y.C., The Ex-Criminal Tribes of India, *National Publishing House,* New Delhi, 1979.

Simhadri, Y.C., 'Caste and De-notified Tribes', *The Journal of Social Work,* 1977.

Simhadri, Y.C., Institutional factor and Tribal Criminality: An Analysis of Yerukula tribe in Andhra Village, the Eastern Anthropologist, Vol. 27, No. 1.

Simhadri, Y.C., 'Changing Criminal Behaviour of an Ex-Criminal Tribe in an Indian village', *Indian Journal of Criminology, 1976, 4(1).*

Simhadri, Y.C., *De-notified Tribes, A Sociological Analysis,* Classical Publishing Company, New Delhi, 1991.

Singh, K.S., *People of India,* National Series, Vols. 4-6: India's Communities, Anthropological Survey of India, Calcutta, 1988.

Singh, K.S., *Tribal Situation in India,* Indian Institute of Advanced studies, Shimla, 1972.

Singha, Radhika, 'Providential Circumstances: The Thuggee Campaign of the 1830s and Legal Innovation', *Modern Asian Studies,* 27:1, 1993.

Singha, Radhika, *Despotism of Law,* Oxford University Press, New Delhi, 1988.

Singhal, D.P. *Gypsies: Indians in Exile,* Folklore Institute, Archana Publications, Meerut, 1982.

Siva Rao, Digavalli Venkata, 'Mana Police Vyavasta' (Telugu), Vijayawada (n.d.)

Siva Rao, Digavalli Venkata, 'The Lambadis and Culture Contact', *Triveni,* Machilipatnam, 1945.

Slcak, P.A., *Vagrants and Vagrancy in England 1598-1664,* Economic History Review, 2nd series, No. 27, 1974.

Sleeman, Col. James L., Thug or a Million Murders, *Pilgrims Book Pvt. Ltd.,* Delhi, 1998 (First Indian Reprint).

Sleeman, W.H., *Ramaseeana or a Vocabulary of the Peculiar Language used by the Thugs,* G.H. Huttmann, Military or Phan Press, Calcutta, 1836.

Sleeman, W.H., *Rambles and Recollections of an Indian Official,* 2 Vols. London, 1844.

Sleeman, W.H., *Report on the Depredations Committed by the Thug* Gangs of Upper and Central India, Culcatta.1840.

Smith, Vincent A., *The Oxford History of India,* Oxford University Press, Oxford, 1999.

Solveing *Smith, By Love Compelled, The Story of 100 years of the Salvation Army in India and Adjacent Countries,* Salvationist Publishing, St. Alboans, England, 1981.

Somasundaram, A.M., Vagrants and Nomads, Vanyajati, 1958.

Somerville, Augustus, *Crime and Religious Belief in India,* Calcutta, The Criminologist Industry Press, 1929.

Spooner, Brian, *The Cultural Ecology of Pastoral Nomads,* Addison-Wesley Module in Anthropology, No. 45, Reading, Mass: Addison-Wesley, 1973.

Sreenivas, M.N., *Caste in Modern India and other Essays,* Asia Publishing House, New York, 1962.

Sreenivas, M.N., *Social Change in Modern India,* The University of California Press, Berkeley, 1967.

Srinivas, M.N., "The Myth of Self-sufficiency of the Indian Village", Economic and Political Weekly, VoL.12, 1960.

Srinivas, M.N., India's Villages, *West Bengal Government Press,* Calcutta, 1955.

Srinivasa Raghava Iyenger, Memorandum of the Progress of Madras Presidency During Last Forty Years of British Administration, Madras, 1983.

Srivastava, R.S., "Crime and Society', *Indian Journal of Criminology,* Madras, 1974.

Sreenivasa Varma, G., *Yerukula Dialect,* Madras, 1978.

Srivastava, S.P., *A Social psychological Study of Barawara: An Ex-Criminal* Tribe of U.P., Unpublished Ph.D. thesis, Lucknow University, 1970.

Starti, O.H.B., *Reformation of Offenders in India, A Hand book for the use of Workers Amongst Delinquents in India,* Bombay, 1935.

Statistical Outline of India 1998-99, Tata Services Limited, Bombay, 1999.

Stein, B., *Integration of the Agrarian System of South India,* in Frykenberg R.E., (ed), Land Control and Social Structure in Indian History, OUP, Madison, 1969.

Stein, B., *Peasant State and Society in Medieval South India,* OUP, Delhi, 1980.

Stepan, Nancy, *Idea of Race in Science: Great Britain 1800-1960,* Oxford, 1982.

Stoddart, B., *The Unwanted Commission: National Agitation and Local Politics in Madras City,* South Asia ,V, 1975.

Stuart, H.A., *Census of India,* 1891, Vol.XIII, Madras, 1893.

Stuart H., Blackburn, 'The Kallars: A Tamil "Criminal Tribe" *Reconsidered', Journal of South Asian Studies,* New Series, Vol.1, No.1, March 1978.

Subbarayan, V., *Forgotten Sons of India,* New Delhi, 1949.

Surajit Sinha, *'Tribes and Indian Civilization, Transformation Process in Modern India',* Man in India, 1981.

Suryanarayana, M., "Marine fisherfolk of North-East Coastal Andhra Pradesh", *Anthropological Survey of India*, Calcutta, 1977.

Sutherland and Cressay, *Principles of Criminology*, New York, 1955.

Syed, Siraj-ul-Hasan, Caste and the Tribes of H.E.H., the Nizam Dominions, Delhi, 1909.

Sykes, G.A., and Matza D., "Techniques of Neutralization; A Theory of Delinquency", *American Sociological Review*, Vol. XXII, December.

Takkar, A.V., Tribes of India, New Delhi, 1950.

Taylor, Meadows, *The Story of My Life*, (Autobiography), New Delhi, 1886.

Taylor, Meadows., *Confessions of a Thug*, New Delhi, 1885.

The Telegraph, *'MP Tribals Driven to Crime'*, Calcutta, 31 July 1998.

The War Cry, *Salvation Army Monthly, 1930-40*, Salvation Army Office, Madras.

Thompson, E.P., *Whigs and Hunters, The Origin of the Black Act*, England, 1975.

Thorton, E., *History and Practices of Thugs*, London, 1837.

Thurston, Edgar, *Castes and Tribes of South India*, Vol. I to VIII, Cosmo Publications, New Delhi, 1909.

Thurston, Edgar, *Ethnographic Notes in Southern India*, Vol.I and II, Government Press, Madras, 1906.

Tod, James, *Annals and Antiquities of Rajasthan*, 2 Vols. London, 1829.

Topinard, Paul, *Anthropology, Translated by Bartley*, Robert T.H., London, 1878.

Tribal Cultural Research and Training Institute, *Tribal Welfare Activities in Andhra Pradesh*, Hyderabad, 1987.

Tribal, 1970, (Bi-Annual Bulletin devoted to the Study of the life and Cultural of Tribes of Andhra Pradesh), 1968 to 1969, Vol. VI and VII, Hyderabad, 1970.

The Scheduled Tribes of Andhra Pradesh, *Tribal Cultural Research and Training Institute*, Tribal Welfare Deptt., Hyderabad, 1961.

Tripathi, Chandra Paul, *Denotified Community of Rajasthan*, New Delhi, 1963.

Troisi Jesh, *Social Movements among the Santhals, Social Movements in India*, Vol. II, *ed.*, M.S.A., Rao, New Delhi, 1979.

Troisi, J., "Tribal Religion: Religious beliefs and Practices among the Santhals", *Manohar Publications*, New Delhi, 1978.

Tupper, C.L., *Punjab Customary Law, UNESCO*, Calcutta, 1881.

Tupper, C.L., *Population Census Methods*, Population Series No. 4. *Lake Success, UNESCO*, New York, November 1949.

Tupper, C.L., *Race Questions in Modern Science*, UNESCO, 1957.

Vanikar, P.G., *Missionary Approach to Tribal Welfare*, Tribal Souvenir, 1984.

Varma, Paripurnananda, *Crime Criminal and Convict*, Ramaprasad and Sons, Agra, 1963.

Varma, R.C., *Indian Tribes through the Ages*, New Delhi, 1990.

Veeraiah, Palaparti, *"What we did 1924-64", The Report of the 7th Conference for Scheduled Tribes and Tribal Areas,* Guntur, November, 1964.

Veerendranath, Yendamuri, *Stuartpuram Police Station (Telugu Novel),* Navasakti Book House, Vijayawada, 2004.

Venkata Rao, V., *A Century of Tribal Politics,* New Delhi, 1976.

Venugopal Rao, S., 'Crime, Society and the Police', *Indian Express, (n.d.)*

Venugopal Rao, S., 'The Police Service: Some Compulsions and Contradictions', *Indian Journal of Public Administration, No. XXIV, 1978.*

Venugopal Rao, S., Crime in Our Society, A Political Perspective, *New Delhi, 1983.*

Venugopal Rao, S., 'Some Compulsions and Contradictions', *Indian Journal of Public Administration,* 1979.

Venugopal Rao, S., 'The Strategy of Meeting of the Challenge of Socio-Economic Offenders', *Indian Journal of Criminology,* Madras, 1974.

Venugopalarao, V., *Facets of Crime in India,* Bombay, Allied Publishers, 1962.

Vernon and Samuel B. Rutash, *Encyclopedia of Criminology,* New York, 1949.

Vidyarthi, L. P. & Rai, B.K., "The Tribal Culture of India", Concept Publications, New Delhi, 1978.

Vidyarthi, L.P., *Crime, Society and the Police,* Vanyajati, (n.d).

Vidyarthi, L.P., *Cultural Contours of Tribal Bihar,* Calcutta, 1964.

Vilas, A., Sangava,"Phanse-parathis of Kolhapur: A Tribe in transition", *Sociological Bulletin, XIV, No.1, March 1967, 81.*

Vold, George B., *Theoretical Criminology,* New York: Oxford University Press, 1958.

Vyas, N.N, and Mann, R.S., "Indian Tribes in Transition", Rawat Publications, Jaipur, 1980.

Waite, Arthur Edward, *The Mysteries of Magic,* London, 1897.

Walsh, Sir Cecil., 'Crime in India'. *With an Introduction on Forensic Difficulties and Pecularities,* Ernest Benn Ltd., London, 1930.

Ward, Robert E., (ed), *Studying Politics Abroad,* Little Brown and Co., Boston, 1964.

Washbrook, D.A., *The Emergence of Provisional Politics: the Madras Presidency,* 1870-1920, Cambridge, 1976.

Watson, Bernard, *A Hundred Years' War,* Hodder and Stoughton, London, 1964.

Weber, M., *The Theory of Social and Economic Organization,* New York, 1964.

Weber, Max, *The Religion of India,* The Free Press, Glencoe, III, 1958.

West, D.J., *The Young offender,* OUP, 1968.

Westley, William, A., *Violence and the Police,* London, 1970.

Whyte, William F., *Street Corner Society,* University of Chicago, Chicago, 1943.

Wilson, Margaret S., "Pioneers in Criminology", *Journal of Criminal Law and Criminology and Political Science, VL (May, 1954)*, 3.

Wilson, John, *Caste in India, 2 Vols,* London, 1877.

Wilson, *Code of Tribal Customs in Sirsa.n.d.*

Winfred, D.J., *Glimpses of Police Work in Tinnevelly,* Madras, 1914.

Wiser, W.H., *The Hindu Jajmani System,* Locknow: Locknow Publishing House, 1936.

Wood, C., *Peasant Revolt: An Interpretation of Moplah Violence in the nineteenth and Twentieth Centuries,* in C., Dewey and A.G., Hopkins (ed), *The Imperial Impact.*

Woodruff, Phillip, *The men who ruled India: The Founders,* Jonathan Cape, London, 1953 (Sixth impression 1955).

Yaseen Saheb, S., "Demogenetic study of Kodava and Amma Kodava populations of kodagu district", unpublished report, Anthropological Survey of India, Mysore.

Yeasts, M.W.H., *Census of India 1931, Vol.* XIV, Madras, 1932.

Yogesh, Atal, "Conceptual Framework for the Analysis of Caste", *Sociological Bulletin, XVI (September, 1967), 60.*

Young Pauline, V., *Scientific and social Surveys and Research,* New Jersey: Prentice-hall, Inc., 1960.

Zelditch, (jr.) M., "Some Methodological Problems of field Studies", *American Journal of Sociology, 67: 566-76.*

Zinhin, Taya, *Caste Today,* London: Oxford University Press, 1963.

Index